breaking through

HOW THE POLGAR SISTERS CHANGED THE GAME OF CHESS

Susan Polgar
with Paul Truong

EVERYMAN CHESS

Gloucester Publishers plc   www.everymanchess.com

First published in 2005 by Gloucester Publishers plc (formerly Everyman Publishers plc), Northburgh House, 10 Northburgh Street, London EC1V 0AT

First published 2005 by Gloucester Publishers plc

British Library Cataloguing-in-Publication Data
A catalogue record for this book is available from the British Library.

ISBN 1 85744 381 0

Distributed in North America by The Globe Pequot Press, P.O Box 480, 246 Goose Lane, Guilford, CT 06437-0480.

All other sales enquiries should be directed to Everyman Chess, Northburgh House, 10 Northburgh Street, London EC1V 0AT
tel: 020 7539 7600 fax: 020 7379 4060
email: info@everymanchess.com
website: www.everymanchess.com

EVERYMAN CHESS SERIES (formerly Cadogan Chess)
Chief advisor: Garry Kasparov
Commissioning editor: Byron Jacobs

Typesetting by First Rank Publishing, Brighton.
Edited by Jonathan Tait.
Cover design by Horatio Monteverde.
Production by Navigator Guides.
Printed and bound in the US by Versa Press.

CONTENTS

CHAPTER ONE

Susan

Our family background

My grandparents fortunately survived the horrors of the Holocaust. Otherwise my parents and the Polgar sisters would not be here today. Both my parents were born right after World War II in 1946. As a strange coincidence, my father is only two days older than my mother.

My father, Laszlo, was born in Gyongyos, Hungary, a medium-sized town about an hour's drive away from the capital, Budapest. My mother, Klara, was born in a small village called Vilok (or Tiszaujlak in Hungarian) in the territory of today's Ukraine. At the time when she was born it was part of the Soviet Union. This area is right next to the Ukrainian/Hungarian border where many of the population speak Hungarian. At home my mother and her family spoke only Hungarian, while all her education was done in Ukrainian and Russian.

As the borders of the Soviet Union were basically kept locked in those days, it was very fashionable to have pen pals abroad. In my mother's region the obvious choice was Hungary as they spoke the same language. During her college years, my mother also put an advert in one of the Hungarian youth magazines. She was looking to correspond with young Hungarian males with similar interests, mainly to improve her writing skills. She received about 250 responses. However, this was not the way my parents met.

Here is the recollection from my mother, Klara: 'My family and Laszlo's family happened to know each other. His mother was on a visit in Vilok and told my mother that Laszlo would like to come for a visit too. My parents dictated an invitation letter to send to Laszlo: "Please come to visit. I am looking forward to meeting you!", which I had to sign. However, the next day I wrote my own letter explaining to Laszlo that I did not actually write the first letter and would have never written to a guy first. Laci (a nickname for Laszlo) wrote back with great pleasure. We discovered that we were both educators. After a while the other 30-40 pen pals dropped out and he remained the only one.

'We met in person for the first time in 1965, during my visit to Budapest. Laszlo was enthusiastically telling me about his dreams. He told me he would like to have six children, not knowing yet that they would be with me. He said he would teach them a lot with specific goals in mind and nurture them with great love. I just listened and upon my return to home, I told my parents that I met a very interesting person. But I had a hard time imagining ever marrying him.'

While they mutually respected each other, at that point romantic interests were one sided. However, they have continued to exchange letters, mostly about educational issues as they shared the same profession.

After about a year and a half, my mother felt that 'Laszlo is the most special out of all the guys I ever met.' Soon the subject changed and Laszlo wrote the first love letter... and at the end he proposed!

Klara: 'Then Laszlo came to Vilok for a visit. After the November 7th day parade (in 1966), we announced to my parents that we were getting married. Shortly after the engagement, Laszlo received the order to serve his army duties. For six months, we could not see each other. A few months later we got married and settled temporarily in Gyongyos.'

Soon the newly-weds moved to Budapest and bought their own home fully from loans. They both worked very hard to try to pay off the debt as soon as possible. I was born one day short of my parents' second wedding anniversary, in Budapest on April 19th 1969.

My early childhood; discovering the wonderland of chess

According to my mother, I was a very active and intense child, who could not sit still for two minutes. Therefore, she felt that it was a miracle when I was introduced to chess and, because of chess, started to calm down. She could hardly believe her eyes when one day, coming home from work, she saw my father and me sitting at the table patiently playing chess.

It was 1973, less than a year after the famous Fischer-Spassky match, when I discovered chess. One day, as I was at home alone with my mother, I was in search for a new toy. I opened one of the cabinets and I found a bunch of strange pieces that looked interesting!

I bombarded my Mom with questions: 'What is this? What do you do with them? How do you play with it?' She answered 'It is a chess set. You have to wait until Daddy comes home and he can teach you how to play'. My Mom did not know anything about chess at that time. My father was just a hobby player. Prior to my discovery of chess, he tried to teach my Mom but she showed no interest. The next day, my Dad gladly started his introduction to the royal game.

As a teacher by profession, he knew how to teach me. He was methodical and very patient. After introducing the chess board and the pieces, for some time we only played 'pawn wars'. That means games where only the pawns participate without the rest of the army. The goal of the game was whoever queens a pawn first wins. Then later we added the kings and playing all the way to checkmate. Parallel to these games, my father also gave me many checkmate puzzles to solve. Another thing we liked to do was going over short games from a book called 'Opening Traps'.

The joys and the difficulties of being labeled as a 'wunderkind'

For several months we were playing games, learning how to set up checkmate traps and going over short mastergames. Sometime after my fourth birthday, I entered my first chess tournament. I remember everybody being shocked that such a tiny little girl wanted to enter the competition. My home city, Budapest, is divided into twenty three districts. I was born in the thirteenth, 'Angyalfold' (the English translation would be Angel's Land). My first tournament was a regional qualifying scholastic tournament, which I won. My next tournament was the one that made probably the biggest impact on my future.

All the children who qualified from the district tournaments were getting together to compete for the title 'Budapest Champion'. It was held in four sections, 1st-4th grade (ages 6-10) and 5th-8th grade (ages 11-14), separately for boys and girls. Almost all of the girls that qualified for my section (up to 4th grade) were twice my age or older. At that point I did not realize the importance of that event in my life. I just looked at it as one chess game at the time. I was having fun. During the

tournament, everything went great. I won game after game, and my final score was 10-0!

The fact that such a young girl won the Championship was already a sensation in itself, but winning *all* my games certainly added a lot to people's amazement.

Basically, after this victory my life changed forever. The media right away labeled me as a 'wunderkind' and began following me with curious eyes for the rest of my career. In those years, the Hungarian press was divided into two groups. A smaller group that was very supportive and sympathetic towards me, and the other which was very pessimistic and negative about my future. There was a large group of people (journalists among them) who thought this success was a one-time accident and that I would burn out very quickly. My parents had to endure an awful amount of attacks from a lot of people, including close family members. They said 'a little girl should play with dolls and with sand in the playground, not sit at a chessboard and move wooden pieces'.

However, my mother saw that I enjoyed the challenge of chess and that is why she supported my father in staying with the game. Of course I also played with other toys. I played outdoors with the neighboring kids probably just less than the average child. Also at that time I was going to nursery school, so I was in a traditional environment anyway until the early afternoon.

My parents did a smart thing by enrolling me in a Russian language nursery school where I was the only Hungarian. All the other kids were children of the

Soviet diplomats residing in Budapest. My mother taught me a little bit of Russian before, but probably not more than a couple of hundred words. Whether I liked it or not, I had to pick up Russian quickly as nobody there knew more than 'hi' and 'bye' in Hungarian. After a summer of stay-away camps with them, my Russian became almost better than my native tongue. Later during my chess career, knowledge of the Russian language came in handy many times.

When I was turning six, my parents had to make another serious decision as it was time for me to go to school. However, they felt that it would be a waste of time for me, because there was very little that I would learn in school as I was so much more advanced. I already knew how to read and write, and in math I was many years ahead of my grade. Both my parents as teachers were quite confident that they could help me with all my academic development. Also they believed that for children well above (or below, for that matter) the average, school can be very harmful. People have a hard time accepting the different. So after a lot of thinking, they decided to apply for a permit to school me at home. In those days, that was practically unprecedented in Hungary.

At high school age, numerous athletes in different sports were practically home-schooled, or else showed up for classes only randomly, in order to have more time to practice or to travel to competitions.

However, it was an original idea to keep a child at home from grade 1 to improve her chess skills! My parents went through hell for this decision and had to overcome a lot of hurdles. At one time, the authorities came to our house with the police (with machine-guns!) to warn my father that he was breaking the law by not letting me attend school. Luckily, my parents did not get scared and told the policemen that the 'case' was still pending. The policemen made a written record of the visit and left. Altogether it took about nine months of correspondence back and forth until the Ministry of Education finally gave permission.

The way it worked was that I had to pass a standardized test in all subjects at the end of the school year. As long as I passed I would move on to the next grade. When I was 4-5 years old, my day would be divided three ways (besides sleeping and having meals, etc. of course) into chess, math and play time. After a couple of years, I stopped focusing on math and studied it only to pass the yearly exams at school.

On the way to becoming a Master

After my early sensational success at the age of four, the next five years or so were pretty similar as regards my chess training. I was absorbing a lot of new information from books and from different coaches, especially my father. He focused mostly on improving my tactical and calculation skills. I also studied great games by different grandmasters to have a better understanding of strategy, did some exercises to improve my visualization by memorizing master games, played blindfold chess and, last but not least, I was learning a lot about endgames. The opening was the part of the game that I spent the least time on.

In addition, I was playing a lot of practice games at home with my father and friends, or in one of the several outdoor parks, or at my chess club. I rarely left my home-town for tournaments; mostly I played in club tournaments that lasted for several weeks, with just a couple of games a week. The team championships (representing Voros Meteor, and later, after a merger, MTK-VM) were also an important part of my life. I really enjoyed playing for a team and developing friendships with my team-mates. Even now, thirty years later, I still love team competitions and their unique atmosphere.

Here is one of my favorite games from those early league games:

| ☐ **Susan Polgar** |
| ■ **Laszlo Kiss** |
| Budapest 1980 |
| *King's Indian Defense* |

---

1 d4 ♘f6 2 c4 g6 3 ♘c3 ♗g7 4 e4 d6 5 f3 0-0 6 ♗e3 e5 7 d5 ♘h5 8 ♕d2 f5 9 0-0-0 ♘d7 10 ♗d3 ♘c5 11 ♗c2 a5 12 b3 ♘a6 13 a3 f4 14 ♗f2 g5 15 ♘ge2 g4 16 ♖he1 ♕g5 17 ♔b2 ♘f6 18 ♘c1 h5 19 ♘d3

♘h7 20 b4 b6 21 bxa5 bxa5 22 ♗a4 ♘b8 23 c5 ♗a6 24 ♘b5 ♗xb5 25 ♗xb5 h4 26 h3 g3 27 ♗g1 ♕d8 28 c6 ♘g5 29 ♔a2 ♕c8 30 ♖b1 ♗f6 31 ♘b2 ♔f7 32 ♗f1 ♔e7 33 ♘c4 a4 34 ♖b7 ♔d8

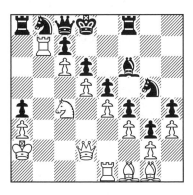

35 ♗b6! cxb6 36 ♘xb6 Black resigned

One time, at the age of ten, I participated in the final of the Hungarian Women's Championship. I only finished sixth but became a national woman master. It was another sensation. Right after my game ended, our country's leader, Janos Kadar, personally came to congratulate me!

Until 1980, I played only within Hungary and I improved steadily year by year. Here is a small chart:

Age	Category in Hungary	Approximate American equivalent
7	3rd	B
8	2nd	A
10	1st	expert
11	candidate master	master
13	master/FIDE master	FIDE master

I was eleven years old when, for the first time in my life, I traveled abroad for a chess tournament to participate in the Esperanto Chess Festival in Ceske Budejovice, Czechoslovakia. I had a lot of fun and made a lot of new international friendships. We went on excursions, singing, swimming and more. It is really amazing how Esperanto made communication so easy between all the participants from different nations. Esperanto is a very easy, logical, neutral, artificial international language. The main difference between Esperanto and other popular languages (as, for example, English) is the fact that no nation has the 'home court advantage' when learning it.

That was the time when I discovered that, through chess, I could expand my horizons and see other countries, get to know different cultures, and meet interesting new people all the time. This aspect of chess gave me extra motivation to improve my game.

Around 1981, I started to play in more serious international tournaments with masters and International Masters. I was invited to another Esperantist chess festival in Varna, Bulgaria. It was quite a strong tournament with most of the best local players participating alongside the Esperantists from the surrounding countries. Varna is a beautiful harbor town on the shores of the Black Sea. We fell in love with the warmth of the Bulgarian people. Many of them invited us to their homes for dinner, showed us around, and offered to help in any way they could to make us feel at home. In the following three years, we went back to Bulgaria frequently and I participated in more than twenty tournaments. I even picked up enough Bulgarian to get by.

In 1982 in Balatonbereny (Hungary), I had a good tournament. In the last round with the black pieces, I faced a very experienced player, Dr. Liptay,

who was much higher rated than me. I needed to win to make the FIDE Master norm. Most people were skeptical that I could do it, but I played well and succeeded in a long hard-fought game.

☐ **Laszlo Liptay**
■ **Susan Polgar**
Balatonbereny 1982
King's Indian Defense

---

1 d4 ♘f6 2 c4 g6 3 g3 ♗g7 4 ♗g2 0-0 5 ♘f3 d6 6 0-0 ♘c6 7 ♘c3 ♗g4 8 d5 ♘a5 9 ♘d2 c5 10 h3 ♗d7 11 ♕c2 e5 12 dxe6 ♗xe6 13 b3 ♕d7 14 ♔h2 d5 15 cxd5 ♘xd5 16 ♗b2 ♘c6 17 ♘de4 ♘db4 18 ♕c1 b6 19 a3 ♘a6 20 ♘b5 ♘d4 21 ♘xd4 cxd4 22 ♕f4 f5 23 ♘g5 ♖ad8 24 e3 ♗xb3 25 exd4 ♗d5 26 ♖fe1 ♖fe8 27 ♗xd5+ ♕xd5 28 ♘f3 ♖e4 29 ♕d2 ♖xe1 30 ♘xe1 ♘c5 31 ♖d1 ♘e4 32 ♕e2 ♕b3 33 ♘f3

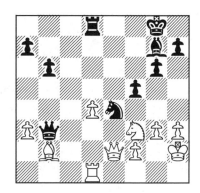

33...♘xf2! 34 ♖d2 ♘e4 35 ♖c2 ♕d5 36 ♕c4 ♕xc4 37 ♖xc4 ♖d7 38 a4 ♔f7 39 ♖c6 ♔e7 40 g4 ♘d8 41 gxf5 gxf5 42 ♔g2 ♗f6 43 ♔f1 ♖g3 44 ♘e5 ♖g3 45 d5 ♗xe5 46 ♗xe5 ♖xh3 47 ♔g2 ♖d3 48 d6 ♖d5 White resigned.

Soon afterwards I made the other two required norms and became both a Hungarian national master and a FIDE Master. As the FIDE Master title is considered higher than the Hungarian national master, I received the latter automatically.

The appearance of my sisters, and chess in their lives

I very clearly remember the days my two sisters were born. In a cold winter day (November 2nd 1974), I was in the middle of a chess lesson when my father and I got the news my baby sister was born. At that time my parents thought it would be cute to name all their children with a 'Zs' starting letter (in Hungarian that exists as one double-letter, pronounced something like 'Zh' in English). That is why they named her Zsofia, which in English would be Sofia or Sophia.

Less than twenty months later (on July 23rd 1976) we got another addition to the family. If the baby was a boy, my parents were considering naming him Zseni. The translation of that name would be 'Genius'! As I previously mentioned, the idea was for all children to have a Zs starting letter for their names. When I asked my father recently why they wanted that, he said: 'It was a silly idea, but at the time we were poor and I figured when you went to school and label your clothes, one child could inherit from another without needing to change the initials!' However, the baby was another girl, named Judit.

I was about five and a half when Sofia was born, and a little over seven at Judit's birth. So I remember both my sisters as babies vividly. I can clearly see a picture in my mind when my mother, wearing a yellow and brown checkered dress, came home from the hospital carrying Judit, who had very distinct red hair.

My sisters already were very different as babies. Judit was always calmer and more easy going, while Sofia was more demanding. Sofia was a strong-willed and stubborn child. She was very talented in drawing, in chess and a number of other things.

I used to call Judit as the 'little angel'. She was very calm, always willing and wanting to help everyone. Very early on, she was already always looking for challenges. Here are a few small examples...

On our early trips, whenever the rest of the family would take the escalator, she would prefer to take the stairs; and despite being the youngest, she usually wanted to carry the bags, preferably the heaviest ones.

Growing up Sofia used to be very skinny while Judit was a little more on the chubby side. However, when Judit turned ten, all of a sudden she changed. She decided overnight that she would go on a diet. She proved her strong will-power, that if she sets her mind on something she will get it. She has always been very diligent and hardworking towards her goals.

My sisters never needed any formal introduction to chess. They were watching me play and practice all their lives. However, normally I would be in the 'chess room' behind closed doors. That door had a small window in the top part which they would peep through. They always wanted to be taught to play chess, but had to be patient until my parents felt that they were old enough to start learning. Sofia was about four and a half and Judit was close to five years old when they each learned how the pieces move. Unlike Sofia and me, who were taught from the first steps by our father, Judit got introduced to the very basics by our Mom. By then, she had picked up enough chess knowledge to do that.

My father felt, from his experience with his two older daughters, that five was the most ideal age to introduce chess to a young child. Even though many four year olds can learn the rules and more, it usually goes at a much slower pace than it would a year later. Therefore, he thinks that in most cases it is not worthwhile the effort to start prematurely.

One of my first coaches, Mrs. Eva Karakas, was looking forward since the birth of Sofia to teaching her chess, and in 1979 she started giving her lessons.

My first trips beyond the 'iron curtain', and my first world title

My first trip to the West was in 1981 to England. Prior to this I had only been to other countries of the eastern block: Bulgaria, Czechoslovakia, the Soviet Union and Yugoslavia. England was really a shocking contrast with the above countries in those days. For the first time I saw everything being lit so colorfully. The shops had plenty of choices – and astronomical prices compared to our currency.

I was sent as the Hungarian representative to the World Under-16 Girls'

Championship, which was held in Westergate, England (West Sussex). I was accompanied by my parents and my coach, Gyula Forgacs. It was quite an adventure even just getting there. First, the Ministry of Sport by mistake handed the wrong passport to my coach. It was somebody else's passport with the same name. We were already driving to the airport when we realized the mistake. So, after the error had been corrected, we were already in time pressure. Then we had to face another problem, we were running out of petrol. We were so late that we didn't even have enough time to stop at a petrol station. We were just 'praying' we would make it to the airport on time. We did, but sure enough on the way back the car would not start. As we joked after the tournament, the hardest part was to get to the tournament, not winning it!

This was the first World Championship I ever participated in. The tournament itself was very interesting. My main rivals were the local star Teresa Needham, and Jolanta Rojek from Poland. My toughest game was versus Ms. Rojek. After I defeated both of them I was in good shape, and in the last round against the American, Baracca Shabbaz, I could play it safe and agree a draw (with an extra pawn in a rook endgame) to guarantee first place. It was a fun event where, typically for all-girls tournaments, most players got along well. We were playing outdoors in between rounds, dining together and making friendships of many years.

After the event, we were fortunate to spend a few days in London. That is one of the numerous good sides of being a professional chess player: being able to see the world throughout one's travels. Despite being on an extremely tight budget, in London we were able to see Big Ben, Westminster Abbey, Buckingham Palace, Trafalgar Square, the Changing of the Guard, some museums, etc. I even got to see Madame Tussaud's wax museum (needing only a child's ticket). Unfortunately, my parents could not afford to come in.

During our stay in London, as a sideshow of the Lloyds Bank tournament, I played a four game blitz exhibition match against the Boys' U-16 World Champion, which I won 2½-1½.

After we returned from the World Championship, instead of a congratulatory note, an unpleasant surprise awaited my mother. By the time we got back, she had missed a few of the meetings prior to the beginning of the school year. As a result, she got a disciplinary note from the principal of the school at her job. She decided to quit. In retrospect, it was probably a good thing for the family. However, it felt quite painful back then.

Fighting for equality;
challenging a male-dominated game

When I started to play chess, it was strange for me to see that so few girls and women also played. I questioned why they had separate championships. I felt that, in chess, there should be no difference in abilities between the sexes. As strange and distant as it may sound today, 20-30 years ago a lot of people honestly doubted, many could not even imagine, that women could come close to grandmaster standard in chess. It

took a lot of 'proof' to gain respect and recognition.

Today, I still feel that women who take chess as seriously and professionally as their male colleagues can be equally successful. However, I understood over the years that along the way (in the meantime), girls need more encouragement, support, and help – including all-female events.

Throughout my career, at different times I was not even allowed to compete in some events because they were 'only for men'. The most painful experience was when, after qualifying to the 'Men's Chess World Championship' from the overall Hungarian Championship, I was not allowed to represent my country. One of the reasons was that it was for men only.

I am proud that, because of my success, I paved the road for the future, as at the following FIDE congress (in 1986) the name of the event was changed to 'The World Chess Championship'. They eliminated the word "men's". Today, for girls around the world, the doors are open at chess tournaments.

Difficulties with the authorities,
and overcoming them

As a pioneer, I had to face a lot of difficulties over the years. After the home schooling issues were solved, the next big issue was: how could a little girl play against boys and men?

Another problem my parents had was they did not obey the standards of our Chess Federation. Namely, when a young player traveled abroad to represent the country, usually one of the officials of the Chess Federation would travel with the player. My parents being quite conservative minded could not agree to that. They felt that a teenage girl should not travel with a stranger without parental supervision. In those days, a trip beyond 'the iron curtain' was considered almost like winning the lottery, so it is no wonder my parents did not gain sympathy of the Chess Federation.

My father developed a theory why none of the women players became grandmasters. He carefully studied the life stories and developments of great male champions. Then he searched for the answer: what do men do differently then women, and why do women stay behind?

He believed that one can only achieve high results if one has high expectations in the first place. In the case of chess, in order to become a World Champion or even a grandmaster, one has to have the highest goals. Also, it is important to have similar training methods and competition challenges to the more successful players. Getting strong competition in chess in the 1980s certainly meant competing against men. All along our dreams and goals were to become a top ten grandmaster in the world. That is why for many years I avoided women-only events. As a punishment, our family got 'blacklisted' by the Hungarian Chess Federation.

Another aspect at the time was that we felt certain people were prejudiced against us because we are Jewish. In Hungary, throughout the eighties, there was no 'open' or official anti-Semitism. However, behind our backs and 'off the record', we knew it existed.

Even being No. 1 in the world did not help much

After we found out the news that, on the July 1984 world rating list, I was ranked number one (together with Pia Cramling), we were hopeful there would be changes in the attitude of the Hungarian Chess Federation towards us. Unfortunately, not much changed for almost another year. I was still not allowed to travel to the West. Even until after the 1988 Olympiad, the only improvement was that I was finally allowed to travel, although still not as freely as other Hungarian chess players.

It was quite absurd that Hungary, instead of being proud of their own player leading the world rankings, the president of the Hungarian Chess Federation, Sandor Szerenyi, was strongly lobbying with FIDE (in written requests and at the FIDE congress in Manila) to remove me altogether from the world rankings.

In 1986, I finally got a chance to play in the Final of the Hungarian Championship. It was a long and grueling event with 15 rounds. Before the tournament started, it was announced at the opening ceremony that the top three finishers would represent Hungary at the next stage of the World Championship. Therefore, my main goal was to reach one of those three qualification spots. I played very solid chess: twelve draws, three wins, with no loss. At the end, I tied on second place with my coach IM Laszlo Hazai. I was very happy and looking forward to being the first woman ever to compete in the 'Men's' World Championship. Unfortunately, it was an event in which I was not allowed to participate.

The Soviet Chess Federation was used to seeing their players dominate the chess world and the world rankings. However, by late 1986 it was clear that in the January 1987 list my rating was going to be 2495, 65 rating points ahead of the Soviet World Champion, Maia Chiburdanidze. During the Chess Olympiad in Dubai, they held the FIDE congress where an unthinkable decision was made. All women players in the world would receive 100 bonus points except for me!!! So when the official world rating list came out, I had 2495 and Maia had 2530 with the added 100 point gift! It was amusing, that even with this colossal injustice, I still remained the third-ranked player in the world and only 35 points behind Maia. According to the rumors, this was part of some political favors owed by FIDE to the Soviets. There was no proper logic to this and there was definitely no justification for it. But when you deal with chess politicians, they can turn a chicken into a turkey without blinking an eye.

This is how the Gulf News commented on the issue: 'This is the worst thing that FIDE has ever done...'

Unfortunately, another sad political decision was made. I was not allowed to represent Hungary in the 'Men's World Championship'. It was not quite clear, (but neither does it matter much) whether the Hungarian Chess Federation or FIDE (or both!?) made the decision that a woman cannot participate in a 'Men's World Championship'.

At that time, I was the top rated 17-year-old player in the world of either gender! Before I heard about those two

very unfair and outrageous decisions, I felt that I was on the top of the world. When I first got the news I thought it was just a bad joke, but soon I had to come to the realization that it was the sad reality. It was very hard for me to believe that, after all the discriminations I had to face from my own Chess Federation, now the International Chess Federation did not treat me fairly either.

I did not give up the fight, but I certainly was somewhat discouraged and very disappointed.

The Breakthrough:
Winning the Olympiads

Even though I was the number one ranked woman player in Hungary since 1981 and number one in the world since 1984, I did not participate in any Olympiads until 1988. In the Hungarian press, which was often censored those days, it was falsely portrayed that I refused to defend our national colors.

It reminded me of the famous saying: 'Nobody can be a prophet in their own land'. While the whole world recognized my rating and accomplishments, in Hungary I had to face a lot of opposition from my own Chess Federation. Unfortunately, at that time the former first lady of Hungarian Chess, WGM Zsuzsa Veroci, had great influence. She and her father, Bela Veroci, were both board members of the Hungarian Chess Federation. Obviously they were biased and had a conflict of interest any time they voted against, or other ways influenced, decisions involving me. But that did not seem to interest anyone in the leadership of the HCF in those days. As a communist party member, she had very powerful (political) connections.

Finally in 1988, my sisters and I, alongside Ildiko Madl, were selected for the Hungarian national team to represent our homeland. The rankings of the top Hungarian women prior to the Olympiad were the following:

Susan Polgar	2490
Judit Polgar	2365
Sofia Polgar	2345
Ildiko Madl	2345

For about two decades, Zsuzsa Veroci and Maria Ivanka were the foundation of the Hungarian national women's team. They both were very bitter when they found out that they did not make the team this time. I had for many years been the top-ranked Hungarian player, so they had some time to get used to me. But now came two young girls, 12 and 14 years old, who were also rated higher than them. To some degree it is understandable. They had a hard time dealing with the fact that there were 'new kids on the block' – and all from the same family.

Even though it should have been obvious that the team would consist of the four top-ranked players, there was an incredible amount of opposition to the 'changing of the guards'. After a lot of discussion and argument, the team captain, Janos Tompa, finally made a (chess) politically courageous decision and selected the four top-rated women in the country to represent Hungary at the Olympiad.

We knew we had plenty of 'well-wishers' who could not wait to see us

crawl back in failure. That just gave us extra motivation to win and quiet all of our critics. Since my childhood this was the first time I had participated in an international women-only competition. The whole world's eyes were on me to see whether I would be able to justify my 'high' rating, that according to the politicians was 'collected' against men.

The Olympiad started smoothly, but then a tragedy happened. The fiancée of our team-mate Ildiko, IM Bela Perenyi, was on his way from Hungary to support us and to participate in one of the side events at the Olympiad. Unfortunately, he never made it to Greece, as on the way he was killed in a car accident. It was quite admirable that, after such shocking and sad news, Ildiko was still able to play well and even score a win against our big rivals, the Soviet Union.

I played all 14 games on the top board without a break. I scored 10½ points and did not lose a single game. I proved to all the doubters that chess is chess and playing versus the world's top women players is the same as against men. My rating was 'for real', no matter what gender my opponents were.

Here is my game versus the United States:

□ **Anna Akhsharumova**
■ **Susan Polgar**
Thessaloniki Olympiad 1988
Dutch Defense

1 d4 f5 2 ♘c3 d5 3 ♗f4 ♘f6 4 e3 c6 5 ♗d3 g6 6 ♘f3 ♗g7 7 ♘e2 ♗e6 8 c3 ♘bd7 9 h3 ♘e4 10 ♕c2 h6 11 ♗e5 ♘xe5 12 ♘xe5 ♗xe5 13 dxe5 ♕c7 14 ♘f4 ♔f7 15 ♘xe6

♔xe6 16 f4

16...♛b6 17 ♛c1 ♞g3 18 ♖g1 g5 19 ♔f2 gxf4 20 ♔f3 ♞e4 21 ♔xf4 ♛c7 22 ♔f3 ♛xe5 23 ♔e2 ♖hg8 24 ♛e1 ♛h2 25 ♔f1 ♞g3+ 26 ♔f2 ♖af8 27 ♗e2 ♞e4+ 28 ♔f1 ♖g3 White resigned.

Thanks to Judit's outstanding performance, we were in the chase for the medals all along. The last round was a real thrill ride. The whole chess world was curious to see if we would be able to break the Soviet dominance. A lot of players told us as much and one could almost physically feel it in the air, the chess world was ready for a change...

We both had 31 points but on paper the Soviets had an easier pairing. They faced the Dutch national team and everybody expected an easy walkover (a 3-0 victory) as the Soviets were higher rated by hundreds of points on each board. We played against Sweden, who were not very strong on board two and three, but had Pia Cramling (one of the top-ranked women players in the world) on board one.

The Soviets could not handle the tension and drew all three games against their much lower-rated opponents, hoping that we would not catch up with them. Judit won relatively quickly, but Ildiko only drew, so everything came down to my game against Pia. In the middlegame I achieved a huge advantage, but spoiled it in time pressure. By the time we adjourned the game, I was in trouble. So calculators were out to see who had better tie-break points in case I lost the adjourned game. Luckily, in the resumption Pia made a mistake and I found a resourceful way to save the game.

Therefore, there was no tie. Our teenage team won – a clear half point ahead of the previously unbeatable Soviet team! We were certainly in a celebratory mood. This was an incredible breakthrough for the Polgar sisters.

Upon our return to Hungary, everything changed. Overnight, from being the black sheep we became national heroes. After red lights for so many years, suddenly green lights appeared everywhere. Our lives changed tremendously for the better. We were greeted by many already at the airport, and then we were invited to one reception after another. We received the highest honors any civilian in Hungary can get. In 1989, we were also invited to the American Embassy to meet with First Lady Barbara Bush and President George Bush during their visit to Hungary.

We had numerous endorsement offers, both within Hungary and beyond. We had significant contracts with AB (an insurance company), Controll (a computer company) and Mephisto (a chess computer company).

Two years later, in 1990, we returned to the Olympiad (in Novi Sad) with the same team as the top seeds and as defending champions. Naturally, we had more pressure, but we also were more experienced. Our team leader was the Hungarian-American GM Pal Benko, our captain was IM Laszlo Hazai, and our coach FM Miklos Morvay.

Just as in Thessaloniki, again I was on the top board and played all 14 games. This time I scored 11 points and again went undefeated (8 wins and 6 draws). I also won the individual gold medal for the highest percentage on board one.

This time we started OK, but unfortunately lost the crucial match against the Soviets, despite my win against the reigning World Champion, Maia Chiburdanidze. Then history repeated itself. Before the final round we were again tying with our Soviet rivals, this time each having 32 points. Again we got the tougher challenge, but at least our destiny was in our hands. The draw was: Soviet Union vs. Yugoslavia C; Hungary vs. Czech & Slovak Republics.

Yugoslavia is a very strong chess nation, but of course this was not their best line-up, it being their C team. This time all six players handled the pressure well and both the Soviet team and ours scored a perfect 3-0! We tied for first with a record 35 points out of the possible 42, the highest ever for the Women's Olympiad. The third finisher, China, was two matches (6 points) behind with only 29 points. (See page 124 for my last round game.)

At that point we just had to worry about who had better the tie-break, which was based on all our opponents total scores. On December 3rd, a little after 9pm, we found out that we had won the Gold again!

Besides winning the team gold for Hungary, each sister also won the individual gold on boards one, two and three. This time Ildiko Madl, our reserve player, played only two games and won both times.

Again the welcome back home was overwhelming for us, including a reception on our honor with the Hungarian President, Arpad Goncz, in the Parliament.

Making history: becoming the first woman the earn a GM title

Back in the 1980s becoming a Grandmaster was very difficult. There were only about five hundred GMs in the world. The elite used to be considered 2600 rated and above. Only the very best (about ten players) would make that. One becomes a Grandmaster by performing as a 2600 player in twenty four games (or more) from two or three tournaments. Besides that, the candidate has to have an actual rating of 2500 or higher.

I became an International Master in 1984 and thought it would not be so difficult to make the next step to the highest title. But actually it took longer than I thought, partly because of the unexpected things I had to face in 1986, as well as many other incidents.

In 1985, the borders suddenly opened for me. Between December of 1982 and April of 1985, I was not allowed to accept any invitation and travel to the West. Finally, thanks to some good friends like Mr. Retsagi, Frederic Friedel, Robert Entel, Israel Parry (representing the Western media) and others, things changed. The above-mentioned friends were from Hungary, West Germany, USA and England respectively. They all put pressure on the Hungarian Chess Federation to let me play outside of the Eastern block. Also, the fact that I was the top-ranked female player in the world certainly helped.

The ice broke when, in April 1985, I was allowed to play a small exhibition match vs. GM John Nunn in Hamburg, Germany, through the organization of Frederic Friedel.

Shortly after, I also played in the world's strongest open tournament of those times, the New York Open. The organizer/sponsor, Jose Cuchi, was very kind and invited both my sisters and parents as well. However, the borders did not quite open for the whole family. The officials were afraid that if the entire family was in America together, we might not come back. Therefore, only my mother, Sofia and I went for the first overseas trip.

New York, New York... there is no place like New York! That was my first impression. As they say, you either love or hate New York. I certainly fell in love with New York. We stayed and played at the (then) Penta Hotel right across the street from Madison Square Garden. I felt that one day I would live in New York. I didn't know when or how, or even why, but it remained a secret dream for many years. After this first visit, I was glad to be invited back to the US almost every year, until I eventually moved there in 1994 because

of 'accidental' personal reasons. This was also the first time I met my long-time friend and co-author of this book, FM Paul Truong.

Here is the first game I ever played in the US:

> ☐ **Douglas Bellizzi**
> ■ **Susan Polgar**
> New York Open 1985
> *English Opening*

1 c4 e5 2 ♘c3 ♘c6 3 ♘f3 f5 4 d4 e4 5 ♗g5 ♗e7 6 ♗xe7 ♘cxe7 7 ♘g5 h6 8 ♘h3 ♘f6 9 e3 g5 10 ♗e2 d6 11 ♕c2 ♘g6 12 0-0-0 c6 13 f3 exf3 14 gxf3 ♕e7 15 ♕d3 ♗d7 16 ♖he1 0-0-0 17 e4 ♖he8 18 ♗f1 fxe4 19 fxe4 ♘h4 20 ♘f2 ♘h5 21 ♗h3

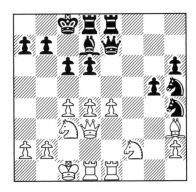

21...g4! 22 ♗xg4 ♗xg4 23 ♘xg4 ♕g5+ 24 ♘e3 ♘g2 25 ♕d2 ♘xe1 26 ♖xe1 ♘f6 27 ♘f5 ♔d7 28 h4 ♕xd2+ 29 ♔xd2 h5 30 ♔c2 ♘g4 31 b4 ♖f8 32 c5 dxc5 33 bxc5 b6 34 cxb6 axb6 35 ♘a4 ♔c7 36 ♖b1 ♖a8 37 ♔b3 ♘f2 38 ♘c3 ♘xe4 39 ♘xe4 ♖xf5 40 ♖g1 ♖f3+ 41 ♔b2 ♖d8 42 ♘g5 ♖f2+ 43 ♔c3 ♖e8 44 ♔d3 b5 45 a3 ♖fe2 White resigned.

Returning to the chess event itself in 1985, the press treated me as a world sensation. I made the cover of the New York Times twice and was in the news on practically all the major television stations. I was not quite yet 16 and the number one ranked female player in the world. On top of it all, in round seven I defeated the Philippine grandmaster, Eugenio Torre (who has been a World Champion candidate), with the black pieces. He was my first ever GM victim!

Here is the game:

□ **Eugenio Torre**
■ **Susan Polgar**
New York Open 1985
Torre Attack

---

1 d4 ♘f6 2 ♘f3 e6 3 ♗g5 c5 4 c3 cxd4 5 cxd4 d5 6 ♘c3 ♘c6 7 e3 ♗e7 8 ♗d3 0-0 9 0-0 a6 10 ♖c1 h6 11 ♗h4 ♘d7 12 ♗xe7 ♕xe7 13 e4 dxe4 14 ♗xe4 ♘f6 15 ♗xc6 bxc6 16 ♘a4 ♗d7 17 ♘e5 ♖fb8 18 ♘xc6?

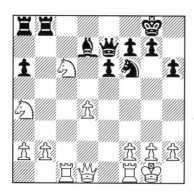

In this critical moment of the game I gained the advantage with a tricky move:

18...♕e8! 19 ♘xb8 ♗xa4 20 b3

♗b5 21 ♘xa6 ♖xa6 22 ♖e1 ♖xa2 23 ♖a1 ♖xa1 24 ♕xa1 ♕b8 25 f3 ♕f4 26 ♔h1 ♘d5 27 ♕b2 ♘b4 28 ♕f2 ♘d3 29 ♕e3 ♕c7 30 ♖a1 ♕c2 31 h3 ♗c6 32 ♖a6 ♗d5 33 ♖b6 f5 34 ♖xe6 ♗xe6 35 ♕xe6+ ♔h8 36 ♕d6 ♕c1+ 37 ♔h2 ♕f4+ 38 ♕xf4 ♘xf4 39 g4 ♔g8 40 b4 ♘d5 41 b5 f4 42 ♔g2 ♔f7 43 ♔f2 ♔e6 44 ♔e1 ♘b6 45 ♔d2 ♔d5 46 ♔c3 g5 and White resigned.

All the way I had good chances to win one of the big money prizes, until the last round when, unfortunately, I lost to GM Dmitry Gurevich. But altogether I had a pretty good score: 5½ out of 9.

In the next couple of years, I gained a lot of experience and had some good results, but still short of the GM norm.

I made my first Grandmaster norm in Royan, France, in the summer of 1988. Royan is a beautiful sea resort on the French Atlantic coast. In this 10-player invitational tournament, as usual I was in the chase for a GM-norm. This time I got that one lucky game which helped me break the ice. The Soviet-Israeli GM Murey played a good game against me, but on the forty-first move he made a careless one and fell into a trap.

□ **Jacob Murey**
■ **Susan Polgar**
Royan 1988

In this position my opponent played 40 ♗c4, pinning my knight. I had to make the last move of the time control and, as a last resort, sacrificed my bishop with 40...♗xg4. Then I went to the bathroom to freshen up. On my walk back to the stage, I was getting ready to resign. To my surprise, I saw on the demonstration board that GM Murey had taken my bishop and played 41 fxg4. He totally forgot about the discovered check 41...f3+ and then the queen on b8 falls. So he sadly resigned.

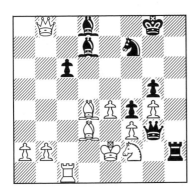

In Royan I finished second, behind only three-times World Championship finalist, Victor Korchnoi.

As they say the first norm is the hardest. It was certainly so in my case. The second norm came about a year later in León, Spain. I had a steady tournament with 5 wins and 6 draws, finishing undefeated in first place.

I clearly recall the fun times I had in León with my mother, Sofia and GM Jozsef Pinter, who also participated in the tournament. The good mood certainly helped my result.

After the Novi Sad Olympiad, we flew to India for the Triveni GM tournament in New Delhi. Judit and I tied for third place behind Anand and Kamsky. I always had trouble playing against Anand, but Judit used to beat him on a regular basis.

Here is the trick that Judit pulled on him in New Delhi:

☐ **Judit Polgar**
■ **Viswanathan Anand**
New Delhi 1990

20 ♘xe6! ♖xd2 21 ♘d4+ ♔f6 22 ♔xd2 winning a pawn and the game.

During that tournament there was a special dinner for the participants and some guests, which India's Prime Minister, Rajiv Gandhi, also attended. He showed great interest in chess and was very kind to us. Unfortunately, a few months later, he was assassinated.

My third and final GM norm was achieved in Pamplona, Spain, at the end of 1990. This event has a very special atmosphere as it is usually held over the Christmas/New Year Holiday season. In that middle-sized town, which is famous for its yearly bull runs, New Year's Eve is also very special. It is almost like a carnival, with thousands of people dressing up like slaves, celebrities, babies, and even the devil. There were countless costumes. It was quite a spectacle.

In a very strong event I played quite solidly with two wins and seven draws and no losses. I was happy and very proud to be the first woman ever actually to 'earn' the highest chess title of International Grandmaster. Here is a key game I won in that important tournament:

□ **Leonid Yudasin**
■ **Susan Polgar**
Pamplona 1990/91
Sicilian Defense

---

1 e4 c5 2 c3 d5 3 exd5 ♕xd5 4 d4 ♘c6 5 dxc5 ♕xc5 6 ♗e3 ♕a5 7 ♘f3 ♘f6 8 ♗c4 e6 9 0-0 ♗e7 10 ♘d4 ♗d7 11 ♘d2 ♘xd4 12 ♗xd4 ♗c6 13 ♖e1 0-0 14 ♘b3 ♕g5 15 g3 ♖ad8 16 f4 ♕h6 17 ♕e2 ♘e4 18 ♕e3 b6 19 ♖ad1 ♘d6 20 ♗d3 ♕h5 21 ♗e5 ♘f5 22 ♕f2

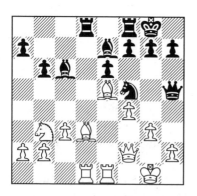

22...♘h4! 23 ♗e2 ♘f3+ 24 ♗xf3 ♗xf3 25 ♖xd8 ♖xd8 26 h3 ♗b7 27 ♔h2 ♖d3 28 ♗d4 ♕d5 29 ♕e2 ♗f6 30 ♖g1 ♗xd4 31 ♘xd4 ♕e4 32 ♕xe4 ♗xe4 33 ♖e1 f5 34 g4 ♔f7 35 ♖e2 ♖d1 36 ♔g3 h6 37 ♘f3 ♖d3 38 ♖f2 g5 39 fxg5 hxg5 40 h4 f4+ 41 ♔g2 gxh4 White resigned.

Two women, Nona Gaprindashvili and Maia Chiburdanidze had received the GM title prior to 1990. However, they did not meet all the necessary requirements as men must do. They received their titles in recognition of being Women's World Champions. Until today, only five women have ever earned the Grandmaster title the same way I did. My sister Judit earned the GM title one year later. Then there followed Pia Cramling, Antoaneta Stefanova, and Humpy Koneru.

Four other women have been awarded the GM title as merit recognition: Xie Jun and Zhu Chen as Women's World Champions, and recently Alexandra Kosteniuk and Zhaoqin Peng for winning the European Women's Championship – a new rule which was created by FIDE to give more women Grandmaster titles.

This is a very controversial issue which, I think, does not help women gain more credibility in chess. Many people feel that women should not be given 'Men's' Grandmaster titles unless they earn them the same way men do. Otherwise, what is the point? Women already had the Women's Grandmaster title. Many also argued that it was bad enough before, that FIDE selectively gave the Grandmaster title to some Women's World Champions. Now FIDE give out the same title to the European Women's Champion. Some even joked about what FIDE will do next... give the title to the World Girls Under-10 Champion? What used to be the elite title has now been somewhat tarnished.

I was the highest-ranked Hungarian

junior player for many years, but did not get a chance to measure myself against the best of my peers from around the world until 1988. It was therefore a great pleasure to return to Australia for the World Junior Championship in Adelaide. The tournament was held on the premises of a college, while the local students were on vacation. With both the girls' and boys' Championships being held simultaneously, it was also a lot of fun outside the serious chess games. Several chess marriages developed from that trip...

I was the only girl in the boys' event. It was probably the strongest ever World Junior Championship with names such as Ivanchuk, Gelfand, Adams, Akopian, just to mention a few. Surprisingly, the then 16-year-old French player, Joel Lautier, won on tie-break ahead of all the favorites. I did quite well winning three games and drawing the rest without a single loss. It was a good result but in the end I missed first place by one point.

Here is my best win from that event, against one the four Soviet players:

> □ **Susan Polgar**
> ■ **Grigory Serper**
> Adelaide 1988
> *Grünfeld Defense*

1 d4 ♘f6 2 c4 c6 3 ♘c3 d5 4 e3 g6 5 ♘f3 ♗g7 6 ♗d3 0-0 7 0-0 ♗g4 8 h3 ♗xf3 9 ♕xf3 e6 10 ♖d1 ♘bd7 11 b3 ♘b6 12 ♗b2 ♘c8 13 ♘e2 ♘d6 14 ♘g3 ♕a5 15 ♕e2 ♖ad8 16 ♕c2 ♖d7 17 a4 ♕d8 18 ♘f1 ♘h5 19 c5 ♘c8 20 g4 ♘f6 21 f4 ♘e8 22 ♘h2 f6 23 ♘f3 ♖e7 24 ♖f1 ♘c7

25 b4 a6 26 ♕h2 ♘e8 27 ♖ad1 ♘c7 28 h4 f5 29 g5 h5 30 gxh6 ♗xh6

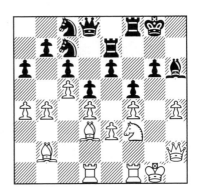

31 h5 ♖g7 32 ♔f2 gxh5 33 ♕xh5 ♖f6 34 ♘e5 ♘e7 35 ♖g1 ♘e8 36 ♗c3 ♘c7 37 ♖xg7+ ♗xg7 38 ♖g1 ♕e8 39 ♕g5 ♖f7 40 ♗e2 Black resigned.

I had a good tournament in Brno in October 1991. I was very excited to drive for the first time in my life to a foreign tournament. It was a very close field with only half a point difference between first and eight places. I won on tie-break ahead of GM Shirov, GM Epishin and others.

Playing the world's elite and meeting the World Champions

Botvinnik

Mikhail Botvinnik is considered as the father of the modern Soviet school of chess, which dominated the chess world since the end of World War II. He was probably the first player who took chess very professionally, approaching the game partly as science. He was ahead of his time in the way he approached the game. His opening analyses often went deep into the middlegame and at times even to the endgame.

He also is looked at as an icon for the way he understood chess strategy. Botvinnik originated many ideas that today we call standard. Since my childhood, I have studied most of his games, and many are evergreen classics. I recommend it to anybody who wants to improve their positional understanding of chess.

Botvinnik was also a pioneer in computer chess. I met Mikhail Botvinnik for the first time at the Chess Palace in Moscow in 1981, but only for a brief moment. The second and last time we met was in 1994 in Tilburg at the Women's Candidates tournament (which I won). We stayed in the same hotel and spoke together several times.

Smyslov

I also met Vassily Smyslov more or less at the same time and place as Mr. Botvinnik. However, I since met Mr. Smyslov many more times, and even across the chess board. We first played at the Politiken Cup in Copenhagen in 1986. In that game my famous opponent offered a draw in just fourteen moves, which I accepted.

Mr. Joop van Oosterom, one of the greatest (if not *the* greatest) chess sponsors, felt that women and veteran Grandmasters needed more support and recognition. That is why he created the 'Dance tournaments', where a small group of top women players would battle against the Greats of the past. They were all superbly organized events where chess players were treated royally.

Between 1992 and 1995 both Smyslov and I participated in all four of those yearly events. In all of the 'Dance' tournaments, the players (male versus female) faced each other twice with alternating colors.

The first of the series, the 'Tumba' tournament, was held in 1992 in Aruba, where Mr. Van Oosterom and his family resided a good part of the year. It is a very pleasant Caribbean island near Venezuela with a Dutch flavor. We all stayed in the luxurious Hyatt Regency right on the beach.

In that event, GM Smyslov first had the white pieces against me. He played rather cautiously and the game ended in a draw after forty nine moves in a position with only two pawns and a rook on each side. In the second game in Aruba, I had the white pieces. I was quite happy with the outcome of the early middlegame. I gained a small but steady advantage with a clear target, an isolated pawn. Unfortunately for me, my experienced opponent defended accurately and managed to hold the game to a draw.

Our next meeting over the chess board was at the Mikhail Tal Memorial blitz tournament in Moscow 1993. Even though Vassily played a different opening than in Aruba, we reached a similar type of isolated pawn position. This time, however, I was able to win the game. Probably the short time control (in blitz only five minutes are given to each side) also affected the outcome.

The 1993 'Walzer' event was hosted at our neighbors in Vienna. In the game where I had the white pieces, we started similarly to our encounter in Moscow.

Then I played differently and soon we got into a 'Stonewall' set-up. I had some advantage after the opening, but have blundered a pawn soon after. However, I did not give up fighting and actually found some compensation for the pawn. Later on I managed to turn things around and even win!

| □ **Susan Polgar** |
| ■ **Vassily Smyslov** |
| Vienna 1993 |

Smyslov's last move was 38...♖a2, threatening to mate me along the second rank. The position looked bad for White. In this crucial moment of the game, I found a cute simplifying combination 39 ♕xa2! ♘xa2 40 ♖c8+ ♔h7 41 ♖h8+! ♔xh8 42 ♘g6+ and the knight endgame with two extra pawns was a simple technical win.

In our other game in Vienna, I had a lucky escape. I misplayed the position early on and got into difficulties needing to give up my queen for rook and bishop. However, I managed to build a 'fortress' which even the endgame virtuoso Smyslov was not able to break through, and the game ended in a draw.

The small principality of Monaco is the other home of our beloved chess sponsor, Joop van Oosterom. This time the 'Palladienne' Ladies vs. Veterans Tournament (in 1994) was organized right in his 'backyard' in Monte Carlo. The site was the exceptional Hotel Metropol, where we saw such celebrities as Luciano Pavarotti, among others. Most cars pulling up were Rolls Royces, Bentleys or sports cars such as Ferrari, Porsche and Lamborghini.

The pairings brought us together in round one. I had White and GM Smyslov chose the same opening as back in 1986, the Meran, although a different variation of it. I did not get much out of the opening and at some point I even had to be a little bit careful, but eventually the game ended in a draw in forty two moves in a rook endgame.

In the second game, as Black I mixed up the variations in the Sicilian and got into a very difficult middlegame. I managed to survive until the endgame but, typically of the best days of Smyslov, with great patience he 'squeezed' it to a win.

The last event I played with the great Vassily was in Prague (in 1995) at the 'Polka tournament'. Despite it being so close to Budapest, that was the first time I actually spent more than a few hours (traveling through) in Prague. I discovered how amazingly beautiful it is with its special bridges and the Royal Palace.

Here in the first game, I had White and the game again (!) ended in a rook endgame with two pawns each, resulting in a draw. It is kind of ironic that, as a child, I used to study 'religiously' an endgame book by Smyslov and Leven-fish, called 'Theories of rook endgames'. Smyslov is also a respected endgame composer.

In my last game against Vassily Smyslov, I was Black. He used the same Rossolimo variation as in Monte Carlo. He played slightly differently on the fifth move, but nevertheless I managed to equalize out of the opening. However, unfortunately, soon after I made some mistakes and lost rather quickly.

Mr. Smyslov, besides being a great World Champion chess player, is also a wonderful singer. He has his own re-cord and even sang in the famous 'Bol-shoi' theater in Moscow. I had the pleasure of listening countless times to his special voice.

I will certainly cherish forever the memories of our chats, the discussions about the chess world, music and more, and of course our many interesting games.

Tal

My very first meeting with Mikhail Tal is very dear to my heart. I was only twelve years old and was on a visit to Moscow with my family. Coincidentally, at the same time there was a strong invitational Grandmaster tournament going on in town. One of my coaches, Peter Szekely, participated in the event. Therefore, we went to visit him and to observe the tournament. It was in a typical setting for Eastern Europe at the time: the players would play on stage with huge demonstration boards relaying the moves. It felt like being in a theater and watching a 'play'. The spectators could whisper to each other, dis-cuss the positions, trying to predict what moves will come next. Such events were a very important part of chess culture in the Soviet Union, Hungary and the rest of the Eastern European countries.

During my visit to the tournament the 'magician from Riga', as he is commonly referred to, was in the middle of his game against the Armenian grand-master, Rafael Vaganian. Tal had some serious health problems but, nevertheless, he was kind of a 'chain smoker'. This turned out to be my 'luck'! During one of his walks up and down the hall-way to smoke, my mother was brave enough to go up to him and tell him how much I admired him and his games. And yes, by the way, my dream was to play a blitz game against him! Would he be willing to play a 12-year-old girl from Hungary?

Tal was known to like to play blitz and was considered as one of the very best in the world even at that time. Some years later, in 1988, he still won the World Blitz Championship in Canada. I was shocked and very pleasantly surprised about his answer, which was something like: 'Sure. I have already heard legends about the Polgars. Wait a minute, let me see what I can do...'

A few minutes later, we saw the Vaganian-Tal game ended! Apparently after my mother's question, he went back to his board and offered a draw so we could play blitz! Vaganian accepted the draw offer. Minutes later we were actually playing blitz in the analysis room being surrounded by dozens and dozens of spectators! To my great joy and to the amazement of the entire crowd watching, in the first game I had the initiative, sacrificed two pieces and almost... won. But in the end the attack was only good enough for a draw by perpetual check. While I immensely enjoyed the remaining five games as well, I have not much to brag about. But it was an experience I could never forget. And the kindness and passion for chess from Tal forever stayed in my heart.

Exactly ten years later in 1991, I finally played Tal under classical chess conditions at an international tournament in San Francisco. I had the black pieces and to my surprise, after just fifteen moves, Mikhail offered a draw, which I accepted as the position was about even.

At this event I got to know Tal a little better in a more social environment. He was very sociable, friendly and funny. Tal was known, admired and loved for his colorful, fearless, combinative style. At times, he would make sacrifices even when it might not be one hundred percent sound, but other grandmasters would somehow chicken out.

At the tournament in San Francisco I won the brilliancy prize with a 'Tal-like' combination against the strong American grandmaster, Larry Christiansen.

◻ **Susan Polgar**
◼ **Larry Christiansen**
San Francisco 1991

See following diagram

---

19 ♗xg6 fxg6 20 ♕xh6 ♘h7 21 ♕xg6+ ♔h8 22 ♗xe7 ♕xe7 23 c4! (the final point – if the bishop moves away,

♖d7 is killing. Black had to return the piece and remain down in material and with an exposed king) 23...♕h4 24 cxd5 ♕xf2+ 25 ♔h1 ♖f6 26 ♕e4 exd5 27 ♕d5 and I won on move 50.

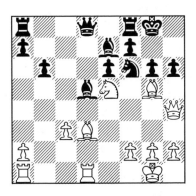

Unfortunately, I discovered after the tournament that things would not have been simple at all if Black had played the superior 19...hxg5! 20 ♕xg5 fxg6 21 ♕xg6 ♔h8, as after 22 ♖d3 ♘h7 23 ♖h3 ♗h4 Black can successfully defend. Therefore, it was a nice game but not perfect.

The next time I saw Tal was in Cologne, Germany, at a rapid event. I saw him one more time on a boat excursion in New York, together with Garry Kasparov and others. As I witnessed several times that his weakness was the 'bottle' and that perhaps made things worse for his health. However, I believe that he drank to ease the physical pain that he had for most of his life and not for pleasure, since it was said that no medicine could help subside his pain. Many others have also confirmed to me the same thing. Unfortunately, soon afterwards he got very sick and died at the young age of 55.

Spassky

I first met Boris Spassky in December 1985 at the OHRA tournament in Brussels. It was a beautifully organized event and perhaps the strongest competition that I had had in my career up to that point. It was a really great experience to get the opportunity to play against top level grandmasters. In our game, Boris simply outclassed me and I lost without too much resistance. Perhaps I had too much respect for him at the board. But in the end, I finished with a respectable 50% score in that event.

I had the pleasure to share the dinner table daily with Boris and the other players (who included grandmasters Korchnoi, Nunn, Speelman, Sax, Van der Wiel and others). Boris is a great storyteller with a very unique style.

Boris was originally from Leningrad (St. Petersburg) and was the tenth Chess World Champion in history. He is a player with a very deep understanding of chess. Boris had an incredible career winning many world-class events. The highlight was beating Tigran Petrosian to win the World Championship in 1969. However, it is somewhat unfortunate that many people will remember him more for losing his title to Bobby Fischer in the controversial 'match of the century'. He and Bobby will forever be linked. As Boris personally told me, after he lost his title he was considered a 'black sheep' in the Soviet Union. They viewed him as a traitor who let 'the system' down. They withdrew most of the privileges he used to have. As if he was not trying his best his best to win.

Spassky married a very nice and classy French woman named Marina.

He moved to France and became a French citizen in 1978. Boris himself admitted that he lost most of his competitiveness and motivation after losing the world title to Bobby in 1972. Although he remained a top ten player for a while after that, he never had to same fire again.

A year and a few months after the tournament in Belgium, I was invited to Cannes and to Monaco where we saw each other again. In Cannes, again having the black pieces, I managed to make a draw. I no longer had the same butterflies as I did the first time we played.

After those tournaments, Boris invited us (my mother and I) to visit him and Marina in Paris on our way back home. He gave us a 'tour of Paris at night' in his Mercedes. Then Marina and Boris treated us to a nice home-made dinner. He was already in the process of writing a book on his life and games, and showed me some interesting discoveries from the future book that night.

Next time we met was at the other end of the world in Wellington, New Zealand. That trip also belongs to the very pleasant ones. It was really interesting to see the geysers they have there and to learn about the Maori culture. Boris again had the white pieces and totally surprised me with the King's Gambit. I put up a decent fight but he outplayed me at the end.

The next time we saw each other was in my home-town in 1993 when he played my sister Judit a ten game match. (See more about that later in Judit's section.) In the same year, Bobby Fischer moved to Budapest, not long after he and Boris played their second controversial match in 1992. Bobby became an everyday guest at our family home.

It is amazing that over all these years Bobby and Boris always remained good friends, despite their hard-fought and well-publicized chess matches. Therefore, when Boris found out that Bobby was in Budapest, he flew to Hungary to visit his 'good old friend'. Boris visited us in our home and we also went out to restaurants together during his visit. While the two chess legends do not agree on everything, they do have great mutual respect for each other and always had very lively debates. They certainly have one thing in common: they both love good food.

Just as against Smyslov, I also played against Boris in the 'Ladies vs. Veterans' events. We drew three of those games and I lost one.

The last time I saw Boris was in 2003 in Fort Lauderdale, where he was inducted to the Chess World Hall of Fame. He and Marina stayed at the same hotel with Lev Alburt, Paul Truong, Sam Palatnik and me. Boris and I even gave a team simul (I started the game and halfway through Boris took the games over) at the Chess Hall of Fame. During dinner, and on our way back and forth from the hotel and the Chess Hall of Fame, Boris told us many wonderful stories.

At the induction ceremony, Boris gave an extremely entertaining acceptance speech and answered all questions with passion. Among many things he said, he felt that his peak was in the late 1960s, whereas in 1972 Fischer already was a stronger player than him.

Some months later, around his birthday, I spoke to Boris on the phone when I interviewed him for one hour on behalf of the World Chess Network (WCN). As Robert Byrne said in the film 'Clash of the Titans': 'he is truly a classic gentleman'.

Karpov

Anatoly Karpov was *the* chess icon when I started to play chess more seriously. He defeated Victor Korchnoi in 1974 and earned the right to challenge Bobby Fischer for the World Championship title in 1975. He was declared the World Champion when Fischer refused to defend his title. Living in Hungary, which was under great Soviet influence at the time, we were exposed to a lot of Soviet propaganda. But regardless of any propaganda, the fact is that his games were great and his strategical understanding of chess is exceptional. Therefore, I grew up following his games and my style was greatly influenced by him.

I first saw Anatoly Karpov when I was around six or seven years old; he was visiting Budapest and gave a lecture. We first met over the board in a competition in Bilbao, Spain in 1987. Those were the years when he and Garry Kasparov were playing their endless matches. Karpov was still in his prime. It was an honor to get invited to such an event. That was the biggest purse tournament of my life up to that point.

Anatoly was very friendly with me right from the start, except when sitting across the chess board. I vividly remember during one of the excursions on the free day, he showed me how to eat lobster and clam, which was a new experience to me at the time.

In our game, I had a strange feeling. I really liked my position for a long time and then suddenly when the position opened up, all his pieces found themselves on the right squares while mine lost co-ordination. This is something he was so good at. A few moves later, I had a horrible position. Instead of a long passive defense, I decided to gamble and made an unsound combination, hoping that in time pressure he might not find the best respond. I had no such luck against somebody of Karpov's caliber.

During the Bilbao tournament, I had a very memorable last round in one of the longest games I have ever played. I had Black against the Swedish grand-master, Ulf Andersson. He was chasing after Karpov to win the tournament. Besides the prestige at stake for both of us, $5,000 difference in prizes was on the line. The Swedish grandmaster is famous for his success and liking of endgames, so I knew I would have to play a long game. He played his favorite Exchange variation against the King's Indian, making sure that the queens were off the board quickly. However, I was well prepared and got a nice position. I even got a favorable endgame at one stage, but misplayed it and let him off the hook. After that, I had to suffer defending a worse endgame for hours to come.

In those days, the time control was a lot slower than today. We used to have two hours each for the first forty moves, and then an hour each for twenty moves. Typically, after one or two time controls, the game would be adjourned. This was prior to the time when chess computers became strong. However, even without computer assistance, all players used to analyze the adjourned position in the break, usually with the help of their coach or friends. Therefore, I think the current 'no adjournment' is a lot fairer.

My game with Anderson got adjourned twice in the same night, both times only for a short time (I think a two-hour break). If it had not been the last round, normally we would have continued it the following morning.

On move 90, he missed a winning opportunity. Later, we got a queen, knight and one pawn vs. queen and bishop endgame. He tried for 115 moves to win, but I defended until about 4:30 in the morning (!) and managed to hold on to a draw.

☐ **Ulf Andersson**
■ **Susan Polgar**
Bilbao 1987

In the above position, my opponent played 90 b6?, and after 90...a2 91 b7 a1♛ 92 b8♛+ ♚c1, the best White could get was forcing me to give my bishop up for the f-pawn, but queen and knight does not win objectively against a queen.

Instead after 90 ♘a5? a2 91 ♘b3, Black has a pretty saving move 91...♗d4!!. On the other hand 90 ♘b4! ♗c3 91 b6 ♗xb4 92 ♔xb4 a2 93 b7 a1♕ 94 b8♕ leads to a theoretically won queen endgame. According to the endgame tablebase, White will checkmate in 46 moves and it is 100% precise! It was not an easy continuation to find in the small hours of the morning.

The next time we played was in the blitz section of the Melody Amber tournament. That is a spectacular yearly event that Mr. Van Oosterom sponsors, named after his first-born daughter. It is usually held in Monte Carlo, but in 1992 it was for the first time in a breathtaking place, just about a mile away in Roquebrune. Although it was only a five minute game, I won a nice game and checkmated Anatoly in 36 moves.

| □ **Susan Polgar** |
| ■ **Anatoly Karpov** |
| Roquebrune 1992 |
| *Queen's Indian Defense* |

---

1 d4 ♘f6 **2** c4 e6 **3** ♘f3 b6 **4** g3 ♗a6 **5** b3 ♗b4+ **6** ♗d2 ♗e7 **7** ♗g2 c6 **8** 0-0 d5 **9** ♘e5 ♘fd7 **10** ♘xd7 ♘xd7 **11** ♗c3 0-0 **12** ♘d2 f5 **13** ♖c1 ♗a3 **14** ♖b1 ♗d6 **15** b4 ♕c8 **16** ♕b3 b5 **17** c5 ♗c7 **18** e3 ♕e8 **19** f4 h6 **20** ♘f3 ♔h7 **21** ♔f2 ♘f6 **22** ♘e5 ♗xe5 **23** dxe5 ♘g4+ **24** ♔e2 ♘xh2 **25** ♖h1 ♘g4 **26** ♗f3 ♕g6 **27** ♖h4 ♔g8 **28** ♕c2 ♕e8 **29** ♖bh1 ♗c8 **30** ♗xg4 fxg4 **31** ♖xg4 ♔h8 **32** ♖g6 ♕f7 **33** g4 ♔g8 **34** ♖hxh6 a5 **35** ♖g5 axb4 **36** ♕h7 mate.

A few months later, we met again over the board in Madrid. This time it was at a regular classical time control and we played an interesting game. He got a microscopic advantage and I was convinced that I should be able to hold it. However, I did not understand where I went wrong and I lost. In fact, for many years, I was not quite sure what I should have done differently. Finally in 2004, during the Women's Olympiad Training Program session with Garry Kasparov, Garry, Paul Truong, the girls and I analyzed the critical position and, after about half an hour, we came to a conclusion on how to improve and easily draw the game.

The following year, I was invited as a participant to the Melody Amber tournament in Monaco. This time I played in the main events, in the Rapid and the 'Blind' sections. The latter is an interesting format which works in the following way: Both players sit in front a computer screen looking at the empty 64 squares. Once they are ready to move they just move the mouse cursor from a square to another square. We had to remember the entire games in our head and try to play high level chess. If somebody forgets where a piece is and makes an illegal move, he or she loses the game right away. So those competitions require the utmost concentration.

In the rapid game we drew in 49 moves. The game was mostly around equal, but I made some mistakes towards the end and then had to fight to hold. Despite having an extra bishop my opponent could not win because of the 'wrong corner'.

In the blindfold game, in a close to even endgame, I 'overlooked' my bishop and lost.

In 1994, we were back again in the same place (Monte Carlo), at more or less the same time, with mostly the same participants. This time I defeated Anatoly in the blindfold game, but lost in the rapid.

I had to wait another decade to play Anatoly again. Then we played a special six-game promotional exhibition match in Lindsborg, Kansas. This event was put together by Mikhail Korenman (a friend of Karpov) and Paul Truong. The original idea was to show the mainstream media the diversity of chess by playing two rapid games, two blitz games, and two advanced chess games (where each player is allowed to consult their laptop computers). Due to the tragic situation with Bobby Fischer, Anatoly and I decided at the last minute to change the two advanced chess games to two Fischer random games, to honor Bobby Fischer and what he had contributed to chess.

The match took place in a small town in Kansas with only about 3000 population. However, the support for chess in Lindsborg and in Kansas was simply phenomenal. The town threw an incredible parade. It seemed like the entire town was there cheering us on.

On the first day, we played the two rapid games. I drew the first and lost the second game. In the second day, we started with two Fischer random games, followed by two blitz games. I won the

first Fischer random game to even the score to 1½-1½ but lost the second one. In the first blitz game, I drew; which meant I had to win the final game with the white pieces to tie up the match. I did and the final score was 3-3.

Kasparov

I first heard of Garry Kasparov in the late seventies. He was a top junior player at the time, but already a lot of people foresaw the future in him and predicted that he would be the next world champion. I started closely following, studying and admiring his games. His style was very refreshing after the dryer, though no less successful era of Karpov. Garry played many brilliant games in 1980. I believe that was his breakthrough year to the international arena.

I did not meet him personally until 1988 when he was already World Champion. We both participated at the 28th Chess Olympiad in Thessaloniki, and led our respective teams on board 1 to the team gold medal. Then we spoke at length. There was even a famous picture of him and me talking that was published many times over. He was very friendly to me and my family. He was in absolute amazement at Judit's incredible performance in that event (she scored 12 wins and only 1 draw in a winning position).

On one of the free days, we all went for a long walk. My parents and I were asking Garry's advice on how to improve our training methods, etc. We asked him about what was his 'secret' to such an amazing rise in his late teenage years. He said that his coaches wisely and patiently waited until he was ready to face stronger and stronger fields. Therefore, he never faced a tragic tournament result (a minus score) that could psychologically harm his confidence for future events. Among other things, he recommended that we avoid overly strong tournaments where we would be expected to finish in the second half of the field.

The next time I saw Garry was in Linares at the 'Wimbledon of Chess' in 1994. I was Judit's and Gata Kamsky's second at that tournament. We stayed at the Hotel Anibal on the same floor and bumped into each other regularly.

Everything was cordial and friendly until the infamous game between Garry and Judit. We (Judit, Gata and I) prepared for hours before their first ever clash. We anticipated the Sicilian Najdorf, Garry's favorite against 1 e4. We planned to surprise him with a rare order of moves and I vividly recall the excitement in our analyses. Unfortunately, quite early on the 9th move, he already avoided our preparation and Judit did not get an advantage out of the opening. Then, slowly, slowly Garry outplayed Judit in the middlegame. After Judit's 36th move, Garry had a clearly better position. That is when the infamous incident took place, right in front of all the spectators including myself, as well as a TV camera which turned out to be filming it!

□ **Judit Polgar**
■ **Garry Kasparov**
Linares 1994
Sicilian Defense

---

1 e4 c5 2 ♘f3 d6 3 d4 cxd4 4 ♘xd4 ♘f6 5 ♘c3 a6 6 f4 e6 7 ♗e2 ♗e7 8

0-0 ♕c7 9 ♕e1 ♘bd7 10 a4 b6 11 ♗f3 ♗b7 12 ♔h1 ♖d8 13 ♗e3 0-0 14 ♕g3 ♘c5 15 f5 e5 16 ♗h6 ♘e8 17 ♘b3 ♘d7 18 ♖ad1 ♔h8 19 ♗e3 ♘ef6 20 ♕f2 ♖fe8 21 ♖fe1 ♗f8 22 ♗g5 h6 23 ♗h4 ♖c8 24 ♕f1 ♗e7 25 ♘d2 ♕c5 26 ♘b3 ♕b4 27 ♗e2 ♗xe4 28 ♘xe4 ♘xe4 29 ♗xe7 ♖xe7 30 ♗f3 ♘ef6 31 ♕xa6 ♖ee8 32 ♕e2 ♔g8 33 ♗b7 ♖c4 34 ♕d2 ♕xa4 35 ♕xd6 ♖xc2 36 ♘d2

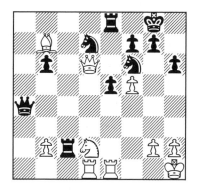

Garry was in serious time pressure, having no more than a couple of minutes left to reach the time control at forty moves. He touched his knight and moved it from d7 to c5, and let the knight go for a fraction of a second. As he suddenly noticed what Judit's next move would be (a fork with ♗c6), he changed his mind and moved the knight from c5 and put it on f8.

Many spectators witnessed what happened but could not believe their eyes, including the arbiter Mr. Falcon who was standing right next to the table! Judit looked in disbelief at the arbiter with a questioning expression... 'Did this really just happen? Have you seen the same what I've seen?' Judit was stunned. At such high-level competition this was absolutely unprecedented. I am 100% sure that if it had involved a less famous player than Garry, the arbiter would have intervened. But because it was Garry, and because it took place too fast, they gave him the benefit of the doubt. I also think that, since it took place so quickly and Garry was so focused in the game, he may not have realized it.

Garry made the necessary moves to reach the time control, although he missed a simple win on move 40. Judit, being quite upset about the lack of intervention by the arbiter, made a final error the next move and lost the game. These were the final moves: 36...♘f8 37 ♘e4 ♘8d7 38 ♘xf6+ ♘xf6 39 ♕xb6 ♘g4 40 ♖f1 e4 41 ♗d5 e3 42 ♗b3 ♕e4 43 ♗xc2 ♕xc2 44 ♖d8 ♖xd8 45 ♕xd8+ ♔h7 46 ♕e7 ♕c4 White resigned.

Ironically, the 'blunder' that Garry wanted to avoid turned out, in the after the game analyses, to be not as bad as it seemed. While Judit would win an exchange Garry could have saved the game to a draw with perpetual check.

Unfortunately, this memorable knight move temporarily ruined our relationship with Garry. It took some time until Judit and Garry spoke again. Now after many years, all of this is history and they are back to having a good relationship.

I next saw Garry at the Chess Olympiad in Moscow that same year. Despite not having much contact during the tournament, he was very supportive of my Candidates semi-final match versus Chiburdanidze to be held in St. Petersburg.

After my relocation to America, I saw Garry only randomly at different chess functions in New York. Then in early 2003, the Kasparov Chess Foundation decided to support my initiative of the 2004 US Women's Olympiad training program. To my very pleasant surprise, Garry closely involved himself with the progress of our training, including conducting two sessions personally. He was very respectful and friendly with me and the whole team. Since I had never had a chance to face Garry in a tournament, I was always curious to know what it is like to play against the world's best. When I mentioned this to Michael Khodarkovsky, he told Garry, who graciously accepted to play some blitz game with me.

Garry's confidence in our team was certainly helpful to us and maybe even somewhat intimidating to our opponents. You can read more about it in the 'Ultimate Breakthrough' section of this book.

No matter what one's opinion of Garry, everyone agrees that he has been one of the most colorful and dynamic champions ever. There were many memorable matches: versus his great rival Karpov, *Deep Blue*, *Deep Fritz*, *Deep Junior*, etc. He is also arguably one of the greatest champions in the history of the game. He has solidly held his No.1 ranking for more than 20 years. In this modern era of chess, this is something that will be very difficult, if not impossible, to duplicate.

Anand

The 19-year-old 'Vishy' Anand first amazed the world of chess at Wijk aan Zee in 1989 (and at other tournaments later) with his incredibly fast play. While most players usually use up all their time on the clock and barely make the time control, Anand seemed to play as if it was rapid chess. He finished his games using less than an hour, compared to his opponent's two or three hours. This is a true phenomenon in top-level competitions. Incidentally, my sister Judit used to play the same way in her early teenage days, but later she grew out of it.

During the tournament, we (Vishy, my sisters and I) became good friends and invited him to visit us in Budapest. To our delight, Vishy accepted the invitation and shortly after the tournament he came to stay with us for about a week. Like most Hindus, he was a strict vegetarian back then. Some years later, being on the European chess circuit, it probably was complicated to maintain that diet. Therefore, he added fish and chicken to his diet.

At that time, Vishy was completely engrossed in chess. He was eager to play blitz or analyze at any time. In between, he would listen to music or meditate. We could clearly see his talent and the unlimited boundless future of his chess career. We always joked around and had a lot of fun. In addition, we of course played tons of blitz. The impact that Vishy made for chess in India is unsurpassed. He is a national hero in his homeland and he revolutionized Indian chess.

The Bobby Fischer I know

As so many others of my generation, I was greatly influenced by the chess frenzy that Bobby created right around when I started to play chess. Fischer played Spassky for the World Champi-

onship in July and August of 1972 in Reykjavik, Iceland. I do not remember exactly but it was definitely within six months of that time when I first saw a chessboard. I do remember from back then my father talking about the Fischer phenomenon and how amazing his chess play was. Obviously at that time, and for a long time to come, I never could imagine that I would ever play chess with Bobby or even meet him.

After winning the World Championship title in 1972, Bobby decided to retire and did not defend his title in 1975. The chess world was very sorry and disappointed by the disappearance of Fischer from the scene. He brought fire, excitement and, yes, sometimes scandals to the chess community. But most of all, he played many great games and had amazing victories. He practically defeated the Soviet chess machine all by himself. He virtually single-handedly created professional chess as such.

He was the first one with the star power to command serious financial conditions from chess organizers. After his 1972 match, he had lucrative endorsement contracts in his hands. Unfortunately, he never signed any of them. Had he have been more business and marketing oriented, most likely chess professionals even today could benefit from it. But even so, we chess professionals have to be very thankful for what Bobby did for the sport, and not complain of how much more he could have done.

It is amazing that even now, more than 30 years after the chess match of the 20th century, there is still a mystic, excitement about what would happen if

Bobby returned to competitive chess. The chess world can probably thank a young Hungarian woman, Zita Rajcsanyi, that we saw Bobby Fischer come back one more time. Zita is about a year older than Sofia and was a promising junior player in the late eighties. She wrote a fan letter to Bobby and probably did not expect an answer. But surprising as it seems, a meeting was set up and Zita flew to California to meet Bobby in person. They got involved and Zita convinced Bobby to play again.

In 1992, on the 20th anniversary of the 1972 Fischer-Spassky match, a Yugoslav Bank owner sponsored a politically highly controversial rematch with $5,000,000 prize funds between the same two players. That was the time when the US had an embargo forbidding Americans doing any kind of business with Yugoslavia. Bobby, however, did not obey the order of the US Government and traveled to Sveti Stefan, a beautiful resort off the coast of Montenegro. Prior to the start, Bobby received another notice from the White House warning him about the consequences if he played the match. He literally spat on the letter. The whole world saw it on television, creating yet another Fischer scandal.

Both former world champions were twenty years older and not quite on the top of their games. However, they did play many interesting games and some very high level ones too. Bobby won the rematch quite convincingly, 17½-12½, even though, to quote Boris: 'I did not want to lose the match, but also I did not mind that Bobby won.'

After the match was over, Bobby went into hiding. Officially the US government was after him and he kept a 'low profile' in a small Yugoslavian town, Kanjiza, near the Hungarian border.

I believe it was sometime late May 1993 when our old acquaintance/friend, Janos Kubat, a Hungarian/Yugoslav, drove my parents and sisters to meet Bobby in his hiding place. I was in Peru at the time and envied them for the honor of meeting the American chess genius. Apparently, Bobby was disappointed that I did not go as well and he wanted to meet me. Therefore, another visit was arranged. After my return from South America, I drove my family in my VW Passat for another trip across the border. Bobby was protected by a professional bodyguard, as well as his good friend Filipino grandmaster Eugenio Torre. Bobby was staying in a modest hotel room. His main activities were listening to the radio, reading, analyzing, and playing chess. He was constantly following the chess news and games. I was surprised to see how tall and big he is. He was slightly overweight, though I would not call him fat, and seems to have enormous hands and feet. He was very friendly and open with me right away, and had a lot of questions, including about my recent trip to Peru. He was in the process of analyzing the games between the two World Champions right after him, Anatoly Karpov and Garry Kasparov. Fischer was completely convinced that the Soviets usually prearranged the results of important championship games.

I was fascinated to watch his analysis. In some endgame positions where, after an adjournment, one side made obvious (according to Bobby) mistakes and blew the game, he viewed at it as proof that a player of this caliber would never make such mistakes unless they did so on purpose.

By the way, it also showed the tremendous professional respect that Bobby had for his colleagues. While I personally did not agree with Bobby's theory, I can also imagine some occasional games were not being played out at full strength, especially games ending in a draw. However, I did not feel that there was any need to debate with Bobby on this issue. I do my debate on the chessboard.

After I first met Bobby, I felt he was not happy hiding and living like a fugitive in a small place to which he had no connection whatsoever. My family and I suggested to him that he move to Budapest, a much bigger city where he could go to restaurants, movies, meet chess players or do many other things.

A few weeks later, Bobby, together with his bodyguard and GM Torre, packed up and moved to Budapest. At that point Zita and Bobby were not together anymore. However, in Budapest, besides our family, Bobby found some old friends as well: Pal Benko, Lajos Portisch and Andor Lilienthal, grandmasters more or less from his generation. I also introduced him to some of my friends to keep him company.

After Bobby arrived in Budapest, I often drove him and his companions around, showing him my beautiful home-town. We often had lunch or dinner at our place, and went out to restaurants together, which was one of his favorite things to do. He was especially fond of caviar and Japanese cuisine. Another thing Bobby loved in Budapest was our world-famous mineral baths.

Even though Bobby's reign as World Champion was brief, the impact he made on chess will live on forever. While I disagree with many unfortunate comments that he has made, I will always respect his genius and vision of the game. I was very sorry to hear about his arrest in Japan. I hope that he will be granted citizenship in Iceland and live out his life in peace.

Blitz and Rapid World Championships, May 1992

The Hungarian Chess Federation, with the help of my father, organized the Women's World Championship in Blitz (5 minute) and Rapid (30 minute) chess in Budapest in 1992. It was done at nice settings at Hotel Beke and Aqiuncum, located right on the banks of the Buda side of the Danube river. The Van Oosteroms were one of the sponsors and were present during the tournament. 27 participants representing 24 countries showed up, including former Women's World Champion Maia Chiburdanidze, both my sisters and many other top women chess players.

The blitz event was first on the schedule. It was a fierce fight between Judit and me for the World Championship title. She was rated No.1 in the world and I was No.2. She won our individual game, but I scored 22½ out of the other 25 games to finish half a point ahead and won the tournament.

Judit came second with 22 points. Alisa Galliamova was third with 20 points and Sofia finished fourth with 19½ points.

The 15-round World Rapid Championship was played over a three day period. I scored 12 points out of 15 without a single defeat to win the World Rapid Championship, ahead of Sofia, Maia Chiburdanidze and Judit, who all scored 11½. (The placements were decided on tie-breaks in that order.)

Here is my encounter from round 10:

□ **Susan Polgar**
■ **Susan Arkell**
Budapest 1992
Queen's Gambit

---

1 d4 d5 2 c4 e6 3 ♘f3 c5 4 cxd5 exd5 5 ♗g5 ♗e7 6 ♗xe7 ♕xe7 7 dxc5 ♕xc5 8 ♘c3 ♘f6 9 e3 ♘c6 10 ♗b5 0-0 11 0-0 ♗g4 12 ♖c1 ♕b4 13 b3 ♖fd8 14 ♗xc6 bxc6 15 ♘a4 ♖ac8 16 ♕d4 ♕a3 17 ♘e5 ♗e2 18 ♖fe1 ♗b5 19 ♘c5 a5 20 ♖c2 ♖e8 21 ♖d1 h6 22 f4 ♖e7

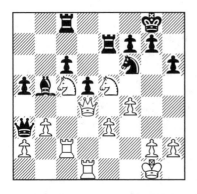

23 ♕b2 ♕xb2 24 ♖xb2 ♘e4 25 ♘xe4 dxe4 26 a4 ♗a6 27 ♖c2 c5

28 ♖d6 ♗b7 29 ♘c4 ♖a8 30 ♘b6 ♖b8 31 ♖xc5 ♗a6 32 ♖xa5 ♗d3 33 ♖c5 Black resigned.

Later that same year, we had another trip down under. The distant continent is one of my favorite places in the world. The only thing I do not like about it is that it is so far from the rest of the world! During this visit, I won the Australian Rapid Open Championship in Sydney.

Entering the Women's World Championship for the first time

For many years prior to 1992, I did not care about entering in women-only events, including the World Championships. One of my earlier goals was to achieve the Men's Grandmaster title.

I finally earned that highest title of Men's Grandmaster in early January of 1991, becoming the first woman ever in chess history to accomplish this feat. In one way, it was a great satisfaction; it felt like mission accomplished. On the other hand, I was not quite sure what was my next big goal.

Originally I dreamt of becoming one of the top ten players in the world. However, with all the unexpected chess-political hurdles, the religious and gender discrimination along the way, I lost so much energy, time and faith in being able to have a fair chance to compete, I no longer had the proper desire to make all the necessary sacrifices.

Also, around that time I had a turning point in my life in more than one way. As a normal process at that age, I felt the need for independence. I moved out from my parents' home to live on my own and I started to travel by myself. I learned to drive and got my driving license. It may sound nothing special for most people in America, but in our family no one owned a car or had a driver's license at that time. In addition, I wanted to have a normal social life. Up to then, I had devoted practically my whole life to chess, competing and fighting to make the game fairer for all, regardless of age, gender or religious belief.

With all those changes in my life, I had a new goal with my chess career. I felt that I was ready to quiet down all the doubters about my abilities to play against women. Strangely enough, many women players felt throughout the eighties that there was a difference playing against men rather than women. They felt it was less demanding playing against men. Many claimed that it was easier for me to collect rating points against men, but that there was no way I could perform the same against women. Even with gold medals in the 1988 and 1990 Olympiads, they were still not convinced. It sounded totally absurd to me and just did not make any logical sense. While some said it purely out of jealousy, to the defense of others I think many honestly believed so.

My argument was if it was so easy to 'collect' rating points playing against male players, how come none of them were able to do it until I came along, and then my sisters? Even though Gaprindashvili and Chiburdanidze had success in some events, the facts showed that many other top-ranked women were playing in open tournaments against men with lesser success. It was not as easy as they claimed.

In 1992, I had the encouragement of my boyfriend at the time, as well as the full support of our friend and sponsor Joop van Oosterom, to show what I could do in the Women's World Championship.

The Candidates tournament was held in Shanghai, China. Before the trip, I was a little worried. I felt that I was going into the lion's den since, out of my eight opponents, three were Chinese. In those days, one used to hear rumors of horror stories about playing in communist countries. According to some players, the locals would use all means possible to gain a 'home court advantage' against foreigners at important title events.

Fortunately, nothing could be further from the truth in China. The Chinese organizers were great hosts and the players were all good sports. The place where we stayed, and where the tournament was held, was in the outskirts of Shanghai. It was in a breathtaking gated park that was reserved for Chinese leaders and important foreign guests. In the middle of the park, there were a few buildings with a hotel and a few restaurants. I love Chinese food, so I really had a field day. Chinese food in China is somewhat different than elsewhere, but it is clearly better.

I did quite well against the top Chinese players, scoring 5½ out of 6. We played a double round robin, meaning that we all played each other twice with alternate colors.

Besides my boyfriend, GM Julio Granda Zuniga from Peru, I had the former top non-Soviet player in the world, GM Bent Larsen, and his wife

Laura with me. This was only possible thanks to Mr. Van Oosterom's generosity. Unfortunately, my boyfriend and I had some personal difficulties right before the tournament. Therefore, I did not begin play in quite the right frame of mind. I was most thankful to Mrs. Larsen for her moral support during those tough moments.

Fortunately, things got temporarily resolved after a couple of days and I managed to have a spectacular start of 9½ out of 10. Amazingly, looking retrospectively at the crosstable, I could have lost all of my last six (!) games and still won the event! I ended up drawing them and finished ahead of second place by 3½ points.

After I passed the first step successfully I had two more to go in order to win the title. According to the regulations, despite my convincing victory in the Candidates tournament, the winner and the runner-up had to play a match to decide who would be the challenger to the Chinese World Champion, Xie Jun.

My opponent in the Candidates final match was Nana Ioseliani from the republic of Georgia. I first met Nana in 1981, when we were introduced at the Chess Palace in Moscow. She was already a star back then, even though she was only nineteen. She accepted my challenge to a blitz match and I came to visit her in her hotel. I won the first match and she requested a rematch within a few days. We met again and, overall, the score was balanced. However, it was only at the Candidates tournament that we played an official game the first time. There I won with the black pieces and drew with White.

Here is one of our games from Shanghai:

□ **Nana Ioseliani**
■ **Susan Polgar**
Shanghai 1992
Sicilian Defense

1 e4 c5 2 ♘f3 ♘c6 3 ♗b5 e6 4 0-0 ♘ge7 5 c3 a6 6 ♗a4 b5 7 ♗c2 ♗b7 8 a4 ♘g6 9 ♖e1 ♖c8 10 axb5 axb5 11 d4 cxd4 12 cxd4 ♘b4 13 ♗b3 ♖xc1 14 ♕xc1 ♘d3 15 ♕e3 ♘xe1 16 ♕xe1 ♗e7 17 ♘c3 0-0 18 ♘xb5 ♕b6 19 ♗c4

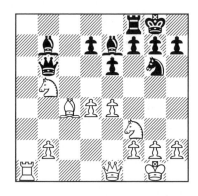

19...f5 20 e5 ♗xf3 21 gxf3 ♘h4 22 ♕c3 ♕b7 23 ♗e2 ♖c8 24 ♖a7 ♖xc3 25 ♖xb7 ♖c1+ 26 ♗f1 ♘xf3+ 27 ♔g2 ♘h4+ 28 ♔g1 ♘f3+ 29 ♔g2 ♗h4 30 ♖xd7 ♖c2 31 ♔xf3 ♖xf2+ 32 ♔e3 ♖xf1 33 ♖c7 f4+ 34 ♔d3 f3 35 ♘d6 h5 36 ♘e4 f2 37 ♘xf2 ♖xf2 38 b4 ♖xh2 39 b5 ♖b2 40 ♖c5 ♗e7 41 ♖c7 ♔f7 White resigned.

Mr. Van Oosterom was very excited about my results in China and offered to host the match versus Nana in Monaco, in February 1993, with the prize fund of $100,000. He told me that if I won, he would sponsor the World Championship Final with an unprecedented total prize fund of $1,000,000!

Before the match, all agreed that I was the clear favorite. I had just come back with a convincing victory in Shanghai and was exactly 100 points higher rated than Nana. I was also leading in our personal score.

This time I had Grandmaster Boris Gulko with me as my second, along with my boyfriend Julio. This was a mistake. I should have known better than to have my boyfriend at the match after what happened in Shanghai. When things go well in your personal relationship, you can perform 100 points better. When things go badly, you can lose to anyone. Things started pretty well. I won the first two games, and after five games maintained a two-point lead.

Then things started to go very wrong and I was in one the biggest upsets of my personal life. My personal relationship drastically headed south. I did not know what was going on, but I had a bad feeling. You can say that it was a woman's intuition. My boyfriend acted very strangely, but he would not tell me what was going on. It would have been better if he had broken up with me right there and then. Instead, the anticipation and mystery took a huge toll on me physically, mentally and emotionally. I was a complete wreck and could barely sleep at night; my head was a complete mess. It was one of the most painful times of my life.

I found out later what had happened. My boyfriend not only had someone else, even before we dated, he

actually had a family with this person. He felt guilty but did not know how to tell me. Therefore, he was very indifferent to me, and I felt it the whole time during the match.

I started playing badly. I was no longer the aggressor. I was just holding on for dear life during the games and trying to save my relationship after the game. The match was the best of eight games, and despite my two game lead, my opponent managed to draw level and the final score became 4-4.

So we had to play two play-off games (45 minutes for 60 moves, then 15 minutes for the rest of the game) to determine the winner. I took the lead again by winning the first game, but lost the second. We played two more games with the same time control. This time I had the black pieces first and won, taking the lead 6-5. In the final game, I had White. All I had to do was not lose and I would be in the World Championship.

I guess it was 'easier said then done'. I felt like the sinking Titanic. It was one of those feelings that I could not control. My emotions were like a yo-yo and once again I allowed my opponent to tie the match. I never once trailed in the match, but to her credit, Nana's fighting spirit brought her back each time. I also have to add that she was very well prepared for the match and full of surprises for me. Her two very capable seconds, Konstantin Sakaev and Igor Efimov, certainly deserve credit as well.

So, according to the FIDE rules, in the case of a tie after twelve games there would be a drawing of lots!!! Prior to the match, I was very confident in myself and did not seriously consider the possibility of there not being a decisive result after so many games. I also did not expect what had happened in my personal life. It was a series of big miscalculations on my part and I had no one to blame but myself.

During the match, I contacted the International Chess Federation about modifying that drawing of lots rule. I requested to have the challenger for the World Championship match decided over the chessboard and not by means of luck. Unfortunately, they declined my request. As you may imagine, at this point nothing went my way. It was like Murphy's law: when something is wrong, everything is wrong. So, the drawing of lots was made and Nana won.

Even though I felt that it was not ideal or fair to decide the match by luck, I had no one to blame but myself. I really had all the opportunities to win the match within the twelve games and, no matter what happened in my life, I was the one who failed to capitalize on those chances. Prior to the match, I felt that I was well prepared. I was motivated and in a good mood. Not making it through this match was probably the biggest disappointment in my entire chess career.

After the match with Nana, Julio returned to South America. We did not meet again until I went to Peru for a pre-planned chess related trip there. He kept delaying telling me what he already probably decided during or prior to my match with Ioseliani. As I found out upon my arrival in May in Peru, our relationship never had a chance. It was over before it started. He had a Peru-

vian girlfriend long before we dated and he had two children with her. He simply forgot to mention about these little details... the whole time.

Success at the second attempt

As a semi-finalist in the previous World Championship, I was able to start at the Candidates tournament stage in the next cycle. In September 1994, I was back in the ring. This time the event was hosted in Tilburg, Holland.

The famous Tilburg super-tournaments used to be the most elite event of the year in the 1970s and '80s. It is always a pleasure to compete in the Netherlands, as the people are very hospitable and friendly and love chess.

I had a pleasant discovery from the window of my hotel room. There was a very tempting Indonesian restaurant! Ever since my first trip to Holland back in 1985, and then my later visit to Indonesia, I have been a big fan of their cuisine. I even learned how to cook some of my favorite Indonesian dishes.

At this tournament, I borrowed one of Judit's coaches, GM Lev Psakhis, as my second. Lev was playing in a parallel knockout tournament. Unfortunately for him, he was eliminated at an early round, but from then on, Lev was able to help me full time with my preparations for the games.

Judit and my mother also joined me from about halfway through the tournament. It was perfect team work. Lev usually had some good ideas on which direction to go in the opening, Judit helped with actual analyses, and my mother gave me moral support. I wished I'd had my Mom and sisters with me in my match against Nana in the previous cycle. It could have made all the difference in the world.

The tournament started well for me, though I was somewhat lucky. In the first round, I played against Maia Chiburdanidze. She reached a better position but then in time pressure she made a blunder, lost a pawn, and then the game.

Things continued pretty smoothly, although this time I did lose one game in the tournament: against Maia with the black pieces. At the end, I won on tie-break over Maia with a score of 10½ out of 16. With this victory, I again qualified for the semi-finals of the World Championship. This time my opponent was also Georgian, the four-time World Champion Maia Chiburdanidze.

Right after the Tilburg tournament I moved to New York, and in November I got married in Israel. It was unclear until December when and where the match with Chiburdanidze would be held. During the closing day of the 1994 Olympiad in Moscow, GM Zurab Azmaiparashvili managed to interest some Russian officials in it. Zurab is the top Georgian player and, as it turned out, he was going to be Maia's second against me.

I had a training session in New York with Lev Psakhis getting ready for the next stage. Finally it was sorted out and the match would be in St. Petersburg in February 1995. With the motto 'never change a winning team', I had Lev Psakhis, Judit and my mother on my side in St. Petersburg, with the addition of my husband.

I first met Maia in 1977 in Budapest when I was still only eight years old. She was playing in the Alfoldy Memorial women's invitational tournament. She was sixteen and her mother was accompanying her. She was the clear winner of that event. A year later she became the youngest ever Women's World Champion at seventeen.

She defended her title successfully three times until 1991, when the Chinese superstar Xie Jun dethroned her. For thirteen years Maia was clearly a class above the rest of the women players who entered the Women's Championship. For all those years, I (as well as my sisters) stayed away from those women-only events, so she did not have to worry about competition from the Polgar sisters.

However, since 1984, there was a continued fascination in the chess world and media as to how the top-rated player would do against the World Champion. So this was a long-awaited clash that many were eager to see.

Prior to the big match our score in classical time control games was the following: I had won three, lost one and drawn four. In ratings, I was 2545, Maia was 2520. So the general feeling was that I was the slight favorite, but not by much. We were also expecting a close match.

In the first game, I had the white pieces. I got a small advantage out of the opening, but after an inaccurate move, Maia got the opportunity to make a combination with a rook sacrifice and force a draw by perpetual check.

In the second game, Chiburdanidze

surprised me in the opening and I got a worse position. She made a very nice queen sacrifice, gaining a rook, a bishop and a pawn in return. Normally that material distribution is balanced, but in this case I underestimated the dangers that awaited me in the resulting endgame. I fought hard and managed to defend, though I think that with perfect technique she could have won the game. I felt relief. Things could have been worse. I think this was a crucial point of the match from the psychological aspect.

In game three, Maia played the Queen's Gambit Declined again. Lev prepared me with a surprise and I varied from the first game on the fifth move. The preparation worked out very well and I won rather quickly in 32 moves.

In the fourth game, I repeated the same King's Indian Defense from game two. I quickly equalized and then, after a mistake of Maia's on move 18, took over the initiative and won a nice game, again in 32 moves!

At this point I had a two point lead, which is huge in a best of ten match. However, with the memories of my match against Nana Ioseliani in the back of my mind, I knew it was definitely premature to celebrate. I guess I had learned my lesson and was extremely cautious this time. I knew the match is not over until it is over.

In the fifth game, we repeated the same opening as in game three. This time I did not trade my bishop for the knight, but decided to keep it on the board by retreating it. I got a very pleasant and slightly better position with practically no risk of losing. Unfortu-

nately, I made some inaccuracies when approaching the time control and we agreed to a draw on move 41.

Even though I was disappointed to spoil a better game, it still brought me closer to the ultimate goal of 5½ points. This score of 3½-1½ was scarily reminiscent of the tragedy against Ioseliani in Monaco, but I was determined to have a different end result. I was psychologically and mentally sound this time. I did not have the same personal problems, and my mother and sister were there as well.

Game 6 was the last critical moment. I had Black, which is always a slight disadvantage, but I knew if I did not lose this game, things would be alright. On move seventeen, I made an exchange sacrifice; on the next Maia missed an unexpected quiet move which neither of us saw during play. That was probably the last chance for the match to have changed course. Later on in the game, I managed to develop a winning attack against the white king.

At this stage all I needed was one point from the last four games. It could be either two draws or a win. At the beginning of the seventh game my opponent, understandably, switched from the peaceful Queen's Gambit to the more aggressive King's Indian Defense. This was the same opening I used against her in all my games with the black pieces. I responded with one of White's most ambitious lines: the Four Pawns Attack. I had the killer instinct and I wanted to finish off the match. I managed to achieve a solid advantage out of the opening and then increase it little by little to a win!

I had done it! I made it to the final! Even though the score 5½-1½ was one-sided, it did not feel like that during the match. One lucky break at various stages of the match could have led to a completely different outcome.

We went to celebrate at a Chinese restaurant and started the psychological and mental preparation for my match against Xie Jun. Even with the schedule of the match itself, we had managed to find some time to see the beautiful city of St. Petersburg, the City of the Tsars. We spent a wonderful day at the Hermitage, saw the Peter and Paul Fortress, the Winter Palace, walked on the famous Nevsky Prospect, and a lot more.

The restaurant in the hotel was not the greatest, so I really appreciated my mother preparing some of the meals in our suite. My mother was very instrumental in the success of all three sisters during our chess careers. Talking of food, I have not eaten so much caviar in my life as during that match. Amazingly it was freely available in the local supermarkets at a very low price.

There was a whole year between the end of the semi-final match and the Final, since FIDE had some difficulties coming up with a proper venue. In the end, the well-known Spanish chess organizer, Luis Rentero, saved the situation and brought the match to Jaen in Spain. However, it was somewhat disturbing not to know until about only two months prior to the start of the match when, where, or even if it would be played at all. Therefore, I had to be in constant preparation to play in a relatively short notice.

I had some training sessions with IM Laszlo Hazai, and GMs Zurab Azmaiparashvili (who was Maia's coach against me less than a year before!), Yuri Shulman, Boris Alterman, and of course Lev Psakhis. Besides studying and preparing, I needed practice too. I played some training games with local New Yorkers, such as IM Victor Frias (who sadly died just recently), and GMs Joel Benjamin, Gennadi Sagalchik, Maurice Ashley and Ilya Gurevich.

At last it was time to travel to Spain. I knew that it would be a long match and I would have to be very calm, relaxed and patient. The whole match was expected to take almost a month. We had to play sixteen games, one per day, with a few days off in between. We also allowed a few days for acclimatization prior the match to get over the jet-leg.

Game 1

The match really started badly. I wanted to surprise my opponent straight away, but somehow I mixed up the planned move order and ended up unpleasantly surprising myself. I quite quickly got into a horrible position and Xie completely outplayed me. In the endgame she made a mistake, so that at one point I probably could have held on to a draw, but I missed my chance and it never came back. The Chinese World Champion demonstrated good technique and defeated me. I was devastated, but my attitude was: OK, there are fifteen more games to catch up, so nothing is lost yet.

Game 2

I felt I needed some recovery time after the unexpected and tragic loss with the white pieces. So, having Black, my pre-game goal was to hold on and play cautiously. For the first time of my life I played the Rauzer variation of the Sicilian and got no problems out of the opening. In the final position, where my opponent offered a draw, I was actually slightly better, though I realized it only after the game.

Game 3

I think I made a unexpected surprise for Xie on the first move, when I started with 1 e4, something I have not played since my childhood. She responded as expected with 1...e5 and I played the Scotch, which was once my favorite, though I was ten years old when I last played 1 e4 in a serious tournament game. The Scotch became fashionable again in the early 1990s, thanks to some new discoveries by Garry Kasparov and his team of seconds. I got a minimal advantage, but was still not quite back to my full energy, and I settled for a draw on move nineteen.

Shortly after the end of the third game, both Xie Jun and I received a very disturbing and shocking letter from the technical director of the match, Mr. Luis Rentero. He had decided to fine us both $25,000 and called us 'chess tourists'. He complained that the last two games of the match had ended in relatively quick draws.

Mr. Rentero is famous for his contracts during the Linares super-tournaments, where most players have to sign not to agree to a draw in less than forty moves, or else they will be fined. However, the big difference was that our match was an official FIDE

event to decide who would be the Women's World Champion, whereas the Linares tournament is a private event. He had no right and no authority to interfere the way he did. There was *no* such stipulation in our contracts.

Obviously the ultimate goal for both sides is to win or retain the World Championship title. How many moves were played in each game was unimportant. In other words, it was part of my match strategy, after the trauma of losing the first game, to gain time and get back on my feet. Now if Games 2 and 3 were both decisive in 15-20 moves each, would we both be fined as well since there were so few moves? Could an organizer decide in the middle of a match that all games must, for example, be played with 1 h4 - ? All conditions put forth by the organizers may be acceptable prior to the signing of the contracts. Then the players can decide whether to accept or reject. But to make up rules as we went along was totally unprofessional and absurd.

The first reaction from both camps was the same. After such an insult we wanted to pack up and leave. But after calming down from the initial shock, we decided to stay and deal with it through the press and other ways. We would not let this matter go quietly. Eventually, Mr. Rentero backed off and the match resumed.

Game 4

The opening was a repeat of Game 2 and the game was probably the wildest of the entire match. We castled on opposite sides and marched our pawns forward against the opponent's kings. In the critical moment, Xie sacrificed a pawn but missed an opportunity to take the upper hand. That one mistake was enough for me to seize the initiative. I kept my pawn advantage and later won the game by trapping her queen. This was an important comeback for me. With this victory, I equalized the score at 2-2 and never trailed in the match again.

While I am sure that Xie was hurt by this loss, in a way she was still in the lead because as a defending champion she had 'draw odds', meaning that if the final score was 8-8, she would retain her title.

Game 5

It seems that Xie was satisfied with the results of the opening in the third game as she invited it again. This time I played differently on the tenth move. She right away made some mistakes and, as a result, her king remained in the center for the rest of the game. As happens so often in such situations, a powerful offensive can end things quickly, as it did in this game in only twenty-five moves. Finally, I took the lead and never relinquished it.

Game 6

Now that I was leading, my strategy was to play safely, especially with black. I switched to a new surprise opening variation, one that I had never played before in my life, and prepared it especially for this occasion. The preparation worked out fine. I equalized quite easily, and after most of the pieces got traded off, we drew the game in 28 moves.

Game 7

Again, and for the third and last time during this match, I used the Scotch. My opponent and her coaches prepared an improvement on Game 5. The new move came on the eighth move. Xie was ahead in development and it felt a little scary as my opponent seemed to play with a lot of self-confidence, noticeably content with her position. The climax of the game came early on move 15. My king hadn't castled yet and Xie started a dangerous-looking combination. To her disappointment, I found a rather unusual refutation of her idea. I carefully calculated the variations and came to the conclusion that she could not take advantage of the situation, so I willingly let my king move into a 'discovered check'. That was the response she overlooked. Xie had no choice but to sacrifice her queen and transpose to a hopeless endgame the exchange down. This victory for me was a great step towards the final goal.

Game 8

I believe this was the crucial and decisive game of the match. I repeated the same variation for Black as in Game 6. This time the surprise effect had worn off as my opponent had time to prepare. Xie improved on move twelve and obtained a somewhat better position. It was a very tense fight as she went right after my king. However, after mutual inaccuracies in time pressure, I think Xie probably missed her last chance to turn the match around. When we reached the fortieth move and the end of time pressure, I was an exchange up and had a close to winning position. She did not give up fighting, but after another twenty moves, she ran out of defensive resources. At the midway point in the match, the score was 5½-2½ in my favor.

Game 9

I switched from the Scotch to the Four Knights, mostly for its surprise value, but it didn't work out too well. I did not have any advantage throughout the game. We reached an opposite-colored bishop endgame and settled for a draw on move 37.

Game 10

In a match like this, the games as Black are always critical. With the white pieces, it is much simpler to achieve a comfortable position. With the black pieces, one first needs to equalize, which is not always so simple. In this game I switched, for the first time during the match, from the Sicilian to the Open variation of the Ruy Lopez. Right out of the opening, skipping the middlegame, we transposed to an almost equal endgame with only the four rooks and a pair of bishops on the board, and six pawns each. I had a weakness in my position (an isolated pawn), while my opponent was completely safe, so I had to be on the defensive for most of the game. But I managed to hold on, at and the end made a draw by repetition of moves.

Game 11

After all the king's pawn games, I decided (together with my team) to switch back to my regular queen's pawn opening. Even though prior to the match, I am sure that this was the main focus of the Chinese team, at this point in the match I think it was unexpected! As we had hoped, Xie responded with her usual Grünfeld Defense. I played a somewhat forgotten version of the Fianchetto variation and managed to get a very comfortable and practically 'no risk' position, which was exactly what I was hoping for. Slowly I took control of the open d-file and increased my advantage little by little. After reaching the time control, I was a pawn ahead in a winning rook and knight endgame. On move 47, my opponent threw in the towel being faced with unavoidable checkmate.

At this point, the score was 7½-3½. Only one more point was needed for the world title, and I had five more chances to score this point.

Game 12

I tried to repeat the opening I used in Game 10, but Xie chose to avoid it with a not too ambitious, solid variation. This was her best game of the entire match. She was more experienced and familiar with the type of closed Ruy Lopez structure we obtained, and outplayed me fair and square. This was an unpleasant loss, but I still had four more chances left.

Game 13

Having the white pieces, my goal was to play safely for 'two results'. I was expecting my opponent to play for a win at all cost, as every draw would bring her closer to losing the crown. Honestly, we were convinced that Xie would switch from the Grünfeld to an even sharper opening, such as the King's Indian Defense. However, Xie repeated the same

Grünfeld as in Game 11. We had prepared a different surprise this time and it worked perfectly for me. I got into a clearly better endgame straight out of the opening. Soon, on move 20, she allowed a pin and I won a piece. On the 24th move, she resigned the game and graciously congratulated me on becoming the new World Champion.

February 25th 1996 was certainly one of the happiest days in my life. I was glad to share it with my family who, apart from my sister Sofia, were all there for the last game. I would like especially to thank my parents for their lifelong support of my career, and Judit and Lev for all their help in this entire World Championship cycle.

Family life

After the break-up with my first serious boyfriend, Julio, I felt that I wanted to start a new chapter in my life. In retrospect, I made a mistake by allowing things to escalate too quickly and I made a too sudden decision to accept the marriage proposal. I had known my future husband only for a very short time; because of the distance between New York and Budapest, it was difficult logistically to get to know each other better. Despite there being things I did not like from when we first dated, we had good and happy times and I closed my eyes to ignore the problems. Unfortunately, these problems escalated.

I was supposed to have a match to defend my World Champion title some time early in 1998. However, despite all efforts made by FIDE, they failed to hold the match in a timely fashion. According to FIDE rules, I was supposed to be given six months notice about who my challenger was to be, and where or when I would have to play. I waited to hear from them, but nothing happened until the end of 1998, nearly a year late. FIDE then announced that the World Championship match would be in March/April of 1999.

Later on they told me that I would have to travel to China, my opponent's homeland, and that they could only raise $100,000 for my match with Xie Jun. These things were both seriously wrong and also against FIDE rules. A World Championship match is supposed to be held in a neutral country, which obviously China was not. And the minimum prize fund is supposed to be $200,000 rather than $100,000. But it did not seem to bother FIDE that they violated three of their own rules.

In the meantime, since I there was no sign of any match at the beginning of 1998, my husband and I decided to start a family in summer of 1998. I became pregnant with my first son, Tommy, who was eventually born on March 6th 1999. This was when FIDE decided to have the illegal World Championship match. I naturally requested a postponement. After numerous correspondences back and forth, FIDE declined and would not allow me a fair opportunity to defend my title.

So I had three complaints in order of importance:

1) To get a delay for the start of the match (to recover from childbirth). It was FIDE who had failed to organize the World Championship match in early 1998, the time I was supposed to defend my title.

2) To have a neutral country host the match. China was obviously not a fair and neutral country for a match with Xie Jun, and FIDE should have known better.

3) To put up at least the minimum required prize fund of $200,000 and not just 50% of it.

In addition, FIDE did not give me sufficient notification of the match. I would have been willing to compromise on one or two of these issues, but not on all three. Therefore, FIDE stripped me from my title without play. The ironic part was that they delayed the match until July anyway, when Alisa Galliamova played instead of me.

I felt that it was a great injustice and sued FIDE. I could not allow the World Chess Federation to pull a stunt like this. I easily won the case and was awarded a symbolic $25,000 compensation. However, the moral victory was more important to me.

The pregnancy with Tommy went quite smoothly and I was very happy. Despite all the anticipation and psychological preparation, having a baby is a life-changing experience in a woman's life. There are certain feelings she can only really understand from her own experience. I truly enjoyed my first year in my new role as a mother. I was a fully devoted mom, nursing for 11 months, and cooking fresh home-made food daily.

During the pregnancy with my second child, one night I felt like competing again. I just showed up, without any special training or preparation, at the Marshall Chess Club. I entered in the NY Blitz Championship and won it ahead of several strong grandmasters, including Max Dlugy (former World Junior Champion) and Igor Novikov, etc.

My second son, Leeam, was born less than 20 months after Tommy on November 22nd, 2000. Ever since, they have been the central part of my life.

The comeback, partly in a different role

After winning my fourth World Championship title, I decided to take a break from the professional chess circuit. Except for a few small exhibitions, I stayed mostly in New York. In 1997, I had decided to fulfill one of my childhood dreams and opened a Chess Center in Queens. I knew it would not be a money-making machine (to put it mildly), but it was something I really wanted to do. It was (and still is) something I enjoy and that the local community needs and appreciates. I have been lucky to meet some very nice people who help out in various ways. Without the support of the numerous volunteers, the Chess Center would have closed long ago.

In September 1997, I also started teaching at the Mott Hall School in Harlem, in a chess program sponsored by the Harlem Educational Activities Fund. It was a very interesting experience teaching in a regular classroom, and the first time I had ever worked in a 'normal' or 'regular' job environment. It was a real pleasure to teach those children critical thinking through chess. They mostly came from underprivileged families, which made my experience even more special. Most of them fell in love with the game and some of them still play competitively. But more significantly, they also learned very important life skills.

After being a full-time mom between 1999 and 2001, I felt I wanted to be more actively involved in promoting chess in the United States. In the spring of 2001, an idea was born. I set my mind to organizing an international event, giving an opportunity to our young and talented players to play for norms in a Grandmaster tournament. In June, the Mayor's Cup was officially underway at the Elmhurst Hospital in Queens. We had the honor of Mayor Giuliani, NY City Sports Commissioner Ken Podziba, and the Director of the Elmhurst Hospital opening the event, which included ten invited players from five different countries.

That is when I started to work officially with an old friend of mine, Paul Truong. We had known each other for many years, ever since my very first visit to New York back in 1985. During the Mayor's Cup, Paul helped out a lot. At the same time we talked at length about promoting chess and decided to work closely together in more projects to promote chess in the US. I felt that this was a wonderful idea since Paul had had tremendous success in Marketing, Public Relations and Promotion for over 15 years. He also understands the chess world, as he was a chess child prodigy in his own right. We also started to write for numerous chess publications, including Chess Life and ChessCafe.com. In 2002, we co-wrote our first book together: *Teach Yourself Chess in 24 Hours*, which was published by Macmillan.

In the summer of 2002, I had the opportunity to meet the USCF Executive Director, Frank Niro, at my club. He expressed his desire for me to help out US chess, which I agreed to do. Towards the end of 2002, I visited the USCF headquarters in New Windsor, and during the meeting with Frank Niro, a very serious decision was made. Mr. Niro asked if I would be willing to represent the United States in the 2004 Chess Olympiad in Spain. He told me it would mean a lot to US chess, and that the USCF would support our team as much as they could. He was very passionate about making US chess better, so I agreed!

My main condition to come out of retirement was to make sure that the team would have a proper training program. I take the Olympiad very seriously since I have never lost an Olympiad game and have never come home with less than two medals (team and individual). I wanted the team to work together and gel as a unit in order to have a chance. We both understood that such a program was not easy to put together, since it requires a lot of funding, time, leadership and organizational skills, and this is a monumental task. Up to that point, the US Women's Team had never won a single Olympiad medal. What we wanted to do would rewrite history.

The first very promising sign, changing the entire equation, was when Paul Truong agreed to be the Business Manager and Captain of the US Women's Olympiad Training Program. Both Frank and I were very happy. No one has ever succeeded in handling even one of these tasks, and yet we were asking Paul to do both at once, for no pay, for two years!

Not only that, we had full confidence that he could pull both of them off.

I did not know what it would be like to compete again after an 8½ year break from the world arena. On one hand, people were telling me that it is like riding a bike. Once you know how to ride a bike you never forget. On the other hand, eight and a half years was a very long time! In the end, things worked out as in a fairy tale.

Many teams came in with very high expectations, such as China, Russia, Georgia, Ukraine, India, etc. We were not the only ones, but we succeeded. You can read more about the 2004 Olympiad in the 'Ultimate Breakthrough' chapter of this book.

In 2002, I also founded The Susan Polgar Foundation. It is a 501(c) (3) non-profit organization. Our mission is 'to promote chess with all its social, educational and competitive benefits throughout the United States for young people of all ages and especially for girls.'

An event I am very proud of is the Susan Polgar National Invitational for Girls, which is mainly sponsored by the Susan Polgar Foundation. In its inaugural year in 2004, this special event was held in Fort Lauderdale, alongside the Denker Tournament of High School Champions as well as the US Open. In our first year, there were 34 girls participating from across the country. The rule is that each state is entitled to nominate one girl to the tournament. She can be the top-rated girl in the state or be the state girls' champion. The main idea is to encourage more girls to compete in chess.

Paul and I are continuing to work on many more incredible projects. I have two ultimate breakthrough goals:

1) Revolutionize chess in America and eventually around the world. I want to take chess to the next level of popularity, such as other mainstream sports like tennis or golf, etc.

2) I firmly believe in the importance of chess to develop learning and life skills for children. Therefore, I want to push chess into the forefront of education. My next major project is 'Excel Through Chess', where I would like to bring chess to classrooms everywhere.

Once I am done with these goals, I am sure I will come up with more. Being an ambassador of chess is to promote the game positively. Stay tuned for many more breakthrough ideas!

Games and Combinations

Games

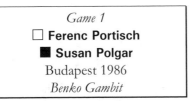

Game 1
☐ **Ferenc Portisch**
■ **Susan Polgar**
Budapest 1986
Benko Gambit

This game was played at the Hungarian Team Championship. In Europe many countries have a national team championship. In Hungary we used to play fortnightly from September to May. I really enjoyed those matches on a social level, and also gained a lot of experience from the games.

1 d4

My opponent in this game is an International Master. He is the brother of the Hungarian chess icon, Lajos Portisch.

1...♘f6

In those days, against 1 d4, I used to alternate between 1...d5 and 1...♘f6. I would decide just before a game, depending on the tournament situation and who my opponent was.

2 c4

The most logical follow-up to the previous move, controlling the central d5 square.

2...c5

This is just a temporary pawn sacrifice.

3 d5

If White accepts the pawn with 3 dxc5, Black wins the pawn back after 3...e6 and equalizes comfortably.

3...b5

This is the Volga/Benko Gambit. I first saw the Volga Gambit in the late 1970s in some Soviet tournaments. In Soviet publications that's how it used to be called. I used to like it a lot; it was like love at first sight; at that time it was somewhat of a culture shock to give up a pawn so early. As compensation Black usually gets very easy and active play along the a- and b-files. White has to play very accurately to neutralize the activity of the black pieces in order to obtain and maintain any advantage. That is why most people use the gambit as an occasional surprise weapon, instead of having it as their main response to 1 d4. If someone anticipates it, they can refresh their memory and prepare for it right before the game, and then the gambit would not have the same effect.

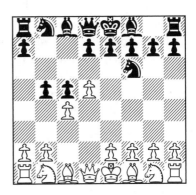

When I first started traveling to the West, I realized that people in the US and other Western countries call it the Benko Gambit, after the famous Hungarian-American Grandmaster, Pal Benko, who happens to be a very good old friend of mine.

4 cxb5

The most popular response to the sacrifice is to accept it; another one is 4 ♘f3.

4...a6

This is the point: to open the a- and b-files.

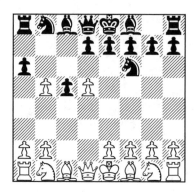

5 bxa6

White has several reasonable alternatives, such as 5 e3, 5 f3, 5 b6 or 5 ♘c3.

5...g6

This is the modern approach. For many years Black took back on a6 (5...♗xa6) automatically. In recent years, Black has preferred to delay the recapture, to see how White developed the pieces. In some cases Black is better off taking back with the knight.

6 ♘c3

Since White cannot save the a6 pawn, the right thing to do is continue developing.

6...♗xa6

Now it was time to take the pawn. If Black delays the recapture any further with, let's say, 6...♗g7, then after 7 e4 White gets a favorable position.

7 e4

This is one of the two old main lines and has a very direct plan: to advance with e4-e5 as soon as possible! In this position, White allows the trade of bishops on f1, even though it stops him from castling. The other main plan here is to fianchetto the bishop with 7 g3.

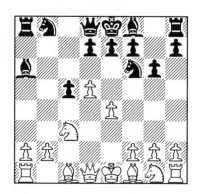

7...♗xf1

With this move, Black forces the white king to move.

8 ♔xf1

White had no choice.

8...d6

This prevents e4-e5 and also opens room on d7 for the knights.

9 ♘f3

Another good developing move, controlling the center.

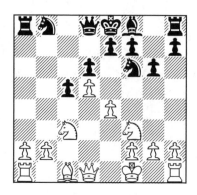

9...♗g7

There is no doubt that the bishop has to develop to the a1-h8 diagonal, where it is most powerful in this opening.

10 h3

A more common plan is 10 g3, followed by 11 ♗g2 to castle artificially.

10...0-0

The king is now safe. Therefore, after this move Black can focus on attacking on the queenside.

11 ♔e2

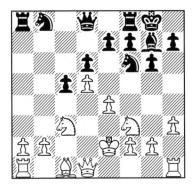

This is a very unusual and not the very best move. White's idea is to allow the rook to go from h1 to e1 as in the usual lines (e.g. after g3 and ♔g2, or ♔g1-h2), and then retreat the king back to f1. However, the king not supposed to wander around in the middle with almost all the pieces still on the board.

11...♘a6!

The knight aims towards the d3 square. The more standard route is via d7 and c5. However, at this moment I felt that there might be an additional route, a6-b4-d3, keeping the d7 square available for the other knight.

12 ♖e1

The rook has to come out of the corner, if it wants to participate in the battle.

12...♕b6

12...♘b4 13 ♔f1 ♕b6 was also possible, with transposition to the game.

13 ♔f1

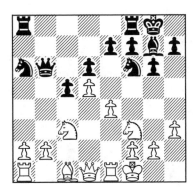

The king finally managed to reach safety. White is a clear pawn ahead, but as you can see, the black pieces are very active. The white bishop on c1 has trouble getting out, and Black's threats are coming quickly. Therefore, Black has more than enough compensation for the pawn.

13...♘b4

Threatening 14...♕a6+ and then ...♘d3.

14 ♖e2

After 14 e5 dxe5 15 ♘xe5 ♖fd8 White cannot hold on to the d5 pawn.

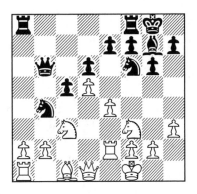

14...♕a6

Pinning the rook and preparing ...♘d3.

15 ♘e1

Stopping ...♘d3.

15...♘d7

Beginning another very common maneuver, ...♘f6-d7-e5, to give support to the other knight in fighting for the d3 square.

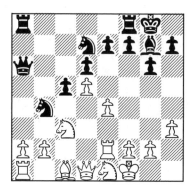

16 ♗f4

With the idea of meeting 16...♘e5 with 17 ♗xe5, stopping the knight from getting to d3.

16...c4!

A key move in the Benko Gambit! It further magnifies the weakness of the d3 square and opens up c5 for the knight on d7.

17 ♗e3

After 17 a3 White is not really attacking the knight because of the pin along the a-file. I planned simply to improve my position by 17...♖fb8. On the other hand, 17...♘c5 would be a mistake because, after 18 axb4 ♕xa1 19 ♕xa1 ♖xa1, the knight on c5 is hanging.

17...♘d3!

Finally mission accomplished, the knight got to d3! Black is now threatening 18...♘xb2! 19 ♖xb2 ♗xc3.

White had plans to answer 17...♘e5 with 18 ♗d4, or 17...♘c5 by 18 ♗xc5.

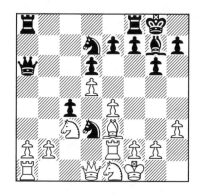

18 ♕c2

If 18 ♘xd3 cxd3 19 ♖d2 ♘e5!, with the dangerous threat of 20...♘c4, gives Black the advantage.

18...♖fb8

Now all the black pieces are actively participating in the attack on the queenside.

19 ♖b1

A must! Black quickly wins material after 19 b3 cxb3! 20 ♕xd3 ♕xd3 21 ♘xd3 ♗xc3 or 19 ♘xd3 cxd3 forking the queen and rook.

19...♖b7!

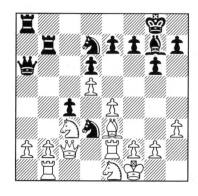

Black doubles the rooks on the b-file

and puts more pressure on White's b2 pawn. Black has more than enough counterplay on the queenside for the sacrificed pawn.

20 ♖d2

After 20 b3, I could choose to win the pawn back right away with 20...♘b4 21 ♕d2 ♗xc3 22 ♕xc3 ♘xa2, or else play 20...♘xe1 21 ♖bxe1? cxb3 22 axb3 ♖c7! (not 22...♖c8? 23 ♕a2! and the white knight escapes) 23 ♗d2 ♗xc3 24 ♗xc3 ♖ac8 and White loses the bishop because of the pins. 21 ♔xe1 cxb3 22 axb3 ♖c8 23 ♗d2 is a better option, though 23...♗d4 still gives Black a nice position.

20...♘7e5

Ideally, Black wants to keep a knight on d3 because it paralyses White's play. That is why Black's last move to connect the knights was very important.

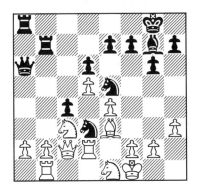

21 ♔g1

Black gains material after 21 ♗d4 ♘xe1 22 ♖xe1 ♘d3 23 ♗xg7 ♖xb2.

21...♖ab8

After 21...♘xe1 22 ♖xe1 ♘d3, White would still be able to hold the position by simply protecting b2 with 23 ♖b1.

22 b3

White is in trouble after 22 ♘xd3 cxd3! 23 ♕d1 ♘c4 24 ♖xd3 ♘xb2.

22...cxb3

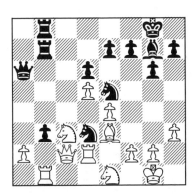

We have reached one of those critical moments of the game when enough positional improvements have been made, and now it is 'action time'.

23 axb3

The rook could not take back because it needs to hold on to the knight on e1.

23...♘xe1

Removing the rook from its defense of the b3 pawn.

24 ♖xe1

The rook cannot protect both.

24...♖xb3

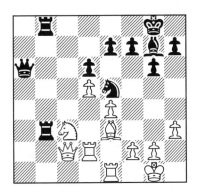

Regaining the pawn and maintaining

an active position. Black now threatens to win a piece by using a discovery with 25...♖xc3 26 ♕xc3 and then 26...♘f3+ winning the white queen.

25 ♗d4

On this move my opponent made the decisive mistake. 25 ♘d1 was a better defense.

25...♘c4!

This wins material by force.

After 26 ♖d3 ♘a3 27 ♕d2 ♖b2 28 ♕e3 ♗xd4 29 ♖xd4 ♘c2 forks the 'family'.

26...♘a3

Forcing the queen to move. There are four choices but all of them have some drawbacks.

27 ♕e2

The other choices were no better:

a) 27 ♕c1 ♖c8! and the knight cannot get out of the pin.

b) 27 ♕d2 ♗xd4 28 ♕xd4 ♘c2 again forks.

c) 27 ♕d3 ♗xd3 28 ♖xd3 ♗xd4 29 ♖xd4 ♖xc3 just loses the knight.

The game continuation is a tricky-looking move and it seems to save the game. Now if I trade queens, the knight takes back and things are OK for White.

27...♕a5! White resigned

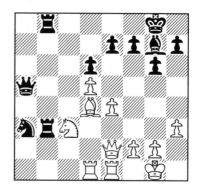

It is quite amazing that this quiet move won the game for me!

White cannot avoid material loss. Basically the knight on c3 is trapped; for example, if 28 ♗xg7 ♔xg7 29 ♘a2, then 29...♖b2 forks and wins the knight.

Game 2
□ **Susan Polgar**
■ **Ljubomir Ljubojevic**
Bilbao 1987
Old Indian Defense

There is a special story connected with this game. Grandmaster Ljubojevic ('Ljubo' as most of the chess players call him) had voiced his view with the organizers that they should not be inviting female participants (Chiburdanidze and me) to such a prestigious event. Ljubo claimed that the tournament was too strong for women! Ironically, he lost against both of us!

1 d4

In the mid to late 1980s I started most of my games with this move.

1...♘f6

The queen's pawn openings (1 d4 d5) are considered more peaceful.

2 ♘f3

One of the points of this move order is to avoid the Benko Gambit, which I have used as Black, e.g. against F. Portisch (see Game 1).

2...d6

This is a less often used set-up than 2...e6, followed by 3...b6 to play the Queen's Indian, or 2...g6, to play the Grünfeld or King's Indian Defense.

3 g3

At that time of my career I had a special liking towards fianchettoing my bishop(s). Naturally 3 c4 is also possible with more focus on play in the center.

3...♗g4

Black still has the option to transpose to the King's Indian Defense with 3...g6.

4 ♗g2

Developing and preparing to castle.

4...♘bd7

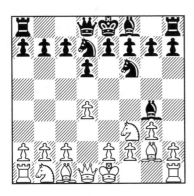

With this move, Black prepares ...e7-e5. Another interesting plan is 4...♕c8 with the idea of trying to trade bishops with ...♗g4-h3. If White answers with 5 h3, Black could play 5...♗d7 and White would have some difficulties castling (without losing the h3 pawn).

5 c4

Now that Black is about to approach the center with ...e7-e5, I have to prepare to deal with it. My last move controls the central d5 square and gains some space on the queenside.

5...e5

With this pawn advance, Black prepares to develop the bishop on e7.

6 ♘c3

Developing and controlling the central d5 and e4 squares.

6...c6

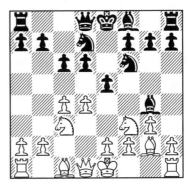

This is a typical move that makes sense in this position. It takes control of the d5 square and also reduces the potential power of White's bishop on g2. Instead after 6...e4? 7 ♘g5 Black would lose the e-pawn. White would be attacking the pawn three times while Black protects it only once, so there is no way Black can hold on to it.

7 0-0

In most of my games it is my first priority to put my king in safety.

7...♗e7

Now after 7...e4 8 ♘g5 d5, I planned to open the e-file with 9 cxd5 cxd5, followed by 10 f3, and White is better developed.

8 h3

Now Black cannot keep his pair of bishops.

8...♗xf3

After 8...♗h5 White would continue with 9 ♘h4, followed by g3-g4 or ♘f5, trading the knight for one of the bishops.

9 exf3

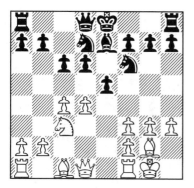

The normal recapture, of course, would be with the bishop. I do not think that what I played is bad. However, if I had the same position today, I probably would choose the more conservative 9 ♗xf3. My idea at the time was to advance the f3 pawn to f4, where it can nicely control the e5 square and prevent a black knight from getting there. I also had in mind the possible long-term plan of creating a kingside pawn storm with g3-g4-g5 and f3-f4-f5.

9...exd4

There was no need to rush with this trade. I would prefer 9...0-0.

10 ♕xd4

Now White's target is quite obvious: the weakened d6 pawn on the half-open d-file.

10...♕b6

Black would like to trade queens and then, after 11 ♕xb6 ♘xb6 12 b3, play

12...d5 and get rid of the weakness.

11 ♕d2!

At first, this looks like a weird place for the queen, being right in front of the bishop. However, Black cannot take advantage of the temporary awkwardness of White's position. My next move would be 12 b3 to develop the bishop on the c1-a3 diagonal.

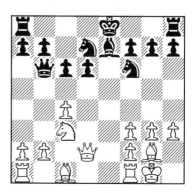

11...0-0

It is time for Black to castle. It would be far too risky to castle on the queenside, because the black c7 pawn has already moved to c6. After 11...0-0-0 White would start a queenside attack with 12 ♖b1 and then b2-b4.

12 b3

Preparing for the development of the bishop.

12...♘c5

12...♘e5 would not make sense as, after 13 f4, the knight would need to leave.

13 ♖e1

Occupying the open file by attacking the bishop.

13...♖fe8

Naturally, the bishop did not have to move.

14 ♗b2

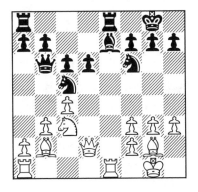

Finally, both sides are fully developed and the strategical middlegame phase begins. On the immediate 14 ♗a3, I did not like 14...♕a5 15 ♗b2 and 15...d5!.

14...a5

A good idea! The threat is ...a5-a4 to destroy White's healthy pawn structure on the queenside.

15 ♗a3

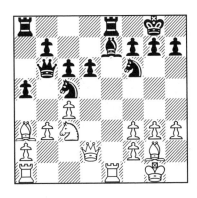

This works better now because the black pawn on a5 prevents the queen from going there. The idea of the move is to meet 15...a4 with 16 b4.

Perhaps 15 ♘e4 right away is even more accurate. For example, 15...♘fxe4 16 fxe4 a4 17 b4, and now 17...a3 loses because of the pin with 18 ♗d4.

15...♗f8

Getting away from the cute threat of 16 ♖xe7! ♖xe7 17 ♕xd6.

16 ♘e4!

This forces the trade of knights, which enables me to get rid of my doubled pawns on the f-file.

16...♘fxe4

If Black traded with the other knight, the d6 pawn would be under pressure straight away.

17 fxe4

No more doubled pawns! That is certainly an achievement for White.

17...♖ad8?

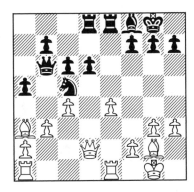

This is the most obvious-looking move, but it leads to long term passivity. Black would have been better off sacrificing the d6 pawn with 17...g6 18 ♗b2 and now 18...♗g7 19 ♗xg7 ♔xg7 20 ♕xd6 ♖ad8 21 ♕f4 ♘d3. White can escape from the fork by playing 22 ♕e3. However, Black has decent compensation after 22...♕d4. Black will get control of the d-file and some important dark squares such as d4, c5 and b4.

18 ♗b2!

The bishop has fulfilled its mission on a3 – time to get back to the long diagonal.

18...♛c7

Now it is too late for 18...g6 as 19 ♛d4 would land Black in big trouble, while after 18...a4, 19 b4 is next.

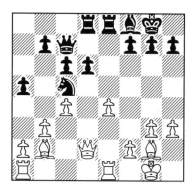

19 ♖ad1

Centralizing the rook. The nice thing about these types of positions is that White has all the time in the world to slowly improve the position, without needing to worry much about Black's counterplay.

19...♖d7

Getting ready to double the rooks on either the e or d-files.

20 ♗c3

Provoking further weakening of the queenside.

20...b6

In this position, I had to make perhaps the most difficult decision of the game. I had to find a plan to open up the position. To my big surprise, my world-famous opponent offered a draw here. Normally, I would consider a draw against someone his caliber acceptable. However, I felt that my position was already too good to accept a draw. After some thought, I decided to continue the fight and go for the win.

Black's move protects the a5 pawn

but weakens the one on c6. As ugly and passive as it looks, it was perhaps better to play 20...♖a8.

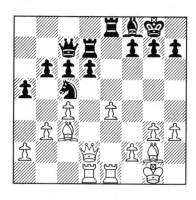

21 ♔h2

My plan was to prepare f2-f4 and eventually break through with e4-e5 at the perfect moment. That is why the reason why I wanted my king off the g1-a7 diagonal.

21...♛c8

Black has no productive plan.

22 ♖e3

To double the rooks on the e-file and improving my position.

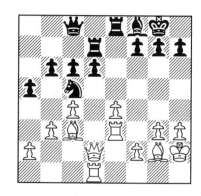

22...♖de7

Putting pressure on the e4 pawn.

23 ♖de1

Protecting the e4 pawn. It would be

a blunder to take the pawn with 23 ♕xd6 because Black could then skewer with 23...♖d7.

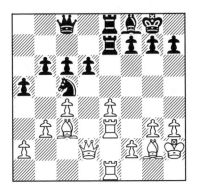

23...♕c7

Protecting the d6 pawn.

24 f4

Over the last few moves my goal was to slowly but surely improve the positions of my pieces. The first step of the plan has been accomplished.

24...f6

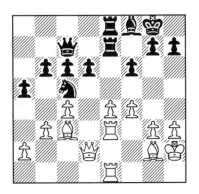

Black is trying to prevent the e4-e5 plan, but By doing so, he has considerably weakened the light squares on the kingside. If Black had played 24...g6 instead, then the natural 25 ♕d4 would be a mistake, because after 25...f6 26 ♕xf6 ♗g7 27 ♕h4 ♗xc3 28 ♖xc3

♘xe4 29 ♖ce3 d5 Black is OK! However, I could still keep the advantage with 25 ♕b2, not letting the black bishop to get to g7.

25 ♕f2

Relocating the queen to f3 to keep one eye on the c6 pawn, as well as on the kingside.

25...♖e6

Black is just making waiting moves.

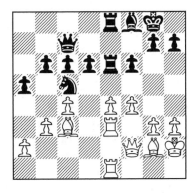

26 ♕f3

Following up on the plan of the previous move.

26...♔h8

After 26...♕e7, 27 f5 would suffocate the rook on e6. If Black plays 26...♖6e7, White would have a choice between the immediate 27 e5 or continuing similarly to the actual game.

27 ♔h1

To get off the second rank while keeping it available for the rooks, as you will see why in the next few moves.

27...♔g8

Here my opponent was already in time trouble. He made some 'waiting moves' to get closer to the time control. But no matter what, Black is in a difficult position.

28 h4!

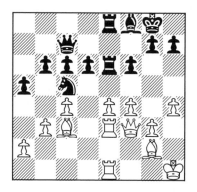

A multipurpose move! It prepares the activation of the bishop via h3-f5, as well as the h4-h5-h6 advance.

28...♔h8

When these are the best moves (shuffling the king back and forth between g8 and h8), one can safely say that it usually is a bad sign.

29 ♗h3

Finally, the up to now modest light-squared bishop gets an important role.

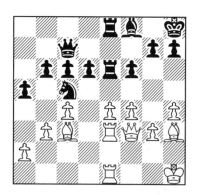

29...♖6e7

There is no other place for the rook.

30 h5

This pawn advance of h3-h4-h5 greatly improved White's position.

30...♖f7

Continuing to wait, since there is really nothing better.

31 ♗f5

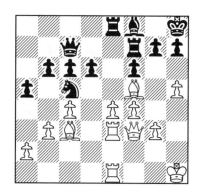

Threatening the beautiful combination of 32 ♗g6! hxg6 33 hxg6 and then checkmating on the h-file with the queen.

31...♖d8

By moving away from the h5-e8 diagonal, 31 ♗g6 lost its threat, as the rook on f7 can simply retreat without losing the rook on e8.

32 ♖d1

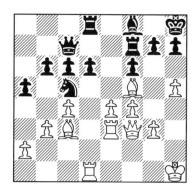

Perhaps not necessary, but I just wanted to kill even the idea of possible counterplay by a ...d6-d5 thrust. I did not want to give Black any chances.

32...♗e7

Black had to be careful over which

waiting move to make. For example, 32...♖e7 would leave the f6 pawn weak and then 33 h6 gains strength.

33 ♖e2!

The rook is a lot more flexible on the second rank. It can have potential on the d, g or h-files.

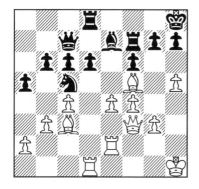

33...♖ff8

Black had seven more moves to make to reach the time control (move 40), when he would have more time to think again. Therefore, he just tried to make a logical, obvious and safe move.

34 ♖h2

At this point I was also short on time. So I made moves that might not be the most energetic or aggressive, but would still allow me to maintain the advantage until I had time to calculate more deeply.

34...♖fe8

Clearing the f8 square for another piece.

35 ♖hd2

I still was not comfortable with allowing ...d6-d5; although, looking at it some years later, perhaps 35 ♕g4 was more accurate. Then if 35...d5 36 exd5 cxd5 37 cxd5 ♘e4, the game would have ended in spectacular manner with

38 ♕g6!! hxg6 39 hxg6+ ♔g8 40 ♗e6+ ♔f8 41 ♖h8 mate.

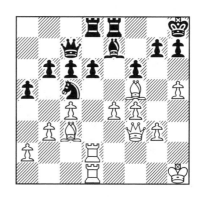

35...♘d7

Bringing the knight to f8 for defense.

36 ♗b2

I was hoping that the g7 and f6 pawns would be gone (from their current positions), and I could get some mating threats along the a1-h8 diagonal with ♕c3.

36...♘f8

Now at least the h7 and g6 squares are covered. But the problem comes on the dark squares.

37 h6!

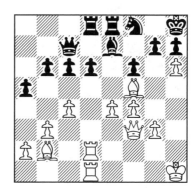

Finally! 'Action time'!

37...g6

After 37...gxh6 38 ♕h5 Black is in even more trouble.

38 ♗h3

A temporary retreat.

38...♔g8

Getting out of the pin.

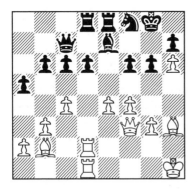

39 g4!

It is crucial to open the a1-h8 diagonal. Therefore, I need to eliminate Black's f6 pawn.

39...♘e6

On most other moves, 40 g5 would be the answer anyway.

40 g5

With a discovered attack on the knight.

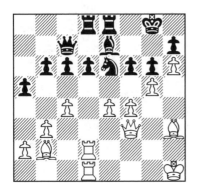

40...♘c5

Trying to put pressure on the e4

pawn.

41 gxf6

This is much better than 41 ♗xf6. The bishop on b2 is the jewel of White's position. It would be a waste to trade it off.

41...♗f8

A discovered attack on the e4 pawn and on h6 at the same time.

42 f7+!

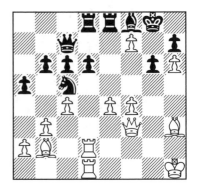

A very important sacrifice! I wanted to get rid of the pawn on f6 to open up the deadly a1-h8 diagonal.

42...♔xf7

After 42...♕xf7 43 ♕c3 the white queen is unstoppable on the a1-h8 diagonal.

43 f5

Now all the files and diagonals opened up to expose the weakness of the black king. There is no hope left for Black.

43...♔g8

The king is trying to run to safety.

44 fxg6

Further opening up the position. This is better than 44 ♕c3 ♖e5.

44...hxg6

After 44...♗xh6, White would play 45 ♖g2.

45 ♕f6

White is threatening 46 ♕h8+ ♔f7 47 ♕h7+ ♗g7 48 ♕xg7 mate.

45...♕h7

Protecting the h8 square and the g6 pawn.

46 ♖g2 Black resigned

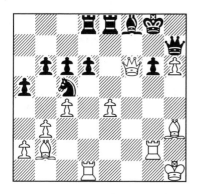

Due to the deadly threat on g6. I am very proud of this game.

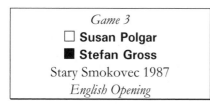

> *Game 3*
> □ **Susan Polgar**
> ■ **Stefan Gross**
> Stary Smokovec 1987
> *English Opening*

1 d4

This game was played at a grand-master tournament in a small, but beautiful mountain city in Czechoslovakia.

1...♘f6

My opponent is one of the local International Masters.

2 ♘f3

This move prevents a few gambit variations, such as the Benko or the Budapest, and simplifies some of White's opening preparation.

2...g6

After this, Black will still have a choice between the King's Indian or the Grünfeld, depending where the black d-pawn moves.

3 g3

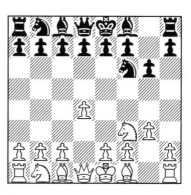

This is one of the more solid ways to fight the King's Indian or Grünfeld.

3...♗g7

Black is getting ready to castle.

4 ♗g2

Sometimes I prefer to play c2-c4 first. It is just a matter of taste.

4...0-0

Black's last two moves were quite automatic.

5 0-0

Again 5 c4 is a logical and sound alternative.

5...c5

At this moment, Black has two other good options in 5...d6 or 5...d5.

6 c4

It would be too greedy to capture with 6 dxc5 and, after 6...♘a6, try to hang on to the pawn with 7 ♗e3 ♕c7 8 ♕d4?, because of 8...♘e8 followed by ...♗xb2.

6...cxd4

Another common move is to protect the pawn on c5 with 6...d6.

7 ♘xd4

Taking back with 7 ♕xd4 would break the rule of not bringing your queen out early! After the natural 7...♘c6, White would lose time by having to move the queen again.

7...♘c6

A good developing move. A trade on c6 would only help Black.

8 ♘c3

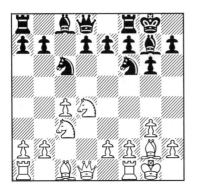

Now if Black moves either the b- or d-pawns, White would take the knight on c6 with 9 ♘xc6. 8 b3 would be a blunder since it would open the a1-h8 diagonal prematurely, allowing Black to win material by 8...♘xd4 9 ♕xd4 ♘e8.

8...♘xd4

Otherwise Black has difficulties getting the bishop on c8 out.

9 ♕xd4

Now the white queen has been forced to advance, but the difference (compared to the comment on move seven) is that Black cannot chase it away with ...♘b8-c6.

9...d6

Opening the diagonal for the bishop on c8. None of the knight moves would result in any gain for Black.

10 ♕d3

At first it seems that 10 b3 would be

a big mistake, because 10...♘e4 11 ♕xe4 ♗xc3 12 ♖b1 ♗f5 wins the rook on b1. But after a deeper look we can find 13 ♕f3 ♗xb1 14 ♕xc3 ♗f5 15 ♗h6, when White gains the sacrificed material back with a favorable position. 12 ♗g5 is also a good option, so 10 b3 is quite playable. Nevertheless, I prefer the continuation of the actual game, removing the queen from of a potential discovered attack.

10...♘d7

With the idea of relocating the knight to either e5 or c5. Having the knight on c5 will attack the white queen and protect the b7 pawn at the same time, helping the development of the bishop on c8.

Other common and logical moves are 10...a6 or 10...♖b8 to prepare the ...b7-b5 advance.

11 b3

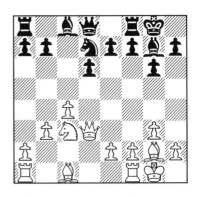

Now it is completely safe to play 11 b3. This move accomplishes two goals at once. It prepares the development of White's bishop to b2, and also protects the c4 pawn to free up the white queen. Therefore, if Black plays ...♘d7-e5, the queen will be free to move away without the necessity of guarding the pawn.

11...♘c5

After White's last move, the c4 pawn now being safe, this move is now a lot more logical than ...♘d7-e5.

12 ♕d2

It may seem illogical and unnatural to put the queen in front of the bishop, but it is only a very temporary problem as White's next move will be 13 ♗b2.

12...♖b8

The rook gets out of the pin along the h1-a8 diagonal, to prepare counter-play with ...b7-b5.

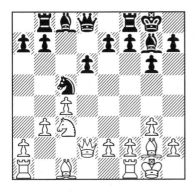

13 ♗b2

The only logical move! 13 b4 would be premature, allowing Black to use the pin effectively by playing 13...♘a4.

13...a6

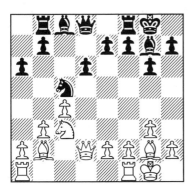

There is a famous trick that Black could have fallen into if he was not careful: 13...♕a5 14 ♖ad1 and now 14...♖d8? would be a big mistake, because White wins a pawn by 15 ♘d5! ♕xd2 and now the intermediate check of 16 ♘xe7+ ♔f8 17 ♗xg7+ ♔xg7 18 ♖xd2.

14 ♘d5

It is usually a good idea to centralize the knight when you can. Here the important point is that if Black chases the knight away with ...e7-e6, the d6 pawn would become a long term weakness.

14...♗xb2

Black could only worsen his position by avoiding the trade of bishops.

15 ♕xb2

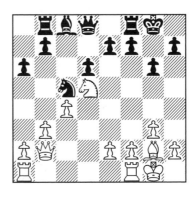

Now the queen takes control of the long (a1-h8) diagonal. It puts in the back of my mind some checkmate potential, either by pushing the h-pawn up to h4-h5-h6 (followed by ♕g7 mate), or maybe somehow luring the black queen away from protecting the e7 pawn and then mate with ♘xe7.

15...b5

This is the only opportunity Black has for counterplay.

16 cxb5

16 b4 would let the advantage slip out of White's hands. The knight would not need to move as Black can play 16...bxc4 creating a pin on the b4 pawn.

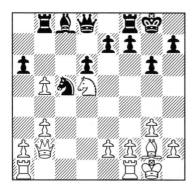

16...axb5

Taking back with the rook is also playable, although I don't think it's a considerable improvement on Black's position.

17 ♖fd1

This is one of those 'it just fits the position' kind of moves, putting the rook on the half-open file.

17...♗b7

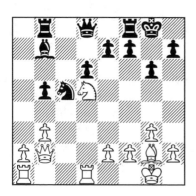

Black's best bet is to try to trade the bishop for White's powerful knight. Chasing away the knight with 17...e6 would now be outright suicidal, as

White wins with 18 ♘f6+ ♔h8 (things end even more quickly after 18...♔g7, when it is White to move and mate in five! 19 ♘h5+ ♔h6 20 ♕g7+ ♔xh5 21 ♕xh7+ ♔g5 22 ♕h4+ ♔f5 23 ♕f4 mate) 19 ♖xd6! ♕xd6 20 ♘e8+ and by this discovered check, Black loses the queen.

It is time to decide what plan to choose next. Here are my choices:

a) Trying to create a passed pawn on the a-file by preparing a2-a4.

b) Trying to attack the isolated b5 pawn.

c) Advancing the h2 pawn to h6 to create additional threats, due to the weakened dark squares near the black king.

18 h4

I chose to start with plan 'c' while maintaining the option to implement plan 'a' or 'b' later as well.

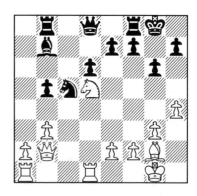

18...♗xd5

Black has solved one problem in getting rid of the knight. However, due to the exchange, White's bishop has now gained more power.

19 ♖xd5

I chose to recapture with the rook because I felt that, in some variations after h4-h5, it may come handy along the fifth rank in the kingside attack.

19...♘d7

This is a bit too passive. 19...b4 20 h5 e6 was a better defense, although after 21 h6 f6 22 ♖d4 White still has favorable chances.

20 h5

Moving along as planned.

20...♘f6

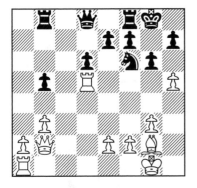

At first it seems that Black has just made a fork by attacking White's rook on d5 and the pawn on h5, but White has a defense in mind.

21 h6

White can save both! With this move, White indirectly protects the rook.

21...♖b6

Of course the rook could not be taken, as checkmate would follow with 22 ♕g7 mate.

22 ♖ad1

A preventive move.

22...♕c7

If Black had played 22...e6, I planned a cute combination with 23 ♖xd6! ♖xd6 24 ♖xd6 ♕xd6 25 ♕xf6 and checkmate is unavoidable without major material loss.

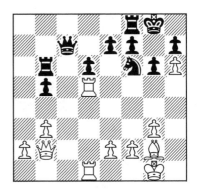

23 ♖c1

Taking control of the open file with tempo.

23...♖c6

Moving the queen away with 23...♕d7 was a more solid defense.

24 ♖xc6

Definitely the best choice, forcing the black queen into a discovered attack.

24...♕xc6

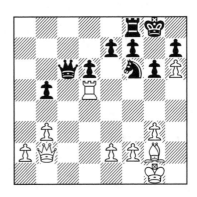

Even though the white rook can go almost anywhere and create a discovered attack; there is nothing that would win material immediately.

25 ♖f5

A tricky move, which could be deadly as my opponent was short on time.

25...♕e8

The only move. On 25...♕b6 White can win by sacrificing with 26 ♖xf6! etc., or if 25...d5 26 ♖xd5!.

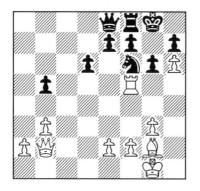

26 ♖f4

Now the rook is finally under real attack, so it is time to put it on a safe square. Here the same sacrifice with 26 ♖xf6 exf6 27 ♕xf6 does not work because of the saving move 27...♕e5.

26...♕d8

Black had a reasonable alternative in 26...♕c8, as 27 ♖xf6 exf6 28 ♕xf6 fails to 28...♕c1+ picking up the h6 pawn.

27 a4

Time to create a passed pawn on the a-file!

27...e5

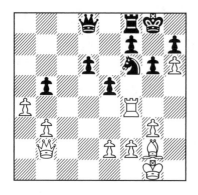

Black tries to stop any threat from the white queen down the long diagonal. Had Black gone hunting for the h6 pawn, then the passed a-pawn would have become too fast to defend, e.g. 27...bxa4 28 bxa4 ♕a5 29 ♖b4 ♕g5 30 ♖b7 e5 (or 30...♖e8 31 ♗c6 ♖c8 32 ♖b8) 31 a5 ♕xh6 32 a6.

28 ♖b4

Attacking the b5 pawn a second time.

28...♕a5

A very resourceful and tricky move!

29 ♕d2

White would get in big trouble by being greedy with 29 ♖xb5? ♕e1+ 30 ♗f1 (or 30 ♔h2 ♘g4+) 30...♘e4! 31 e3 ♘d2.

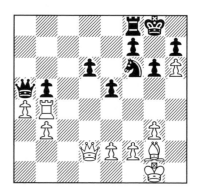

29...bxa4

Here Black is in serious difficulties already, but the best hope for some 'complications' was probably 29...♘g4 30 ♕xd6 ♖d8.

30 bxa4

After the more aggressive 30 ♕xd6, Black can steer into a rook endgame a pawn down with excellent drawing chances: 30...♘e8 31 ♕e7 axb3 32 ♖b8 ♕c7! (but not 32...♕a4? 33 ♗d5) 33 ♖xe8 ♕xe7 34 ♖xe7 ♖b8 35 ♗e4 b2 36

♗b1 ♔f8 37 ♖xe5 ♖d8 38 ♔g2 ♖d1 39 ♗c2 b1♕ 40 ♗xb1 ♖xb1.

30...d5

If Black protects the pawn on d6 with 30...♖d8, White can continue with 31 ♕g5 ♘e8 32 ♖b7 creating a killer attack.

31 ♕g5

Getting out of the pin by tactical means!

31...♘e8

Black could not accept the gift with 31...♕xb4, as after 32 ♕xf6 mate on g7 would follow.

32 ♕e7

32 ♖b8 is also good.

32...e4

The game would have lasted somewhat longer after 32...♕c7 33 ♖b7 ♕xe7 34 ♖xe7 e4 35 a5. Nevertheless, the result would be the same.

33 ♖b8

Attacking the knight a second time.

33...♕xa4

Black protected the knight and took a pawn.

34 ♕e5

Now the problem comes on g7 again!

34...f6

Otherwise 35 ♖xe8 removes the guard of the g7 square and ♕g7 mate follows.

35 ♕e6+

To chase the king away from the rook on f8.

35...♔h8

Black has no alternative.

36 ♕e7 Black resigned

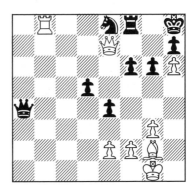

Attacking the rook on f8, while after 36...♔g8 37 ♖xe8 Black gets mated on g7.

Game 4
□ **Susan Polgar**
■ **Uwe Bönsch**
Dortmund 1990
Queen's Gambit

1 d4

Just a couple of months prior to this game, I suffered a very painful loss against the same opponent in the last round of the World Championship Zonal tournament. I was eager to have my revenge.

1...♘f6

This came as a small surprise as the German GM usually favors 1...d5.

2 c4

If White wants to have the option of playing the Nimzo-Indian then this move is a must.

2...e6

Here White has to decide whether to allow the pin after 3 ♘c3 ♗b4, or to avoid it by 3 ♘f3 or 3 g3.

3 ♘c3

This allows 3...♗b4, which is called the 'Nimzo', after the great player Aaron Nimzovich.

3...d5

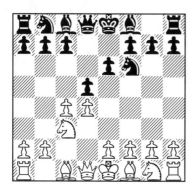

Transposing to a quieter game: the Queen's Gambit Declined.

4 cxd5

This is the Exchange variation. 4 ♗g5 and 4 ♘f3 ♗e7 5 ♗f4 are the two main alternatives.

4...exd5

4...♘xd5 is also playable, although not very popular. It transposes to another opening, the Semi-Tarrasch, after 5 e4 ♘xc3 6 bxc3 c5 7 ♘f3.

5 ♗g5

White certainly wants to develop the bishop prior to playing e2-e3. The f4 square is also a good option.

5...c6

Black can set a trap here with 5...♘bd7 and now if 6 ♘xd5?, despite

the pin on the f6 knight, 6...♘xd5! 7 ♗xd8 ♗b4+ 8 ♕d2 ♗xd2+ 9 ♔xd2 ♔xd8 and Black has gained a material advantage. Of course White does not have to take on d5 but can, and should, play a calmer 6 e3 or 6 ♘f3.

6 e3

In this variation, it is quite important to fight for the control of the b1-h7 diagonal. It is considered as a small success for Black if the bishop manages to occupy the f5 square safely.

6...♗e7

If now 6...♗f5, Black has to count on 7 ♕f3 ♗g6 8 ♗xf6 ruining the pawn structure on the kingside.

7 ♕c2

To prevent ...♗f5. 7 ♗d3 is also OK with the same purpose.

7...♗g4

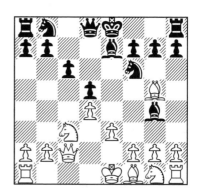

An unusual move. Normally you would want to wait until a knight is developed to f3 to make such a move. I guess the idea is that, after the natural 8 ♗d3, Black will try to exchange the light-squared bishops with ...♗g4-h5-g6.

Instead, 7...♘e4 would be a mistake as White wins a pawn with 8 ♗xe7 ♕xe7 and 9 ♘xd5. The common moves are 7...♘bd7 or 7...0-0.

8 ᐃge2

8 ᐃd3 and 8 h3 are also good.

8...ᐃxe2

This was very surprising to me. To make such an effort to trade the bishop for the knight is not common. Although, what else can Black do? After 8...ᐃh5 9 ᐃf4 is the answer. Therefore, the whole plan with 7...ᐃg4 is questionable.

9 ᐃxe2

White has gained the advantage of the 'bishop pair'. Black has no compensation for this whatsoever.

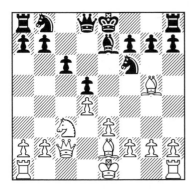

9...ᐃbd7

If 9...h6 or 9...ᐃe4 then 10 ᐃf4 in either case.

10 0-0

In the Queen's Gambit Declined Exchange variation, White can choose between castling to the kingside or the queenside. The first is a lot safer and normally leads to a stable positional game. The second often becomes a crazy 'pawn storm' race.

10...0-0

Both sides are fully developed. Now it is time to formulate plans.

11 ᐃd3

This puts the bishop on a more important diagonal, to control the e4 center square and put pressure on the h7 pawn. After the immediate 11 f3, Black could play 11...ᐃh5 and force the trade of dark-squared bishops.

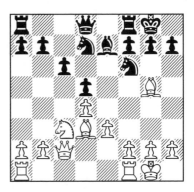

11...ᐃe8

This move has two purposes: to clear the f8 square for the knight and to occupy the half-open e-file.

12 f3

White's plan is to prepare the e3-e4 pawn advance with ᐃae1, ᐃh1, and ᐃg5-h4-f2.

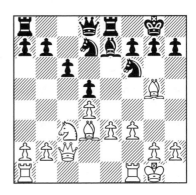

12...ᐃf8

This defends the h7 pawn so Black is now ready to play 13...ᐃh5.

Considering that White already has played f2-f3 and weakened the e3 pawn, it is a logical reaction to play 12...c5.

However, it has some tactical difficulties at the moment: 13 dxc5 ♘xc5 14 ♗b5 ♖f8 15 ♖ad1 and Black has trouble with the d5 pawn.

13 ♗h4

Relocating the bishop to f2 to protect the d4 pawn, before advancing the e-pawn.

13...a6

An understandable idea, preparing ...c6-c5 by preventing ♗b5. However, it is a little slow.

14 ♖ad1

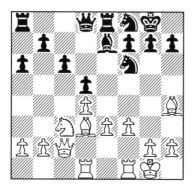

Preparing to open up the position.

14...♘g6

14...c5 would lose a pawn after 15 ♗xf6 ♗xf6 16 dxc5, and Black cannot win the pawn back because of the discovered attacks such as 16...♖xe3 17 ♘xd5 ♕xd5 18 ♗xh7+ or 16...♗xc3 17 ♕xc3 ♖xe3 18 ♗xh7+.

15 ♗f2

Now White's pieces are ideally positioned for the breakthrough with e3-e4.

15...♗d6

Again 15...c5? loses the d5-pawn, this time to 16 dxc5 ♗xc5 17 ♗xg6 hxg6 18 ♘xd5.

16 e4

It is certainly good timing to play e3-e4, as there is an immediate threat of a pawn fork with 17 e5.

16...dxe4

If Black does not trade, and plays instead 16...♗f4, White advances further with 17 e5 ♘d7 18 g3 ♗h6 19 f4 with a great position.

17 fxe4

Renewing the fork threat.

17...♘g4

Looking for counterplay.

18 e5

This advance not only attacks the bishop, but also blocks the attack on the h2 pawn.

18...♗c7

Black does not have time to trade with 18...♘xf2? because he loses material after 19 ♕xf2.

19 ♗c4

Now the new target is the f7 pawn.

19...♖e7

Black has to defend the pawn. If he plays 19...♗b6, White gets a winning advantage with 20 ♗xf7+! ♔xf7 21 ♗h4+ (or 21 ♕b3+ ♔f8 22 ♘a4 ♗a5 23 ♗g3+ ♘f6 24 exf6 gxf6 25 ♕xb7 also works) 21...♘f6 22 exf6 ♘xh4 23 ♕xh7.

20 ♔h1

This move releases the g1 square for the bishop. In general, when the f2 pawn is gone, it is a good idea to get the king off the g1-a7 diagonal, just to make sure there is no surprise check or pin by the black bishop. 20 ♘e4 is also good.

20...♘xf2+

Otherwise 21 ♗g1 and the knight on g4 gets in trouble.

21 ♕xf2

Putting more pressure on the f7 pawn.

21...♕d7

Again Black has to defend the pawn.

22 ♘e4

Time to bring more ammunition to the kingside.

22...♖f8

Black is trying to protect the f7 pawn as much as possible.

23 ♕f3

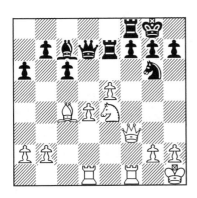

In many cases, one target is not enough to create a winning advantage. Therefore, White is looking for a second one on h7. The queen will head to h5.

23...♕e8

Moving the queen away from a potential ♘e4-c5 attack. and protecting the rook on f8. After 23...♘h8 24 e6

would be possible due to the pin on the f7 pawn.

24 ♕h5

Threatening 25 ♘f6+! gxf6 26 exf6 and 27 ♕h6 next, or else 25 ♘g5 h6 26 ♘xf7 winning for White.

24...♔h8

Moving the king out of the pin.

25 ♖d3

Bringing another piece into the attack. 25 ♘g5 h6 26 ♖f5 would have been even more energetic.

25...h6

Black loses quickly after 25...f5 26 ♖h3 h6 27 ♘f6! ♕c8 28 ♕xh6+! gxh6 29 ♖xh6+ ♔g7 30 ♖h7 mate, or 25...b5 26 ♘f6! gxf6 27 ♖h3 and the mate on h7 is unstoppable.

26 ♖df3

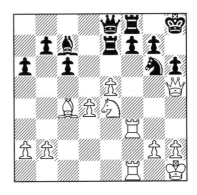

The knight is trapped! White threatens to play 27 ♕xg6 taking advantage of the pin down the f-file. Also good is 26 ♘f6 ♕c8 27 ♘g4 ♔h7 28 ♖h3 and then 29 ♘xh6. White is clearly winning.

26...♘xe5

Black tries a last trick. If instead 26...b5 27 ♕xg6 bxc4 then 28 ♘g5! hxg5 29 ♖h3+ ♔g8 30 ♕h7 mates.

27 dxe5

There is nothing to be afraid of, as

long as you see White's next move .

27...♖xe5

Now Black forks the queen and the knight.

28 ♖xf7!

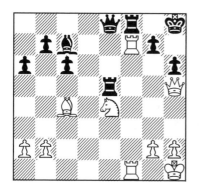

This is a crushing move for White.

28...♖xf7

28...♖g8 29 ♕g6 ♖xe4 does not save the game either, as 30 ♗d3 ♕e5 31 g3 wins the rook.

29 ♕xf7 Black resigned

After either 29...♖xe4 30 ♕f8+ ♔h7 31 ♗g8+ ♔h8 32 ♗d5+ ♔h7 33 ♕f5+ or 29...♕xf7 30 ♖xf7 ♖xe4 31 ♖f8+ ♔h7 32 ♗d3, White will be a rook up.

Game 5
□ **Maia Chiburdanidze**
■ **Susan Polgar**
Novi Sad Olympiad 1990
Sicilian Defense

Chiburdanidze was the Women's World Champion in from 1978 until 1991. Therefore, she was the reigning champion when this game was played, although I had a higher rating than Maia since 1984 (when I became the No.1 woman player in the world). Since I did not compete in the Women's World

Championship cycle until 1992, for many years the press and chess fans were curious as to who was stronger. The few encounters we had prior to this game all ended in draws.

1 e4

It used to be hard to prepare against Maia because she had a very wide opening repertoire.

1...c5

I was inviting a sharp struggle by choosing the Sicilian Defense. I knew that this game could impact on the medal race, so I was aiming for a win to help Hungary win the Gold.

2 ♘f3

The main move; White maintains the option of playing either the open Sicilian (with d2-d4) or a side variation.

2...♘c6

I usually like this move, which allows me to decide a few moves later between the Accelerated Dragon and the Sveshnikov variation.

3 ♗b5

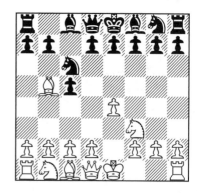

This is the Rossolimo variation. At one time, it was considered an unambitious sideline. However, in recent years it became very popular as many of the top players started employing it with

success. Unlike the more direct 3 d4, which leads to more aggressive play; in this variation White aims for a more positional game.

3...g6

The next piece to develop is my bishop on f8. 3...e6 is an equally good alternative.

4 0-0

In general it should be a priority to get the king to safety by castling. In this case, White could have delayed it by one move with a trade on c6. After exchanging the bishop for the knight, Black is forced to take back with a pawn, creating doubled pawns on the c-file, though Black would have compensation by the advantage of the pair of bishops. In this variation, it is a matter of taste whether or when to take on c6.

4...♗g7

After Black's previous move, this is a must continuation.

5 ♖e1

5 c3, preparing d2-d4, and 5 ♘c3 are also common choices.

5...e5

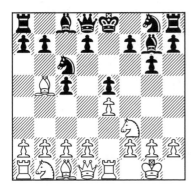

This was a big decision. On one hand, it takes control of the e5 and d4 center squares, and stops White from

playing e4-e5 (for example after 5...♘f6). On the other hand, it weakens the d5 square and limits the scope of the black bishop on g7.

6 c3

This was White's last opportunity to trade on c6 which, actually, I would think is the most logical move. Otherwise why did the bishop go to b5 the first place?

6...♘ge7

Once the two black knights are connected, then after 7 ♗xc6 ♘xc6 Black would gain the advantage bishop pair without needing to have doubled pawns.

7 b4

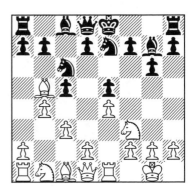

This move came as a total surprise to me, as it is very rarely seen at the professional level. After the calmer 7 d3 0-0 8 ♗e3 d6, Black gets comfortable play by preparing ...f7-f5.

7...d6

At this juncture of the game, the psychological aspect played a big role. I was not too curious to find out what Maia and her coaches prepared for me if I accepted the pawn sacrifice. Although I have no doubt that Black could take the pawn without any tragedy, at the same time I think that White would get compensation in the form of activity. That is why I chose the more practical approach, rather than walk into the home preparation of my opponent. I did not want her to have any psychological advantage.

8 bxc5

In my opinion, this was a strategical error. Opening the d-file only helps the black queen gain power. Perhaps 8 a3 was better.

8...dxc5

At this point, I really liked my position. I thought the only chance White might have to fight for an advantage was if the d-pawn could advance to d4 at the right moment.

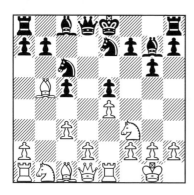

9 d3

I expected 9 ♗a3 b6 10 d4 exd4 and then either 11 cxd4 0-0 or 11 ♘xd4 ♗d7 (but not 11...cxd4 12 ♗xe7). However, Black is fine in both of these variations. Therefore, objectively speaking, my opponent probably made the right choice.

9...a6

It is time to find out which way will the bishop go.

10 ♗a4

After 10 ♗c4, Black can play 10...♘a5 and the bishop cannot escape the trade.

10...0-0

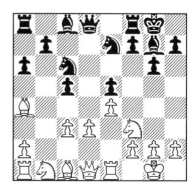

Finally, the black king is in safety and the knight on c6 is no longer pinned.

11 ♗e3

Developing the bishop and attacking the c5 pawn at the same time.

11...♕d6

Protecting the pawn and preparing space for the rook to come to d8. 11...b6 would be fine as well.

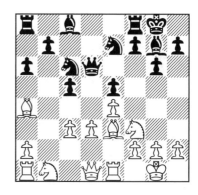

12 ♗c2

Black has some difficulties after 12 ♘bd2 ♕xd3 13 ♗xc5 b5 14 ♗b3 ♕xc3 (too greedy) 15 ♖c1 ♕d3 16 ♗d5, because of the bishop pins. It is better not to take the d3 pawn but to play 12...b5.

12...h6

A prophylactic move. Without it, should Black decides to play ...♗c8-e6 or ...f7-f5, then ♘f3-g5 could be an unpleasant response.

13 ♕c1

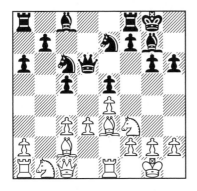

I believe my opponent anticipated my plan of playing ...f7-f5 in the near future. Therefore, she probably thought it was to White's advantage to lure the black king to h7 on the same diagonal as the bishop on c2. In addition, the white queen is eyeing the a3 square to put pressure on the c5 pawn.

13...♔h7

13...g5 would not be a bad choice either. However, I did not want to give up my plan of playing ...f7-f5 with the ability, after e4xf5, of recapturing with my g6 pawn.

14 ♘bd2

Finally all the white pieces are developed, though Black has a small space advantage.

14...b6

Securing the safety of the c5 pawn. White would gain some initiative after 14...b5 15 ♘b3 c4 16 dxc4 bxc4 17

♘c5.

15 ♘c4

Attacking the queen and the b6 pawn.

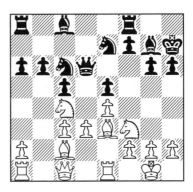

15...♕c7

The most obvious move, which saves them both.

16 ♖b1

Putting more pressure on the b6 pawn.

16...♖b8

Simply protecting the pawn. During the game, I did not like 16...b5 17 ♘cd2 ♕d6 18 ♘b3. While writing these comments, however, I found a nice improvement with 17...♘d4!.

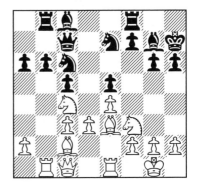

17 ♕a3

White seems to search in the wrong

direction. Black is solid on the queen-side and ready to launch an attack on the kingside. The white queen will be missed soon in the defense of the king.

17...f5

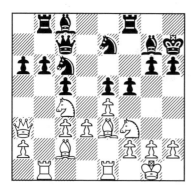

Finally! I wanted to play this move for a while, but it had to be well pre-pared.

18 exf5

If White does not capture the pawn, Black would play ...f5-f4 followed by ...g6-g5 and ...♘e7-g6 with a nice attack.

18...gxf5

Any other recapture would be a se-rious positional mistake, because it would leave the e5 pawn isolated. It is somewhat unusual to keep the bishop on c8 undeveloped for this long, but it is doing a job by protecting the a6 pawn. Note that the bishop could not develop on b7, because it would lock the rook's protection of the b6 pawn.

19 ♗d2

Getting away from some future ...f5-f4 attack, as well as opening the e-file for the rook.

19...♘g6

This is an ideal square for the knight, guarding the black king as well as aim-ing towards the kingside attack.

20 ♘e3

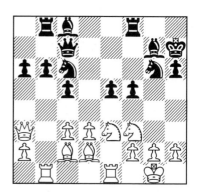

The knight is heading towards the d5 square. Just as over the past several moves, White has a hard time coming up with a good plan. I think the knight should have stayed on c4 to attack the two targets at e5 and b6. Perhaps it was time to get the queen back to the king-side.

20...♘ce7

Preventing White from playing ♘e3-d5.

21 ♕b3

It would have been better for the knight to return to c4.

21...♗d7!

I wanted to get the bishop to the long diagonal a8-h1. I did not want to ease White's problems by 21...♗b7 22 ♕xb6 ♕xb6 23 ♖xb6 ♗xf3 24 ♖xb8 ♖xb8 25 gxf3.

22 h3

This is not a good idea. As we shall see, my opponent was trying to make a hideaway square for the knight on h2. But that does not look too promising.

22...♗c6

Threatening to capture on f3 and ruin White's pawn structure.

23 ♘h2

After 23 ♗d1 ♘f4 24 ♕c2 ♖bd8 the d3 pawn is in trouble.

23...♘f4

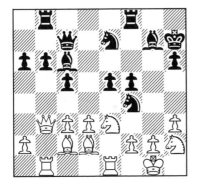

A dream place for the knight to attack the d3 and g2 pawns. The best part is that it cannot be chased away with 24 g3, because the pawn on h3 would be unprotected.

24 ♖bd1

Too slow, although White cannot do much to address the future problems on the kingside.

24...♕d6

Preparing to swing the queen over to g6.

25 f3

Trying to reduce to power of the black bishop on c6.

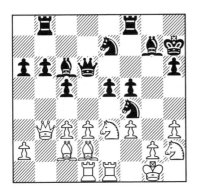

25...♕g6

This creates a pin and threatens to win a pawn with 26...♘xh3+.

26 ♔h1

Getting out of the pin to avoid losing the pawn.

26...♘ed5

Trying to remove the guard of the g2 square. If 27 ♘xd5 ♕xg2 mate would follow.

27 ♘hf1

After 27 ♖g1, Black can increase the pressure with 27...♘e2 28 ♖ge1 ♘df4.

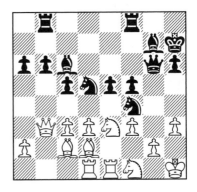

27...♘xe3

Now it's time to cash in! It is obvious that Black has an overwhelming attack. But in most attacks there will eventually be a point when one needs to actually calculate variations or combinations that lead to material gains or checkmate.

28 ♘xe3

The only sensible recapture to protect g2.

28...♕g3?!

Both my opponent and I had few minutes left on our clocks to reach the time control (on the 40th move). Because of the time situation, I was not able to find the quickest way to win with 28...♗xf3! 29 gxf3 ♕g3 and White is helpless, for example 30 ♕c4 e4 31 d4 ♕xh3+ 32 ♔g1 ♗xd4 33 cxd4 ♖g8+ 34 ♔f2 ♕xf3 mate.

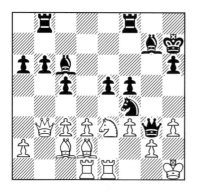

29 ♖f1

Reinforcing the f3 pawn. The threat from Black is 29...♘xg2 30 ♘xg2 ♗xf3 31 ♖g1 ♕h3 mate.

29...♘xh3!

Time to act! Otherwise ♗d2-e1 would chase the queen out.

30 d4

If 30 gxh3 ♕xh3+ 31 ♔g1 ♗f6 32 ♘g2 ♖g8 33 ♖f2 ♗h4 wins, or 30 ♗e1 ♕g5 31 gxh3 ♕xe3.

30...♘f4!

After 30...♘f2+ 31 ♖xf2 ♕xf2 32 ♘xf5 White would get some counterplay.

31 ♗e1

White could not grab the pawn with 31 ♗xf5+? because, after 31...♖xf5, the knight on e3 cannot take the rook as it is tied up defending the g2 pawn.

31...♕g5

Because of the miss on move 28 I now have to work a little harder.

32 d5

Eliminating the bishop's attacking power towards g2 and f3.

32...♗d7

Bringing additional protection to the f5 pawn.

33 ♗b1?!

33 ♖f2 would be a better defense, preventing 33...♘e2.

33...♘e2

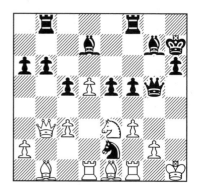

Black threatens to checkmate down the h-file.

34 ♘g4

This is possible because of the pin on the f5 pawn.

34...e4

Cutting off the bishop on b1 which was pinning the f5 pawn. After the direct 34...♕h5+ White would have blocked with 35 ♘h2.

35 ♘h2

The knight was under attack and simply had to move away.

35...♗e5

Threatening a deadly pin with 36...♕h5.

36 ♖f2

Trying to get some protection for the h2 square.

36...♕g3

This is more precise than 36...♕h5 37 g4.

37 f4

After 37 ♘f1 ♛h4+ White gets mated.

37...♗xf4

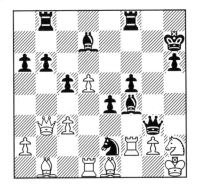

Renewing the same threats.

38 ♖xf4

White has no choice.

38...♛xf4 White resigned

Black is an exchange and two pawns up. White's position is hopeless.

This was my first ever victory against Maia, and it helped my sisters and I capture our second consecutive Olympic gold medal for Hungary over the Soviet team.

Game 6
□ **Susan Polgar**
■ **Peter Lukacs**
Hungarian Championship 1991
English Opening

---

1 ♘f3

This was a planned surprise deviation from my usual starting move 1 d4.

1...d5

This game was played in the Super Hungarian Championship. My sister Judit caused a worldwide sensation by being the first woman ever to win a national championship. This prestigious

event included legendary Hungarian GMs such as Portisch, Sax, and Adorjan. I finished in fourth place one point behind Judit, but ahead of Portisch.

2 c4 e6

Capturing the pawn on c4 would only bring temporary gain for Black, as after 2...dxc4 the pawn can be regained by various manners, such as 3 ♛a4+, 3 ♘a3 or 3 e3.

3 g3

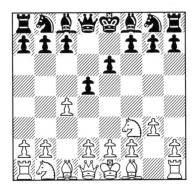

My opponent is a very well-known theoretician. That is why I wanted to get him away from the main lines in which he is an expert. The main move is 3 d4, which would transpose to the Queen's Gambit.

3...♘f6

Typical development for the knight.

4 ♗g2

On this move, or the next two moves, White can still play d2-d4 and the game would transpose into the Catalan. 4 cxd5 would help Black, since after 4...exd5 the bishop on c8 becomes more active.

4...♗e7

Preparing to castle. Other alternatives are 4...dxc4 and 4...c5.

5 0-0

White still does not need to worry about Black capturing the c4 pawn, as ♕a4+ or ♘e5 wins the pawn right back.

5...0-0

Now that the king is away from e8, Black can now think about capturing the c4 pawn.

6 b3

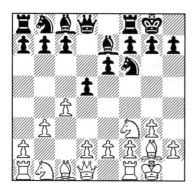

This solid move is the final sign of my intention to avoid a theoretical battle in the opening. The idea of this move is simple: it protects the c4 pawn and prepares ♗c1-b2. Instead, 6 d4 would have still transposed to a regular Catalan.

6...c5

A logical move to control the center. 6...b6 is another possible set-up.

7 cxd5

I wanted to stop Black from pushing ...d5-d4, which would lock up my bishop on b2.

7...♘xd5

After 7...exd5, I planned to play 8 d4 with transposition to the Tarrasch Defense. In that opening the d4 pawn most often gets traded for the c5 pawn; Black has an isolated d-pawn, but tries to get activity and counterplay in the center.

8 ♗b2

Practically a must, as otherwise ...♗e7-f6 would be unpleasant.

8...♘c6

A good developing move and controlling the center.

9 ♘c3

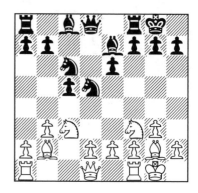

Finally the last minor piece is developed. White has somewhat better piece development, while Black has a stronger presence in the center.

9...♗f6

This is a wise move to create a pin on the c3 knight. If 9...b6 10 ♘xd5 ♕xd5? then 11 ♘e5 and Black gets into big trouble along the h1-a8 diagonal, while after 10...exd5 11 d4 and White has a nice harmonious position.

10 ♕c2

Protecting the bishop on b2 and freeing up the knight. 10 ♕c1 is also good with the same purpose.

10...b6

This is not the most ambitious choice. I would personally prefer either 10...♘xc3 11 ♗xc3 e5 or 10...♘cb4 11 ♕c1 b6 with balanced positions in both lines.

11 ♘xd5

It is action time. If White wants to

gain some initiative, it is best to do so while Black is temporarily behind in development.

11...exd5

Taking back with the queen loses again due to the discovered attack, so Black has only two choices. The alternative 11...♗xb2 would invite some very interesting and complicated variations. Of course the simple 12 ♕xb2 exd5 13 d4 is available with a tiny advantage for White. However, there is a crazy move 12 ♘xb6 and if Black captures the knight, White will take the bishop and maintain an extra pawn. Therefore the key reply is 12...♗xa1 13 ♘xa8 ♗f6, and after 14 ♕xc5 ♗b7 the white knight has no hope, but there is an interesting way to rescue the knight on a8 by 14 ♘g5 ♗xg5 15 ♗xc6 ♕xd2 (if 15...♗d7 16 ♗f3) with approximate equality.

12 d4!

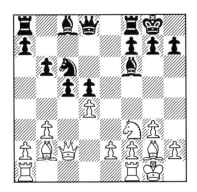

This was the whole idea of my previous move. The c5 pawn is pinned, because the knight on c6 is unprotected.

12...♘xd4?

After this Black gets an unpleasant position with a weak, isolated d5 pawn, and no counterplay. 12...♗a6 13 dxc5

♖e8 14 ♖fe1 ♗xb2 15 ♕xb2 bxc5 would have been a more active and promising way to play.

13 ♘xd4

This forces Black to double up his pawns on the d-file.

13...cxd4

Taking back with the bishop and allowing the trade would only help White.

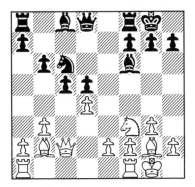

14 ♖ad1

White attacks the d4 pawn a second time and Black has no way of holding on to it.

14...♗e6

If Black tries to get tricky with 14...d3 15 ♖xd3 ♗f5, White has 16 e4 utilizing the pin along the d-file.

15 ♗xd4

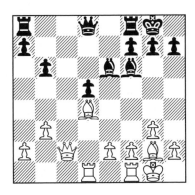

Finally, I have regained the pawn. Now the plan is simple: to target the d5 pawn. First of all, I have to make sure that it will be blockaded, which means that White will keep a piece on d4, stopping the d5 pawn from advancing, and can then just go after it.

15...♖c8

Occupying the open file with tempo.

16 ♕b2

Threatening to trade on f6 which would ruin Black's pawn structure on the kingside. After the more direct attack on the target by 16 ♕d3 ♗xd4 17 ♕xd4, Black can indirectly protect the pawn with 17...♕e7 18 ♗xd5 ♗xd5 19 ♕xd5 ♕xe2. Of course White is not forced to capture the pawn, and would secure the e2 pawn first.

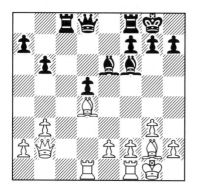

16...♗xd4

Otherwise 17 ♗xf6 comes.

17 ♖xd4

Better than 17 ♕xd4, which would transpose to the position discussed after 16 ♕d3. In general, when attacking a target with a queen and rook(s), it is more effective to have a rook in front and the queen behind.

17...♖c5

17...♕f6 18 ♖fd1 ♖c5 19 ♕d2

would transpose and reach the same position as in the game.

18 ♖fd1

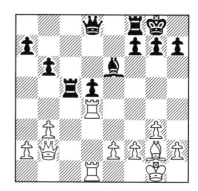

In this type of position, patience is the key. It would be premature to use the pin with 18 e4, because Black can create a counter-pin with 18...♕f6 and save the pawn, i.e. 19 exd5 ♗xd5.

18...♕f6

This pin temporarily holds the pawn.

19 ♕d2

Moving out of the pin, so I now have four pieces eyeing the d5 pawn.

19...♖fc8

19...♖d8 would protect the pawn, but it moves into a pin and allows White to win the pawn with 20 e4.

20 ♗xd5

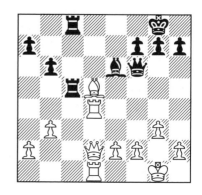

Finally the target has fallen! Black gets a pawn back, but the two pawns are not of equal value in this case. This is an excellent example that demonstrates the importance of the control of the center.

20...♖c2

With this fork Black regains the pawn, but the rook will now be far from the action.

21 ♕d3

It is important for tactical reasons to keep the queen on the d-file.

21...♖xa2

Black has managed to maintain a material balance, but not equality.

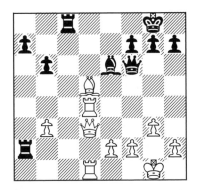

22 ♗xe6

This forces Black to weaken the seventh rank and creates a new pawn weakness.

22...fxe6

22...♕xe6 23 ♖d8+ was out of question because of Black's back rank problem.

23 ♖e4

Attacking the newly created target: the e6 pawn. Now the threat is 24 ♕d7.

23...♖e8

Protecting the e-pawn.

24 ♕d7

The main idea of this move is to lure the black queen to the seventh rank, so that the white rook can later land on d7 with tempo.

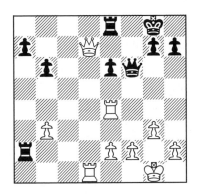

24...♕e7

After 24...♖e7 Black loses his queen by 25 ♕c8+ ♕f8 26 ♖d8 or 25...♔f7 26 ♖f4.

25 ♕c6

The black king would find safety on g6 after 25 ♕xe7 ♖xe7 26 ♖d8+ ♔f7 27 ♖f4+ ♔g6. So it was better for me to maintain the pressure by keeping the queens on the board.

25...♖a5

25...♕f7 26 ♖d7 ♕g6 would have been a better defense.

26 ♖d7

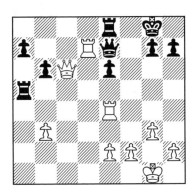

As so often occurs when a rook

comes to the seventh rank, the game is over.

26...♛f8

If Black holds on to the e6 pawn by 26...♛f6, he loses another pawn with the discovery 27 ♖xg7+.

27 ♖xe6

And the pawn is gone!

27...♜c8

Black would lose even faster after 27...♜xe6 28 ♛xe6+ ♚h8 29 ♖e7 followed by 30 ♖e8.

28 ♛b7

White is planning to create a triple attack on the seventh rank with 29 ♖6e7.

28...♜c1+

Finally an active move, but a little too late.

29 ♚g2

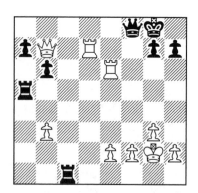

Black is only one pawn down, but the bigger problem is that White completely dominates the board.

29...♜f5

Looking for some disturbance on f2, hoping for a miracle save.

30 f3

A defensive move is needed. Black's seventh rank problem still remains.

30...♖f7

Black is helpless against either 31 ♖de7 or 31 ♖6e7.

31 ♖xf7 Black resigned

Since if 31...♛xf7 32 ♛b8+ ♛f8 33 ♖e8 wins.

> *Game 7*
> □ **Susan Polgar**
> ■ **Zbynek Hracek**
> Brno 1993
> *Nimzo-Indian Defense*

1 d4

I won another nice game against the same Czech GM three years before (see Combination 13).

1...♞f6

This is the same starting move as in our earlier encounter.

2 c4

In the previous game, I played 2 ♞f3.

2...e6

The other main option is 2...g6 leading to some riskier openings.

3 ♞c3

The other main choice is 3 ♞f3, avoiding the Nimzo-Indian and inviting the Queen's Indian.

3...♝b4

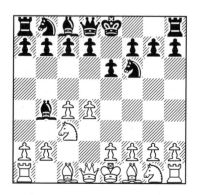

This is the Nimzo-Indian Defense. By creating a pin on the c3 knight, Black stops White's plan of advancing in the center with e2-e4.

4 ♕c2

With the idea that, if and when Black captures on c3, White would recapture with the queen. In many other variations of this opening, Black gets to trade on c3 forcing White to recapture with the b-pawn, thus creating doubled pawns on the c-file.

4...0-0

4...c5 and 4...d5 are other popular choices.

5 a3

Chasing the bishop away to get rid of the disturbing pin.

5...♗xc3+

Black had no other choice. It is impossible to maintain the pin with 5...♗a5 because of 6 b4 ♗b6 7 c5 trapping the bishop. It would also be illogical to retreat to e7 as it gives up the fight in the center and allows e2-e4.

6 ♕xc3

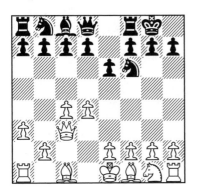

Now White has gained the advantage of the pair of bishops, without needing to double up the pawns on the c-file. However, White wasted two

queen moves and a pawn move (a2-a3) to achieve this, so Black is ahead in development.

6...b6

Preparing to develop the bishop to its optimal post at b7.

7 ♗g5

Making a pin is usually a good idea as it limits the mobility of a certain piece (here it is the knight on f6).

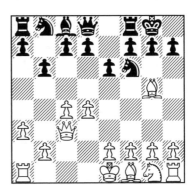

7...♗b7

Black would lose a pawn after 7...♘e4? 8 ♗xd8 ♘xc3 9 ♗xc7.

8 e3

Another possible plan was 8 f3 to prepare e2-e4.

8...h6

Chasing the bishop away. This move can sometimes be useful because it eliminates any back rank problems later on.

9 ♗h4

The only logical answer is to maintain the pin.

9...d6

Black wants to develop the knight from b8 to d7. In this position, it was not so healthy to put it on c6 because it would stand in the bishop's way.

10 f3

Otherwise the bishop on f1 would have a hard time getting out, because it needs to guard the g2 pawn.

10...♘bd7

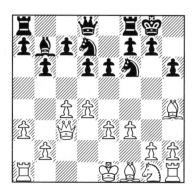

Until this move was played the black queen was tied to the knight on f6, as otherwise ♗xf6 would ruin Black's pawn structure on the kingside. Now the two knights are connected so, if required, the knight from d7 will be able to recapture.

11 ♗d3

A natural developing move. 11 0-0-0 or 11 ♘h3 are interesting alternatives.

11...c5

The black pieces are developed, so it is time to open up the position (i.e. trade pawns) somewhere. Considering that the white queen is on c3, the c-file seems to be the most logical place to try.

12 ♘e2

There is a need to react to Black's offer to trade. Best is simply to continue to develop.

12...cxd4?!

A little premature; there was no rush to make this exchange. It was better to play 12...♖c8, with the idea of ...d6-d5 or now ...c5xd4 and ...d6-d5.

13 exd4

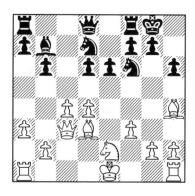

During the game I did not even consider any other move. I wanted to keep my space advantage and good control of the center. While writing these comments, I thought that perhaps I should have considered 13 ♕xd4 as well, with the plan of targeting the d6 pawn.

13...♖c8

After 13...d5 I planned to play 14 c5.

14 b4

Again preparing to meet 14...d5 with 15 c5.

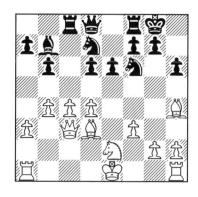

14...e5

White would win a pawn after 14...♘d5 15 ♗xd8 ♘xc3 16 ♗e7. If instead 14...♗a6 White has to get out of the pin with 15 ♕b3.

15 0-0

Finally White has completed development. 15 d5 would be good strategically, but it does not work tactically, because the pin along the c-file allows 15...♗xd5.

15...b5?!

This is a very natural and logical move, trying to utilize the pin. But as we shall see, after a pawn sacrifice, White gets more than enough compensation. In fact Black would have been better not initiating any action, but played more calmly with 15...♖e8, for example.

16 c5!

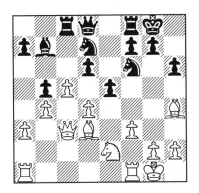

Before making this move I had to be ready to sacrifice a pawn, but this was the only way to keep the initiative.

16...exd4

My opponent decided to accept the pawn.

17 ♘xd4

The knight is wonderfully centralized on d4 and ready to jump to f5.

17...a6

Apparently this was my opponent's secret hope. Now that the b5 pawn is secured, Black can go after my c5 pawn with full force.

In a previous game, Black took the pawn straight away and things ended badly: 17...dxc5 18 ♘f5 c4 19 ♗c2 ♗d5 20 ♖ad1 ♗e6 21 ♖d6 ♖e8 22 ♖fd1 ♖c7 23 f4 ♗xf5 24 ♗xf5 ♕b8 25 ♗xd7 ♖xd7 26 ♖xd7 ♘xd7 27 ♖xd7 ♕xf4 28 ♕f3 ♕c1+ 29 ♕f1 ♕e3+ 30 ♗f2 ♕xa3 31 ♗d4 Black resigned (Gulko-De Firmian, US Championship 1989).

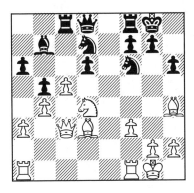

18 ♘f5!

Much better than passively hanging on to the c5 pawn.

18...dxc5

Practically a forced move. After 18...♘e5, I would continue to increase pressure along the d-file with 19 ♖ad1 (but not 19 ♘xd6 because of ♕xd6!).

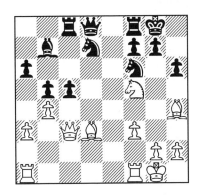

19 ♖ad1

Even though I had just sacrificed a pawn, there was still time for this quiet move. The direct attempt to advance with 19 ♘d6 at once does not achieve anything.

19...cxb4

After 19...c4, I planned 20 ♗b1 with similar ideas as in the game, plus the additional weapon, ♕c3-c2, with potential mating threats on h7.

20 ♕xb4

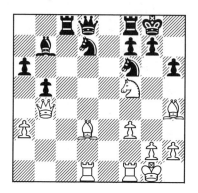

Black has a very difficult position despite being a pawn ahead. He is in two pins by White's bishop on h4 and rook on d1. Also, the knight jumps to e7 or d6 look very threatening.

20...♔h8

Solving the most direct problem (♘e7+) by getting out of the check. 20...♖e8 would also stop the fork on e7 but would create a new one with 21 ♘d6, while after 20...♖c7 the rook would not find peace for long because of 21 ♗g3.

21 ♘d6

Now all the white pieces (except for the rook on f1) are in their ideal positions.

21...♖b8

The best way to defend the bishop,

keeping the a5-d8 diagonal open for the black queen. If 21...♖c7, White gets an overwhelming position after 22 ♘xb7 ♖xb7 23 ♗e4 ♖c7 24 ♗xf6 gxf6 (24...♕xf6 is even worse due to 25 ♖xd7! ♖xd7 26 ♕xf8 mate!) 25 ♗f5 and the pin on the d-file is overwhelming.

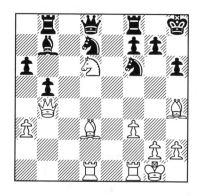

22 ♗f5!

Putting more pressure on the pinned piece, and threatening to win material with 23 ♘xb7 ♖xb7 24 ♗xf6. After 22 ♘xb7 Black escapes trouble with 22...♕b6+ 23 ♗f2 ♕xb7.

22...♗c6

22...♕b6+ 23 ♗f2 ♕c7 24 ♖c1 ♗c6 25 ♖fd1 does not seem to be an improvement.

23 ♗xd7!

It is time to convert the positional advantages into material gains.

23...♗xd7

After 23...♕xd7 24 ♗xf6 gxf6 25 ♕f4 ♔h7 26 ♘f5 Black would be completely lost.

24 ♘e4!

It is amazing how the knight jumps from one great spot to another, reacting to the changes and needs of the position.

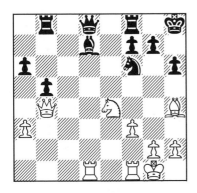

24...a5

Black's position is also hopeless after 24...♕b6+ 25 ♗f2 ♕e6 26 ♘xf6 gxf6 27 ♖fe1 ♕c6 28 ♕f4 or 27...♕f5 28 g4.

24...g5 would solve the problem of the existing pin on the h4-d8 diagonal, but would create other problems along the a1-h8 diagonal. It is usually possible to defend against one threat, but more threats would be too much to handle. 25 ♘xf6 ♕xf6 26 ♗f2 (threatening ♗f2-d4) 26...♕f5 and now 27 ♕d4+ forks and wins the bishop.

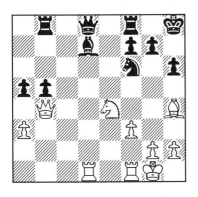

25 ♕b2!

The best place for the queen. 25 ♕d4 looks also attractive, but that would give the black bishop a chance to get out of the pin with 25...♗f5. White

is still better after 26 ♕xd8 ♖fxd8 27 ♖xd8+ ♖xd8 28 ♘xf6, but Black gets some practical counter-chances with 28...♖d3.

25...♕b6+

After 25...♖b6 White wins a piece with 26 ♗xf6 gxf6 27 ♘c5.

26 ♗f2

Of course! Defending the check and counter-attacking at the same time!

26...♕c6

White gets a mating attack after 26...♕e6 27 ♘xf6 gxf6 28 ♖fe1 ♕c6 29 ♖xd7 ♕xd7 30 ♕xf6+ ♔h7 31 ♗d4 ♖g8 32 ♖e7.

27 ♘xf6

The most direct way. 27 ♖d6 is good as well.

27...gxf6

The queen had to stay put to protect the bishop on d7.

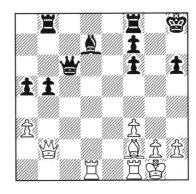

28 ♕d2

A double attack on Black's bishop and the pawn on h6.

28...♗f5

Trying to defend along the b1-h7 diagonal.

29 ♕xh6+

White has only just regained the sacrificed pawn, but has a winning attack.

The game lasted only one more move.

29...♔g8

After 29...♗h7 30 ♗d4 is decisive.

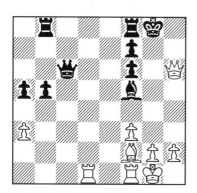

30 ♖d4 Black resigned

There is no defense against the threat of ♖d4-h4. For example, 30...♗h7 31 ♖g4+ ♗g6 32 ♖h4 or 30...♕c2 31 ♖c1.

Game 8
□ **Susan Polgar**
■ **Kiril Georgiev**
Pardubice 1994
Queen's Gambit

1 d4

My opponent in this game was the top Bulgarian grandmaster for many years.

1...d5

The most conservative response.

2 c4

I played 2 ♘f3 in many of my games, too.

2...e6

This is the Queen's Gambit Declined. 2...dxc4 would be the Queen's Gambit Accepted.

3 ♘c3

Now 3...♘f6 or 3...♗e7 are the stan-

standard QGD continuations.

3...c6

This move transposes to the Semi-Slav Defense.

4 e4

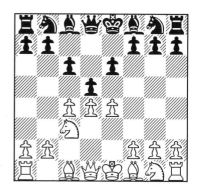

The most ambitious move, but risky as it often involves a pawn sacrifice.

4...dxe4

This is the best answer. After 4...♗b4, White would gain some space advantage with 5 cxd5 exd5 6 e5.

5 ♘xe4

Now if Black develops with 5...♘f6, White continues 6 ♘xf6 ♕xf6 7 ♘f3 and maintains a slightly better position.

5...♗b4+

After this check White has to decide whether to play solidly or go for a riskier and more complicated game. Naturally White has to block the check, as after 6 ♔e2 White would lose the right to castle.

6 ♗d2

I choose to give the pawn up. This is called an 'speculative' pawn sacrifice. What that really means that it is a long term plan. There is no immediate or clear visible way to get the material back or to checkmate. The pawn is usually given up for certain dynamic factors,

1975 Playing Blitz

Susan, Judit and Sofia in 1979

The family at home 1989 with the chess
library in the background

On stage receiving our first Olympic medals with team member
Ildiko Madl and team captain Janos Tompa, Thessaloniki 1988

The sisters with the First Lady and President Bush Budapest 1989

The sisters with team-mate Ildiko Madl showing off the Olympic
Gold medals and trophies Novi Sad 1990

Three sisters with Mom in Brno 1991

The three sisters in New York Central Park 1992

Where are we traveling next?
The three sisters at home in Budapest

Olympiad Gold 1988, 1990, 1994

The Polgar family on a sightseeing cruise in Sydney with the Opera
building in the background. 1992.

Sofia 1993

Judit in New York with the
World Trade Center in the
background 1994

Judit visiting the Polgar Chess
Center 2003

such as the pair of bishops, preventing the opponent from castling, a lead in development. After the more conservative 6 ♘c3 Black's best answer is 6...c5.

6...♛xd4

Black took the pawn! After 6...♛xd2+ 7 ♛xd2 White has some space advantage, while Black has difficulties activating the bishop on c8, and sometimes White can get a nice outpost for the knight on d6.

7 ♗xb4

This is the idea behind the pawn sacrifice. Now Black cannot easily castle to the kingside.

7...♛xe4+

Regaining the piece back and forcing White to block the check.

8 ♗e2

This is another pawn sacrifice. 8 ♘ge2 also leads to an interesting game; for example, 8...♘a6 9 ♗f8! ♚xf8? 10 ♛d8 mate. Naturally Black does not have to take the bishop on f8, but should rather play 9...♘e7 and give up the g7 pawn.

8...♘d7

Preparing ...c6-c5 to close the a3-f8 diagonal, so as to be able to castle. If Black plays 8...♘e7 instead, he would

still have difficulties getting the king to safety because it would need to guard the knight on e7. 8...♘a6 is another good attempt to chase the bishop away. But if Black grabs another pawn with 8...♛xg2, White gets a very strong attack after 9 ♛d6 ♘d7 10 0-0-0, and now Black cannot take the rook with 10...♛xh1 because 11 ♗f3 traps the queen.

9 ♘f3

White must continue to develop. After 9 ♛d6 Black would give the pawn back with 9...c5 to activate the bishop.

9...c5

If 9...♘e7 10 ♗xe7 ♚xe7 Black would permanently lose the right to castle, and White would have sufficient compensation or the pawn after 11 ♛d2 followed by 12 0-0-0.

10 ♗c3

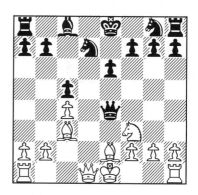

Attacking the pawn on g7.

10...♘gf6

This is the most natural response, developing while protecting the attacked pawn. However, perhaps 10...♘e7 was a better move. Then if 11 ♗xg7 ♖g8 12 ♗c3 ♖xg2 wins the pawn back again. It is better not to hunt for the g7 pawn, but continue with 11 0-0

0-0 12 ♗d3 and White has good compensation, because the black queen is in an awkward position.

11 ♕d6

Again stopping Black from castling.

11...♕c6

Black is trying to chase the queen away, but it has a price: Black will have doubled pawns. If instead, 11...b6, Black does not have enough time to get the bishop to b7, because White occupies the diagonal first with 12 ♘d2 ♕b7 13 ♗f3. Now 13...♕b8 seemingly saves the rook, but not quite, since after 14 ♕c6 the rook is trapped.

12 ♕xc6

A slightly surprising decision. Very rarely is it a good idea to trade queens a pawn down, but this is an exception. 12 ♕g3 0-0 13 ♖d1 was also well playable, though

12...bxc6

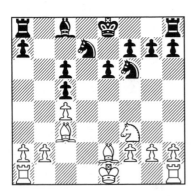

Now Black has two problems: the doubled c-pawns and the prospectless bishop on c8.

13 ♘d2

To free the f3 square for a more important piece, the bishop. The knight may go to b3 to attack the c5 pawn, and perhaps to a5 as well.

13...♗b7

Black is preparing to castle on the queenside. But somehow I would have bad feelings about putting a bishop behind the c6 pawn, which has no hope to advance and open the long diagonal.

14 0-0-0

14 ♗f3 would also have been good, with similar ideas as in the game.

14...0-0-0

14...h5 was a possible improvement, preventing my future plan of g2-g4.

15 ♗f3

On 15 ♘b3, I did not like 15...♘e4.

15...e5

A mistake! This makes more holes in Black's position. After 15...♘b6 16 g4! ♘a4 17 ♗xf6 gxf6 18 ♘e4 ♖d4 19 b3 White wins back either the c5 or f6 pawn with a clearly superior position. It was the last chance for Black to play 15...h5 preventing my next move.

16 g4!

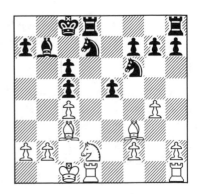

This is the key move of the game. The idea is to kick the knight from f6 by playing g4-g5, and pave the road for White's knight to d6 via e4.

16...h6

Preventing the direct 17 g5. If 16...♖he8, White would continue the plan with 17 g5 ♞g8 18 ♞e4.

17 h4

White is not abandoning the plan but brings up reinforcements. It is crucial to recapture on g5 with a pawn, in order to chase the knight away from the e4 square.

17...h5

If Black stops g4-g5 by playing 17...g5 himself then 18 ♞e4 ♞xe4 19 ♝xe4, followed by 20 ♝f5, and Black is in bad shape with too many weak squares and pawns.

18 gxh5!

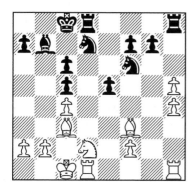

When circumstances change, plans need to change as well. After 18 g5 I did not want to allow 18...♞g4, although White is better after 19 ♞e4.

18...♚b8

In anticipation of ♞d6+. After 18...♞xh5 19 ♞e4 Black has no defense against ♞d6+ and losing material similarly to the game.

19 ♜hg1

Now that the g-file has been opened, White gets an additional target: the g7 pawn.

19...♞xh5

If Black protects the pawn with 19...♜h7, White wins an exchange 20

♞e4 ♞xe4 21 ♝xe4 ♜xh5 with 22 ♝a5. Or if 19...♜dg8 White can play either 20 ♜g5 or choose to win a pawn with 20 ♞e4 ♞xe4 21 ♝xe4 ♚c7 22 ♝f5 ♝c8 23 ♝xd7 ♝xd7 24 ♝xe5+.

20 ♞e4!

Finally the knight comes! This is even better than 20 ♝xh5 ♜xh5 21 ♜xg7. Black has to face too many threats: 21 ♝a5, 21 ♞d6, and attacks on the c5, e5 and g7 pawns.

20...♝c8

Black is lost also after 20...f5 21 ♞d6 e4 22 ♝xh5 ♜xh5 23 ♞f7 or 20...f6 21 ♝xh5 ♜xh5 22 ♜xg7 ♝c8 23 ♞xf6 utilizing the pin.

21 ♞d6

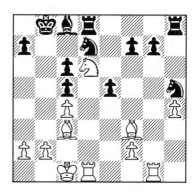

Now the knight has arrived on d6, the black position completely collapses.

21...f6

This loses an exchange straight away, but after 21...♜df8 White also wins with 22 ♝xc6 (threatening 23 ♞xc8 and winning a piece) 22...♞hf6 23 ♜xg7 ♜xh4 24 ♞xf7 ♜xc4 25 ♞d6.

22 ♞f7

Forking the two black rooks, and threatening 23 ♞xd8 winning a whole rook.

22...♜df8

The rook on h8 needs to defend the knight on h5.

23 ♘xh8

Now finally the positional advantage is transformed into material gain.

23...♖xh8

This holds on to the knight, but Black still loses more material.

24 ♗xh5

Removing the defender of the g7 pawn.

24...♖xh5

And now another pawn falls.

25 ♖xg7

Attacking the knight on d7.

25...♘b6

If Black protects the knight with 25...♔c7, then 26 ♗a5+ chases the king away and White takes on d7 anyway.

26 ♖d8

Pinning the bishop.

26...♖xh4

If 26...♘xc4 27 ♖gg8 ♘b6 28 ♗a5, followed by 29 ♗xb6 and capturing the bishop on c8.

27 b3

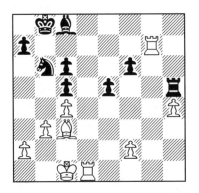

Simply protecting the pawn on c4; the bishop on c8 cannot run away. It is best not to give your opponent any chances.

27...♖f4

Black has no defense.

28 ♗a5 Black resigned

And Black cannot avoid losing the bishop.

Game 9
□ **Susan Polgar**
■ **Pia Cramling**
Tilburg 1994
Queen's Gambit

1 d4

This game is from the Candidates Tournament of the Women's World Championship. Winning that event was my first step on the way to winning the title in 1996.

1...d5

This came as a surprise to me. The Swedish grandmaster almost always employs the King's Indian or the Benoni Defenses which start with 1...♘f6.

2 c4

I first met Pia in 1981. We have been rivals since the mid 1980s, but have always had friendly relations.

2...e6

Two other equally good moves are 2...c6 or 2...dxc4.

3 ♘f3

In my game vs. Kiril Georgiev, I played 3 ♘c3 c6 4 e4 (see Game 8).

3...c6

Black plays similarly to my opponent in the above-mentioned game. Black's main opening idea is to solve the problem of the bishop on c8 by developing it to b7 after ...d5xc4, ♗f1xc4, ...b7-b5, and soon after open up the a8-h1 diagonal with ...c6-c5.

4 ♕c2

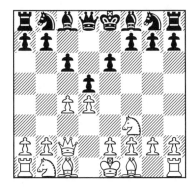

I chose this move mostly for psychological reasons. In the past I have always played 4 e3 or 4 ♘c3 in this position. Obviously Cramling had prepared something against those, so I decided to deviate to avoid her pre-game preparation.

4...dxc4

Black continues the normal way according, to the plan described in the previous comment. 4...♘f6 is also possible.

5 ♕xc4

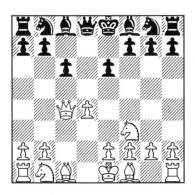

Generally speaking, it is not advisable to get the queen out so early in the game. This time I made an exception. The idea of White's early queen moves is to provoke Black into playing ...b7-

b5, and by delaying ♘b1-c3 White tries to block Black's weakened c6 pawn and prevent ...c6-c5.

5...b5

Black gains a tempo by attacking the queen.

6 ♕c2

The best place to retreat the queen, keeping an eye on the c5 square and the c6 pawn.

6...♗b7

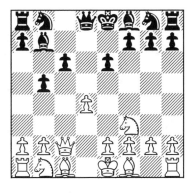

Now the battle is over the c5 square. If Black is able to play ...c6-c5 without losing a pawn, she will equalize the game. If White is able to prevent it, the black bishop is likely to have a sad future and a bad position altogether.

7 e4

Occupying the center and opening up the diagonal for the bishop on f1. An alternative idea would have been 7 ♘bd2 followed by ♘b3, putting more pressure on the c5 square.

7...♘d7

With this developing move, Black prepares to play ...c6-c5. However, there is one more problem to solve: the b5 pawn needs protection before the c6 pawn can be pushed.

8 ♘bd2

After 8 ♗e3 a6 (protecting the b5 pawn) 9 ♘bd2 ♖c8 10 ♘b3, Black has to play aggressively with 10...♗b4+ (10...♘gf6 would be too slow, as 11 ♘c5 arrives just in time) 11 ♘fd2 (or 11 ♗d2 c5 12 ♗xb4 cxb4) 11...c5! (a temporary pawn sacrifice solves Black's problems) 12 dxc5 ♘gf6 13 f3 (if 13 ♗d3 ♘g4) 13...♘xc5! 14 ♘xc5 (or 14 ♗xc5 ♘d7) 14...♛b6 15 ♖c1 ♘d7 and, because of the pins, Black wins the piece back with a good position.

8...♘gf6

Black misses the chance to liberate the queenside with 8...a6 9 ♘b3 ♘gf6 10 ♗d3 c5 11 dxc5 ♘xc5 12 ♘xc5 ♗xc5. In this line 10 ♘c5 is bad due to 10...♗xc5 11 dxc5 ♛e7 12 b4 a5 or 12 ♗e3 ♘g4.

9 a3

Preparing b2-b4 to clamp down on the c5 square.

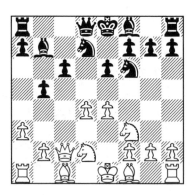

9...♛b6?!

After this, Black never gets to liberate the position. She should have played 9...a6 10 b4 (if 10 ♘b3 then 10...c5 is possible because the e4 pawn is hanging) 10...a5 11 ♖b1 axb4 12 axb4 ♖a4 13 ♛c3 ♗d6 14 ♗d3 (if White forks with 14 e5 Black has the intermediate

move 14...♘d5, attacking the white queen, and can then capture the b4 pawn) 14...♛e7 15 ♗a3 e5 with a complicated position.

10 b4!

Putting a permanent stop to the ...c6-c5 advance.

10...a5

Attempting to get counterplay.

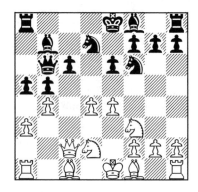

11 ♖b1

Protecting the b4 pawn. Naturally not 11 bxa5, which would give up the fight over the crucial c5 square, making all of White's previous moves irrelevant.

11...axb4

At least Black will have control of the open a-file.

12 axb4

Maintaining the blockade of the c5 square.

12...♖a4

Attacking the b4 pawn a second time.

13 ♛c3

The only way to protect the pawn.

13...♗d6

The sacrifice with 13...e5 14 ♘xe5 ♘xe5 15 dxe5 ♘g4 is not good, because 16 ♛g3 protects both the e5 and f2 pawns.

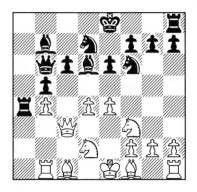

14 ♗d3

Black did not have to worry about 14 e5, because of 14...♘d5.

14...e5

Seeking some counterplay. 14...0-0? would lose material immediately to 15 ♗c2 ♖aa8 16 e5 since 16...♘d5 17 ♕d3 now threatens mate on h7.

15 dxe5

I took the pawn understanding that it was only a temporary material gain.

15...♘g4

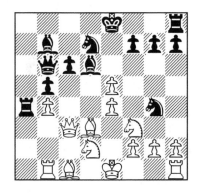

This was the point of Black's previous move.

16 0-0

Black had tried some tricky play. I could not take on d6, because of 16 exd6 ♕xf2+ 17 ♔d1 ♘e3 mate.

16...♘gxe5

16...♘dxe5 17 h3 ♘xd3 18 ♕xd3 would have been even worse.

17 ♗c2

Chasing the black rook back so there will be less pressure on the b4 pawn.

17...♖a8

Black has no choice but to retreat.

18 ♘d4

A general rule of thumb: when you have space advantage, keep the pressure on the opponent and avoid trading pieces.

18...♘g6

Clearing the e5 square for the bishop and preventing the f2-f4 pawn advance. After 18...0-0, White gets an advantage with 19 ♘f5 c5 20 ♕g3 g6 21 f4.

19 ♘2f3

If 19 ♘f5 ♗e5 20 ♘xg7+ ♔d8 and White loses the knight on g7.

19...♘de5

Now Black could not castle, 19...0-0?, because of 20 ♘f5 ♗e5 21 ♘xe5 ♘gxe5 22 ♗e3 (unpinning the f-pawn) 22...♕c7 23 f4 and Black loses the knight.

20 ♘f5

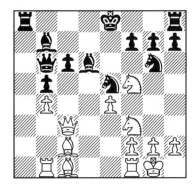

A very strong move, attacking the bishop on d6 and the pawn on g7.

20...♘xf3+

The bishop could not retreat to f8 because the knight on e5 would not have enough support.

21 ♕xf3

Maintaining the double threat on Black's bishop and pawn.

21...♗e5

Now Black has protected everything, but White still has the initiative.

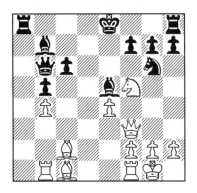

22 ♗e3!

Better than 22 ♗b2 ♗xb2 23 ♖xb2 0-0 24 ♕c3 f6 25 ♗b3+ ♔h8 26 ♖d2 which also gives White a clear edge.

22...♕c7

Now Black attacks the pawn on h2.

23 ♗c5

Preventing Black from castling king-side. It may sound silly, but during the game I spent about 10 minutes calculating the variations arising from 23...0-0-0. Afterwards Pia reminded me that she had lost her right of queenside castling because her a8 rook had already moved.

23...♗c8

If Black takes on h2 with 23...♗xh2+ 24 ♔h1 (threatening to trap the bishop with 25 g3) 24...♗e5, I would proceed 25 ♖bd1 ♖d8 26 ♖xd8+

♕xd8 27 ♖d1 with an overwhelming advantage.

24 ♖bd1

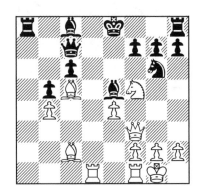

Black's position is falling apart. The king is stuck in the center for the rest of the game, while all of White's pieces are active and ready for the attack.

24...♗xf5

If 24...♗xh2+ 25 ♔h1 ♗e5, White would be winning after 26 ♗d6 ♗xd6 27 ♘xd6+ ♔f8 28 ♗b3.

25 exf5

Opening up the e-file and putting the black king in greater danger.

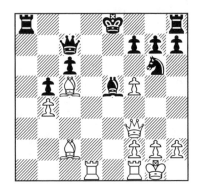

25...♘e7

Blocking the a3-f8 diagonal to allow kingside castling.

26 ♖fe1

Putting the other rook on the open e-file and indirectly stopping Black from castling.

26...♖d8

Again 26...0-0 was losing, to 27 f6! gxf6 (or 27...♗xf6 28 ♗xe7 ♗xe7 29 ♕e4! winning a piece) 28 ♗xe7 ♕xe7 29 ♕g4+! ♔h8 30 ♕f5 with unavoidable mate on h7.

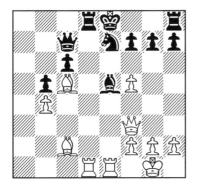

27 ♗xe7

Time to collect!

27...♖xd1

27...♔xe7 28 ♕g3 would just be a transposition of moves.

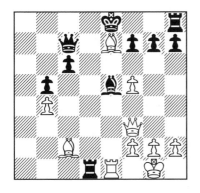

28 ♗xd1!

Accuracy is needed until the very end! The rook needs to stay on the e-file.

28...♔xe7

Now Black will suffer because the king has no safety, but the queen was busy protecting the c6 pawn (if 28...♕xe7 29 ♕xc6+).

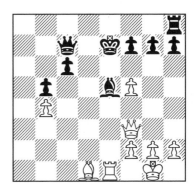

29 ♕g3

The key move, utilizing the fact that the black bishop is pinned.

29...♔f6

If 29...f6 then 30 ♕xg7+ and Black is completely lost.

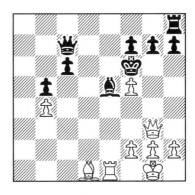

30 ♕h4+

Mercilessly attacking the vulnerable king. This is one of the reasons why I always encourage players to learn the basic principle of chess: castling the king into safety as soon as possible in the game.

30...g5

30...♚xf5 31 f4 ♗xf4 32 ♗c2 mate.

31 ♕h6+

Chasing the king further out.

31...♚xf5

31...♚e7 32 ♕g7 wins.

32 ♗c2+

32 g4+ ♚f4 33 ♕h3 followed by 34 ♕g3 also leads to mate in three.

32...♚f4

The king can only go forward.

33 ♖e4+

33 ♕h5 also does the job.

33...♚f5

The only move.

34 g4 mate

This was a nice gesture from Pia for the spectators! It is very rare among Grandmasters to see a game end with an actual checkmate.

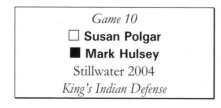

Game 10
□ **Susan Polgar**
■ **Mark Hulsey**
Stillwater 2004
King's Indian Defense

1 d4

This is a game from a special tournament organized by Mr. Frank Berry, in which the 2004 US Women's Olympiad training squad challenged all comers from Oklahoma and the neighboring states.

1...♘f6

I was expecting this first move from my opponent, as he likes to play the King's Indian Defense. I did some research on my opponent prior to the game, because I was told by my trainer that he is a very solid player.

2 c4

I also played 2 ♘f3 in many games in the past. I try to vary from time to time just to make things more interesting.

2...g6

As expected.

3 ♘c3

To prepare e2-e4.

3...♗g7

This is the King's Indian Defense. Black does not directly occupy the center, as in the Queen's Gambit, but attempts to attack it a little later from the sides.

4 e4

There are many different approaches against the KID, but I believe occupying the center with the c, d and e-pawns is the most straightforward one.

4...d6

Opening up the diagonal for the bishop, as well as preventing White's e4-e5 advance.

5 h3

This is partly a preventive, and partly a preparatory move. Without it, when White plays ♗c1-e3, Black can annoy the bishop with ...♘f6-g4; the pin with ...♗g4 after the knight comes to f3 may also be unpleasant for White. It also prepares a potential future g2-g4 advance. This line became popular and brought a lot of success for White in the early nineties. The more traditional moves are 5 ♘f3 or 5 ♗e2.

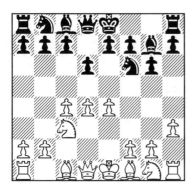

5...0-0

The most natural and best move, putting the king in safety.

6 ♗g5

White is provoking ...h7-h6 to weaken Black's kingside.

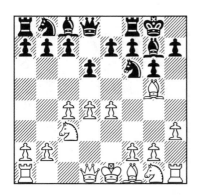

6...h6

An inaccuracy; 6...c5 straight away is perhaps more accurate. After the immediate 6...e5? 7 dxe5 dxe5 8 ♕xd8 ♖xd8 9 ♘d5, Black would lose a pawn.

7 ♗e3

White voluntarily lost a tempo by making two bishop moves in a row. But

after ♕d1-d2, attacking the h6 pawn, Black will also have to waste a move protecting it.

7...c5

A temporary pawn sacrifice which it is not wise to accept. The other popular set-up starts with 7...e5.

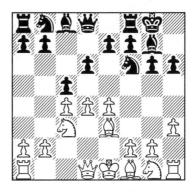

8 d5

After 8 dxc5 Black responds with 8...♕a5, and if 9 cxd6 then 9...♘xe4 gives very good play thanks to the pin along the a5-e1 diagonal, the power of the g7 bishop, and the fact the white king is still a long way from castling. White does better not being greedy and to give the pawn back with 9 ♗d3 dxc5.

8...e6

White gained a space advantage with the last move. Therefore, Black tries to open up the position.

9 ♗d3

I was also considering 9 dxe6, but did not like that the black knight would then get access to the weakened d4 square, via c6.

9...♘bd7

9...exd5 seems more logical to me.

10 ♘f3

Now that the black knight is gone from b8 and is further from the d4 square, I considered 10 dxe6 fxe6 11 ♘f3 targeting the backward d6 pawn.

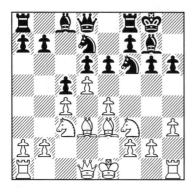

10...exd5

If Black locks up the center and the bishop on g7 with 10...e5, White would have noticeable space advantage and a very comfortable position.

11 exd5

11 cxd5 is also a normal way to recapture, and would transpose to a Benoni-like position.

11...♖e8

Black occupies the open file, which is a smart thing to do.

12 0-0

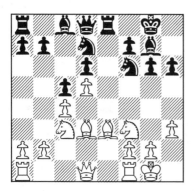

White is fully developed and has a space advantage and stands slightly better. If Black plays passively, White will try to take control the of the e-file.

12...♘h5

Black is looking for some activity by preparing ...f7-f5. If Black tried to trade a pair of knights with 12...♘e5, I planned 13 ♘xe5 ♖xe5 14 ♕d2 ♔h7 15 ♗f4 ♖e7 16 ♖ae1 and then trade a pair of rooks and occupy the e-file with my other rook.

13 ♕d2

Gaining time by attacking the pawn on h6.

13...♔h7

On 13...g5 I planned 14 g4 ♘hf6 15 ♖ae1 ♘f8 16 ♕c2.

14 ♖ae1

I considered 14 g4 ♘hf6 15 ♖ae1 right away, too.

14...f5

White also has a strong position after 14...♘e5 15 ♘xe5 ♖xe5 and now 16 f4 ♖e7 17 f5.

15 g4!

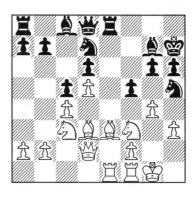

This is a very important move; otherwise the knight returns from h5 to f6 and Black has a decent position. Despite looking dangerous to open up in front of my own king, it greatly strengthens White's attack.

15...fxg4

Otherwise Black loses the pawn on f5.

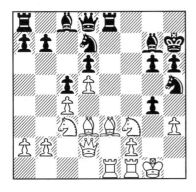

16 hxg4

White gets nothing after 16 ♗xg6+ ♔xg6 17 ♕d3+ ♔f7 18 ♕f5+, because 18...♘df6 protects everything and Black wins.

16...♘hf6

Black is also in trouble after 16...♗xc3 17 ♕xc3 ♘g7 and 18 ♔g2 followed by ♖h1.

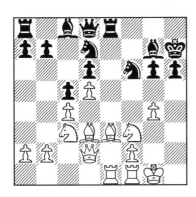

17 g5

This is better than 17 ♕c2 ♘f8 18 ♗xg6+ (Black gets enough counterplay after 18 ♘h4 ♘xg4 19 ♗xg6+ ♔g8 20 ♗xe8 ♕xh4 21 ♗f4 ♘e5 22 ♗xe5 ♗xe5, and White even loses after 21 f4? ♗xc3 22 bxc3 ♗f5) 18...♘xg6 19 ♘h4

♗xg4 (but not 19...♘e4? 20 ♘xg6) 20 ♕xg6+ ♔h8 21 ♗xh6 ♖g8 22 ♗xg7+ ♖xg7 23 ♕h6+ ♔g8 24 ♘g6 ♘h7 with complications.

But 17 ♗xh6!? was also interesting after 17...♗xh6 (17...♘xg4? is a lot worse due to 18 ♗xg6+! ♔xg6 19 ♖xe8 ♕xe8 20 ♕g5+ ♔f7 21 ♕xg7 mate) 18 g5 ♗g7 19 gxf6 ♗xf6 20 ♘e4 with a strong attack.

17...♘g4

After 17...hxg5 18 ♘xg5+ Black is lost.

18 gxh6

I had to see some long variations and fine points prior to deciding on 16 g4, which was a very committal move.

18...♘de5

The key variation was 18...♘xe3 19 hxg7 ♘xf1. It took me some time to figure out the winning move here. Can you find it?

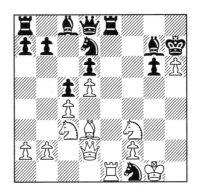

20 ♕g5!! – a beautiful quiet move that wins the game! For example, 20...♕xg5+ 21 ♘xg5+ ♔xg7 22 ♖xe8 and the black knight on f1 gets trapped after 22...♘d2 23 ♖e2 ♔f6 24 f4.

Black also loses after 18...♗xh6 19 ♗xh6 ♖xe1 20 ♖xe1 ♘xh6 21 ♗xg6+ ♔xg6 22 ♖e6+ ♘f6 23 ♕g5+ ♔f7 24

♕xh6 ♗xe6 25 ♘g5+ ♔e8 26 ♘xe6
♕e7 27 ♕h8+.

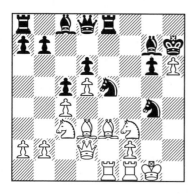

19 ♘g5+!

This in-between move wins a piece.
After 19 ♘xe5 ♗xe5 Black would get
some counter-chances.

19...♔g8

Moving into a discovery with
19...♔xh6 would be deadly, too, after 20
♘e6.

20 hxg7

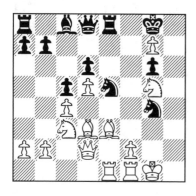

As a result of the attack started on
move 16, White has gained a piece. The
rest is a matter of technique, as they say.

20...♘xd3

If 20...♘xe3 21 ♕xe3 and the black
knight has no good discoveries.

21 ♕xd3

Attacking the g6 pawn.

21...♗f5

My opponent actually thought he
was doing OK here, until he realized
that after 21...♘xe3 I don't have to recapture but can play 22 ♕xg6!.

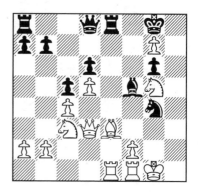

22 ♘ce4

At first I was hesitant moving into
this ugly pin, but after a deeper look I
realized that there was nothing Black
can do to take advantage.

22...♘e5

If Black puts more pressure on the
knight with 22...♕e7, White can play 23
♗f4 and defend the knight on e4.

23 ♕e2

Finally the queen is out of the pin.

23...♔xg7

With some ideas of counterplay
down the h-file after ...♖h8 and ...♗xe4,
♘xe4, ...♕h4.

24 ♔g2

Getting ready to counter Black's
plan with ♖h1.

24...♕e7

There is nothing Black can do, except hope for a blunder.

25 ♗f4

Threatening 26 ♘xd6 ♕xd6 27
♗xe5+.

25...♘f7

Defending against the above threat.

26 ♕d2

The most accurate way.

26...♕d7

Black cannot stop the white queen getting to c3.

27 ♕c3+

The queen is deadly on the long diagonal.

27...♘e5

Black loses even faster after 27...♔f8 28 ♘h7+.

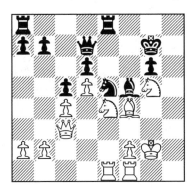

28 ♘xd6 Black resigned

And Black cannot avoid further material losses.

Combinations

Combination 1
☐ **Susan Polgar**
■ **Zoltan Endrody**
Budapest 1977

I was not yet 8 years old when I played this game, against an adult male opponent in one of the local tournaments in my home-town, Budapest.

21 ♖xf6!

Here I sacrificed an exchange in or-

der to force the king out of safety.

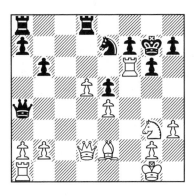

21...♘xd5

This was a desperate move by my opponent. In the post game analysis, he told me that he thought after 21...♔xf6 22 ♘h5+ gxh5 23 ♕h6 mates. He did not notice that the check can be blocked with 23...♘g6. I saw this defense, however, and would have played 22 ♕h6 threatening 23 ♘h5 mate! If Black avoids the mate with 22...♘g8, White continues with the sequence 23 ♖f1+ ♔e7 24 ♕g7.

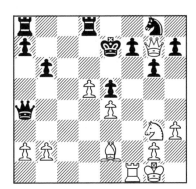

I have to admit that I stopped calculating at this point. I felt that I had a winning attack, because the black king is too vulnerable. The following variations could occur:

a) 24...♕e8 25 ♗b5! (deflecting the queen) 25...♕xb5 26 ♕xf7+ ♔d6 27 ♖c1 (preventing the escape of the king to the c-file, and with the threat of 28 ♕e6 mate) 27...♕d7 28 ♖c6+ ♕xc6 29 ♕e6+ ♔c7 30 ♕xc6+ and White is winning because the e5 pawn will soon be lost too.

b) 24...♖f8 25 ♕xe5+ ♔d8 26 ♕d6+ ♔e8 27 ♘f5! (with the threat of 28 ♘g7 mate) 27...gxf5 28 ♖xf5 ♘e7 29 ♖e5 ♕d7 and all Black's pieces come to help the king, but White wins with the sneaky 30 ♗b5!.

The best Black can do is give a check with 24...♕d4+ (in order to protect the pawn on e5), when White continues 25 ♔h2 ♖f8 26 ♗g4 and 27 ♗e6 next.

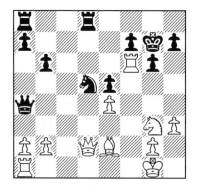

22 ♖xf7+!

A second sacrifice!

22...♔xf7 23 exd5 ♕d4+

This forces the exchange of queens and thus solves the problem of the vulnerable king, but in the process loses another pawn.

24 ♕xd4 exd4 25 ♖d1

And Black cannot take 25...♖xd5 because of 26 ♗c4 pinning the rook. White soon won.

Combination 2
□ **Susan Polgar**
■ **Jozsef Nemeth**
Ceske Budejovice 1980

This game I played at my first ever international tournament outside of Hungary, at an 'Esperanto Festival' in Czechoslovakia.

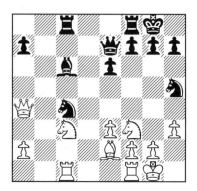

At this point, my opponent offered a draw. He assumed that, after 17 ♕xc4 ♗xf3 18 ♕a4 ♗xe2 19 ♘xe2, the position is equal. But he forgot about the 'back rank' problem. I declined the draw offer and continued...

17 ♕xc4 ♗xf3

and now...

18 ♕xc8!

This was what my opponent completely overlooked. Trying the same idea with a different move order, such as 18 ♘d5, would not work. Black can respond with 18...exd5 19 ♕xc8 and is better after 19...♗xe2, with two pieces for a rook.

18...♖xc8 19 ♘d5!

A discovered attack!

19...♕c5

If Black protects the rook on c8

with his queen then, after exchanging rooks 20 ♖xc8 ♕xc8, 21 ♘e7+ forks and wins the queen.

20 ♘e7+

The simpler 20 ♖xc5 ♖xc5 21 ♗xf3 works too.

20...♔f8

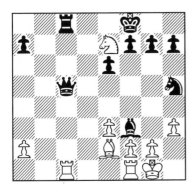

21 ♘xc8!

This move is the point of the combination! 21 ♖xc5 ♖xc5 22 ♗xf3 ♔xe7 was not good.

21...♕xc1

If Black moved the queen away then, after 22 ♗xf3, White has two rooks and a bishop for the queen which is a winning advantage.

22 ♖xc1 ♗xe2 23 ♘xa7

After all the fireworks were over, and I was up an exchange and a pawn. I converted the material advantage to a win in a few more moves.

Combination 3
□ **Smirnov**
■ **Susan Polgar**
Teteven 1981

In the early to mid 1980s, I used to play many tournaments in Bulgaria, where I always felt welcome. In fact,

because I spent so much time there with my family, I actually learned some of the language. Some people even half-jokingly called me an 'honorary Bulgarian'.

I played this game against the Soviet representative, who was a promising young player in those days.

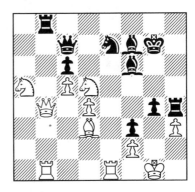

White has just happily captured the pawn with 34 ♘b6xd5, hoping to win at least a pawn after 34...♘xd5 35 ♕xb8. Instead, I made a surprising move which changed the whole complexion of the game. Black to move and win!

34...♕h2+!

After this queen sacrifice, the black rooks take over the h-file and win the game.

35 ♔xh2 ♖xh3+ White resigned

After 36 ♔g1 ♖bh8, the mate on h1 is unavoidable.

Combination 4
□ **Teresa Needham**
■ **Susan Polgar**
Westergate 1981

I was twelve years old when I played this game in England at the World Championship for Girls under 16, which I won. This was my favorite game from that event.

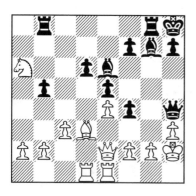

22...♗h6!

Opening the g-file and allowing the bishop to participate in the attack.

23 ♖h1?

This makes things easier. The following analysis shows what would have happened otherwise.

a) 23 ♘xb8 ♖xg2+! 24 ♔xg2 ♕xh3+! 25 ♔g1 f3 26 ♕xf3 (if 26 ♕f1 then 26...♕g4+ 27 ♔h1 ♗f4 and White is helpless against ...♕h4+ and ...♕h2 mate) 26...♕xf3 27 ♗f1 ♕g4+ 28 ♗g2 (or 28 ♔h1 ♗f4) 28...♕g8! and White cannot save the knight, because of the threat of ...♗h3.

b) 23 ♕f1 f3! 24 g3 ♗f4 (threatening to capture on g3) 25 gxf4 ♗xh3 26 ♕xh3 ♖g2+ wins.

23...♗xh3! White resigned

If 24 gxh3 f3! clears the f4 square for the bishop and White is lost.

Combination 5
□ **Janos Orso**
■ **Susan Polgar**
Kecskemet 1983

Here my opponent expected the repetition of moves with 27...♕c4 28 ♖c1 ♕e4 29 ♖e1 and so on. However, I had something else in mind...

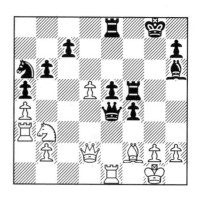

27...♕b4

Allowing the fork with...

28 ♕d3

And the surprise I prepared was...

28...e4 29 ♕xa6 e3 30 ♔f1 f3 31 ♗g3 e2+ White resigned

He saw the following variation: 32 ♔g1 f2+ 33 ♗xf2 ♕xe1+! 34 ♗xe1 ♖f1 mate.

Combination 6
□ **Susan Polgar**
■ **Vladimir Dimitrov**
Ivailovgrad 1984

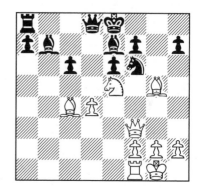

This was a very eventful game; at one point there were four queens on the board. In this position my opponent was up a pawn. However, the black king has no hope for safety, and because of its vulnerability I was able to find a winning combination.

20 ♗xe6!

This is a good example for one of the most elementary chess recommendations: castle early in the game and keep your king safe. This is what can happen when you do not!

20...fxe6 21 ♗xf6 ♕xd4

After 21...♗xf6 22 ♕h5+ ♔e7 23 ♕xh7+ ♔d6 24 ♘f7+, Black would lose the queen.

22 ♕h5+ Black resigned

If 22...♔f8 23 ♕f7 mate, or on 22...♔d8 23 ♘f7+ and again Black loses the queen.

Combination 7
□ **Susan Polgar**
■ **Krastjo Dimitrov**
Targoviste 1984

My opponent in this game was a legendary Bulgarian master.

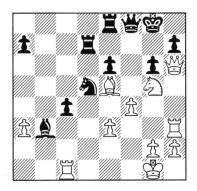

Black's main problem here was the

weakness of the dark squares along the a1-h8 diagonal. The key to winning is to exploit that weakness.

34 ♕xg6+! ♖g7

If 34...hxg6 35 ♖h8 mate. Black tries to get away with losing 'only' an exchange.

35 ♖xh7! Black resigned

The same idea again. If 35...♖xg6 36 ♖h8 mate.

Combination 8
□ **Susan Polgar**
■ **Peter Hardicsay**
Hungary 1985

This combination is one of my all time favorites. In the *Hungarian Chess Magazine*, it was named as one of the most spectacular games of the year.

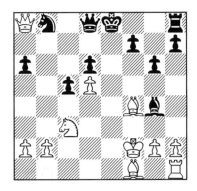

17 ♗b5+!

This is the beginning of a Morphy-style combination. (Paul Morphy was a legendary American chess player in the nineteenth century, who implemented countless beautiful sacrifices during his spectacular career.) I sacrificed the bishop with check in order to gain time to bring the more important rook into action.

17...axb5 18 ♖e1+ ♔f8

There is no escape on the other side either. If 18...♔d7 19 ♕b7+ ♕c7 20 ♖e7+! and Black loses the queen.

19 ♗h6+ ♔g8

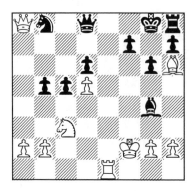

20 ♖e7!

I know it is a matter of taste, but I loved that move. It stopped 20...♕h4+, which could give Black some breathing room, and also threatened a potential ♖e7-b7 to attack the pinned knight on b8. Now Black's position is paralyzed.

20...♗d7

Although I had already calculated my next move in advance, I paused for couple of seconds, took a deep breath and then played:

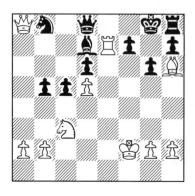

21 ♕xb8!

My opponent was totally shocked by this move, and to play it gave me great aesthetic pleasure. Even though it was not the only win, it was the most beautiful one in my eyes! The other win was 21 ♘e4 ♕xe7 22 ♕xb8+ ♗e8 23 ♕xe8+! ♕xe8 and 24 ♘f6 mate.

21...♕xb8 22 ♘e4 Black resigned

To end the combination with a quiet move is rather rare. There is no defense against 23 ♘f6 mate.

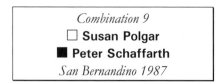

Combination 9
□ **Susan Polgar**
■ **Peter Schaffarth**
San Bernandino 1987

This game is from an open tournament in Switzerland. After just thirteen moves, I had the opportunity to end the game in only three more.

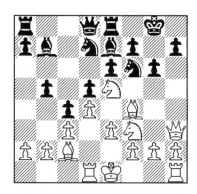

14 ♘xf7! ♕b6

Black could not accept the sacrifice, because after 14...♔xf7 15 ♘g5+ (but not the fancy 15 ♕xe6+, intending 15...♔xe6 16 ♘g5 mate, since Black can defend with 15...♔g7!) 15...♔g8 16 ♕xe6+ ♔g7 17 ♕f7+ ♔h8 18 ♘e6 and Black either loses the queen or gets mated on g7.

15 ♗xg6! ♖f8

After 15...hxg6 White mates in two moves: 16 ♕h8+ ♔xf7 17 ♘g5.

16 ♘3g5 Black resigned

Combination 10
□ **Susan Polgar**
■ **Liu Shilan**
Thessaloniki Olympiad 1988

This game was played in the Hungary-China match at the 1988 Chess Olympiad. As China were one of our main rivals in the quest for the gold medal, it had very special importance.

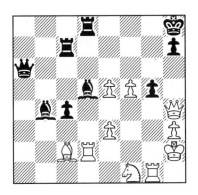

My opponent's last move was 37...g6-g5, with the idea of answering 38 ♕xg5 with 38...♖g8 and then to capture the rook on d2. But there is an unexpected alternative.

38 ♖xd5! ♖xd5

Black could not take the queen because of checkmate on the eighth rank.

39 ♕xg5 Black resigned

Threatening 40 ♕g8 mate. If Black tries to guard with the queen, 39...♕a8 or 39...♕c8, then 40 ♕f6 mate; while if Black plays 39...♖c8, then 40 ♕g7 mate. There is no defense to the multiple threats.

Combination 11
□ **Susan Polgar**
■ **Zurab Azmaiparashvili**
Dortmund 1990

In this game my opponent was a famous Georgian Grandmaster. Several years later, Zurab helped me with my preparations for my 1996 World Championship match vs. Xie Jun.

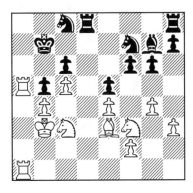

In this game my opponent employed his favorite opening, the Modern Defense. In the above position, White has some space advantage and the control of the a-file. However, it is not so simple to see how to proceed.

I decided to sacrifice a knight for only two pawns, believing in the strength of my connected passed b- and c-pawns.

28 ♘xb5! cxb5 29 ♖xb5+ ♔c7 30 ♖a6

Perhaps 30 ♖ba5 would have been an even stronger choice, opening the way for the b-pawn.

30...♖d1 31 ♖ba5 ♘d8 32 ♔c2 ♖h1 33 b5 ♖xh3 34 ♘d2 h5 35 gxh5 gxh5 36 ♘c4

Despite having only one pawn for

the piece, White has a winning advantage. Practically all the white pieces are in position to attack the black king. In addition, the dangerous passed b- and c-pawns make Black's position hopeless.

36...♘b7 37 ♖a1 ♗f8

This loses straight away.

38 ♖c6+ ♔b8

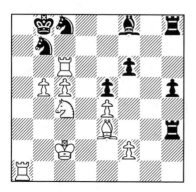

39 ♖a8+!

Another cute sacrifice!

39...♔xa8 40 ♖xc8+ ♔a7 41 c6+ ♖xe3 42 fxe3 Black resigned

White's passed pawns are too strong.

Combination 12

□ **Susan Polgar**

■ **Miodrag Todorcevic**

Pamplona 1990

This was one of my victories from the tournament in which I made my third GM norm, thus becoming the first woman ever to earn the Grandmaster title.

The traditional Pamplona tournaments are held annually from around Christmas until early January. It was a very special time of the year in Pamplona with its amazing New Year's Eve's Parade.

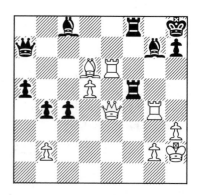

In the above position, after 48 ♖e7 Black can counter-attack with 48...♕b6, aiming at the bishop on d6, and after 49 ♗c7, Black wins with a nice combination 49...♕xc7! 50 ♖xc7 and 50...♗e5+.

Once again, Black's main problem is the back rank.

48 ♕xf5! ♖xf5

Black is losing after 48...♗xe6 49 ♕xe6 ♖g8 50 ♗e5 too.

49 ♖e8+ ♖f8

If 49...♗f8 50 ♗xf8 ♕d7 51 ♗g7 mate.

50 ♗xf8 ♗e5+

If Black takes the rook instead, 50...♗xg4, then 51 ♗c5+ discovered check wins the queen.

51 ♔h1 Black resigned

There is no defense against the threats of 52 ♗g7 or 52 ♗h6 mate. If 51...h5 then 52 ♗g7+ ♔h7 53 ♖h8 mate.

Combination 13

□ **Susan Polgar**

■ **Zbynek Hracek**

Stara Zagora 1990

This game is from the (Men's) World Championship Zonal tournament, the first one in which I was allowed to play. In 1986, when I became the first woman ever to qualify for the Men's World Championship, I was prohibited from competing.

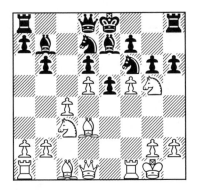

13 ♘e6! fxe6

This loses quickly. However, after the better 13...♕c8, Black's position was not enviable either. White has a very strong position with 13...♕c8 14 ♕a4 g5 15 ♘b5 fxe6 16 fxe6 ♘c5 17 ♘xd6+ ♔f8 18 ♕d1.

14 fxe6

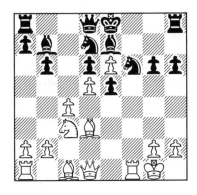

14...♘f8

After 14...♘c5, I planned 15 ♗xg6+ ♔f8 16 b4 ♘a6 17 ♘e4 with a decisive attack. For example, if Black continues 17...♔g7 18 ♘xf6 ♗xf6 19 ♕g4 ♗g5

then 20 ♖f7+! ♔xg6 21 ♕f5+ ♔h5 22 ♕f3+ ♔g6 23 ♖g7+! ♔xg7 24 ♕f7 mate.

15 ♕a4+ ♘6d7 16 c5!

A final blow!, which opens up the diagonal for my light-squared bishop to get into the action.

16...♗c8

There was no defense. If 16...bxc5 17 exd7+ ♘xd7 18 ♗g6 mate, or 17...♕d7 18 ♗b5 pins the queen.

17 exd7+ ♗xd7 18 c6 Black resigned

After the bishop moves, White plays 19 c7+ discovered check, winning the queen.

Combination 14
□ **Lajos Portisch**
■ **Susan Polgar**
Budapest 1991

This game is from the overall Hungarian Championship, where my sister Judit caused a great sensation by winning the event.

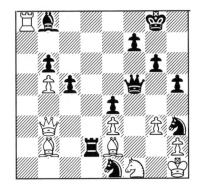

This game was filled with complications and, in the shown position, my situation appeared bad. White has a scary bishop on b2 aiming at my king, and the rook on a8 is pinning my bishop, threatening to mate in a couple of moves. However, I found an immediate solution to all those problems:

36...♕xf1+!!

This was another of my favorite combinations ever.

37 ♗xf1 ♘f2+ 38 ♔g1 ♘f3+ White resigned

39 ♔g2 ♘h1+! 40 ♔xh1 (or 40 ♔h3) 40...♖h2 mate.

Combination 15
□ Susan Polgar
■ Leonid Yudasin
Munich 1991

Grandmaster Yudasin is one my 'favorite' opponents. Despite the fact that his rating has consistently been higher than mine, I have a 4-0 score against him (in classical time control games).

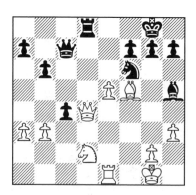

25 exf6!

This move, leaving my queen hanging, is possible due to Black's back rank.

25...gxf6

If 25...♖xd4 26 ♖e8 mate.

26 ♕xf6 c3 27 ♘e4 c2 28 ♕h6 ♗g6 29 ♘f6+ ♔h8 30 ♘e8 Black resigned

There is no defense against the dual threats of 31 ♕g7 and 31 ♕f8 mate.

Combination 16
□ Susan Polgar
■ Ralf Lau
Polanica Zdroj 1991

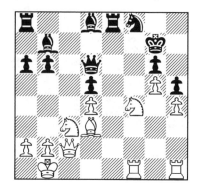

In this position, the key difference is the safety of the two kings.

26 ♗xg6! ♘xg6 27 ♘xh5+ ♔h8

If 27...♔h7 then 28 ♘f6+ ♗xf6 29 ♖xf6 wins.

28 ♘f6 ♖e4 29 ♘cxe4 dxe4

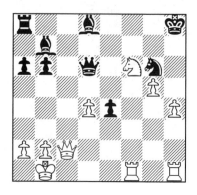

30 ♕d1! Black resigned

One finish was 30...♘f4 31 ♖xf4! ♕xf4 32 ♕h5+ ♔g7 33 ♕h7+ ♔f8 34 ♕g8+ ♔e7 35 ♕e8+ ♔d6 36 ♕d7 mate.

This game was played at a special match between the Polgar Sisters and the Slovenian team (with a guest player, future World Champion Alexander Khalifman).

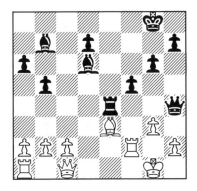

31...♗xg3!

In this position, White suffered because of the weakness of the light squares on the long diagonal.

32 ♖g2

On 32 hxg3 a typical, but nevertheless beautiful 32...♕h1+!! 33 ♔xh1 ♖h4+ 34 ♔g1 ♖h1 mate ends the game.

32...♗xh2+ 33 ♔f1

If 33 ♖xh2 ♖g4+.

33...♕h3 34 ♕d2 ♖xe3 White resigned

This is one of my nicer victories

from the 1992 Rapid World Championship.

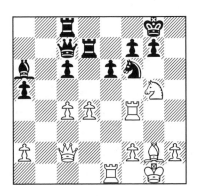

♕h7+ would be a dangerous check if the black knight on f6 was not there. Therefore, White needs to 'remove the guard'.

30 ♖xf6! gxf6 31 ♕h7+ ♔f8 32 ♕h8+ ♔e7

Does the black king escape? Not quite!

33 ♖xe6+!

Another pretty sacrifice!

33...fxe6 34 ♕g7+ ♔e8

If 34...♔d6 35 ♘e4 mate.

35 ♕g8+ ♔e7 36 ♕f7+ Black resigned

Black cannot avoid mate on the following move.

This game was played at the World Championship Zonal tournament, which was held within days of my painful experience in the match versus Nana Ioseliani.

Strategically White is clearly better,

having a better pawn structure and better piece placement. However, the white king is in serious danger and Black's attack comes too quickly.

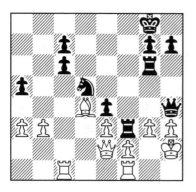

23...♖gxg3!

The only correct way! Sacrificing the other rook with 23...♖fxg3 24 fxg3 ♖xg3 also looks sufficient, but it would be refuted by the pretty 25 ♖f8+! ♔xf8 26 ♕f2+ winning the rook.

24 fxg3 ♕xg3+

Again, 24...♖xg3? would be a mistake, because of 25 ♖f8+! and White would win!

25 ♔h1 ♕xh3+ 26 ♔g1 ♖g3+ 27 ♔f2

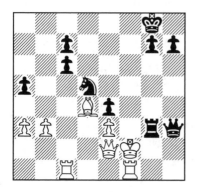

27...♕h4!

The key move of the game! White is

now helpless against the discovered check.

28 ♖h1

If the king tries to run away with 28 ♔e1 then 28...♖xe3+ wins.

28...♖h3+ White resigned

The mate in two cannot be avoided (29 ♔g2 ♕g3+ 30 ♔f1 ♖xh1).

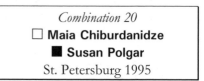

Combination 20
□ **Maia Chiburdanidze**
■ **Susan Polgar**
St. Petersburg 1995

This was the fourth game of my semi-final match in the World Championship.

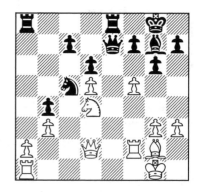

Black has a clear advantage, controlling the open e- and a-files and having a very powerful dark-squared bishop. In this position, I found a nice way to turn my positional advantage to material gain.

22...♘xb3! 23 ♘xb3 ♗xa1 24 ♘xa1 ♕e1+ 25 ♔h2

Black also wins easily after 25 ♕xe1 ♖xe1+ 26 ♖f1 ♖xf1+ 27 ♗xf1 ♖xa2 28 ♘b3 ♖c2 and ...♖c3 next.

25...♕xa1 26 f6

White almost turns things around,

hoping for ♕h6-g7 mate.

26...♔h8 27 ♕h6 ♖g8 28 ♖f4

Threatening 29 ♕xh7+! ♔xh7 30 ♖h4 mate.

28...g5

28...♕c1 also works, since if 29 ♕xh7+ ♔xh7 30 ♖h4+, Black can block with 30...♕h6.

29 ♖xb4 ♖g6 30 ♕h5 ♕xa2 31 ♕f3 ♕a1 32 ♖b7 ♖xf6 White resigned

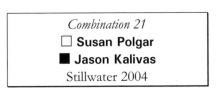

Combination 21
□ **Susan Polgar**
■ **Jason Kalivas**
Stillwater 2004

This is one of my favorites recent victories.

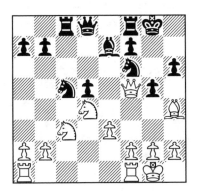

On his last move, Black made an overambitious attack with 15...g5, which I immediately understood was an error. Nevertheless, sacrificing a piece always involves taking some risk and, considering that the positional retreat with 16 ♗g3 also gives White a solid advantage, I took some time to debate whether it was worth going for the sacrifice.

16 ♗xg5! hxg5 17 ♕xg5+ ♔h8

White has two pawns and a strong attack for the bishop.

18 ♘f5

Threatening to checkmate at once with ♕g7+.

18...♘e6

Or 18...♖g8 19 ♕h4+ ♘h7 20 ♘xe7.

19 ♕h4+

But not 19 ♕h6+? ♘h7.

19...♔g8

Now after 19...♘h7 the bishop on e7 would be lost. This is the important difference between the two queen checks.

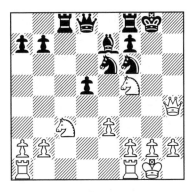

20 f4

Paving the road for the rook to come to f3 and g3.

20...♖c7

The best defense for Black was 20...♗b4, but White wins anyway after 21 ♖f3 ♘h7 22 ♕g4+ ♔h8 23 ♖h3 ♖c7 24 ♘xd5! ♕xd5 25 ♖xh7+! ♔xh7 26 ♕h5+ ♔g8 and 27 ♘h6+ wins the black queen.

If instead 20...♖e8 21 ♖f3 ♘e4 (or 21...♘h7 22 ♘h6+ ♔g7 23 ♕g4+) 22 ♕g4+ ♔f8 23 ♕h5 ♔g8 24 ♘xe4 dxe4 25 ♖h3 wins.

21 ♖f3 ♘e8

Or 21...♘h7 22 ♕h6 f6 23 ♖g3+ ♔h8 24 ♖g7.

22 ♕h6 Black resigned

Supplementary Games

A selection of some important games from my career.

Game 11
□ **Eliska Richtrova**
■ **Susan Polgar**
Novi Sad Olympiad 1990
Sicilian Defense

This was the last round game at the 1990 Olympiad, in the crucial Hungary-Czechoslovakia match.

1 e4 c5 2 c3 d5 3 exd5 ♕xd5 4 d4 ♘c6 5 ♘f3 ♘f6 6 ♗e2 cxd4 7 cxd4 e6 8 0-0 ♗e7 9 ♘c3 ♕d6 10 a3 0-0 11 ♕d3 a6 12 ♗g5 ♖d8 13 ♖fd1 b5 14 ♘e4 ♕d5 15 ♘c3 ♕d6 16 ♘e4

My opponent clearly indicates her willingness to repeat moves and agree a draw. I had to continue to fight for the Gold!

16...♘xe4 17 ♕xe4 ♗b7 18 ♗xe7 ♕xe7 19 ♗d3 g6 20 ♕f4

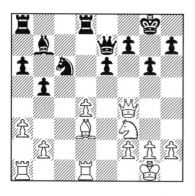

Black has a target in the d4 pawn; though if Black plays too slowly, White has counter-threats with ♕h6 and ♘g5.

20...♘a5 21 ♖ac1 ♗xf3 22 ♕xf3 ♖a7 23 ♗b1 ♖ad7 24 g3 ♘c4 25 b4 ♖xd4 26 ♖xd4 ♖xd4 27 h4 h5

28 ♗a2 ♕d6 29 ♗xc4 bxc4 30 a4 ♕xb4 31 ♕a8+ ♔g7 32 ♕xa6 ♕b2 33 ♖e1 c3 34 ♕a5 ♖d5 White resigned

---

Game 12
□ **Susan Polgar**
■ **Maia Chiburdanidze**
St. Petersburg 1995
King's Indian Defense

The was the final game of my World Championship semi-final match.

1 d4 ♘f6 2 c4 g6 3 ♘c3 ♗g7 4 e4 d6 5 f4 0-0 6 ♘f3 ♘a6 7 ♗d3 ♗g4 8 0-0 ♘d7 9 ♗e3 e5 10 fxe5 c5 11 d5 ♘xe5 12 ♗e2 ♘xf3+ 13 ♗xf3 ♗xf3 14 ♕xf3 ♕e7 15 ♗f4 ♘c7 16 ♕g3 ♖ad8 17 ♔h1 ♗d4 18 ♖ae1 f6 19 ♘e2 ♗e5 20 ♘g1 a6 21 ♘f3 ♗xf4 22 ♕xf4 b5 23 b3 ♖b8

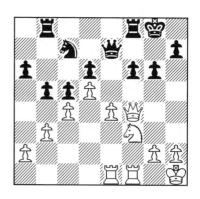

24 b4!

The key move of the game – a nice breakthrough based on the d5-d6 fork.

24...cxb4 25 c5! ♖bd8

If 25...dxc5 26 d6 forks.

26 ♘d4 dxc5 27 ♘c6 ♕d7 28 ♘xd8 ♕xd8 29 ♖c1 c4 30 d6 ♘e6 31 ♕d2 ♕d7 32 ♕xb4 ♘g5 33 ♕c5 ♖e8 34 ♖ce1 ♖e6 35 e5 f5 36 a4

♘f7 37 axb5 axb5 38 ♕c7 ♕xc7 39 dxc7 ♖c6 40 e6 ♖xc7 41 e7 ♘d6 42 e8♕+ ♘xe8 43 ♖xe8+ ♔f7 44 ♖b8 c3 45 ♔g1 Black resigned

---

Game 13
□ **Susan Polgar**
■ **Xie Jun**
Jaen 1996
Grünfeld Defense

This was the thirteenth and last game of the World Championship.
1 d4 ♘f6 2 ♘f3 g6 3 c4 ♗g7 4 g3 0-0 5 ♗g2 d5 6 cxd5 ♘xd5 7 0-0 ♘c6 8 e4 ♘b6 9 d5 ♘a5 10 ♕e1 ♘ac4 11 ♘c3 e6 12 b3 ♕f6 13 bxc4 ♕xc3 14 ♕xc3 ♗xc3 15 ♖b1 ♗g7 16 ♗f4 c6 17 dxc6 bxc6

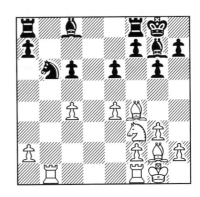

18 ♗d6 ♖e8 19 c5 ♘c4 20 e5 ♗a6 21 ♖fc1 ♖ec8 22 ♗f1 ♘xe5 23 ♘xe5 ♗xf1 24 ♔xf1 Black resigned

CHAPTER TWO

Sofia

Sofia following my footsteps – her first national title at the age of 5!

Sofia was born into the chess atmosphere we already had at home, due to my serious involvement with the game. I think (and my parents agree) that Sofia is the probably most talented of the three sisters. She was only 5 years old when she won her first national title, at the Under-11 Girls' Championship in Debrecen.

However, her problem always has been that she was somewhat lazy, and would give up fights more easily. Also, she always had various interests, and rather than focusing entirely on one thing, she to be more diversified. No one can say whether this is better or not, but it was what she wanted.

Success at the World Youth Championships

Sofia competed in a number of World Youth Championships with varying success. In Puerto Rico (1986), both she and Judit represented Hungary in the World Under-14 Championship. Both were in the hunt for the medals the whole way through. In the end, Sofia (still only 11) won the gold medal as the top girl, and silver medal in the overall competition, behind only the future French No.1, Grandmaster Joel Lautier. Judit, who had just turned 10 at that time, actually had the same number of points as Sofia, but the worse tie-break. Therefore, she finished as the second girl with the silver medal, and won Bronze in the overall championship.

Later in the same year, my sisters also competed in the World Under-16 Championships in Argentina. The tournament was held at probably the coldest place I have ever been to, in Rio Gallegos, Patagonia, not too far from the South Pole.

During that trip we had an exciting excursion to see the penguins right along the Argentine-Chilean border. It was their mating season and there were countless holes in the ground which they used as their 'homes'. There were probably thousands of penguins, all in pairs in their holes, and it was an impressive sight.

In that tournament, Sofia played against the boys, while Judit played against the girls. Sofia scored 6½/11 and finished tied on 6th place. It was a respectable result, as she was the only girl among the best boys under 16 from all around the world. Furthermore, Sofia was only 12, while most competitors were boys around the 15/16-year-old mark. For Judit, the event was somewhat of a disappointment, as she 'only' finished third, half a point behind the Bulgarian, Aladjova, and the Georgian-Soviet, Kakhiani. Both of the above were 'family trips' where I served as my sisters' coach.

In 1988, in Timisoara, while Judit won the World Under-12 Boys' Championship, Sofia played much harder competition in the boys under-14 section. At that young age, two years makes a big difference. Again she did respectably, scoring 6½ out of 11, finishing behind future grandmasters Eran Liss and Gata Kamsky.

Still in 1988, Sofia won the overall (boys and girls) World Under-20 Rapid Championship in Mazatlan, Mexico. We had a lot of fun during that trip. It was a pleasure to escape the cold European winter to the sunny Mazatlan beach. With special permission from the organizers, my sisters were playing in both the junior and the adult championships at the same time. Well, not simultaneously, but in odd hours one event and even hours the other. Sofia also did well in the adult section, and beat the famous Danish grandmaster, Bent Larsen in a great fight.

In 1990, in Singapore, Sofia participated in the overall World Under-16 Championship and again scored 6½ out of 11. A year later in 1991, Sofia proved once more that she could compete successfully with the top juniors in the world. As one of the younger players (16) and the only girl at the World Under-18 in Guarapuava, Brazil, she scored 5½/9. The winner was the future World Champion Vladimir Kramnik. When coming home from Brazil, Sofia proudly showed off the medal she had won. Too bad it was the medal in the ping-pong competition, organized for the chess players and the local people.

Olympic memories

Sofia has played in four Olympiads so far. In the first Olympiad (in Thessaloniki 1988), she was officially the reserve player, but was practically alternating on board 3 with Ildiko Madl. Sofia scored a reasonable 4½/7.

With each Olympiad she moved up a board. In the next three Olympiads she performed very well and above expectation. In Novi Sad (1990), she played on board 3 behind me and Judit. She scored an impressive 11½/13 and won an individual gold medal, besides the Team Gold.

In Moscow 1994, we lost Judit to our 'men's' team. So I was board one, Sofia board two, Ildiko Madl board three, and Tunde Csonkics the reserve. Sofia played all the games and scored again an incredible 12½/14, while going undefeated. We ended up with 31 points, one point behind of the gold medal winners, Georgia, but four points ahead of China and Romania who tied for third place. Sofia again won the gold medal for the best individual performance on board two.

Finally, after my retirement, Sofia was the top board for the Hungarian Women's Team, at the 1996 Olympiad in Yerevan. She proved that she could handle that well too. On board 1, she scored the most points above 70%, 10/14. In her three last Olympiads, she scored nearly 83%!

The first win over a GM

In the early years, both my sisters were playing the King's Gambit, an opening that had been forgotten a century ago.

> □ **Sofia Polgar**
> ■ **Glenn Flear**
> Brussels 1987
> *King's Gambit*

1 e4 e5 2 f4 ♗c5 3 ♘f3 d6 4 c3 ♘f6 5 fxe5 dxe5 6 d4 exd4 7 cxd4 ♗b4+ 8 ♗d2 ♕e7 9 ♗d3 ♘xe4 10 ♗xe4 ♕xe4+ 11 ♔f2 ♗xd2 12 ♘bxd2 ♕d3 13 ♖e1+ ♗e6 14 ♕a4+ c6 15 ♕b4 ♘d7 16 ♕xb7 0-0 17 ♕xc6 ♖ab8 18 b3 ♘f6 19 ♔g1 ♖fc8 20 ♕d6 ♖b6 21 ♕f4 ♖c2 22 ♖ad1 ♘d5 23 ♕h4 ♖b8 24 ♘e4 ♕a6 25 ♘eg5 ♗f5 26 ♖e5 ♗g6 27 ♕g3 ♖d8 28 ♘h4 f6 29 ♖e6 ♕xa2 30 ♖d6 ♖cc8 31 ♘xg6 hxg6

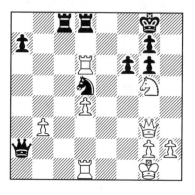

32 ♕h3 fxg5 33 ♖xd5 ♕e2 34 ♖xd8+ ♖xd8 35 ♕d3 ♕xd3 36 ♖xd3 ♖d5 37 ♔f2 ♔f7 38 ♔e3 ♔e6 39 ♖c3 ♖b5 40 ♔e4 ♔d6 41 ♖f3 ♔e6 42 ♖e3 ♔d6 43 ♔f3 ♖b4 44 ♔g4 ♖xd4+ 45 ♔xg5 ♖d2 46 ♖g3 ♔e7 47 ♔xg6 ♔f8 48 ♔h7 ♖d4 49 ♖f3+ ♔e8 50 h3 g5 51 ♔g6 g4 52 ♖e3+ ♔f8 53 h4 a5 54 h5 ♖b4 55 ♔g5 ♔g8 56 ♖e5 ♖xb3 57 ♖xa5 g3 58 ♔h4 Black resigned.

Miracle in Rome (February 1989)

Sofia's career highlight is certainly her astonishing performance at the 'Magistrale di Roma'. It was one of those few situations when the whole family traveled together but only Sofia played. None of us had ever seen Rome before, so we thought it was a good opportunity to combine some tourism while helping Sofia during the tournament. Nobody understood what happened in Rome, but Sofia just kept winning game after game. It did not matter who the opponents were. She won her first eight straight games, only showing 'mercy' in the last round against the Soviet grandmaster, Sergey Dolmatov (rated 2580). Her victims included four grandmasters: the Soviets Alexander Chernin (rated 2580), Semon Palatnik (2470) and Yuri Razuvaev (2550), as well as the many times Romanian Champion Mihai Suba (2515). Her complete games from Rome are given on pages 191-193.

Sofia's pre-Rome rating was 2295. She made an unbelievable performance rating of above 2900. (There are different methods of calculating the ratings, but in all of them her performance is around 2900.) It was clearly a Guinness

World Record performance at that time in any open tournament. As someone wrote: 'the odds against such an occurrence must be billions to one.'

Here is a list of the ever perform-

ances in chess history (according to the calculations of Kevin O'Connell), published by GM Raymond Keene a few years ago.

1.	Fischer	US Championship, 1963	3000
2.	Karpov	Linares, 1994	2977
3.	Kasparov	Tilburg, 1989	2913
4.	Alekhine	San Remo, 1930	2906
5.	Sofia Polgar	Rome, 1989	2879

According to a different and older (1986) source, the list is as follows:

1.	Fischer	Buenos Aires, 1970	2850
2.	Karpov	Waddinxween, 1979	2848
3.	Capablanca	Hastings, 1919	2826
4.	Torre	Manila, 1975	2826
5.	Kasparov	Niksic, 1983	2814

Everything seemed normal during the tournament, except that Sofia had an exceptional appetite. She would eat a huge plate of some kind of pasta as an appetizer, followed by the main course (some kind of meat/fish with potato/ rice and vegetables) and dessert, each lunch and dinner for ten consecutive days. Unfortunately, Sofia has never been able to repeat such a miraculous result (so far).

Becoming an IM

At her amazing 'show' in Rome, Sofia over-fulfilled the IM-norm by an unheard of 3½ points, and the GM-norm by 1½ points. Few doubted it would take her long to get the IM title. Within a few months, she had made three more IM norms at the New York Open, the Berlin Summer Open, and finally in Vejstrup, Denmark, in an all-play-all invitational.

Silver at the Rapid Women's World Championship

At the Rapid World Championship in Budapest (1992), Sofia played really well. Had she not lost in the last round, she could have even won the gold medal. Due to her loss, the Gold and the title of World Women's Rapid Champion went to me.

Here is one of her nice victories:

□ **Sofia Polgar**
■ **Alisa Galliamova**
Budapest 1992

See following diagram

Here Sofia found a nice combination to get a winning advantage: 17 ♖xd7! ♕xd7 (if 17...♘xd7 18 ♘h6+! gxh6 19 ♕xf7 mates) 18 ♘h6+! ♔h8 (if 18...gxh6 19 ♗xf6 followed by 20 ♕g3+

wins) 19 ♘xf7+ ♕xf7 20 ♗xf7 ♖e7 21 ♗a2 bxc3 22 ♗xf6 gxf6 23 ♕xf6+ ♖g7 24 bxc3 ♗c5 25 ♕xe5 ♗a7 26 ♖b1 ♖b8 27 ♖xb7! Black resigned.

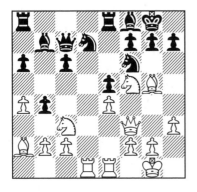

Silver at the World Junior

In her last chance, shortly before her 20th birthday, Sofia played again in the World Junior (under 20) Championship, in Matinhos, Brazil. Before the last round, she was tied for first place on 8½ points with Helgi Gretarsson from Iceland, and Christian Gabriel from Germany. On the last day, Gretarsson was paired against Gabriel, while Sofia had to play the Argentine Hugo Spangenberg. Gretarsson defeated Gabriel, but unfortunately, after a 50-move fight in an equal rook endgame, Sofia had to settle for a draw. Nevertheless, her 9/13 score was good enough for second place. Next to her Rome dream performance, I think this silver medal was Sofia's best ever result in overall competition. It's also the highest ever finishing position achieved by a Hungarian or any girl in the history of the World Junior Championships up to this point.

Diversified interests – 'the artist'

Ever since early childhood Sofia had many interests. I remember as a five-year-old, how she used to love to read and draw. She was caught a number of times late at night sneaking out to the bathroom to read a book. She was also keen on music, arts, movies, shows and sports. Sofia was never the most competitive in anything she did, but she was quite good in many things without too much effort.

Even at chess, she enjoyed the artistic aspect. From a young age, she also composed checkmate problems. Here is one of her favorites, a mate in two that she composed at age 7.

At a summer camp in Wisconsin, where she was one of the main instructors, this composition was printed on the back of the tee-shirts given to all the participants. It was quite a sight to see hundreds of kids running around with this 'tower' on their back.

After her relocation to Israel, she studied arts at Tel Hai College. In 1998, she started her studies in graphic design at the Avni Institute of Arts and Design, Tel Aviv. She recently graduated at Ort College, Rehovot, in interior design and architecture. Her favorite form of art is painting, which she comes back to whenever she has time and inspiration. Sofia's house in Israel is decorated with her own paintings.

Between 1999 and 2001, Sofia worked full time for the KasparovChess.com website in various capacities, from the design of the site to private lessons. She was involved in making this chess community on the web. Her duties included: co-editor of the news section, instructor in the KC University for pre-recording and online lessons, organizing first-class events and doing the live commentaries.

Matches against veterans

In 1992, Sofia played a rapid match versus GM Andor Lilienthal, a chess legend who had once beaten Capablanca. Sofia won by the score 3½-1½. In 1998, she challenged the Hungarian-born American grandmaster, Pal Benko, to a similar match and won 4½-½. You can see one of the finishes from this match in Sofia's combination section.

'The winner pays for dinner OK?'

The way Sofia met her future husband, Grandmaster Yona Kosashvili, was quite funny. We were visiting in Israel with my husband about a year after our wedding. We planned a family reunion in Israel and, knowing that, an Israeli chess organizer, Shay Bushinsky, contacted us about a special blitz tournament, which was a side-event of the European Championship. The main organizer of that big project was Yona Kosashvili. I do not remember too much from the tournament, but for Sofia it was definitely a lifelong memory.

Before the tournament, we were interviewed for Israeli television by a very charming and engaging young chess grandmaster and medical graduate, Yona Kosashvili. Judit and I could see right away the sparkles in their eyes. In the last round, they had to face each other across the chessboard.

Right before the game, Yona presented Sofia with the memorable proposition: 'The winner pays for dinner, OK?' Well, Yona won the blitz game and paid for the dinner like a gentleman. The two hit it off immediately that night. Everything progressed in 'blitz' speed, and within a few weeks Sofia moved to Israel to be near Yona. Prior to becoming a doctor, Yona twice won the Israeli Chess Championship and was the highest scoring member of the Israeli team at the 1990 Novi Sad Olympiad.

The beginning was not easy for the new couple as Yona shortly had to start his army service. Yona was a very patriotic young doctor, who did not mind to be sent to some of the most dangerous places along the Israeli-Lebanese border, in order to save lives. In the first years, they often had to be separated for two weeks or more at a time. Sofia had to go through a lot of nervous moments, listening to the news, hoping and praying daily that Yona was OK.

In 1999, Sofia and Yona got married in Israel. A year and a half later, Sofia gave birth to their first baby boy, Alon, who was born on November 29th, 2000 (exactly a week after my second son, Leeam). Their second boy, Yoav, was born on July 27th, 2003. Currently Sofia is at home as a full-time mom and paints in her spare time. She competes in chess only occasionally. Yona now works as an orthopedic surgeon.

Games and Combinations

Games

Game 1

□ **Sofia Polgar**

■ **Heikki Westerinen**

London 1988

Nimzovich Defense

According to Grandmaster Raymond Keene, this was the most brilliant game of the tournament, with Sofia playing 'in the grand style of Capablanca'.

1 e4

This was a special invitational tournament, in which five women and five men players were invited. Judit won the event.

1...♞c6

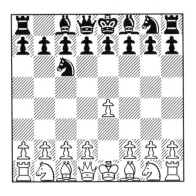

This is a very rare starting move in grandmaster play. The Finnish GM probably wanted to surprise Sofia and avoid the 14-year-old's opening preparation.

2 ♞c3

A sound, but not the most popular response, which would have been 2 d4.

2...♞f6

Here Black had the option to transpose to a normal king's pawn opening with 2...e5, but he wanted to get away from standard theory.

3 d4

Now White is back on track, having good control of the center.

3...e6

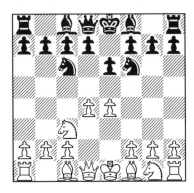

Black is already in a difficult situation in the fight for the center. For example, if 3...e5 4 dxe5 ♞xe5 5 f4 ♞c6 6 e5 and White has the initiative.

4 d5

The obvious 4 e5 ♞d5 5 ♞xd5 exd5 gives Black doubled pawns on the d-file, but he can trade off the d7 pawn soon with ...d7-d6.

4...exd5

After 4...♞e5, the knight could be chased again with 5 f4.

5 exd5

Here Black has to be very careful. White already has a strong advantage.

5...♞e5

This is already a strategically losing move. Black had to try 5...♕e7+ 6 ♗e2 ♞e5.

6 ♕e2!

A very unpleasant pin.

6...♕e7

If Black defends the knight any other way, such as 6...d6 or 6...♗d6, then White would play 7 f4 and win a piece.

7 d6!

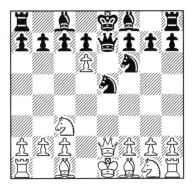

The key move of the entire game! It is a sound, long-term, positional pawn sacrifice.

7...cxd6

The queen could not capture the pawn, because then the pinned knight would get in trouble again.

8 ♗g5

Making another pin, now on the other knight. White is threatening with 9 ♘d5.

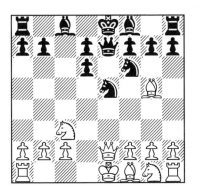

8...♕e6

The queen moves out of the pin. After 8...h6, then 9 ♘d5 does not work because of the tricky 9...♘d3+! 10 cxd3 ♕xe2+ 11 ♗xe2 ♘xd5 and Black is out of trouble, but simply 9 ♗xf6 gxf6 10 ♘d5 wins material.

9 ♗xf6

Forcing Black to recapture with the pawn. 9 ♘b5 also looks tempting, giving Black no choice but to play 9...♔d8.

9...gxf6

After 9...♕xf6 10 ♘d5 ♕d8 11 f4, Black can cause a little commotion with 11...♕a5+ 12 ♘c3 ♕b4, but White comes out ahead at the end after 13 ♕e3 ♕xb2 14 ♖b1.

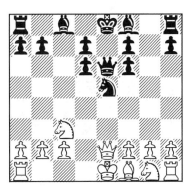

10 f4

Here White must choose whether to play a superior middlegame, or trade queens and 'squeeze' in an endgame. This time Sofia went for the latter.

10...♘g4

Hoping for activity, but it would have been safer to retreat to c6 instead.

11 ♘f3

Despite the fact that White is a pawn down, Sofia was in no rush to win it back. Instead she takes her time to develop calmly.

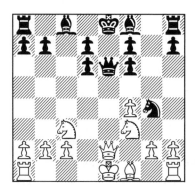

11...&h6

This is not a place with bright perspectives for the bishop.

12 ♘d4

Forcing the trade of queens. Naturally it would be wrong for White to trade on e6, giving Black the opportunity to straighten out the ruined pawn structure somewhat.

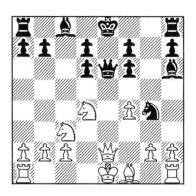

12...♕xe2+

After 12...♕e3 13 ♘d5 ♕xe2+ 14 ♗xe2, Black would collapse even more quickly.

13 ♗xe2

Attacking the knight on g4. 13 ♔xe2 also came into consideration, when Black must make an escape square for the knight; otherwise it would be

trapped with h2-h3.

13...♘e3

The only safe square for the knight. Now two of White's pawns are under attack: g2 and f4.

14 g3

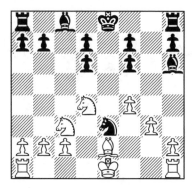

Protecting both pawns at once. The knight on e3 is surrounded by white pieces and is in trouble again.

14...♔d8

To rescue the knight by making room for the rook to protect it.

15 ♔d2

In a position like this, when the queens are off the board, the king is more useful in the middle.

15...♖e8

This is the only way to save the knight.

16 ♗d3

Improving the position of the bishop and attacking the pawn on h7. After 16 ♖ae1 Black could hang in there with 16...♘g2.

16...b6

Trying to develop the bishop on the long diagonal.

17 ♖he1

This is more accurate than 17 ♖ae1, when Black could answer 17...♗b7.

17...♘g4

After 17...♘g2 18 ♖xe8+ ♚xe8 19 ♗e4 Black is completely lost.

18 ♖xe8+

This is a smart trade. White swaps off Black's most active piece.

18...♚xe8

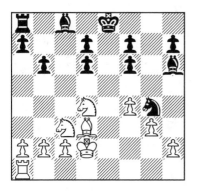

Besides the horrendous pawn structure, Black also has major problems with the co-ordination of his pieces.

19 ♗f5

Here Sofia missed a quicker win with 19 ♘cb5 ♚f8 20 ♗e2 ♘e5 21 ♘f5 and Black loses a piece.

19...♘e5

If 19...♘xh2, the knight will trapped after 20 ♖h1.

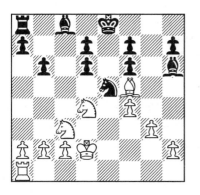

20 ♘cb5

Threatening to fork with ♘c7+ and also to capture the d6 pawn.

20...♚f8

The check with 20...♘c4+ 21 ♚c3 does not improve Black's chances.

21 ♖e1

21 ♘xd6 immediately was good, too, although the d6 pawn cannot be saved anyway.

21...♗b7

If Black plays 21...d5 then 22 ♘c7 wins the pawn anyway.

22 ♘xd6

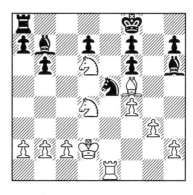

White finally wins the pawn back, and is about to capture another one.

22...♘f3+

Black forces the trade of knights with this check.

23 ♘xf3

Black's only hope would be to reach an opposite-colored bishop endgame where, even a couple of pawns down, the game can often be saved.

23...♗xf3

The bishop on h6 is really a sad sight. It has absolutely no mobility whatsoever.

24 ♗xh7

This is much better than 24 ♗xd7 ♖d8 25 ♖e8+ ♖xe8 26 ♘xe8 ♚e7.

24...♖d8

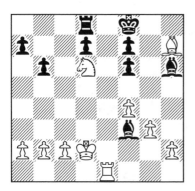

The knight on d6 really paralyses Black's position. The rook cannot get out and the black bishops are out of play.

25 ♗d3

The bishop has done its job on h7. It is time get back to the middle.

25...♗g4

Hoping for 26 ♘f5 ♗xf5 and to get to an opposite-colored bishop endgame.

26 ♔c3

The king gets out of the pin just in case. White did not want to take any chances.

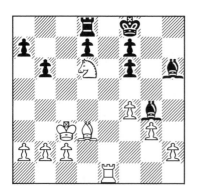

26...♗g7

Trying to activate the dark-squared bishop with ...f6-f5+.

27 ♗f5!

Obviously White does not want to allow the bishop on g7 any play, and therefore simply blocks it again.

27...♗f3

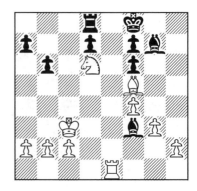

Black's position is totally hopeless, without any counterplay. White can take her time to slowly improve the position.

28 ♔d4

Centralizing the king and making way for the c-pawn to advance.

28...♗c6

This move protects the d7 pawn to free up the rook.

29 c4

Starting to march the pawns up.

29...♖a8

A waiting move. Black has few options here. If 29...♔g8 White would trade rooks with 30 ♖e8+.

30 b4

Threatening 31 b5.

30...a6

If Black plays 30...♖d8, White can play 31 b5 and bring the rook to a3 (via e3) next.

31 b5

White could have made a more 'preparatory moves', but this works perfectly well.

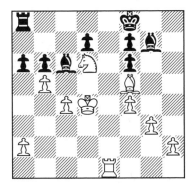

31...axb5

Black finally gets active now, but rather too late. Too many pawns were lost on the way.

32 cxb5

The bishop cannot hold on to the d7 pawn any longer.

32...♗f3

Now the bishop has to move away and White will win a second pawn.

33 ♗xd7

Black cannot capture the pawn on a2 because of the mate with ♖e8.

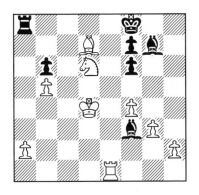

33...f5+

A discovered check looks nice, but it has no effect on White.

34 ♔c4

Black still cannot capture the pawn

because of the back rank problem.

34...♗b2

Clearing space for the king to get out on g7.

35 ♗c6

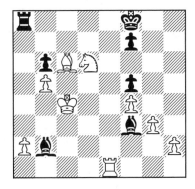

This fork forces the trade of the bishops, after which the c-pawn is unstoppable.

35...♖d8

If 35...♗xc6 36 bxc6 ♖a7, then the king comes to help with 37 ♔b5.

36 ♘b7

Attacking the rook, while the bishop on f3 is still hanging.

36...♖d4+

This loses a piece right away. The game could have lasted a little longer with 36...♖c8 37 ♔b3 ♗f6 38 ♘d6 ♖d8.

37 ♔b3 Black resigned

After 37...♗xc6 38 bxc6 the c-pawn will promote.

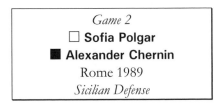

Game 2
□ **Sofia Polgar**
■ **Alexander Chernin**
Rome 1989
Sicilian Defense

This is one of Sofia's games from

the famous tournament in Rome, which was the highlight of her career. You can find the rest of her games from that amazing performance in the supplementary games section. GM Chernin was one of her strongest opponents in Rome.

1 e4

Just like Bobby Fischer, Sofia almost always likes to start with this move.

1...c5

After the game, GM Chernin partially blamed this move for losing! While, objectively, it is certainly not a mistake at all, he felt he had entered into a lion's den. He usually used to play the French Defense, an opening that he was more knowledgeable about than the Sicilian at that time.

2 ♘f3

Sofia was somewhat surprised by her opponent's opening choice, but continued as she normally would with the main line.

2...e6

You can also see Sofia's game versus Fominyh (Game 4) with the same starting moves.

3 d4

This is the Open Sicilian. As usual Sofia has opted for an aggressive battle.

3...cxd4

This trade is almost automatic.

4 ♘xd4

Sofia chooses the usual and most popular recapture.

4...♘c6

Offering a trade of knights, which would strengthen Black's center after 5 ♘xc6 bxc6.

5 ♘c3

White also develops her knight, con-

trolling the e4 and d5 center squares.

5...♕c7

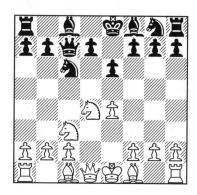

The idea of this early queen move is, in many variations, to make a pin with ♗b4 and put pressure on the knight on c3.

6 ♗e2

Clearing the path for White to castle.

6...♘f6

This is where Fominyh played differently with 6...a6.

7 0-0

7 ♗e3 first is also fine, but it is good to put your king in safety as soon as possible.

7...♗e7

After this the game transposes to the Scheveningen. 7...a6 would be the other option to stay within the Paulsen.

8 ♗e3

White completes the development of all minor pieces.

8...0-0

8...a6 is more common, in order to prevent any ♘c3-b5 move.

9 f4

Threatening to gain space with e4-e5. In the Sicilian, it is crucial for Black to try to stop White from successfully playing e4-e5; therefore, Black's next move is necessary.

9...d6

Preventing 10 e5, as well as opening a way out for the bishop on c8.

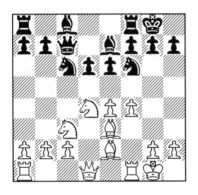

10 ♔h1

A precautionary move. If White plays 10 ♕e1 right away, Black equalizes by 10...♘xd4 11 ♗xd4 e5!, because after the typical pin 12 fxe5 dxe5 13 ♕g3 (which would be dangerous if the king was already on h1), Black can counter-pin with 13...♗c5!.

10...a6

If Black play 10...♘xd4 now, White recaptures with the queen.

11 ♕e1

This is where White has to take a decision to allow ...b7-b5 or not. The

other option is 11 a4.

11...♘a5?!

This is a rarely-played move with the idea of ...♘c4. The main lines start with 11...♘xd4 12 ♗xd4 b5 or 11...♗d7.

12 ♕g3

A small inaccuracy. Instead, 12 ♖d1 would have been more logical, the reason being that if 12 ♖d1 ♘c4 13 ♗c1, the rook will not be locked in on a1.

12...♘c4

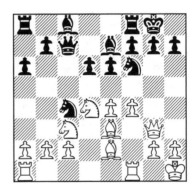

This is the only logical continuation after Black's previous move.

13 ♗c1

The bishop on e3 and the pawn on b2 were under attack, and this retreat defends both.

13...b5

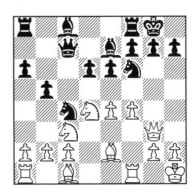

Threatening to play ...b5-b4, to chase the knight away from c3, and then capture the pawn on e4.

14 a3

Preventing Black's threat.

14...♕b6

Another possibility was to complete development with 14...♗b7 15 ♗f3 ♖ac8.

15 ♖d1

Protecting the knight on d4.

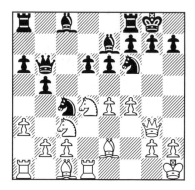

15...♗b7

In the post game analysis, we thought that Black should have tried the pawn sacrifice 15...e5! 16 ♗xc4 bxc4 17 fxe5 dxe5 18 ♕xe5 ♖e8 19 ♕g3 ♗d6, when he has compensation for the pawn. Black is also doing well after 16 fxe5 dxe5 17 ♗h6? ♘h5! 18 ♗xh5 ♕xh6.

16 b3

With this move, White chases the knight back and also enables the dark-squared bishop to develop to b2.

16...♘a5

This is the only safe square for the knight.

17 ♗f3

Protecting the e4 pawn.

17...♖ac8

The rook now occupies the open file and attacks the knight on c3.

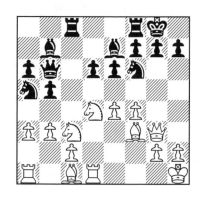

18 ♗b2

Finally the bishop is re-developed.

18...♖fd8?

A crucial mistake. After 18...♖fe8, if White plays 19 ♘d5 ♘xd5 20 ♘xe6 g6 as in the game, the rook is not hanging on d8, but White still has a very strong attack with 21 exd5 fxe6 22 ♗e4 followed by 23 ♗xg6. As ugly as it looks, 18...g6 was probably the best defense. Now White has a winning combination.

19 ♘d5!

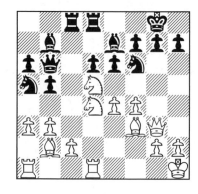

This sacrifice begins the clearing of the long diagonal for the bishop on b2 to gain full power.

19...♘xd5

If Black captures with the pawn, 19...exd5, White wins by 20 ♘f5 ♗f8 21 ♘xg7! ♗xg7 22 ♗xf6.

20 ♘xe6!

The second clearance sacrifice, which definitely cannot be accepted as White threatens checkmate in one with ♕xg7. After 20 ♘f5 g6 would hold.

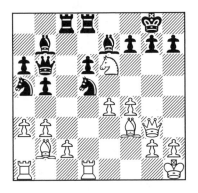

20...g6

To defending against the mate, Black must lose an exchange.

21 ♘xd8

White could have also won the queen for two pieces with 21 ♗d4 fxe6 22 ♗xb6 ♘xb6.

21...♕xd8

If 21...♘e3, then 22 ♗d4 forks.

22 exd5

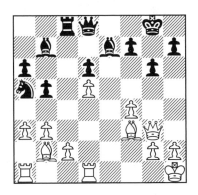

The position has now cleared. White has won an exchange and maintained the initiative as well, thanks to the powerful bishop on b2.

22...♖xc2

Equalizing the pawn count. Now the black rook attacks the bishop on b2, while the knight attacks the b3 pawn.

23 ♖ab1

Protecting the bishop.

23...♗h4

If Black captures 23...♘xb3, White regains the pawn by 24 ♗e4 ♖c4 25 ♗d3 ♖c5 26 ♗xg6 fxg6 27 ♕xb3.

24 ♕h3

Moving out of the attack. 24 ♕g4 would be answered by 24...f5 25 ♕h3 ♘xb3.

24...♗c8

Attacking the queen again. It has no free square to move to, but the attack can be blocked.

25 ♗g4

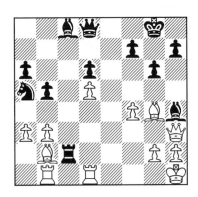

After the trade of the bishops Black wins a pawn.

25...♗xg4

25...f5 was perhaps better, with the continuation 26 ♗f3 ♘xb3 27 g3 ♗e7 28 ♕f1 and now if 28...♘d2? 29 ♕d3.

26 ♕xg4

The queen could not hold on to the b3 pawn any longer. However, White's main focus is not that pawn; she is aiming to take advantage of the weak a1-h8 diagonal.

26...♞xb3

Black won a pawn, but the weakness of the a1-h8 diagonal is still there.

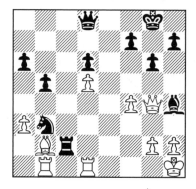

27 g3

27 f5 would have been more precise, opening up the kingside.

27...♗e7

The bishop could not retreat to f6 because White wins the knight after the trade of bishops.

28 f5

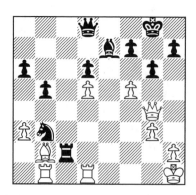

Better later then never! Now White is trying to break the black kingside

wide open.

28...a5?

This leads to even more trouble. The only hope was 28...♕c8!.

29 fxg6

Weakening Black's defense near the king.

29...hxg6

After 29...fxg6 White quickly wins with 30 ♕e6+ ♚f8 31 ♖f1+ ♚e8 32 ♗g7.

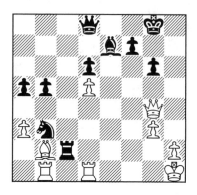

30 ♕h3!

Threatening 31 ♕h8 mate.

30...♖xb2

The key point is that after 30...♗f6 31 ♗xf6 ♕xf6 32 ♖xb3, the rook covers the f3 square.

31 ♖xb2

Now White has two rooks for a bishop, a knight and a pawn.

31...a4

Protecting the knight.

32 ♖f2

Despite the significant material advantage, White looks for a new target to go after, and one is found: the f7 pawn.

32...♞c5

Black had no defense against White's plan. The defense with ...♞d7 and then ...♞e5 is too slow.

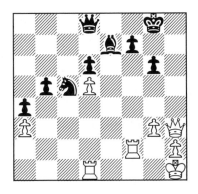

33 ♖df1

To provoke a further weakening on the kingside. This is an excellent example of chess. Keep forcing weaknesses on your opponent; sooner or later, your opponent's position will collapse.

33...f5

After 33...f6 the light squares on the kingside would become weak.

34 g4!

Opening up the f-file and the kingside even more. Black is totally defenseless.

34...♘e4

A beautiful place for the knight, but it does not compensate for the material deficit.

35 ♖g2

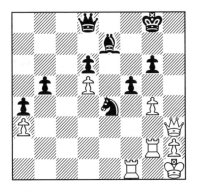

Now Black cannot avoid the opening of more files against his king.

35...♗f6 Black resigned

Realizing how hopeless his position was...

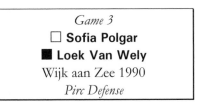

Game 3
□ **Sofia Polgar**
■ **Loek Van Wely**
Wijk aan Zee 1990
Pirc Defense

The very tall and thin GM Van Wely was one of the top Dutch junior players at that time. Some years later he became a world top 20 player with a rating over 2700!

1 e4

All three sisters participated in the same section of this famous event.

1...d6

This opening is named after the Yugoslav grandmaster, Vasja Pirc.

2 d4

Occupying the important center d4 square. This is the most popular continuation.

2...♘f6

Developing the knight while attacking the pawn on e4.

3 ♘c3

Developing the knight and protecting the pawn.

3...g6

Black's development and ideas are practically identical to those in the King's Indian Defense, which is one of the common responses to 1 d4.

4 f4

This is the sharpest and most ambitious variation. 4 ♘f3 or 4 ♗e3 are two of the other common choices.

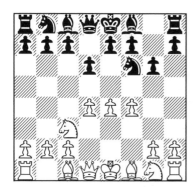

4...♗g7

This is a logical developing move. Always try to remember to develop your pieces and castle your king as soon as possible.

5 ♘f3

On the immediate 5 e5 Black would simply play 5...♘fd7.

5...c5

It is more common and natural to put the king in safety first with 5...0-0. See Sofia's game versus Safranska (Game 8).

6 dxc5

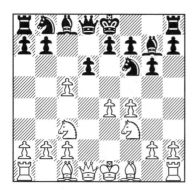

Here White has an interesting alternative in 6 ♗b5+ ♗d7 7 e5 ♘g4 8 e6 fxe6 9 ♘g5, which offers a very complicated game.

6...♕a5

This is Black's idea. By pinning the knight on c3 Black threatens to capture the white pawn on e4. White gets a big advantage after 6...dxc5 7 ♕xd8+ ♔xd8 8 ♘g5 ♔e8? 9 e5 ♘fd7 10 ♘d5.

7 ♗d3

White had to protect the pawn. The materialistic 7 cxd6 does not cause Black any problems after 7...♘xe4.

7...♕xc5

Black's move prevents White from castling.

8 ♕e2

Preparing ♗c1-e3, to chase the black queen from the a7-g1 diagonal, after which White can castle.

8...0-0

Perhaps 8...♗g4 is a more precise move order.

9 ♗e3

Developing and gaining a tempo.

9...♕a5

This is the most active square for the queen.

10 h3

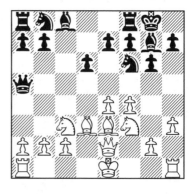

This move is Judit's specialty. It prevents the standard 10 0-0 ♗g4.

10...e5

In an earlier game vs. Hennigan

(London 1988), Judit got an edge after 10...♘h5 11 ♔f2, preventing the fork with ♘h5-g3 and preparing g2-g4.

11 0-0-0

A typical example of the aggressive chess which both Sofia and Judit like to play. The calmer 11 fxe5 dxe5 12 0-0 seems better for White too.

11...♘h5?!

Against Judit a year earlier at the OHRA tournament in Amsterdam, GM Azmaiparashvili played 11...♘bd7 12 g4 d5 13 exd5 e4 14 ♘xe4 ♕xa2 with wild complications. Judit won. In this game, Sofia was ready to challenge Van Wely's opening preparation.

12 f5!

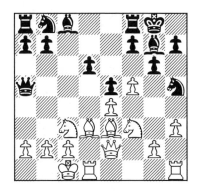

An impressive idea! White allows the fork on g3, sacrificing the rook on h1 for a strong attack.

12...♘g3

Black takes up the challenge. After what happened in the game, Black needs to look for an improvement. One idea could be to trade with 12...gxf5 13 exf5 and then play 13...♘g3. However, White has a dangerous attack in this line as well after 14 ♕e1 ♘xh1 and 15 ♕h4. Similar to the game, 14 g4 is also a possibility.

13 ♕e1

Encouraging the knight to capture the rook.

13...♘xh1

At this point, there was no turning back. Black had to capture on h1. Otherwise, he had just wasted time for nothing.

14 g4!

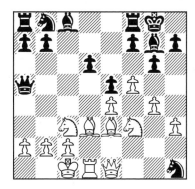

This is an incredible idea! Black has just taken a whole rook and White makes a quiet move!

14...gxf5?

This visibly helps White. After the more dynamic 14...d5, White would play 15 ♘xd5 ♕xe1 16 ♖xe1 ♘c6 (if 16...♘d7? 17 ♘c7 ♖b8 18 ♗xa7 traps the rook, or 16...♘g3 17 f6 ♗h8?? 18 ♘e7 mate) 17 f6 ♗h8 18 ♖xh1 ♗e6 19 g5 with a knight and a pawn for the rook, and it is hard to see how the h8 bishop will come back to play. Therefore, White has more than enough positional compensation.

15 gxf5

Here is what Sofia said in her annotations after the game: 'I think that, despite Black being a whole rook up at the moment, he has no defense.' This shows you Sofia's confidence in her attack.

15...♕d8

Now that the g-file has been opened for the white rook, Black is in trouble. Here are some sample variations:

a) 15...♘d7 16 ♕h4 (White is in no rush to capture the knight on h1) 16...♕d8 (if 16...♗f6? 17 ♖g1+ ♔h8 18 ♘g5 ♗xg5 19 ♕xg5) 17 ♘g5 h6 18 ♖g1 b6 (18...hxg5 19 ♖xg5) 19 ♘d5 ♗b7 20 f6 ♘xf6 21 ♘h7 ♘xh7 (21...♔xh7 22 ♖xg7+ ♔xg7 23 ♗xh6+) 22 ♕xh6 and White is winning.

b) 15...f6 16 ♗c4+ ♔h8 17 ♘h4 threatening 18 ♘g6+ hxg6 19 ♕h4+.

16 ♗c4

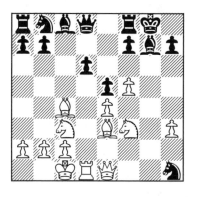

Pinning the f7 pawn. Now the idea is 17 ♗g5 followed by f5-f6.

16...♔h8

White would win easily after 16...♕c7 17 ♕xh1 ♕xc4 18 ♖g1 and now 18...f6 (if 18...♔h8 19 ♕g2 ♖g8 20 f6 or 19...♗f6 20 ♗h6 ♖e8 21 ♗g7+) 19 ♕g2 ♖f7 20 ♗h6 ♕c7 21 ♘d5 ♕d7 22 ♘xf6+ ♖xf6 23 ♗xg7 ♖f7 24 ♗h6+.

17 ♘g5

Hitting two targets at once: the f7 and h7 pawns.

17...♗h6

After 17...f6, White would sacrifice with 18 ♘xh7 to open the h-file.

18 ♕h4

18 ♘xf7+ also gave White a big advantage.

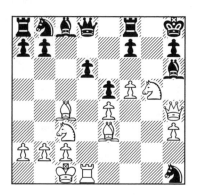

18...♗xg5

If 18...♕f6 19 ♖g1 (threatening to checkmate with 20 ♘xf7+ ♖xf7 21 ♕xf6+ ♖xf6 22 ♖g8) 19...♘d7 20 ♕xh6 ♕xh6 21 ♘xf7+ ♖xf7 22 ♗xh6 and Black cannot avoid major material loses.

19 ♗xg5

Attacking the queen and threatening a deadly check on f6.

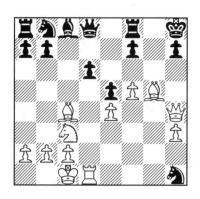

19...f6

The only move to block the attack and delay the end.

20 ♗h6

Attacking the rook on f8 and, even more importantly, the g7 square.

20...♘d7

After 20...♘c6 21 ♖g1 ♕e7 22 ♗xf8 ♕xf8 White has a fancy mate in two with 23 ♕xf6+! ♕xf6 24 ♖g8.

21 ♖g1

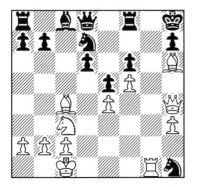

Threatening mate in one with 22 ♗g7.

21...♕e7

Preparing to give up the queen for rook and bishop (if 22 ♗g7+) to avoid the mate.

22 ♕g4 Black resigned

Black cannot defend against both mating threats on g8 and on g7.

Game 4
□ **Sofia Polgar**
■ **Alexander Fominyh**
Rimavska Sobota 1991
Sicilian Defense

This is the last round game from a strong invitational Grandmaster tournament in Czechoslovakia. As usual Sofia played in aggressive, fighting style, with 10 of her 13 games ending in decisive results.

1 e4

No surprise!

1...c5

The Sicilian is the sharpest opening against the king's pawn start.

2 ♘f3

Developing and attacking the central d4 and e5 squares.

2...e6

This one of the three standard choices in this position. The other two are 2...d6 and 2...♘c6.

3 d4

White fights for the center right away. A more peaceful game would arise after 3 d3 or 3 c3.

3...cxd4

As in a typical Sicilian Defense, the idea for Black is to trade the c-pawn for White's center d-pawn.

4 ♘xd4

Naturally, White would not bring the queen out early by 4 ♕xd4 when it could be attacked straight away with 4...♘c6. Therefore, 4 ♘xd4 is the most popular choice.

4...♘c6

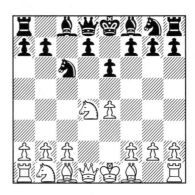

4...♘f6 is also a good move.

5 ♘c3

The alternative was 5 ♘b5, attacking the weakened d6 square, and after 5...d6, to get a Maróczy Bind type of position with 6 c4.

5...♛c7

This is a version of the Paulsen variation, named after the famous master from the 19th century.

6 ♗e2

After 6 ♘db5 Black would keep control of the d6 square by playing 6...♛b8, and then kick the knight back with ...a7-a6.

6...a6

A key move in this variation. It has two purposes: preventing any future ♘b5 jump, and supporting the ...b7-b5 advance to liberate the black bishop on c8 to b7.

7 0-0

The most common road. Another interesting option is 7 f4, with a quick ♗f3 in mind, to disturb Black's plan of ...b7-b5 and ...♗b7.

7...♗c5

This is very rarely played, but it is a 'pet variation' of Grandmaster Fominyh. The 'normal' move is to develop with 7...♘f6. This is another example where it is better to follow general opening principles, rather than looking for an exception to it. Generally speaking, it is better in the opening to develop knights before bishops.

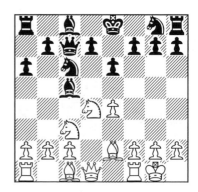

8 ♘b3

The white knight is attacked. Protecting it with 8 ♗e3 is also a reasonable choice.

8...♗e7

Black's idea behind ...♗f8-c5-e7 is the belief that the white knight is worse placed on b3 than it would be in the center on d4. I personally do not buy the idea of wasting a move to accomplish this.

9 a4

This is a typical crossroads in the Sicilian: whether or not to allow Black's ...b7-b5 advance? There are pros and cons in both cases. The game move limits Black's activity on the queenside, but on the other hand it weakens the b4 square.

9...♘f6

Black continues to develop and prepares to castle.

10 f4

With this advance White prepares 11 e5 to chase the knight from f6 away and to gain more control of the center. This would create a very big advantage for White.

10...d6

Preventing e4-e5. In some later

games Fominyh tried instead 10...0-0 and 10...d5 successfully.

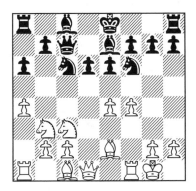

11 ♗f3

This gives more support for the central e4 and d5 squares, as well as making it difficult for Black to develop with ...b7-b6.

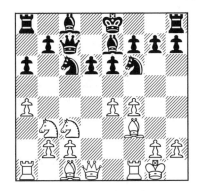

11...♘d7

The start of a dubious maneuvering plan. Black should have castled.

After 11...b6, rather than the immediate 12 e5 dxe5 13 fxe5 ♘d7 14 ♗f4 ♗b7, instead 12 a5! is the correct move and only after 12...bxa5, when Black's queenside is more vulnerable, should White then play 13 e5 dxe5 14 fxe5 ♘d7 15 ♗xc6 ♕xc6 16 ♕g4 with the initiative.

12 ♕e2

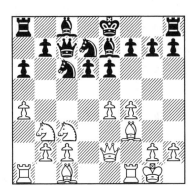

This creates some typical ♘c3-d5 Sicilian sacrifice possibilities.

12...♘c5

After 12...0-0, White could play 13 ♘d5 exd5 14 exd5. Even after 12...b6 White can consider the long-term positional sacrifice 13 ♘d5 exd5 14 exd5 ♘d8 15 ♖e1 ♘f6 16 ♘d4.

13 ♗e3

The alternative 13 ♘xc5 dxc5 would help Black to get rid of the potential weakness on d6.

13...♘xb3

After the game this move was blamed for the loss. This is one of the exceptions when, despite being forced to double the b-pawns, the trade favors White. Black will miss the knight, which is a crucial defender on the kingside. 13...0-0 or 13...b6 are possible improvements.

14 cxb3

Now that the c-file has opened, Black has to be very careful.

14...0-0

If 14...b6 White would immediately occupy the c-file by 15 ♖ac1, with a threat of 16 ♘d5.

15 ♕f2

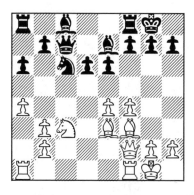

A fine move with two ideas:

1) It takes control of the b6 square.

2) It swings the queen over to the kingside to help in the attack.

15...♗d7

It was probably better to prevent 16 ♗b6 with 15...♗d8. The drawback is that it leaves the d6 pawn more vulnerable.

16 ♗b6

This is a very pleasant move to make. It forces the black queen into a very ugly position.

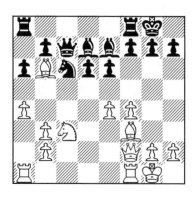

16...♕b8

Not only is the queen in an awkward place, it locks up the rook on a8 as well.

17 ♖ad1

White activates the queenside rook

by putting it on the half-open d-file.

17...♔h8

A typical 'just in case' move. It gets away from the a2-g8 diagonal (which may be important in case Black plays ...f7-f5), and also out of a potential pin once the white queen appears on g3.

18 ♗g4

With the idea that after 18...f5 19 exf5, Black would have to recapture with the pawn, weakening the d5 square.

18...♘a7

After this Black has too many pieces far from the king's defense. As unappealing it may look, 18...f5 probably would give Black the best hope.

19 ♕g3

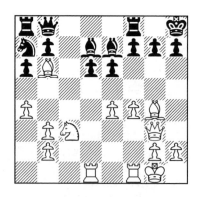

White starts a typical attack on the kingside.

19...♖g8

White has a very strong attack, which Black must address. If instead 19...♘c8, then 20 ♗d4 (threatening 21 ♗xe6) 20...f6 21 ♕h3.

20 ♕h3

Now that the black king is on the h-file, it is logical to move the queen there. White is preparing f4-f5.

20...♗d8

Offering a trade of bishops.

21 ♗xd8

This exchange forces the black rook away from the defense of the king. Retreating the bishop makes sense too, keeping an extra piece on the board to assist in the attack.

21...♖xd8

The queen needs to stay on b8 to protect the d6 pawn. An unusual observation: other than pawns, the only piece that Black has on the kingside is the king itself! This is not a good sign.

22 f5!

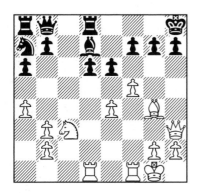

Putting pressure on the e6 pawn.

22...exf5

After 22...e5 the game could have ended the following way: 23 f6! ♗xg4 24 fxg7+ ♔xg7 25 ♕xg4+ ♔f8 26 ♖xf7+! ♔xf7 27 ♖f1+ ♔e7 28 ♘d5+ ♔e8 29 ♕e6 mate.

23 ♗xf5

Forcing the trade of bishops because of the mating threat on h7.

23...♗xf5

The only move, otherwise Black loses the bishop.

24 ♖xf5

Attacking the f7 pawn and threatening the dangerous 25 ♖h5.

24...♔g8

After 24...f6 25 ♖h5 wins by force, e.g. 25...h6 26 ♖xh6+! gxh6 27 ♕xh6+ ♔g8 28 ♕g6+ ♔f8 (or 28...♔h8 29 ♖d3) 29 ♕xf6+ ♔e8 30 ♕e6+ ♔f8 31 ♖f1+ ♔g7 32 ♖f7+ and mate in two more moves.

25 ♘d5

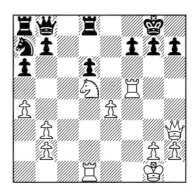

Bringing another piece to the attack. White has many threats, including the idea of trapping the rook on a8 with 26 ♘b6.

25...♘c6

There are some pretty variations after 25...b5 26 ♘e7+, e.g. 26...♔h8 27 ♕xh7+ ♔xh7 28 ♖h5 mate or 26...♔f8 27 ♕xh7 ♔xe7 28 ♖xf7+ ♔xf7 29 ♖f1+ ♔e8 30 ♕xg7 and Black is helpless.

26 ♖h5

Another way to win is 26 ♖g5 (threatening 27 ♕h6 and 27 ♘f6+) 26...♔h8 27 ♖h5 h6 28 ♖xh6+! gxh6 29 ♕xh6+ ♔g8 30 ♘f6 mate.

26...♕a7+

At least Black can say 'I gave a check!' before resigning, since this move has no threat whatsoever.

27 ♔f1

An unusual but good move. The idea is not to let the black queen to get to f2 and help out the defense on the kingside.

27...h6 Black resigned

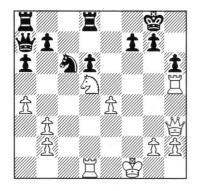

Trying to protect the pawn. Black resigned, however, because there is no defense after 28 ♖xh6! gxh6 29 ♕xh6 (threatening mate with 30 ♘f6) 29...f5 30 ♖d3 f4 (or 30...♔f7 31 ♕h7+ ♔e8 32 ♖g3) 31 ♕g6+ ♔f8 32 ♕f6+ ♔e8 33 ♕g7.

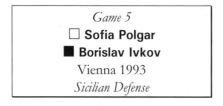

Game 5
□ **Sofia Polgar**
■ **Borislav Ivkov**
Vienna 1993
Sicilian Defense

There was for a decade a wonderful annual event: the Ladies vs. Veterans tournament, organized by the Max Euwe Association and sponsored by Mr. Joop van Oosterom.

1 e4

This game was played at the 1993 tournament in Austria, for six of the top women players and six great veterans.

1...c5

The Sicilian Defense is one of the most popular response to the king's pawn game.

2 ♘f3

Some other less ambitious, but decent choices are 2 c3, 2 ♘c3 or 2 f4.

2...♘c6

When Black uses this developing move, after 3 d4 cxd4 4 ♘xd4, one of the following three variations usually occurs: the Sveshnikov (4...♘f6 5 ♘c3 e5), the Rauzer (4...♘f6 5 ♘c3 d6), or the Accelerated Dragon (4...g6).

3 ♗b5

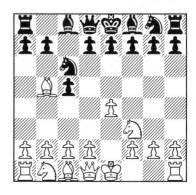

Nowadays this is a popular way to avoid all the above-mentioned choices and get into less analyzed variations. Sofia, and especially Judit, used it numerous times as White as well.

3...e6

Black wants to develop the dark-squared bishop. 3...g6 is also good.

4 ♗xc6

White has traded a bishop for a knight, while Black is forced to double up his pawns. Normally this is considered as an 'even trade'.

The other option was to continue with castling (4 0-0) straight away. However, Black then would connect his knights with ...♘g8-e7, after which he can no longer be forced to double up the c-pawns as in the game. By the way, that is how GM Ivkov continued with reversed colors against Sofia in the same tournament!

4...bxc6

Following the general rule: capture with your pawns towards the center. 4...dxc6 would therefore be a strategical error. After castling White's plan would be to develop the bishop on the long diagonal, with b2-b3 followed by ♗c1-b2, when Black has a passive position.

5 0-0

It is also fine to develop the bishop first with 5 b3 or 5 d3.

5...♘e7

When Black plays ...d7-d5 too soon there are usually difficulties protecting the c5 pawn.

6 b3

White wants to fianchetto the bishop on the more effective a1-h8 diagonal, instead of leaving it on the c1-h6 diagonal.

6...♘g6

Black cannot develop the bishop from f8 to g7, because White occupies the diagonal first after 6...g6 7 ♗b2.

7 ♗b2

Besides developing to its ideal position, the bishop prevents its counterpart

from getting out as it is busy holding on to the g7 pawn.

7...f6

Solving the problem by blocking the white bishop's attack on g7.

8 d4

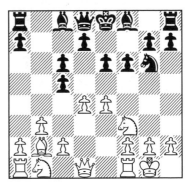

This is one of those situations where White intends to transform one type of an advantage for another. Prior to 8 d4 White had a better pawn structure since Black has doubled pawns. After White's last move, Black is able to trade a less valuable doubled c-pawn for a healthy d-pawn. In return, White will gain control of the semi-open d-file and with a target in mind, Black's d-pawn.

8 e5 is a very different line, though just as interesting.

8...cxd4

Black gladly goes for the trade.

9 ♕xd4

In most games White recaptures with the knight.

9...♗e7

It is true that White brought out the queen early, which is against a basic opening principle. But here Black is unable to chase the white queen away with typical moves such as ...♘b8-c6 or ...♗f8-c5. To avoid passivity Black has to try 9...d5.

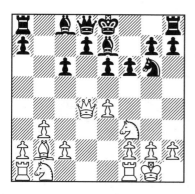

10 c4

With this move White takes further control of the d5 square (preventing the ...d7-d5 advance) and gains more space advantage.

10...d6

After 10...d5 11 cxd5 cxd5 12 exd5 ♕xd5 13 ♕xd5 exd5 14 ♖d1 ♗e6 15 ♘c3 White would get a very pleasant position with a clear target: the isolated d5 pawn.

11 ♘c3

White has completed developing all the pieces.

11...0-0

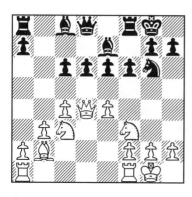

Although the king is now in safety, Black still has three problems to solve:

1) Activating the bishop on c8;

2) Getting rid of (by trading) or properly defending the weak d6 pawn;

3) Crossing his third rank.

12 ♖ad1

The only logical place for the queen-side rook, aiming at the d6 pawn.

12...♕a5

Moving the queen out of a potential pin on the d-file. Black could have also played 12...e5 straight away, opening the diagonal for the bishop on c8.

13 ♕d2

It is obvious that, sooner or later, the white queen had to leave its central position. Now is a good time, while creating a possible discovery threat.

13...♖d8

13...♗b7 would weaken the light squares along the c8-h3 diagonal, and with 14 ♘d4, White could attack the e6 pawn right away. 13...e5 was a better way to develop the bishop.

14 ♘d4

Attacking the c6 pawn. White could also reach a slightly better endgame by tactical means with 14 ♘d5. After 14...♕xa2 15 ♘b4 ♕a5 (if 15...♕xb3 the black queen gets trapped by 16 ♘d4 ♕xc4 17 ♖c1) 16 ♘xc6 ♕xd2 17 ♖xd2

♖d7 18 ♘xe7+ ♘xe7 19 ♗a3, Black loses a pawn. Therefore 14...♕xd2 15 ♘xe7+ ♘xe7 16 ♖xd2 is Black's best.

But typically for her style, Sofia prefers to play with the queens on the board.

14...♕c7

Protecting the c6 pawn and avoiding any future ♘d5 related discovery tricks.

15 f4

White gains some more space advantage with this move.

15...e5

Otherwise White advances with f4-f5.

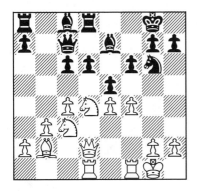

16 ♘de2

The trade with 16 fxe5 would be suicidal for White, as after 16...dxe5 the knight on d4 is stuck in a pin. Instead the retreat also protected the white pawn on f4.

16...exf4

If Black had not taken the pawn, White would push 17 f5 and then activate the rook on f1 via the third rank.

17 ♘xf4

The only sound recapture.

17...♘xf4

This exchange worsens Black's position. I would prefer to centralize the knight with 17...♘e5. Then White has a scary-looking reply in 18 ♘cd5, but Black could just ignore it with 18...♕b7 and stay in the game.

18 ♕xf4

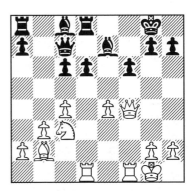

White is finally ready to start the kingside attack. It is amazing that in just another ten moves the game is over.

18...♕a5

I think it was time to complete development with 18...♗e6.

19 ♖d3

Now the rook swings over to the kingside.

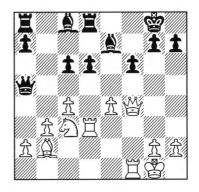

19...♗e6

If Black offers trade of queens with 19...♕e5, White has a cute tactic with 20 ♘d5! ♕xf4 21 ♘xe7+ ♔f7 22 ♖xf4

♔xe7 and while Black seems initially to be OK, after 23 ♖g3! he cannot avoid losing a few pawns; e.g. 23...♖g8 24 ♗xf6+, or if 23...♔f7 24 ♖xg7+! ♔xg7 25 ♗xf6+ ♔g6 26 ♗xd8.

20 ♖g3

White has created a pin with several threats, such as ♕f4-h6, or if Black does nothing White would play 21 ♘d5! cxd5 22 ♗xf6.

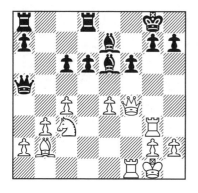

20...♗f7

With the idea of blocking the rook's fire on the g-file with ...♗f7-g6. I would feel more comfortable getting the king out of the pin with 20...♔h8.

21 ♘e2

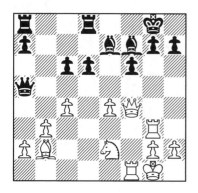

Bringing the knight towards the black king. It is a very strong move,

with an immediate threat of attacking the pawn with 22 ♗xf6.

21 ♘d5 only leads to a draw: 21...cxd5 22 ♗xf6 (or 22 ♖xg7+ ♔xg7 23 ♗xf6+ ♗xf6 24 ♕xf6+ ♔g8 25 ♕xf7+ ♔h8 26 ♕f6+ ♔g8 27 ♕f7+ ♔h8 28 ♕f6+ with perpetual check) 22...♗xf6 23 ♕xf6, since here Black has 23...♗g6. At this point the best White can do is save the game with 24 ♖xg6 hxg6 25 ♕e6+ ♔h7 26 ♕h3+ (26 ♖f3 would be pushing things too far, because of 26...♕e1+) 26...♔g8 27 ♕e6+ also with perpetual check

21...♗g6

The best defense against the pin threat on the g-file.

22 ♕g4

A multipurpose move, which doubles up on the g-file, threatens ♕e6+, and also clears the f4 square for the knight.

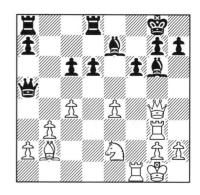

22...♖f8

Preparing to meet 23 ♕e6+ with 23...♖f7. If Black grabs the pawn with 22...♕xa2, White has a pretty straightforward winning attack after 23 ♘f4 ♕xb2 24 ♘xg6 hxg6 25 ♕e6+ ♔f8 26 ♖h3 and Black can only delay checkmate by a couple of moves.

23 ♗c3

White is also better after 23 ♘f4 f5 24 exf5 ♕xf5 25 ♕xf5 ♖xf5 26 ♘xg6 ♖xf1+ 27 ♔xf1 hxg6 28 ♖xg6 ♗f8 with an extra pawn in the endgame.

23...♕xa2

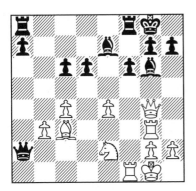

It seems that there is no direct penalty for taking the pawn. But, as we shall see very soon, Black could not afford to lose three moves just to win a pawn. The queen was needed for defense.

24 ♘d4

Protecting the b3 pawn and heading towards the e6 square.

24...♕a6

Avoiding 25 ♖a1 which would trap the black queen.

25 h4!

Pawns are the least valuable pieces in a chess game. Sometimes, however, a little pawn can make all the difference in the world. With this new force in the attack, White cracks open Black's defense.

25...♕c8

Black is hoping to trade queens, which would solve many problems.

26 ♘e6

The rule of thumb is that the attacking side is almost always better off keeping the queens on the board for the attack to succeed.

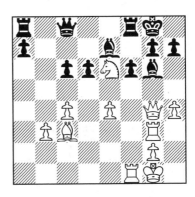

26...f5

Black is lost also after 26...♖f7 27 h5 ♗xh5 28 ♕xg7+! (a nice queen sacrifice!) 28...♖xg7 29 ♖xg7+ ♔h8 30 ♖xe7, or 26...♖e8 27 h5 ♗d8 28 hxg6 ♕xe6 29 gxh7+ ♔xh7 30 ♕xg7 mate.

27 exf5

Now White gains significant material advantage.

27...♖xf5

The bishop could not leave g6 because of the mate with 28 ♕xg7.

28 ♖xf5 Black resigned

After 28...♕xe6 White wins the queen with the discovery 29 ♖f8+!.

> *Game 6*
> □ **Jose Garcia Padron**
> ■ **Sofia Polgar**
> Las Palmas 1994
> *Larsen's Opening*

This was the year when I got married and started (from October 1994) to spend most of my time in New York, away from my family. While we three sisters still miss each other a lot today, it was much harder on all of us at that time, because it was a new experience. After my family's trip to Las Palmas, they were all very excited, telling me what a beautiful place it is and what I had missed out on. In that invitational tournament, Judit played in the A and Sofia in the B section.

1 b3

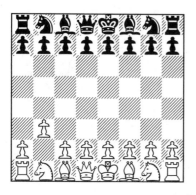

This is the Larsen Opening, named after the world-famous Danish Grandmaster (who, by the way, Sofia defeated in a nice game – see Game 9). For most good players it is only used as a surprise weapon.

1...d5

Against not-so-ambitious openings (those other than 1 e4 or 1 d4), Black can choose many different plans or setups, without needing to worry much about any opening difficulties. 1...e5 would be another common response.

2 ♗b2

After White's first move, this is the only logical follow-up.

2...c6

At the San Francisco International in 1991, I played 2...♘f6 here against the Australian GM, Ian Rogers.

3 e3

Opening up the diagonal to develop the other bishop too.

3...♗f5

Developing the bishop prior to playing ...e7-e6, which would restrict its mobility on c8.

4 ♘f3

With this developing move White controls two important center squares, d4 and e5. A totally different plan would be to include f2-f4, as in a reversed Dutch Defense.

4...e6

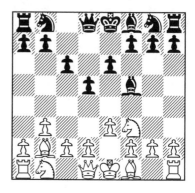

Now that the bishop from c8 is already out, it is fine to move the e-pawn.

5 c4

White is heading towards a 'hedgehog' set-up.

5...♘d7

If 5...dxc4 6 bxc4 ♗d3 Black would only manage to block the d2 pawn temporarily, as after 7 ♗xd3 ♕xd3 8 ♕b3 the black queen is forced to leave.

6 ♗e2

Preparing to castle.

6...h6

This is a typical move in such or similar positions. It makes an escape square on h7 for the bishop on f5. If instead 6...♘gf6 7 ♘h4 and White gets the advantage of the bishop pair.

7 0-0

With this move the white king has reached safety.

7...♘gf6

This developing move, besides controlling the center, also frees up the bishop on f8 from the task of guarding the g7 pawn.

8 ♘c3

A small mistake. When White has a bishop developed on b2 (without having yet locked it up with d2-d4) it is more healthy to develop the knight on d2, as is customary in the 'hedgehog' type of positions.

8...♗d6

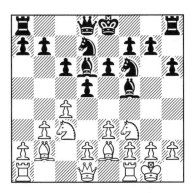

This is the most active place for the bishop.

9 cxd5

This exchange of pawns helps Black.

9...exd5

Better than recapturing with the c-pawn, which would result in a symmetrical pawn structure. Now Black will have additional play along the half-open e-file.

10 d3

Making space for the queen to move out (to d2) and connect the rooks.

10...0-0

Both sides have now completed the opening part of the game by developing all their pieces. At this stage both sides have to look ahead, create their own plans, and try to prevent the opponent's ideas.

11 ♕d2

Here White's best try was the tricky 11 e4, when Black cannot win a pawn with 11...dxe4 12 dxe4 ♘xe4 because White wins a piece with 13 ♘xe4 ♗xe4 and the bishop on d6 is unprotected. However, Black had nothing to fear on simply moving the bishop away after 11 e4.

11...♗h7

Placing the bishop on a protected square, while also avoiding any ideas of a potential e3-e4 advance as mentioned in the previous note.

12 ♖fc1

A strange move! That rook does not belong on c1. 12 ♖fe1, to anticipate actions on the e-file, looks more logical to me.

12...♕e7

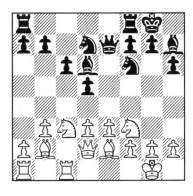

With this move Black keeps the options open for different plans such as:

a) Exchanging dark-squared bishops with ...♗a3.

b) Preparing ...f7-f5-f4 by moving the knight on f6 out of the way.

c) Playing ...♘d7-e5 and, after a trade of knights, to swing the black queen over to the kingside.

13 a3

Ruling out the potential trade with ...♗d6-a3.

13...a5

Preventing any hopes for counterplay with b3-b4-b5. After 13...♘c5 White can hold with 14 ♕d1.

14 ♗d1

White has no real plan and is just making moves to avoid immediate trouble. Meanwhile, Black slowly improves her position.

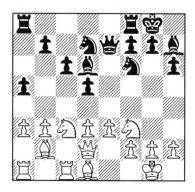

14...♘g4

Another possible move is 14...♘e5, attacking the pawn on d3. If White trades with 15 ♘xe5, then Black would recapture with 15...♕xe5, attacking the h2 pawn.

15 g3

A bad move which unnecessarily weakens the light squares around the white king. 15 ♘e2 would be an improvement.

15...f5

An ambitious move, although the

more peaceful 15...♘de5 may be better. Then Black can try to use the weakness of the light squares by relocating the bishop from h7 to f5 and then to h3.

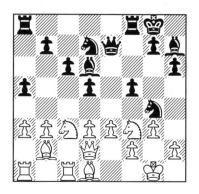

16 ♗e2

Realizing the need to defend the light squares, the bishop runs back towards f1. Sofia energetically stopped this attempt.

16...♘c5

Attacking the b3 pawn.

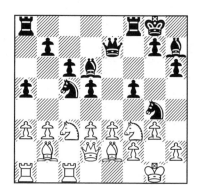

17 ♘d4

If White plays 17 ♕d1, Black can create a very strong attack by the sacrifice 17...♘xe3 18 fxe3 ♕xe3+ and 19 ♔g2 f4.

17...♗e5

Threatening to capture the 'defender' knight on d4, after which the c5 knight can capture the b3 pawn.

18 ♗d1

The white bishop is going back to where it came from, but White had to protect the b3 pawn.

18...♖ae8

Bringing up more reinforcements. The positional alternative 18...♗xd4 19 exd4 ♘e6 also gives Black a clear advantage.

19 ♘a4

White had a difficult position anyway, but it is not wise to provoke Black to attack further.

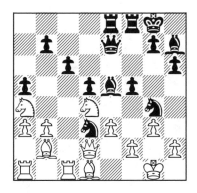

19...♘xd3!

A very nice combination, which is hard to see clearly all the way to the end in all variations.

20 ♕xd3

After 20 ♗xg4 Black can simply recapture with 20...fxg4, because now the knight on d3 is protected. White has no choice but to capture the knight.

20...f4

An attractive discovered attack from the hidden bishop on h7. Black basically sacrificed the knight to break the kingside open and generate a dangerous attack.

21 ♕e2

Black is also winning after 21 ♕d2 ♘xf2! 22 gxf4 (or 22 ♔xf2 fxe3+ 23 ♔xe3 ♗d6+) 22...♘h3+ 23 ♔g2 ♘xf4+ 24 exf4 ♗xf4 25 ♕c3 ♕g5+ 26 ♔h1 ♗xc1.

21...♘xf2!

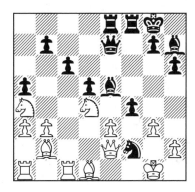

A second knight sacrifice. Now the pawns on e3 and g3 become vulnerable. The problem for White is that his pieces are not properly co-ordinated to fend off the powerful attack.

22 ♕xf2

Here are some sample variations that demonstrate the strength of Black's attack: 22 exf4 (or 22 ♔xf2 fxg3+ 23 ♔g2 ♗e4+) 22...♘h3+ 23 ♔g2 (if 23 ♔h1 ♗e4+ 24 ♘f3 ♗xf3+ 25 ♕xf3 ♗xf4 26 gxf4 ♕e1+ 27 ♔g2 ♘xf4+ wins) 23...♘xf4+ 24 gxf4 ♗e4+ 25 ♘f3 ♖xf4 26 ♕f2 ♕g5+ 27 ♔f1 ♗d3+ 28 ♗e2 ♕g4.

22...fxg3

Another powerful discovery, this time coming from the rook. With a few accurate sacrifices, White's kingside has completely collapsed.

23 ♕g2

Trying to protect the king, but it is too late; the attack is too strong.

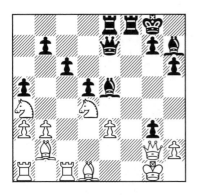

23...gxh2+

Gaining another pawn and a strong one. Now Black's h-pawn is only one move away from the promotion square.

24 ♔h1

The king has no choice but to go in the corner.

24...♗xd4

On the immediate 24...♗e4, White could still block the pin with 25 ♗f3.

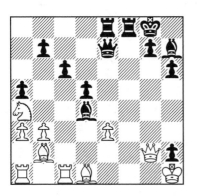

25 ♗c2

To prevent the pin with ...♗h7-e4. White would lose the queen or get checkmated after 25 exd4 ♕e1+ 26 ♔xh2 ♕h4+ 27 ♕h3 ♖f2+ or 25 ♗xd4 ♗e4.

25...♗xc2

After the next few exchanges White

will remain with the problem of an unprotected king. In addition, most of his pieces are out of play.

26 ♖xc2

If White captures the other bishop with 26 ♗xd4, Black again pins the queen with 26...♗e4. The same goes for 26 exd4.

26...♗xb2

Black traded the bishops to avoid any possible counterplay against the g7 square.

27 ♘xb2

The rook recapture would leave the knight on a4 far away from the battle-field on the kingside.

27...♕xe3

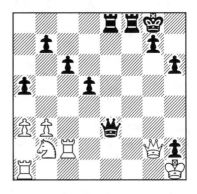

Now Black has five pawns for the knight, while still maintaining a strong attack against the white king.

28 b4

Moving the b-pawn away from the attack. White does not want to capture the h2 pawn as it would only leave the white king more exposed.

28...♖e5

It is time to involve new forces in the attack. The rook can go to f5, g5, or h5 depending on White's play.

29 ♖f1

If 29 bxa5 ♖g5 30 ♕xh2 ♕e4+ 31 ♖g2 then 31...♖f2 wins easily for Black.

29...♖ef5

Forcing White to choose between a trade of rooks or leaving the f-file.

30 ♖xf5

If White plays 30 ♖d1, for example, Black would respond with 30...♖g5 31 ♕xh2 ♖f4 32 ♖e2 ♕f3+ 33 ♖g2 ♖h4.

30...♖xf5

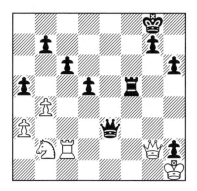

Now White has very serious problems along the first rank.

31 ♖e2

This prevents the check on e1 but allows another one. The white king is now completely vulnerable.

31...♕c1+ White resigned

White cannot avoid losing the queen after 32 ♔xh2 ♖h5+ 33 ♔g3 ♖g5+.

Game 7
□ **Tomaz Marinsek**
■ **Sofia Polgar**
Ljubljana 1994
London System

This game was played at an open tournament in the Slovenian capital.

1 d4

In this game, Sofia proves that she can also play positional, 'slow squeeze' chess, if she wants to. She normally prefers aggressive, attacking chess, though.

1...♘f6

The other very popular move is 1...d5.

2 ♘f3

Avoiding the Benko Gambit, which is very aggressive.

2...c5

This is only a temporary pawn sacrifice. Black has no problem regaining the pawn after 3 dxc5 ♕a5+ or even 3...e6.

3 c3

It is both more ambitious and better to advance the pawn with 3 d5.

3...d5

Now the game has transposed to a queen's pawn opening.

4 ♗f4

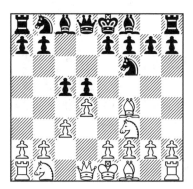

In queen's pawn openings, it is usually best to develop the kingside first. The drawback to White's last move is that it leaves the b2 pawn unprotected.

White could win a pawn by capturing 4 dxc5, but then White lags behind in development and Black gets good compensation after 4...e6 5 b4 a5 6 ♕b3 b6 7 cxb6 ♕xb6.

4...♕b6

Black immediately attacks White's weak point, forcing White to defend. The trade on d4 first (4...cxd4 5 cxd4) and 5...♛b6 is fine too.

In an earlier game, at the 1990 Novi Sad Olympiad, Sofia played 4...♞c6 and won the following nice game against WIM Cathy Forbes: 5 e3 ♛b6 6 ♛b3 c4 7 ♛xb6 axb6 8 ♞a3 ♖a5 9 ♗c7 e6 10 ♗xb6 ♖a6 11 ♗c5 ♗xc5 12 dxc5 ♞e4 13 ♞b5 ♚e7 14 ♞bd4 ♞xc5 15 ♞xc6+ bxc6 16 ♞d4 ♖b6 17 b4 ♞a4 18 ♚d2 e5 19 ♞f3 f6 20 ♗e2 ♗f5 21 ♞h4 ♗e6 22 ♞f3 ♖a8 23 ♖hb1 ♗f5 24 ♖c1 g5 25 h4 g4 26 ♞e1 ♖ba6 27 e4 ♗xe4 28 ♗xg4 ♞b6 29 f3 ♖xa2+ 30 ♖xa2 ♖xa2+ 31 ♚e3 ♗g6 32 h5 d4+ 33 cxd4 ♞d5 mate.

5 ♛c1

This is a mistake, since it is too passive. It was better was to offer an exchange of queens with 5 ♛b3.

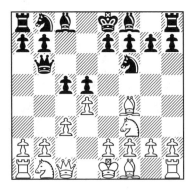

5...♞c6

Black brings the knight out and puts pressure on the d4 pawn at the same time.

6 e3

Protecting the pawn on d4 and opening the road for the bishop on f1.

6...g6

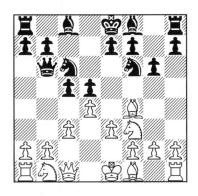

It is a matter of taste. Black could also have developed the light-squared bishop to f5 and then played ...e7-e6. Another tempting option is to go after White's bishop with 6...♞h5 7 ♗g5 h6 8 ♗h4 g5.

7 h3

White makes a hiding place for the bishop on h2, not giving Black another opportunity to catch it with ...♞h5.

7...♗g7

Black resumes developing, clearing space to castle. It is a good practice to get your king safe as soon as possible.

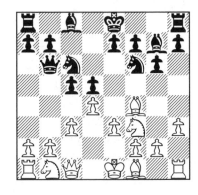

8 ♞bd2

If White tries to prevent ...♗f5 with 8 ♗d3, Black would answer with 8...♞e4.

8...0-0

Following the principle: king safety first!

9 ♗e2

9 ♗d3 would have been more active. Then Black's plan would be to break with ...e7-e5, following some preparation such as 9...♘d7.

9...♗f5

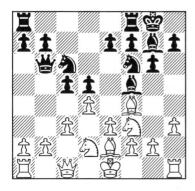

Black has developed all the pieces and has a little space advantage. The black pieces are also more actively located compared to their counterparts; the difference between the two queens is especially visible.

9...♖d8? would be a mistake due to a known trap. White wins material with 10 dxc5 ♕xc5 11 ♗c7! attacking the black rook and also taking away the black queen's last escape square (b6). After any rook move 12 ♘b3 traps the queen.

10 0-0

Now the same trick does not do anything, as after 10 dxc5 ♕xc5 11 ♗c7 there is only one threat (trapping the queen with 12 ♘b3), and Black has time to clear an escape square for on e7 with 11...e6.

10...♖ac8

This is certainly a natural move, considering the white queen's position. Although perhaps 10...♘d7 was more accurate, to prepare ...e7-e5 and prevent 11 ♘e5.

11 ♘e5

White is tries to trade a pair of knights. Piece exchanges usually benefit the side in a more passive position.

11...♘d7

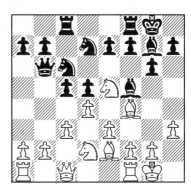

Forcing White to make a decision whether to trade, bring more reinforcements, or retreat. Black wants the e5 square.

11...cxd4 would be another interesting idea, when White cannot recapture on d4, because Black then wins a pawn by 12 exd4 ♘xd4 as the rook on c8 is getting into action. White can avoid losing a pawn with 12 ♘xc6 bxc6 13 exd4, although I like Black's position anyway after 13...c5 14 dxc5 ♕xc5.

12 ♘xc6

White could not keep a knight on e5, because after 12 ♘df3 ♘dxe5 13 ♘xe5 Black wins a pawn with 13...cxd4 14 ♘xc6 ♖xc6 15 exd4 ♗xd4, utilizing the pin again. 13 dxe5 ♗e4 would leave the pawn on e5 very weak as well.

12...♕xc6

Getting out of the way of the b7 pawn.

13 ♘f3

Here Black has two clear plans: to break with ...e7-e5 (prepared by ...f7-f6) or else ...b7-b5-b4. In the game Black accomplished both.

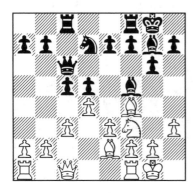

13...b5

Black is gaining more and more space advantage.

14 ♕d2

After 14 dxc5 Black would first attack the bishop on f4 with 14...e5, preventing 15 ♘d4, and then recapture the pawn on c5.

14...c4

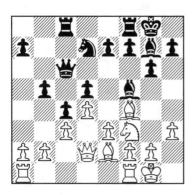

Now the game is at a critical moment. Black is better because she has

full control over whether, when, and where to open the position.

15 ♗h2

If 15 ♘h4 ♗e6 and then ...f7-f6, ...♗f7 and ...e7-e5 would be the plan.

15...f6

This takes full control of the central e5 square. It also prepares the pawn advance ...e7-e5 with the plan, after d4xe5, of recapturing with the pawn.

16 ♖ad1

A preventative move. If Black now insists on 16...e5 then, after 17 dxe5, White wins the d5 pawn.

16...♘b6

Protecting the d5 pawn and eyeing the a4 square which, as we shall see at the very end, will decide the game. 16...g5 is something else to consider, preventing the ♘f3-h4 and f2-f4 plan.

17 ♖c1

Probably White was toying with idea of b2-b3, and so the rook moved over to protect the c3 pawn. That would only help Black's cause, however.

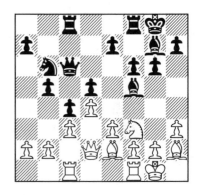

17...♖fe8

The knight went from d7 to b6 to support the d5 pawn. Now the rook takes over that duty to prepare the ...e7-e5 push.

17...♖ce8 may have been a little more accurate, and then if 18 ♘h4 ♗d7 19 f4 Black can play 19...♘c8, jumping towards the weakened e4 square via d6. (With the other rook on e8, the c8 square is not available for the knight.) Then 20 f5 g5 21 ♘f3 ♗xf5 and now 22 ♘xg5 is suicidal, because after 22...fxg5 the bishop on f5 is protected.

18 ♘h4

After 18 b3 Black would continue with 18...e5. The direct 18...cxb3 19 axb3 a5 would allow White to get out of trouble with 20 c4 bxc4 21 ♕xa5.

18...♗d7

Retreating from the knight's attack.

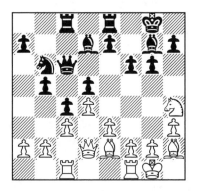

19 f4

Trying to stop Black from playing ...e7-e5.

19...a5

Black has time to prepare everything and only break in the center when the right time comes. After 19...e5, White would simplify the position with 20 fxe5 fxe5 21 dxe5 ♗xe5 22 ♗xe5 ♖xe5 followed by 23 ♘f3, when his position has improved significantly. All of a sudden White has an active game, and the knight will have an awesome outpost on d4.

20 g4

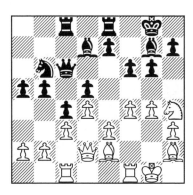

A serious strategic mistake. White would have been better off delaying the ...e7-e5 advance as long as possible with 20 ♘f3.

Instead, after 20 f5 g5 21 ♘f3 ♗xf5 22 ♘xg5 Black maintains some advantage with 22...♕d7 23 ♘f3 ♗e4 and then ...♔h8 and ...♖g8, combining play along the g-file and in the center.

20...e5

The difference between playing ...e7-e5 now and on the previous move is that, if White opens up the position in a similar manner as above, the white king no longer has any pawn protection.

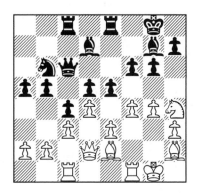

21 ♗f3

By putting pressure on the d5 pawn,

White is provoking the ...e5-e4 push, perhaps hoping to completely block up the position.

21...e4

After locking up the position in the center, Black's focus will shift entirely to the queenside.

22 ♗d1

It is better to keep the bishop on the queenside, as that is where the action will take place.

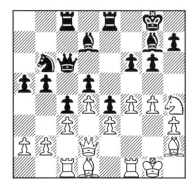

22...♗f8

Black is preparing ...b5-b4, the final step to breaking through on the queenside.

23 a3

White is trying to prevent b5-b4. A favorable inclusion would have been to at least open up the b8-h2 diagonal for the bishop with 23 f5.

23...b4

Anyway! Now White can win a pawn, but only temporarily.

24 axb4

It was better to keep the a-file closed with 24 ♖a1 and allow Black to open the b-file instead.

24...axb4

Recapturing the pawn.

25 ♖a1

After 25 cxb4 Black wins back the pawn quickly with 25...♕b5, and then the b2 pawn will be the next target.

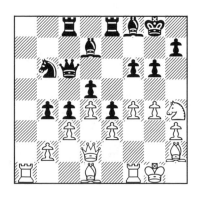

25...♖a8

Balancing out the control of the a-file.

26 ♗c2

26 ♗e2 would have been better.

26...♕b5

26...b3 is a good move as well.

27 ♖fb1

In anticipation of b4xc3, White wants to control the b-file.

27...b3

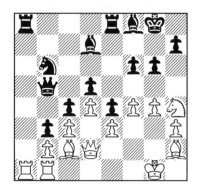

This locks up most of the board, but that one open a-file decides everything. Black is not giving White any opportunity for counterplay.

28 ♗d1

No choice.

28...♖a4

Preparing to double the rooks.

29 ♘g2

A waiting move; there is nothing much White can do.

29...♖ea8

Putting more pressure on the rook on a1.

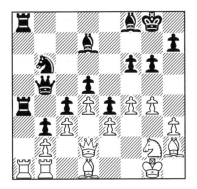

30 ♕c1

Here is a sample variation of what could happen if White exchanges rooks: 30 ♖xa4 ♖xa4 31 ♗g3 ♖a2 32 ♕c1 ♘a4 33 ♘e1 and now 33...♘xb2! 34 ♖xb2 ♗a3.

30...♖xa1

Black forces the trade of all the rooks.

31 ♖xa1

White has no choice but to go along.

31...♖xa1

The rook exchanges are good for Black, since the b2 pawn will be an indefensible target.

32 ♕xa1

It seems that White is OK, but it is not true. White is lost.

32...♕a4 White resigned

This innocent-looking move ended

the game. White cannot hold on to the b2 pawn much longer, and once the b2 pawn is lost, Black's b3 pawn will promote. For example, if 33 ♕xa4 ♘xa4 or 33 ♕c1 ♕a2 followed by ...♘b6-a4 or ...♗f8-a3 decides the game.

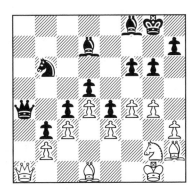

Game 8

□ **Sofia Polgar**

■ **Anda Safranska**

Ljubljana 1994

Pirc Defense

---

1 e4

This game is from the same tournament as Game 7. Sofia's opponent is a Latvian Woman Grandmaster.

1...d6

Black uses the same opening as Van Wely (see Game 3).

2 d4

Whenever you have the chance, it is a good idea to occupy the center with both e- and d- pawns.

2...♘f6

Black develops and attacks the pawn on e4.

3 ♘c3

White also develops the knight while protecting the pawn. It is always ideal when can you combine defending and, at the same time, continue with your own plan.

3...g6

Black wants to develop the bishop on the long diagonal.

4 f4

This is the Austrian Attack, which is considered the most aggressive system against this opening.

4...♗g7

After Black's last move, this is an obvious follow-up.

5 ♘f3

A normal developing move; the knight helps reinforce the d4 pawn and attacks the e5 square.

5...0-0

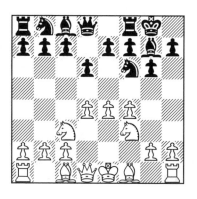

This is the main line in theory. In the earlier game Van Wely played 5...c5.

6 ♗d3

White continues development while keeping in mind to control the center with every single move. 6 ♗e3 is also interesting, as Judit played against Smirin at the 2000 Istanbul Olympiad (see Judit's Game 8).

6...c6

6...♘c6 is a more critical move, as Ftacnik played against Judit at the

World Championship Zonal tournament in 1993. That game continued 7 0-0 e5 8 fxe5 dxe5 9 d5 ♘d4 10 ♘xe5 ♘xe4 11 ♗xe4 ♗xe5 12 ♗f4 ♗xf4 13 ♖xf4 ♘f5 14 ♗xf5 ♗xf5 15 ♕d4 ♗xc2 16 ♖e1 f5 17 ♕c4 ♔h8 18 ♖c1 ♗e4 19 ♘xe4 fxe4 20 ♕d4+ ♔g8 21 ♖xf8+ ♕xf8 22 ♖xc7 e3 23 ♕xe3 ♖e8 24 ♕f2 ♕xf2+ 25 ♔xf2 ♖d8 26 ♖xb7 ♖xd5 27 ♔e3 and White won the endgame.

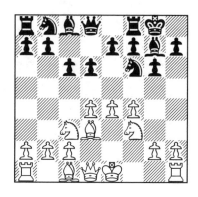

7 0-0

White has a pretty simple plan: get the queen to h4, play f4-f5, followed by ♗h6, and go for the black king.

7...♘a6

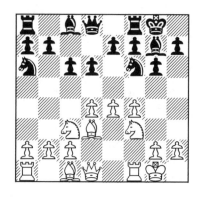

In general, it is not a good idea to develop a knight to the edge of the board. But here it is only for a short

time, as the knight is on its way to c7. The advantage of this maneuver, compared with developing the knight to d7, is that it does not block the diagonal of the bishop on c8.

8 a3

Had White continued with her plan of 8 ♕e1, Black could play 8...♘b4 and then trade the knight for the bishop on d3. The bishop could not run away because it needs to defend the pawn on c2.

8...b6

Preparing to develop the bishop to b7.

9 ♕e1

White proceeds with her plan.

9...♗b7

In a later game, Safranska tried the superior 9...♘c7.

10 f5

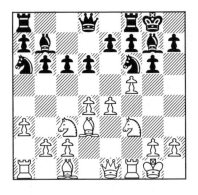

Opening up the diagonal for the bishop on c1. 10 e5 also looks tempting.

10...c5

Black tries to follow the advice: when the opponent attacks on the flank, counter-attack in the center.

11 fxg6

This exchange of pawns weakens the black king's safety.

11...hxg6

After 11...fxg6 12 ♗c4+ ♔h8 13 ♘g5 Black has trouble along the a2-g8 diagonal.

12 d5

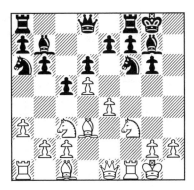

White correctly closes the center to limit Black's counter-chances. In addition, this pawn push limits the mobility of Black's bishop on b7.

12...♘c7

It is time bring the knight back towards the middle of the board.

13 ♕h4

Finally, the queen has made it to h4. Now Black has to be very careful. There is a threat of 14 ♘g5, followed by a 15 ♖xf6 sacrifice, in the air.

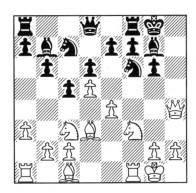

13...♕d7

Black is hoping to trade queens with ...♕g4.

14 h3

An important element in chess to remember: prevent the opponent's plans.

14...♘h7

Defending against 15 ♘g5.

15 ♗h6

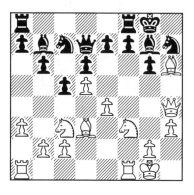

White wants to exchange Black's key defending piece, the bishop on g7.

15...e6

Again Black is looking for some activity, by opening up the e-file and the long diagonal for the bishop on b7.

16 dxe6

White would also stand better after 16 ♖ad1 exd5 17 ♘xd5 ♘xd5 18 ♗xg7 ♔xg7 19 exd5 ♗xd5 20 ♗xg6 fxg6 21 ♖xd5. But Sofia's move was stronger.

16...♕xe6

After 16...♘xe6 White would continue similarly to the game, while if 16...fxe6 then the g6 pawn is weak.

17 ♗xg7

It is best to take on g7 now, before Black has the chance to get away with ...♗g7-f6.

17...♔xg7

Black does not need to worry about

18 ♕xh7+ ♔xh7 19 ♘g5+ as it would result only an equal trade.

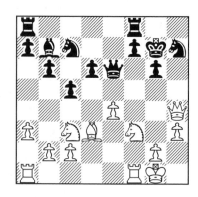

18 ♖ae1

White gets the last major piece involved, and prepares e4-e5.

18...♖ae8

Centralizing the rook to give some more support to the e-file.

19 ♕g3

19 e5 would be premature because of 19...♗xf3, when the pawn on e5 would fall.

19...♔h8

If Black plays 19...f6 to prevent e4-e5, White would respond 20 ♘h4 ♘g5 21 ♘xg6! ♔xg6 22 e5+ ♔h6 23 ♕h4+ ♔g7 24 exf6+ and wins.

20 e5

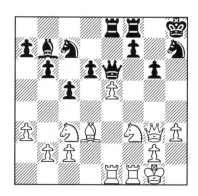

A strong move, exploiting the unfortunate position of the black queen.

20...d5

After 20...♗xf3 21 exd6 ♕d7 22 dxc7 White wins an important pawn, while if 20...dxe5 21 ♘xe5 and Black cannot defend against 22 ♘xg6+ or 22 ♘xf7+.

21 ♘g5

Having exchanged Black's defending, dark-squared bishop, White now wants to exchange the knight on h7 as well, which would leave the black king defenseless.

21...♕e7

After 21...♘xg5 22 ♕xg5 ♕e7 23 ♕h6+ ♔g8, White just brings the rook along the fourth rank to the h-file with 24 ♖f4 and ♖h4.

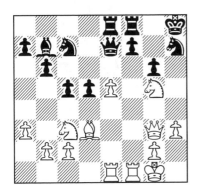

22 ♘xh7

This trade is necessary, to make the f6 square available for the white rook.

22...♔xh7

The black king is in a very vulnerable position now and in big trouble.

23 ♖f6

A very strong move, putting more pressure on the g6 pawn.

23...♘e6

If Black protects the g6 pawn with

23...♖g8, White wins quickly by 24 ♖ef1 ♖g7 25 ♖xf7! ♖xf7 26 ♕xg6+ ♔h8 27 ♖xf7.

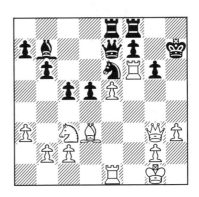

24 ♗xg6+!

And now... action time! This sacrifice destroys all the remaining defenses around the black king.

24...fxg6

Black has no choice. Declining the sacrifice would be even worse.

25 ♕xg6+

White has only two pawns for the bishop, but her attack is much stronger. It is lethal.

25...♔h8

The only move.

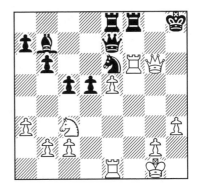

26 ♕h5+

The most accurate continuation. After 26 ♕h6+ ♕h7 27 ♖xe6 White only wins a knight.

26...♔g8

On 26...♕h7, White pins the queen with 27 ♖h6.

27 ♖h6 Black resigned

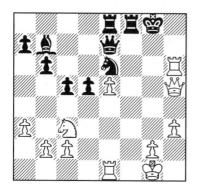

If 27...♖f7 28 ♖h8+ ♔g7 29 ♕h7 mate, or 27...♕g7 28 ♖g6 and Black loses the queen.

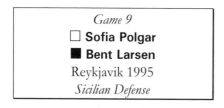

> *Game 9*
> □ **Sofia Polgar**
> ■ **Bent Larsen**
> Reykjavik 1995
> *Sicilian Defense*

In this game, Sofia's opponent is the world-famous Danish grandmaster. At one point, around 1970, he and Bobby Fischer were the two top non-Soviet players in the world.

1 e4

The typical opening choice for Sofia.

1...c5

Grandmaster Larsen is known for his dynamic play. Therefore, the Sicilian suits his style fine.

2 ♘f3

After 2 d4 cxd4 3 ♘f3, in addition to continuing as normal with 3...♘c6,

3...d6 or 3...e6, Black also can protect the pawn with 3...e5!, because after the capture with 4 ♘xe5 White loses the knight to 4...♕a5+.

2...d6

With this move Black is usually hinting that either the Dragon or Najdorf variation will follow.

3 d4

This is the 'Open Sicilian'. White can also choose to avoid the main theoretical debates with 3 c3 or 3 ♗b5+.

3...♘f6

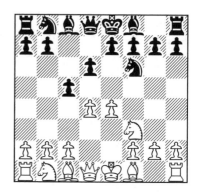

A rare, but perfectly playable move order. Black is trying to throw White off.

4 ♘c3

White cannot take advantage of Black's deviation from the standard 3...cxd4. If White plays 4 dxc5 Black can choose between 4...♕a5+ and 4...♘xe4 5 cxd6 ♘c6. White cannot keep the extra pawn with 6 dxe7 because of 7...♕xd1+ 7 ♔xd1 ♘xf2+.

4...cxd4

Now the game transposes back to the normal lines.

5 ♘xd4

Of course, it would be a mistake to recapture with 5 ♕xd4 (don't bring your queen out early in the game!), because it could be attacked right away with 5...♞c6.

5...♞bd7

This is an unusual move. In most games Black chooses from the following four options: 5...a6, 5...g6, 5...e6 and 5...♞c6.

6 f4

White could also have developed either bishop (to c4 or e2, e3 or g5).

6...a6

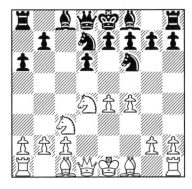

Now we are back to a sideline of the Najdorf .

7 ♞f3

Preparing a possible advance with e4-e5.

7...♛c7

This move prevents the above idea.

8 a4

When Black played 6...a6, he had ...b7-b5 in mind. White's last move aims to stop that, making it a little harder for Black to develop the bishop on c8, since the b-pawn would not stand as well on b6 as on b5.

8...g6

Developing in 'Dragon style' (similar to the Dragon variation).

9 ♝d3

Developing and preparing to castle.

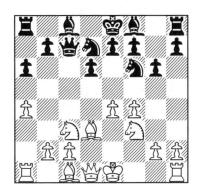

9...♝g7

The black bishop is developed in 'fianchetto' and Black is now only one move from castling.

10 0-0

Before starting an attack, the king should be put in safety.

10...0-0

So far all the pieces have developed except for two bishops, White's on c1 and Black's on c8. Strangely enough, in some openings these bishops sometimes have difficulty finding better squares than their initial positions.

11 ♛e1

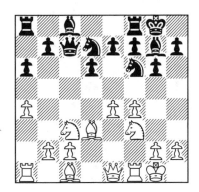

Starting an attack on the kingside by moving the strongest attacking piece closer to the enemy king. The plan is to bring the queen to h4.

11...e6

Judit won a nice game in a computer match vs. 'Junior' (Budapest 1996), when her silicon opponent played 11...♘c5 12 ♕h4 ♘xd3 13 cxd3 ♗e6? 14 ♔h1 ♖ac8 15 f5! gxf5 16 ♗h6 ♗xh6 17 ♕xh6 ♕b6 18 ♖ab1 ♕b4 19 ♘g5 ♖c5 20 ♘e2 ♗d7 21 ♘g3 and Black resigned, due to the deadly threat of 22 ♘h5.

12 ♔h1

In the following year, against the computer program 'Nightmare' at the famous Hague Human versus Computers event, Sofia played the 12th move differently, also with success: 12 f5 gxf5 (it is probably better to ignore White's last move with 12...b6 13 ♕h4 ♗b7) 13 ♔h1 fxe4 14 ♘xe4 ♘xe4 15 ♕xe4 ♘f6 16 ♕h4 d5 17 ♗h6 ♗xh6 18 ♕xh6 ♘e4 19 ♗xe4 dxe4 20 ♕g5+ ♔h8 21 ♕f6+ ♔g8 22 ♘g5 e5 23 ♖a3 e3 24 ♖xe3 Black resigned.

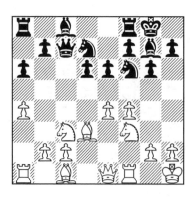

12...♘c5

Black is better off leaving the knight closer to the kingside for defense. At the Sicilian theme tournament in Buenos Aires 1994, Judit played more

strongly against Anand with 12...b6 13 ♕h4 ♗b7 14 f5 ♖ae8.

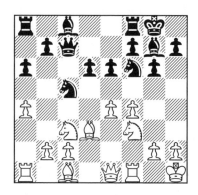

13 ♕h4

The queen has reached its ideal attacking position.

13...b6

Preparing to develop the bishop to b7, but as we shall see, the bishop never makes it there.

14 f5!

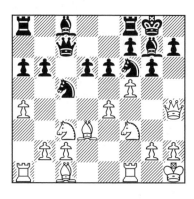

This is a short-term pawn sacrifice to open the files and diagonals against the black king.

14...exf5

Black would face serious trouble after 14...gxf5 15 exf5 e5 16 ♗g5.

15 exf5

Now White threatens 16 ♗g5 and,

when the black knight leaves f6, to push the f-pawn forwards to that square.

15...♘xd3

White also has a very nice position after 15...♗xf5 16 ♗xf5 gxf5, and now either 17 ♘d4 or 17 ♗h6.

16 cxd3

If White tries the tricky 16 fxg6, Black would answer with 16...fxg6, but not the greedy 16...♘xc1? 17 ♘d5! ♘xd5 18 ♕xh7 mate.

16...♗xf5

Black has just won a pawn, but he cannot keep it for too long.

17 ♘d4

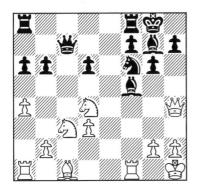

An essential follow-up to White's previous moves.

17...♕c5

If Black grabs another pawn with 17...♗xd3, White gets two pieces for the rook after 18 ♖xf6 ♗xf6 19 ♕xf6, and has a strong attack because of the weakness of the dark squares around the black king.

18 ♘xf5

This destroys the black pawn defense in front of the king.

18...gxf5

White has managed to open the g-file towards the black king.

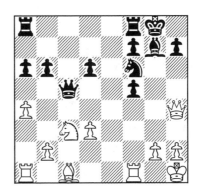

19 d4

Chasing the black queen away from protecting the f5 pawn.

19...♕c4

If Black tried to hang on to the f5 pawn with 19...♕a5, the queen would be too far from the black king's defense. White would continue 20 ♗h6 with a very strong attack.

20 ♖xf5

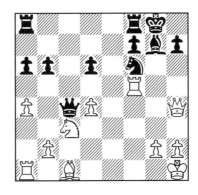

White wins the pawn back while maintaining a strong attack.

20...♘e8

The attack is also very strong after 20...♕e6 21 ♖g5.

21 ♘d5!

Bringing another piece closer to the battlefield.

21...♖a7

If Black captures the pawn with 21...♛xd4?, White wins beautifully with 22 ♘e7+ ♚h8 and 23 ♛xh7+!! ♚xh7 24 ♖h5+ ♗h6 25 ♖xh6+ ♚g7 26 ♘f5+.

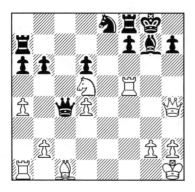

22 ♗e3

Finally, the last piece is developed. It is important to clear the first rank so the rook on a1 can also participate in the game. For example, after the direct 22 ♘e7+ ♚h8 23 ♖h5, all of a sudden Black would checkmate with 23...♛f1.

22...f6

Cutting off the queen to prevent ♘e7+. But Black is simply in a hopeless situation, as all of White's pieces cooperating in the attack against the king.

23 ♛e4!

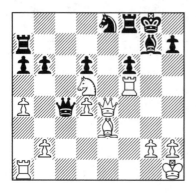

Again White is intending 24 ♘e7+.

23...♖af7

This helps Black lose even faster.

24 ♘e7+

White's attack is decisive.

24...♚h8

Now Black cannot avoid losing material.

25 ♖h5 Black resigned

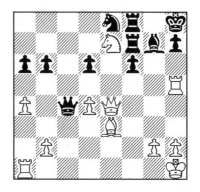

If Black responds with 25...f5, White now has mate in three by 26 ♖xh7+! ♚xh7 27 ♛h4+ ♗h6 28 ♛xh6 mate.

Game 10
□ **Sofia Polgar**
■ **Hans Bouwmeester**
Munich 2000
Ruy Lopez

---

1 e4

This game was played at another edition of the Veterans vs. Ladies tournament, sponsored by one of the greatest chess sponsors ever, Mr. Van Oosterom. These special yearly tournaments were each named after the national dance of the host country. This one in Germany was called the Schuhplattler Tournament.

1...e5

Sofia's Dutch opponent is one of the few strong chess players who also has great talent in music. I remember several occasions when, at the opening or closing ceremonies of different chess tournaments, the legendary Hungarian grandmaster, Lajos Portisch, sang operatic works, while Mr. Bouwmeester accompanied him on the piano. Together, they performed a mini-concert.

2 ♘f3

In their earlier years my sisters used to like to play the King's Gambit (2 f4) a lot. But they changed once they got older.

2...♘c6

2...♘f6, the Petroff Defense, is another quite popular choice.

3 ♗b5

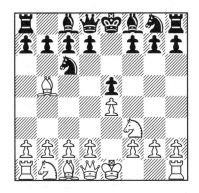

This is one of the oldest and most popular openings. It is called the Spanish Game or the Ruy Lopez, after a 16th century Spanish priest who wrote about it in his famous book of 1561.

3...♘f6

The most common move is 3...a6. Then White cannot win a pawn by 4 ♗xc6 dxc6 5 ♘xe5, because Black regains it immediately with 5...♕d4.

4 0-0

White could have protected the pawn on e4, but it was not necessary. There would have been no problem getting the pawn back with initiative.

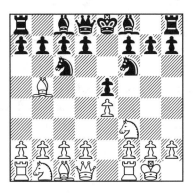

4...d6

If Black captures the pawn on e4, he stays behind in development, White can answer with either 5 d4 or 5 ♖e1, and Black will have to return the pawn soon.

5 d4

White is correctly fighting for the center straight away, while also threatening to exploit the pin with 6 d5 or to capture on e5.

5...♗d7

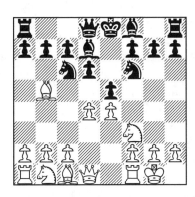

Releasing the knight from the pin. This variation (as Black) was a favorite of a great former world champion, Emanuel Lasker.

6 ♖e1

Protecting the e4 pawn. White could not win a pawn by 6 ♗xc6 ♗xc6 7 dxe5 dxe5 8 ♘xe5 because, after trading queens, the black bishop could capture on e4.

6...♗e7

On 6...exd4 7 ♘xd4 ♘xd4, White would have the intermediate 8 ♗xd7+ ♕xd7, and then 9 ♕xd4 keeps the material balance.

7 ♘c3

White continues to develop.

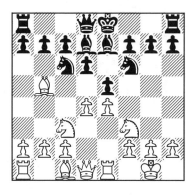

7...exd4

Black can no longer delay the capture on d4, since if 7...0-0, White wins a pawn with 8 ♗xc6 ♗xc6 9 dxe5 dxe5 10 ♕xd8 ♖axd8 11 ♘xe5. Now if Black attempts to exploit White's back rank problem with 11...♗xe4 12 ♘xe4 ♘xe4, White emerges with material gain after 13 ♘d3 f5 14 f3 ♗c5+ 15 ♘xc5 ♘xc5 16 ♗g5 ♖d5 17 ♗e7 ♖e8 18 c4. Or if Black recaptures with other rook, 10...♖fxd8, then 11 ♘xe5 ♗xe4 12 ♘xe4 ♘xe4 13 ♘d3 f5 14 f3 ♗c5+ 15 ♔f1.

8 ♘xd4

Playing 8 ♗xc6 first would give Black the possibility of 8...dxc3.

8...0-0

After 8...♘xd4 9 ♕xd4 ♗xb5 10 ♘xb5 0-0 11 ♗g5, the advantage in space means that White is slightly better.

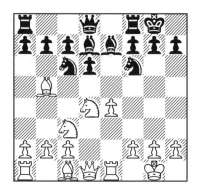

9 ♗xc6

This is one of those exceptions when it is more favorable to trade a bishop for a knight, and keep the knight (at d4) on the board.

9...bxc6

After 9...♗xc6 White continues with 10 ♘f5 ♕d7 11 ♘xe7+ ♕xe7 12 ♗g5 with a better position.

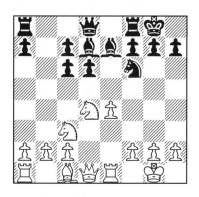

10 ♗f4

White is preparing for a potential

bishop recapture on e5 after e4-e5, ...d6xe5. Had White played 10 b3 instead, Black would have some interesting dynamic opportunities with 10...d5 11 e5 ♗b4.

10...♖b8

Occupying the half-open b-file while attacking the pawn on b2.

11 b3

White puts the pawn on a safer square. After 11 e5 dxe5 12 ♗xe5 Black could not capture the pawn with 12...♖xb2, because the rook would be imprisoned by 13 ♘b3, but Black would be OK after 12...♗d6.

11...c5

Now a similar idea as above would not work. If Black plays 11...d5 here, White would respond with 12 e5 ♗b4 13 exf6 ♗xc3 14 fxg7 ♔xg7 and now 15 ♗e5+ f6 16 ♘xc6.

12 ♘f3

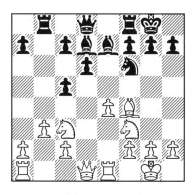

White has a space advantage and the better pawn structure, while Black has a pair of bishops as compensation. Overall, I think White has a more comfortable position.

If White plays 12 ♘f5 instead, Black equalizes with 12...♗xf5 13 exf5 d5.

12...♗e6

Trying to prepare ...c5-c4 to eliminate the doubled c-pawns.

13 ♕d3

Trying to stop the c5 pawn from advancing. After 13 e5 Black would answer with 13...♘h5 14 ♗d2 d5 and if 15 h3, threatening to trap the knight with g2-g4, then 15...g6 clears the g7 square.

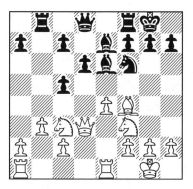

13...♘d7

The black knight is going to b6 to prepare the pawn pushes with ...a7-a5-a4 as well as ...c5-c4. However, this plan seems to be a little too slow.

14 ♘d1

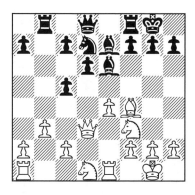

An unusual plan, which really reflects Sofia's way of thinking: attack, attack, attack! The knight is heading towards f5 via e3. 14 ♘d5 or 14 ♖ad1

would have been more natural and probably better moves.

14...a5

A mistake. Black should have played more actively with 14...♗f6, followed by 15 c3 c4 16 bxc4 ♘c5.

15 ♘e3

A good versatile post for the knight, controlling three important squares, c4, d5 and f5, all at once.

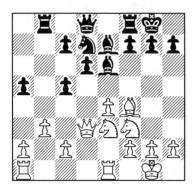

15...♘b6

15...a4 was possible straight away. White would just ignore it and not take the pawn.

16 ♖ad1

White centralizes the last piece.

16...a4

Black follows up his plan which he started on move thirteen.

17 e5

This idea worked out well in this game. Objectively speaking, though, it was not necessarily the best move.

17...d5

This change in the pawn structure helps Black.

18 ♘f5

Creating a strategic threat of 18 ♘xe7+ ♕xe7, followed by 19 ♘g5, forcing the weakening of the dark

squares around the black king with ...g7-g6.

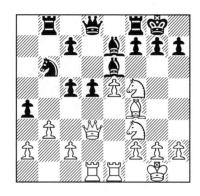

18...c4

This move is the cause of most of Black's forthcoming troubles. 18...h6 was safer.

19 bxc4

More precise than 19 ♘xe7+ ♕xe7 20 bxc4 dxc4.

19...♘xc4

White is also better after 19...♗xf5 20 ♕xf5 ♘xc4 21 e6 or 19...dxc4 20 ♕e4.

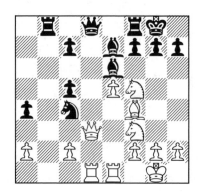

20 ♘xe7+

White now gets a very dangerous attack.

20...♕xe7

At first it seems as if Black is out of

trouble, but after White's next move, new problems arrive.

21 ♘g5!

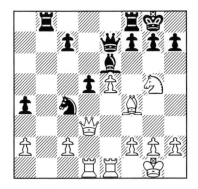

Threatening ♕xh7 mate.

21...g6

Forced, because after 21...f5 White could capture en passant.

22 ♕g3

Preparing the sacrifice we shall see later (at move 25).

22...♘b2

After 22...♖b2, White wins similarly as in the game with 23 ♘xh7! ♔xh7 24 ♗g5 f6 25 exf6 ♕f7 26 ♗h6! ♖fb8 27 ♗g7 ♔g8 28 ♕h4 ♕d7 29 ♕h8+ ♔f7 30 ♕h7.

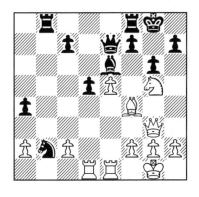

23 ♖d2

The immediate sacrifice with 23

♘xh7 does not work, because of 23...♔xh7 24 ♗g5 ♕b4 and the queen covers the h4 square.

23...c6

Advancing with 23...h5 would have been a better defense, avoiding the ♘xh7 idea.

24 c3

A tricky move to take control of the crucial b4 square.

24...♖b7

This loses. It was Black's last chance to play 24...h5.

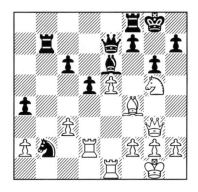

25 ♘xh7!

Now this combination works very well.

25...♔xh7

Black has to accept the 'gift' as after 25...♖fb8, for example, the game is decided quickly with 26 ♘f6+ ♔g7 27 ♗h6+! ♔xh6 28 ♕h4+ ♔g7 29 ♕h7+ ♔f8 30 ♕h8 mate.

26 ♗g5

Now Black has serious problems on the dark squares.

26...f6

There is no choice! Otherwise, if 26...♕d7 27 ♕h4+ ♔g8 28 ♗f6, Black is powerless to stop the coming checkmate.

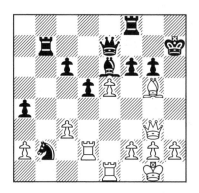

27 exf6!

This is much better than 27 ♗xf6 ♖xf6 28 exf6 ♕xf6.

27...♕f7

After 27...♕d7 28 ♖de2 or 27...♖xf6 28 ♖de2 ♘c4 29 h3, taking care of the back rank problem, Black is lost because he is in too many pins.

28 ♖de2

Black cannot keep the white rooks from ruling the e-file.

28...♘c4

The key variations are 28...♖e8 29 ♖xe6 ♖xe6 30 ♕h3+ ♔g8 31 ♕xe6 and 28...♗f5 29 ♖e7.

29 ♗h6!

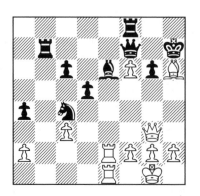

The point of White's combination! She still had to be careful, as 29 ♖xe6?

would lose to 29...♕xe6!.

29...♖fb8

If Black plays 29...♔xh6 then 30 ♕h4 is mate.

30 ♗g7

By reopening the h-file, White threatens mate in two.

30...♔g8

The king runs away, trying to avoid mate.

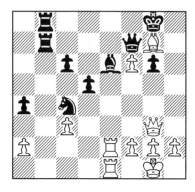

31 ♕h4

White continues to chase the king; the threat is ♕h8 mate.

31...♕d7

Clearing the f7 square for the king to escape.

32 ♕h8+

The most forceful way to win the game.

32...♔f7

It looks like Black has almost survived, and even attacks the white queen right now.

33 ♕h7

Threatening a discovered check. The alternative 33 ♗f8 ♖xf8 34 ♕g7+ ♔e8 35 ♖xe6+ would have won as well.

33...♖b1

Pinning the white rook on e1, trying to minimize White's attack on the e-file.

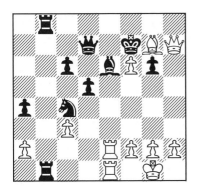

34 ♖xe6

Finally it is time to capture the bishop and end the game.

34...♛xe6

This recapture is possible because of the pin on the e1 rook.

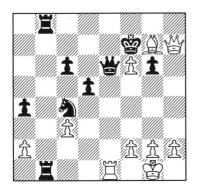

35 ♗h8+!

A pretty move! The bishop goes into the corner and it is a winning move!

35...♚e8

If Black plays 35...♚f8, White mates in four starting with 36 ♛g7+ ♚e8 37 f7+.

36 ♛g8+ Black resigned

Black cannot capture the queen because his own queen is pinned. After the only move, 36...♚d7, White plays 37 ♛xe6+ and Black is completely lost.

Combinations

This is the ending of one of Sofia's victories from the National Scholastic Championship, which she won aged 5.

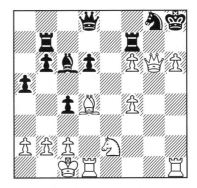

White to play and mate in two!

1 ♛g7+! ♖xg7 2 hxg7 mate

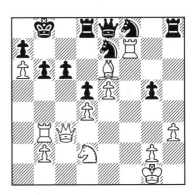

White has an overwhelming attack. Now it is time for action!

1 ♖xb6 + ! axb6 2 ♕b4 Black resigned

Black cannot defend against both 3 ♕xb6+ and 3 ♖xe7.

> *Combination 3*
> □ **Stefan Stefanov**
> ■ **Sofia Polgar**
> Teteven 1984

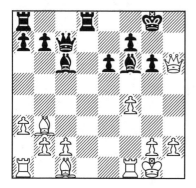

Black exploits White's back rank problem to create a winning attack.

19...♕b6+ 20 ♔h1 ♕f2!

A nice deflection move! The queen cannot be captured because of 21 ♖xf2 ♖d1+ and mate on the following move.

21 ♖g1 ♖d1! White resigned

If 22 ♖xd1 ♕xg2 mate.

> *Combination 4*
> □ **Sofia Polgar**
> ■ **Elliott Winslow**
> New York Open 1987

This game was played at the famous New York Open, which was always one of our favorites events. At that time it was the strongest Open tournament in the world.

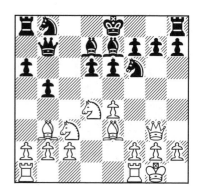

12 ♘f5!

Good timing for this typical Sicilian sacrifice. Black is punished for not castling soon enough.

12...exf5 13 ♕xg7 ♖f8 14 ♗g5 ♘xe4 15 ♗xe7 ♔xe7

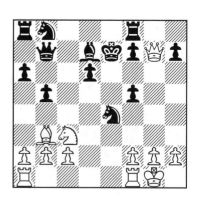

The king is stuck in the middle.

16 ♘d5+ ♔e8 17 ♖ae1 ♘c6 18 ♘f6+ ♔e7 19 ♕g5 ♗e6 20 ♘xe4+ f6 21 ♘xf6 Black resigned

> *Combination 5*
> ◪ **Sofia Polgar**
> ■ **Ulrich Dresen**
> Biel 1987

This game was played at the famous Biel Chess Festival in Switzerland.

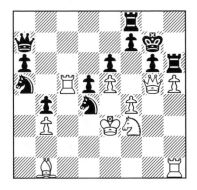

White seems to be in a critical position with the king out on e3 and the rook on c5 under attack. But there is a brilliant, forced combination leading to a winning position for White.

1 ♕xh6+! ♚xh6 2 hxg6+

A discovered check.

2...♚g7 3 ♖h7+ ♚g8 4 gxf7+ Black resigned

4...♖xf7 5 ♖c8+ and the queen is lost.

> *Combination 6*
> □ **Gudmundur Gislason**
> ■ **Sofia Polgar**
> Reykjavik 1988

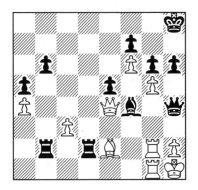

This and the following combination were played at the same tournament in Reykjavik, Iceland, where chess is extremely popular. Even today, people still remember the famous Fischer-Spassky match in 1972. We visited the Icelandic Chess Federation's headquarters, where they keep and treasure the chess board, pieces, table, chairs, and a lot more that was connected with the legendary match of the 20th century.

35...♖xe2! White resigned

Anticipating 36 ♖xe2 ♕xh2+!, followed by 37 ♖xh2 ♖xh2 mate.

> *Combination 7*
> □ **Sofia Polgar**
> ■ **Luitjen Apol**
> Reykjavik 1988

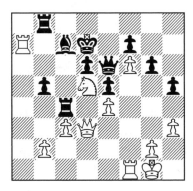

White can win in various ways, but the quickest and most beautiful is...

29 ♕xc4! bxc4 30 ♘xc7 Black resigned

His queen is trapped.

> *Combination 8*
> □ **Sofia Polgar**
> ■ **Rumiana Gocheva**
> Novi Sad Olympiad 1990

This game ends with a mate in three!

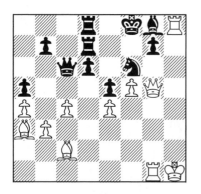

36 ♕xf6+! Black resigned

36...gxf6 37 ♖hxg8+ ♔f7 38 ♖1g7 is mate.

Combination 9

□ **Sofia Polgar**

■ **Vlastimil Jansa**

Rimavska Sobota 1991

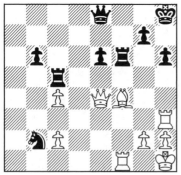

Two of the black pieces are far away on the queenside. Because of this, White can launch a dynamic winning combination on the other side.

31 ♖xh6+! ♖xh6

If 31...gxh6 32 ♗e5 pins and wins the rook.

32 ♗xh6 ♘xc4

After 32...gxh6 33 ♖f6 ♔g7 34 ♖xe6

♕f7 35 ♖e7 pins and wins the queen.

33 ♕h4 ♔g8

The following variations prove that Black is lost:

a) 33...♕h5 34 ♗xg7+ ♔xg7 35 ♕e7+ ♔h6 36 ♖f6+ ♔g5 37 ♕g7+ ♔h4 38 ♕g3 mate.

b) 33...♖h5 34 ♗xg7+ ♔xg7 35 ♕xc4; 33...♘d6 34 ♗xg7+ ♔xg7 35 ♕g3+.

c) 33...b5 34 ♗xg7+ ♔xg7 35 ♕f6+ ♔h7 36 ♖f3 ♖h5 37 ♖g3.

34 ♗xg7!

Another sacrifice!

34...♔xg7 35 ♕f6+ ♔h7 36 ♖f3

Black is helpless against the force of White's queen and rook.

36...♖h5 37 ♖g3 ♕h8 Black resigned

The Czech Grandmaster realized that 38 ♕g6 mates.

Combination 10

□ **Sofia Polgar**

■ **Peter Sinkovics**

Budapest 1992

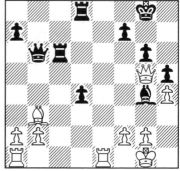

Black's position looks fine, but had forgotten about the serious weakness on f7. Sofia immediately took advantage of this with...

29 ♗xf7+! ♔xf7 30 ♖e7+ ♔f8

If 30...♔g8 31 ♕h6 leads to mate.

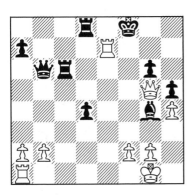

31 ♖ae1

Threatening ♕h6+.

31...♖e6 32 ♖1xe6 Black resigned

Combination 11
□ **Sofia Polgar**
■ **Wolfgang Unzicker**
Germany 1993

In this game, Sofia's opponent is the legendary German Grandmaster.

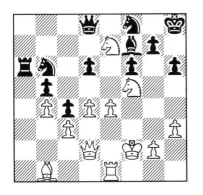

38 ♘xg7! Black resigned

After 38...♔xg7 comes 39 ♘f5+, followed by 40 ♕xh6. Black has no defense against this threat.

Combination 12
□ **Sofia Polgar**
■ **Simon Kerma**
Portoroz 1994

Black's back rank is extremely vulnerable, though it is not so obvious how White can exploit this weakness.

26 ♘xe7!

The first of two sacrifices to gain access to the weak back rank.

26...♖xe7 27 ♕d4+!

A pretty check! If Black accepts the gift, the rook on c3 can get to the crucial c8-square.

27...♘e5 28 ♕xd6 ♖xc3 29 ♕f6+ Black resigned

Mate comes on the next move.

Combination 13
□ **Drazen Sermek**
■ **Sofia Polgar**
Portoroz 1994

In this position, both sides have equal material, but White is forking both the knight and the queen. Sofia found a very nice combination to win the exchange and the game.

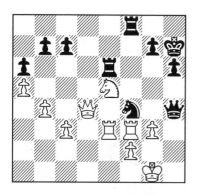

30...♘e2+! 31 ♖xe2 ♕xd4 32 cxd4 ♖xf3 and soon **White resigned.**

Combination 14
□ **Sofia Polgar**
■ **Jose Castellano Ojeda**
Las Palmas 1994

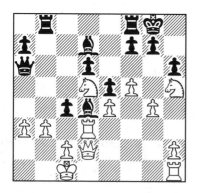

This is a typical Sicilian race when every move counts. In this game, White's attack comes first.

24 ♘hf6+! ♔h8

If Black accepts the sacrifice with 24...gxf6, White plays the quiet 25 ♖h3 and Black cannot avoid mate within a few moves. But not 25 ♕xh6 when Black gets the chance to stop White's attack with 25...♕xa3+ 26 ♔d2 ♕a5+

27 b4 ♕xd5 28 exd5 cxd3.

25 ♖h3 Black resigned

He cannot prevent ♖xh6+ and wins.

Combination 15
□ **Zoltan Gyimesi**
■ **Sofia Polgar**
Hungary 1995

Here Black has a combination leading to promotion of the c-pawn.

37...♕d5! 38 ♕xd5

38 ♕a1 would drop the e6 pawn to 38...♕xe6.

38...♘xd5 39 ♖xd5 c3 40 ♘e5

If 40 ♖d1 c2 41 ♖c1 ♖b1 and the pawn promotes.

40...c2

Capturing the knight with 40...dxe5? would be a mistake, as it allows 41 ♖c5 and White can save the game.

41 ♘d3 ♖b3

Threatening 42...♖xd3 to remove the guard of the c1 square.

42 ♔g2

If 42 ♘c1 ♖b1 43 ♖d2 ♖xc1+ 44 ♔g2 ♖g1+! wins.

42...♖xd3 43 ♖xd3 c1♕ White resigned.

The pawn has promoted.

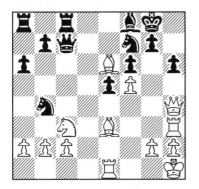

White has a strong attack. It is now time to find the winning combination!
23 ♗xh6! gxh6 24 ♖g3+ ♔h7 25 ♕xf6 Black resigned

He cannot avoid mate in two.

Supplementary Games

Here are all the games from *the* Rome tournament:

1 e4 c5 2 ♘f3 a6 3 c3 ♘f6 4 e5 ♘d5 5 d4 cxd4 6 ♕xd4 e6 7 ♗c4 d6 8 ♕e4 dxe5 9 ♘xe5 ♘f6 10 ♕e2 ♗e7 11 a4 0-0 12 0-0 ♕e8 13 ♘d2 ♘c6 14 ♘df3 ♘xe5 15 ♘xe5 ♔h8 16 a5 ♘d7 17 ♘f3 ♘f6 18 ♗e3 ♗d7 19 b4 ♖c8 20 ♖fc1 ♗c6 21 ♗d3 ♘d5 22 ♗d2 ♗d6 23 ♘e5 ♗xe5 24 ♕xe5 ♕e7 25 ♖ab1 ♖fd8

26 c4 ♘f4 27 ♗c3 f6 28 ♕xf4 ♖xd3 29 ♗d4 e5? 30 ♕f5 Black resigned.

1 d4 ♘f6 2 ♘f3 g6 3 g3 ♗g7 4 ♗g2 c5 5 c4 cxd4 6 ♘xd4 0-0 7 ♘c3 d6 8 0-0 a6 9 h3 ♕c7 10 b3 ♘c6 11 ♘c2 ♗d7 12 ♗b2 ♖ab8 13 e4 b5 14 cxb5 axb5 15 ♘e3 ♕c8 16 g4 h5 17 g5 ♘h7 18 h4 f6 19 f4 fxg5 20 hxg5 ♗d4 21 ♕d2 e5 22 ♘cd5 ♗xb2 23 ♕xb2 ♕d8 24 ♖ad1 exf4 25 ♘xf4 ♕xg5 26 ♖xd6 ♘e5 27 ♘f5 gxf5 28 ♕xe5 ♘f6 29 ♘d5 ♘g4 30 ♘e7+ ♔h7 31 ♕d4 ♗c8 32 ♘xc8 ♖bxc8 33 ♖d7+ ♔h6 34 exf5 ♘f6 35 ♖d6 ♖c2 36 ♖f2 ♖c1+ 37 ♔h2 ♔h7 38 ♕a7+ ♔g8 39 ♗d5+ ♔h8 40 ♖g2 ♕h4 mate.

1 e4 ♘f6 2 e5 ♘d5 3 d4 d6 4 ♘f3 ♗g4 5 ♗e2 e6 6 0-0 ♗e7 7 c4 ♘b6 8 ♘c3 0-0 9 ♗e3 d5 10 c5 ♗xf3 11 gxf3 ♘c8 12 f4 ♘c6 13 ♖b1 ♗h4 14 ♔h1 ♘8e7 15 ♗d3 g6 16 ♕g4 ♘f5 17 ♗xf5 exf5 18 ♕f3 ♘e7 19 ♕h3 ♘c8 20 ♖g1 ♔h8 21 b4 a6 22 a4 c6 23 b5 axb5 24 axb5 ♖a3 25 ♖gc1 ♗e7 26 b6 ♗xc5 27 dxc5 d4 28 ♖d1 ♖xc3 29 ♕h6 ♖xc5 30 ♗xd4 ♖d5 31 ♔g2 ♘e7 32 ♗c5 ♖e8 33 ♖dc1 ♖d3 34 ♗d6 ♘c8 35

♖d1 ♖xd1 36 ♖xd1 ♖g8 37 ♖d3
♘xb6 38 e6 f6 39 e7 ♕e8

40 ♕f8! ♘d5 41 ♖xd5 ♖xf8 42
exf8♕+ ♕xf8 43 ♗xf8 cxd5 44
♔f3 ♔g8 45 ♗b4 g5 46 ♔e3 ♔f7
47 ♔d4 ♔g6 48 ♗e7 h6 49 ♔xd5
♔h5 50 ♗xf6 ♔g4 51 fxg5 hxg5 52
♔e5 b5 53 ♗e7 Black resigned.

Round 4
□ Carlo D'Amore
■ Sofia Polgar
Sicilian Defense

1 ♘f3 c5 2 c4 ♘c6 3 d4 cxd4 4
♘xd4 g6 5 e4 ♗g7 6 ♘c2 ♘f6 7
♘c3 d6 8 ♗e2 0-0 9 0-0 a6 10 ♔h1
♖b8 11 f3 ♗d7 12 ♗e3 ♕a5 13
♘d5 b5 14 c5 ♗e6 15 cxd6 exd6
16 ♗d2 ♕d8 17 ♘db4 ♘xb4 18
♗xb4 ♘e8 19 ♗c3 ♗xc3 20 bxc3
♕c7 21 f4 ♕xc3 22 ♘d4 ♗c4 23
♘c6 ♗xe2 24 ♘e7+ ♔h8 25 ♕xe2
♘g7 26 ♖ac1 ♕f6 27 ♘d5 ♕e6 28
♘c7 ♕e7 29 ♘xa6 ♖bc8 30 ♘b4 f5
31 e5 ♖xc1 32 ♖xc1 dxe5 33 ♖b1
e4 34 ♕xb5 ♕d6 35 g3 ♖b8 36
♕e5 ♕b6 37 ♕c3 e3 38 ♖b2 ♕e6
39 ♕d3 ♕e4+ 40 ♕xe4 fxe4 41
♔g1 ♘f5 42 ♔f1 ♘d4 43 a3 ♖c8

44 ♘a2 ♔g7 45 a4 ♔f6 46 a5 ♔f5
47 a6 ♔g4 48 ♔g2 e2 49 h3+ ♔f5
50 ♔f2 e3+ 51 ♔e1 ♔e4 52 ♖b4
♔d3 53 ♖xd4+ ♔xd4 54 ♘b4 ♔c4
55 ♘c2 ♔c3 56 ♔xe2 ♔xc2 57 f5
gxf5 58 ♔xe3 ♖a8 59 ♔f4 ♖xa6 60
♔xf5 ♖g6 61 ♔f4 ♔d3 White resigned.

Round 5
□ Sofia Polgar
■ Alexander Chernin
See annotated Game 2.

Round 6
□ Sofia Polgar
■ Mihai Suba
Sicilian Defense

1 e4 c5 2 ♘f3 d6 3 d4 ♘f6 4 ♘c3
cxd4 5 ♘xd4 e6 6 ♗e2 a6 7 0-0
♗e7 8 ♗e3 ♕c7 9 f4 0-0 10 ♕e1
b5 11 a3 ♗b7 12 ♗f3 ♘bd7 13
♕g3 ♘c5 14 f5 e5 15 ♘b3 ♘a4 16
♘xa4 bxa4 17 ♘d2 ♖fc8 18 c4
♗c6 19 ♗h6 ♗f8 20 ♗g5 ♘d7 21
f6 g6 22 ♕h4 ♖cb8 23 ♗g4 ♕b6+
24 ♔h1 ♕xb2 25 ♗xd7 ♗xd7 26
♗h6 d5 27 ♗xf8 ♕xd2 28 ♖ad1
♕e3 29 ♖de1 ♕d2 30 ♗h6 ♕a5 31
exd5 ♖e8 32 ♗e3 ♕h8 33 ♗h6 ♕c5
34 ♖e4 ♔g8 35 ♗g7 Black resigned.

Round 7
□ Milan Mrdja
■ Sofia Polgar
Sicilian Defense

1 e4 c5 2 ♘f3 e6 3 d4 cxd4 4
♘xd4 ♘c6 5 ♘c3 ♕c7 6 f4 a6 7
♗e3 b5 8 ♘b3 d6 9 ♗d3 ♘f6 10

♕f3 ♗b7 11 0-0 ♗e7 12 ♕h3 h5
13 ♔h1 ♘g4 14 ♗g1 g5 15 ♗e2
0-0-0 16 a4 b4 17 ♘b5 ♕d7 18
♘5d4 ♘xd4 19 ♗xd4 e5 20 fxe5
dxe5 21 ♗c5 ♗xe4 22 ♕g3 f5 23
♗xa6+ ♔b8 24 ♗b5 h4 25 ♕h3
♕b7 26 ♖ae1 ♘f6 27 ♖xe4 ♕xe4
28 ♗d3 g4 29 ♗xe4 gxh3 30 ♗xe7
♘xe4 31 ♗xd8 ♖xd8 32 gxh3 f4 33
♔g2 ♘g5 34 ♔f2 e4 35 ♔e2 ♘xh3
36 ♘c5 ♖e8 37 ♘d7+ ♔c7 38 ♘f6
♖e5 39 ♖d1 ♔c6 40 ♖d8 f3+ White
resigned.

♔xd5 ♖f3 59 ♗b5 ♘e5 60 ♖xa4
♖xg3 61 ♖a1 ♔g7 62 ♖h1 ♖g5 63
♗e2 ♔g6 64 ♔e4 h5 65 ♔f4 ♔h6
66 ♖h2 ♘g6+ 67 ♔e3 f5 68 ♔f2 f4
69 ♖h3 h4 70 ♖a3 f5 71 ♗f3 ♘e5
72 ♖a5 ♘g4+ 73 ♔g2 ♘e3+ 74
♔f2 ♖g8 75 ♖a6+ ♔g5 76 ♖a7 ♖b8
77 ♖g7+ ♔h6 78 ♖e7 ♖b2+ 79
♔g1 ♖b1+ 80 ♔h2 ♖f1 81 ♗b7
♘g4+ 82 ♔g2 ♖f2+ 83 ♔g1 h3 84
♖e1 ♔g5 85 ♖b1 ♔h4 86 ♔h1 f3
White resigned.

Round 8
□ **Yuri Razuvaev**
■ **Sofia Polgar**
English Opening

---

1 c4 c5 2 ♘f3 ♘c6 3 ♘c3 g6 4 e3
d6 5 d4 cxd4 6 exd4 ♗g4 7 ♗e2
♗g7 8 0-0 ♘h6 9 d5 ♗xf3 10 ♗xf3
♘e5 11 ♗e2 ♘f5 12 ♗d2 ♘d4 13
♖e1 0-0 14 ♗f1 a6 15 ♘e4 ♖e8 16
♗c3 ♘f5 17 b3 ♕c7 18 ♖c1 b6 19
g3 ♘d7 20 ♗h3 ♗xc3 21 ♖xc3
♘g7 22 ♕d2 ♕b7 23 ♕h6 ♘f8 24
♘g5 b5 25 ♖ce3 bxc4 26 bxc4 ♕c7
27 ♖e4 ♘h5 28 ♖h4 ♘f6 29 ♘f3
♖ab8 30 ♘d4 ♖b2 31 ♕c1 ♕b6 32
a4 ♖a2 33 ♕c3 g5 34 ♖h6 ♘g6 35
♗f5 ♖xa4 36 h4 ♕b4 37 ♕c1 ♕xc4
38 hxg5 ♕xc1 39 ♖xc1 ♖xd4 40
gxf6 exf6 41 ♗d7 ♖e2 42 ♖h5 ♖e5
43 ♖h1 ♖dxd5 44 ♔g2 ♖d2 45
♖hd1 ♖ee2 46 ♖xd2 ♖xd2 47 ♖a1
♘e5 48 ♗f5 ♘c4 49 ♔f3 a5 50
♗c8 ♘b6 51 ♗b7 a4 52 ♖b1 ♘c4
53 ♗a6 ♖b2 54 ♖a1 ♘b6 55 ♔e3
d5 56 ♔d4 ♖xf2 57 ♔c5 ♘d7+ 58

Round 9
□ **Sofia Polgar**
■ **Sergey Dolmatov**
French Defense

---

1 e4 e6 2 d4 d5 3 ♘c3 ♗b4 4
♘ge2 ♘f6 5 ♗g5 dxe4 6 a3 ♗e7 7
♗xf6 ♗xf6 8 ♘xe4 ♘c6 9 c3 0-0
10 ♘2g3 e5 11 d5 ♘b8 12 ♘xf6+
♕xf6 13 ♗d3 c6 14 dxc6 ♘xc6 15
♕c2 g6 16 0-0 ♗e6 17 ♖ae1 ♔g7
18 ♕e2 ♖ad8 19 ♗b5 ♖d5 20 ♗c4
♖dd8 21 ♗b5 ♖d5 22 ♗c4 ♖dd8 23
♗b5 Draw agreed

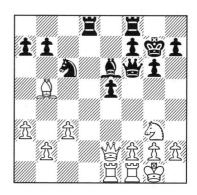

CHAPTER THREE

Judit

In love with chess

From her birth, Judit was exposed to 'chess in the air', though she started to learn the actual rules 'only' around the age of five, the latest amongst the sisters. By then, my father felt that five is the ideal age to start. His explanation was that, while one can possibly teach a four, or even three-year-old, the time and effort invested would not be in proportion to the speed of progress. Children that young have a shorter attention span and it is difficult to keep them focused.

I agree with my father in general; although, in my personal opinion, the age may vary from child to child. I know some children who are ready to be introduced to chess at four or even younger, while others should wait until six or older. A lot depends on the child's overall nurturing and education up to that time of their lives, as well as on their individual, natural maturity. I always felt that Judit was a relatively slow starter, though she is extremely motivated, diligent, hard-working, and disciplined towards her goals in chess and in life.

Unlike Sofia and me, Judit learned the first steps from our Mom. Soon Mrs. Karakas started to give her lessons, too. By the time Judit was five, I was already twelve and Sofia six and a half. Therefore Judit was born into a perfect chess environment. She could always ask somebody in the family for chess advice. Already in my teenage years, I deeply enjoyed teaching and, naturally, my sisters were my first students. I remember as a child, I always used to dream of having my own chess school.

I think for Judit chess was just something very normal. We had a nice collection of chess sets and chess books by that time, and other chess players visited us almost on a daily basis. She traveled with me to some chess tournaments and found it all very natural, exciting and fun. I don't think she ever had any doubt in her mind about what she would be 'when she grew up'.

After some time, while Sofia was ahead by the virtue of being older, the difference was tolerable for them to take lessons together. Perhaps it was not completely ideal for Sofia, but my parents had to compromise for financial and logistical reasons. Sofia and Judit spent all their time together for many years to come, training together, laughing together, crying together and mostly having fun.

Judit was first noticed internationally while we had guests over from Holland and Germany and elsewhere. Between 1982 and 1985, when I was not allowed to accept most of my invitations abroad, as a substitute my parents invited usually several foreign players, who were participating in tournaments in Hungary. They would either come over for the evening or often stay with us for a few days. We would play blitz matches or 4-6 player blitz tournaments. Initially Judit was only a spectator; however, she quite soon joined in the 'party' and started to cause surprises. She already played quite well at age 7, even blindfold.

In 1986, we were all invited to Canada to do some chess exhibitions, as part of the 'Just Say No' anti-drugs campaign led by Nancy Reagan. During the trip, my parents were somehow convinced to leave Sofia there for another week to do some more promotional activities. She had a lot of interesting experiences, including meeting with Bill Cosby, Princess Diana and Prince Charles at the World's Fair in Vancouver. But also she got exposed to some unwanted scenes.

After the extra week finished, we expected her back. The people she was staying with asked for another few days. My parents started to get nervous. With

Sofia having been in Canada for about a month, they felt that perhaps she was actually being kidnapped. My mother decided not to wait any longer and jumped on a plane and tried to pick Sofia up herself. It was not so simple, but with the assistance of one of the members of the group Sofia managed to get to New York to meet up with Mom. Overall it was an exciting, though traumatic trip for Sofia. Perhaps the best thing was that, by the time she came home, she spoke English quite fluently.

After Sofia's return to Budapest, something changed. She skipped a month of discipline and her normal chess training. At the same time, Judit had individual lessons, whereas as before they had always studied together. Slowly but surely, Judit caught up with Sofia, and then surpassed her.

Sensation in New York

In 1986, we were finally allowed to travel to the West as a family. All three of us participated in the different sections of the famous New York Open. By then it was my third trip to the Big Apple, but it was the first for both Judit and my father. For Judit, it was her first trip outside of the eastern block. It was exciting to play daily in the middle of New York City. Judit entered in the unrated section; but it would be naive to think that all the participants were really unrated. Some of her opponents were experienced players with national ratings in their own countries. Judit caused a big sensation by winning her section as the youngest participant, with seven wins and one draw. We made a lot of headlines including the cover of New York Times, which naturally focused on Judit as the young star. Judit won the $1000 first prize; not bad for a 10 year old!

Here is the crucial last round game:

> □ **Judit Polgar**
> ■ **Zoran Simic**
> New York Open 1986
> *French Defense*

1 e4 e6 2 d4 d5 3 ♘c3 dxe4 4 ♘xe4 ♘d7 5 ♘f3 ♘gf6 6 ♗d3 ♗e7 7 c3 0-0 8 ♕e2 c5 9 0-0 cxd4 10 ♘xd4 ♘xe4 11 ♗xe4 ♘f6 12 ♗f3 a6 13 ♗g5 ♕c7 14 ♖fe1 ♗d7 15 ♖ad1 ♖ad8 16 ♕e5 ♗d6 17 ♕e3 ♗xh2+ 18 ♔h1 ♗d6 19 ♗xf6 gxf6 20 ♕h6 ♗c6 21 ♗xc6 bxc6

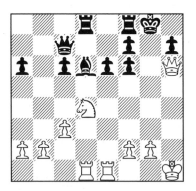

22 ♖e4 f5 23 ♖h4 ♖fe8 24 ♕g5+ ♔h8 25 ♖xh7+ ♔xh7 26 ♖d3 ♗g3 27 ♖xg3 ♕xg3 28 ♕xg3 c5 29 ♘f3 ♖d1+ 30 ♔h2 ♖h8 31 ♘g5+ ♔g7+ 32 ♘h3+ ♔f8 33 ♕b8+ ♔g7 34 ♕e5+ ♔g8 35 ♕xc5 ♖d2 36 ♕c8+ ♔g7 37 ♕xa6 ♖xb2 38 ♔g3 ♖d8 39 ♘g5 ♔f6 40 ♘h3 ♖c2 41 ♕c4 e5 42 ♕h4+ Black resigned.

During the family's visit to New York, we received a serious offer to stay

in the United States and not to return to Hungary. Had we decided to make that big move, I guess our lives would have turned out quite differently. One of the main reasons why we chose to go back was that my grandparents were waiting for us back home. They were survivors of the Holocaust and it would have been unfair to leave them behind.

The following year, Judit celebrated her eleventh birthday during the traditional Biel Chess Festival. She made another sensation by winning the brilliancy prize for the following game:

> □ **Jean Luc Costa**
> ■ **Judit Polgar**
> Biel 1987
> *English Opening*

1 d4 ♘f6 2 c4 c5 3 ♘f3 cxd4 4 ♘xd4 e5 5 ♘b5 d5 6 cxd5 ♗c5 7 ♘5c3 0-0 8 g3 ♘g4 9 e3 f5 10 ♗g2 f4 11 h3

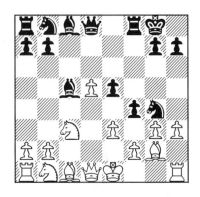

11...♘xf2 12 ♔xf2 fxe3+ 13 ♔e1 ♖f2 14 ♖g1 ♕f8 15 ♕d3 ♘a6 16 a3 ♗f5 17 ♗e4 ♗xe4 18 ♕xe4 ♗d4 19 ♗xe3 ♘c5 20 ♗xd4 exd4 21 ♕xd4 ♖e8+ 22 ♔d1 ♕f3+ White resigned.

The English chess journalist, Leonard Barden called the game: 'the female version of Fischer's Game of the Century'. During the same year, Judit scored her first tournament victory against a grandmaster:

□ **Judit Polgar**
■ **Lev Gutman**
Brussels 1987
Sicilian Defense

---

1 e4 c5 2 ♘f3 d6 3 d4 cxd4 4 ♘xd4 ♘f6 5 ♘c3 e6 6 ♗e2 ♗e7 7 0-0 0-0 8 f4 a6 9 ♗e3 ♕c7 10 a4 ♘c6 11 ♕e1 ♘d7 12 ♕g3 ♗f6 13 ♖ad1 ♖b8 14 ♘xc6 bxc6 15 e5 dxe5 16 ♘e4 ♗e7

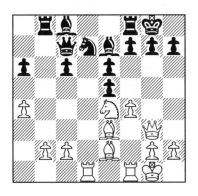

17 f5 exf5 18 ♗h6 g6 19 ♖xf5 ♖b4 20 ♗d3 f6 21 ♖df1 ♖xe4 22 ♗xf8 ♔xf8 23 ♗xe4 gxf5 24 ♗xf5 ♘b6 25 ♗xh7 ♗e6 26 ♗e4 ♘d5 27 ♕h4 ♘f4 28 ♕h8+ ♗g8 29 ♖d1 ♘e6 30 ♔h1 ♗d8 31 ♗f5 ♘d4 32 ♗h3 ♕f7 33 c3 ♕b3 34 ♕h6+ ♔e7 35 ♖f1 ♘e6 36 ♕xf6+ ♔d6 37 ♗xe6 Black resigned.

The Big Year: 1988
According to Judit, this was probably

the most amazing year of her life. She achieved success after success on the world stage.

A girl wins the Boys' Championship!
In 1988, the Youth World Championships were held in Timisoara, in neighboring Romania. Judit entered as the only girl in the World Under-12 Championship, alongside 36 boys. As Timisoara was so close to home (before World War II it used to be a Hungarian town), around midway in the tournament we decided with my mother to jump on a train and visit the rest of the family. I am proud to take a tiny part of the credit for Judit's success, as our pre-game preparations probably helped a bit. I remember a funny story upon occupying our room in the hotel. As normal, I went to switch on the TV. But then I realized that it was only a decoration. It actually had nothing inside!

Judit went undefeated in the tournament with seven wins and four draws. This was an historic event, as never before had any girl won an overall World Championship. I'll never forget the closing ceremony where she received her trophy and a huge bear (almost bigger than her). This was a picture that made the cover of the Hungarian chess magazine, *Sakkélet*.

Here is Judit's game against her main rival, from the Soviet Union:

□ **Porubin**
■ **Judit Polgar**
Timisoara 1988
Sicilian Defense

---

1 e4 c5 2 ♘c3 ♘c6 3 g3 g6 4 ♗g2

♝g7 5 d3 e6 6 ♝e3 ♘d4 7 f4 ♘e7
8 e5 d6 9 ♘f3 dxe5 10 ♘xe5 0-0
11 0-0 ♖b8 12 ♘e4 b6 13 c3 ♘df5
14 ♝f2 ♝a6 15 g4 ♘d6 16 ♘xd6
♕xd6 17 ♘c4 ♕d7 18 ♕f3 ♖fd8 19
♖fd1 ♝b7 20 ♕e2 ♘d5 21 ♝g3 b5
22 ♘e5 ♕c7 23 f5 ♕b6

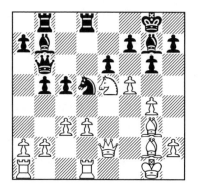

24 ♘d7? ♖xd7 25 ♝xb8 e5! 26
♝xd5 ♝xd5 27 ♝xe5 ♖e7 28 d4
cxd4 29 ♝xd4 ♝xd4+ 30 ♔f1 ♖xe2
31 ♔xe2 ♝c4+ White resigned.

Olympiad: 12 wins and a draw!

The other enormous sensation of the
year was Judit's performance at the
Chess Olympiad in Thessaloniki. We
knew already how well she was playing
from her tournaments in the months
before the Olympiad, but nobody could
even imagine such an incredible result
as scoring 12½ out of 13 and a performance rating of 2694.

Judit was on board two in our Hungarian women's team. At the tender age
of 12, she already played with the self-
confidence and security of an experienced adult. Thinking back, it is quite
amusing that she calmed the rest of the
team down, and we knew we could rely
on her! In a couple of games she had

some luck, as you always need for such
a high score; on the other hand, the one
draw that she allowed was versus the
Soviet Union, where she missed the
win. In most of her games Judit played
very convincingly and simply outclassed
her opponents. Among the players she
defeated was the future Women's
World Champion, Xie Jun.

Here is the game:

□ **Xie Jun**
■ **Judit Polgar**
Thessaloniki Olympiad 1988
Sicilian Defense

1 e4 c5 2 ♘f3 e6 3 d4 cxd4 4
♘xd4 ♘c6 5 ♘c3 ♕c7 6 ♝e2 a6 7
0-0 ♘f6 8 ♔h1 ♘xd4 9 ♕xd4 ♝c5
10 ♕d3 h5 11 f4 ♘g4 12 ♕g3 b5
13 ♝xg4 hxg4 14 ♕xg4 ♝b7 15
♕e2 b4 16 ♘d1 ♔e7 17 ♝e3 ♝xe3
18 ♕xe3 ♖h4 19 h3 ♖ah8 20 ♔g1
g5 21 fxg5 ♝xe4 22 ♕f2

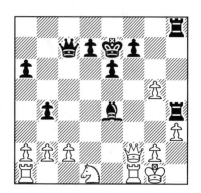

22...f5! 23 gxf6+ ♔f7 24 ♕e3 ♝xg2
25 ♕g5 ♖4h7 26 ♔xg2 ♖g8 27
♕xg8+ ♔xg8 28 ♘e3 ♕c6+ 29 ♔g3
♕d6+ 30 ♖f4 ♖xh3+ 31 ♔xh3 ♕xf4
32 ♘g4 e5 33 ♖g1 ♔f7 34 ♖g2
♕f3+ 35 ♔h2 d6 36 ♖g3 ♕f4 37 c3

bxc3 38 bxc3 ♕d2+ 39 ♔h3 ♕xa2 40 ♖f3 ♕d2 41 ♔h4 e4 42 ♖e3 ♕g2 43 ♔g5 ♔e6 44 c4 a5 45 ♔f4 ♕f1+ 46 ♔xe4 ♕xc4+ 47 ♔f3+ ♔f5 48 ♖e5+ ♔g6 49 ♖e7 ♕d3+ 50 ♔f4 ♕f5+ 51 ♔g3 ♔h5 52 ♖g7 a4 53 ♖g8 ♕d3+ White resigned.

Besides winning two gold medals (the team gold and individual gold on board two), Judit also won the prize for the highest performance rating of the entire Women's Olympiad, and the brilliancy prize (for the most spectacular game) for her game against the Bulgarian Chilingirova (see Combination 2).

The World Under-12 and the Olympiad were not Judit's only successes in 1988. In the spring, as it became a yearly event for us, Judit played the New York Open again and did quite well, achieving her first International Master norm.

In June, we were invited back (after a visit in February) to Iceland to the Egilsstadir Invitational Grandmaster tournament (category 7). Judit and I both played quite well and tied for first with 6½ out of 9. Facing each other, we made a sisterly draw. Judit over-fulfilled the IM-norm by a full point and missed the GM-norm by only half a point. The field included some of the top Icelandic players.

That tournament was quite an exciting experience. That time of the year in that part of the world, it never gets dark! It was quite amusing to look outside the window from our room late at night and still see daylight! Another unusual scene was when we went on an excursion and saw snow on the mountain, while at the same time we could sunbathe in bathing suits!

This event was probably the only one in which our entire family participated in the tournament, although not in the same section.

Judit made her third and final IM norm in Bagneux, France. In order to become an IM, one is required to perform at a 2450 performance level in at least 24 games from two or three tournaments. She became the youngest IM (of either sex) in the world!

Shortly after, Judit went to another international tournament in Bulgaria, which she won with a 12/15 score, two points over the IM-norm!

Right before the Olympiad, she 'collected' another victory at the Duncan Laurie Mixed Challenge in London. Again she scored a point above the IM norm. She became an instant media darling in the British press. Admiring her fierce style she was often called as the 'Skirty-Tal'.

Here are some quotes:

'Chess Prodigy scores her finest victory' or 'Saying Checkmate to Chess Sexists' – *The Independent*.

'Sisters show no mercy' – *The Times*.

'Charmer of 12 who changes all her checks into cash' – *Daily Express*

At that tournament, Judit defeated the then reigning World Under-18 Champion, Michael Hennigan, among others. During the trip, Judit, Sofia and my mother also had the pleasure of seeing the musical 'Chess'.

Judit won another world title in December 1988: the World Under-16 Championship in Rapid Chess. This was held in Mazatlan, Mexico, alongside the overall Rapid World Championship, which Anatoly Karpov won and all three of us participated in. We had very pleasant memories from that trip. The venue was a very nice hotel right on the beach. It felt like a big Mexican 'fiesta'. We were also invited by the Mexican Chess Federation to stay a few days after the event in Mexico City and do some promotion for chess there. We also went see the amazing ancient Pyramids outside the Mexican capital.

To add more icing to the cake, after all the above successes in 1988, Judit also won the Challengers section of the Hastings tournament, scoring 8/10. It was a strong open event with 102 participants, among them many GMs. By that victory, she qualified for the following year's Premier section. That is one of the most famous and traditional international tournaments and has been running since 1895. Hastings is a very pleasant seaside resort town, though not so much in the winter time.

Back then Judit mostly had a straightforward attacking style, but despite her young age, she also won some very fine technical games, such as the following:

| □ **Judit Polgar** |
| ■ **Glenn Flear** |
| Hastings 1988/89 |
| *King's Gambit* |

1 e4 e5 2 f4 exf4 3 ♗c4 ♘f6 4 d3 d5 5 exd5 ♘xd5 6 ♘f3 ♘b6 7 ♗b3 ♗d6 8 ♕e2+ ♕e7 9 ♘c3 ♗g4 10 ♕xe7+ ♔xe7 11 ♘e4 ♗xf3 12 gxf3 ♘c6 13 ♘xd6 cxd6 14 ♗xf4 ♘d4

15 ♔f2 ♘xb3 16 axb3 a6 17 ♖a5 ♔d7 18 b4 ♖he8 19 c4 ♖e6 20 b5 axb5 21 ♖xb5 ♔c6 22 ♖c1 ♖a2

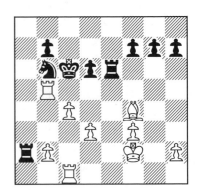

23 ♖b3! ♘d7 24 d4 ♖f6 25 ♗g3 b6 26 ♖e1 d5 27 cxd5+ ♔xd5 28 ♖e7 ♔c4 29 ♖c3+ ♔b4 30 ♖c2 ♔b3 31 ♖d2 ♖a7 32 d5 b5 33 d6 ♖f5 34 ♖d3+ ♔c2 35 ♖c3+ ♔xb2 36 ♖c7 Black resigned.

Remarkable endgame technique from a 12 year old!

As a bonus in March 1989, because of her breathtaking previous year, Judit received the 'Women's Chess Oscar', awarded by the International Chess Journalists (AIPE), with 519 votes.

The first GM norm

After her fantastic year, Judit's rating in January 1989 jumped to 2555, taking over the World's No.1 female ranking for the first time, at the age of 12. She remained at the top for the next fifteen years until January 2005, when she temporarily disappeared from the rating list, having taken a year off to have a family, and I once again became the No.1.

In 1989, Judit was awash with invitations to tournaments and exhibitions. In the first half of the year, she had to get used to her new rating and new expectations. All of a sudden, instead of playing mostly masters and International Masters, rated between 2200 and 2400, in 1989 most of her opponents were between 2400 and 2600.

In the first half of the year, Judit had only two serious tournaments – the usual New York Open and a GM tournament in Salamanca, Spain – and number of small events. She needed some time to generate some new energy and accumulate more knowledge.

In July, Judit finally struck again. At the OHRA tournament in Amsterdam, she had a perfect start with 3/3 over three very strong opponents, GMs Hans Ree, Zurab Azmaiparashvili and IM Friso Nijboer. After England, now the media in Holland also fell into 'Polgarmania'. Despite in the end missing first place in the tournament by half a point, Judit made her first GM norm.

In the games and combinations section you can find Judit's victories over GMs Ree and Hulak. Here is another nice attacking game by Judit from the same tournament:

> □ **Friso Nijboer**
> ■ **Judit Polgar**
> Amsterdam 1989
> *Sicilian Defense*

1 e4 c5 2 ♘f3 e6 3 d4 cxd4 4 ♘xd4 ♘c6 5 ♘c3 ♕c7 6 ♗e2 a6 7 0-0 ♘f6 8 ♔h1 ♘xd4 9 ♕xd4 ♗c5 10 ♕d3 h5 11 f4 ♘g4 12 ♘d1 b5 13 a4 b4 14 c4 ♗b7 15 a5 0-0-0 16 ♗e3 ♘xe3 17 ♘xe3 g5 18 fxg5 ♕e5 19 ♗f3 ♕xg5 20 ♘d1 ♕e5 21

♘f2 ♗d6 22 g3 h4 23 c5 hxg3 24 ♕xd6 ♖xh2+ 25 ♔g1 gxf2+ 26 ♖xf2 ♖g8+ 27 ♗g2 ♖h5 28 ♖c1 ♕h8 29 ♖xf7

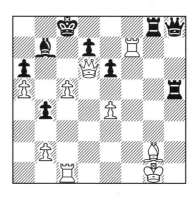

29...♖xg2+! 30 ♔xg2 ♕g8+ 31 ♕g3 ♗xe4+ 32 ♔f2 ♕xf7+ 33 ♔e3 ♗c6 White resigned.

Blindfold chess and meeting... an angel

Because of Judit's amazing success, one night during our visit in Holland, our Dutch friend, IM Leon Pliester, introduced our family to Mr. Joop van Oosterom and his future wife, Muriel. We had a lovely dinner with a chessboard on the table as well. Mr. Van Oosterom used to be one of the top junior players in the Netherlands. He represented Holland at the World Junior Championship in 1955, the year when Boris Spassky won. According to his own tale, Joop understood the difference between the winner and himself and decided to give up his beloved game and instead pursue a (very successful) career in computers. For many years he left chess completely, being fully devoted to his job. However, for a good while he had been sponsoring two teams in the Dutch Chess League, and when we met him, Joop was already retired and greatly enjoyed playing correspondence chess.

We had a very long and interesting conversation, mainly about chess in general, and women's abilities or limits in chess. We believed that, given the same conditions for training and playing in tournaments, women are just as capable as men of achieving the highest results in chess. Mr. Van Oosterom had his doubts about this, but he was curious to find out!

He was so impressed that night, when Judit beat him in a blindfold chess game, that he gave us a Toshiba laptop computer as a gift the next day. In those days, laptops used to cost a fortune, so it was a very big help to us, and was our first portable computer. That was only the beginning of his support for our family. He wanted to sponsor us to give optimal conditions and see how far we could get. We shall be thankful to him for ever. Starting in 1990, for about four years he paid for the cost of our training. He also invited us to special tournaments, which he organized and sponsored. All three of us were also invited to represent his home-town team of Hilversum in the Dutch League. For several years we would play 4-5 games annually on behalf of the team. It used to be a real fun event with great spirit between the team members.

It is really unfortunate that such a wonderful and generous person, who watched his carefully health (playing tennis daily), had a stroke at such a young age (in his early fifties). Regretfully he never fully recovered.

Winning another World Championship

After Judit's victory at the 1988 World Under-12 Championship, in 1990 she arrived in Fon du Lac, Wisconsin as the top seed. She had all the pressure on her to prove that she could win again, this time in the next age group in the World Under-14 Championship. Again she was the only girl participant in the overall section. She scored 9 out 11, but it would not have been enough if her Soviet rival, the future grandmaster, Vasily Yemelin, had won his last game. But he missed his opportunity and Judit won clear first and the world title.

Live TV

In Cologne, there was a yearly TV chess show on one of the main German channels. I participated in them three times, and later Judit took over my spot. The games were played in the WDR TV studio. While the players are sitting in a soundproof glass 'box', the commentators, usually GMs Pfleger and Hort, together with the TV host Mr. Spahn, chat about the game and chess in general. It is great promotion for chess. I hope that other countries follow this great example. In the 1990 edition of the show, Judit won a very exciting game against the German GM Knaak. Each side had an hour for all moves.

□ **Judit Polgar**
■ **Rainer Knaak**
Cologne 1990
French Defense

---

1 e4 e6 2 d4 d5 3 ♘c3 ♗b4 4 e5 c5 5 a3 ♗xc3+ 6 bxc3 ♘e7 7 ♕g4

♕c7 8 ♗d3 cxd4 9 ♘e2 ♕xe5 10
♗f4 ♕f6 11 ♗g5 ♕e5 12 cxd4 h5
13 ♕h4 ♕c7 14 ♗f4 ♕a5+ 15 ♗d2
♕d8 16 g4 e5 17 dxe5 ♗xg4 18
♖g1 ♕d7

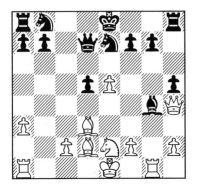

19 f3! ♗e6 20 ♘d4 ♘bc6 21 ♘xc6
♘xc6 22 ♖xg7 ♕c7 23 f4 ♘xe5 24
fxe5 ♕xe5+ 25 ♔f2 ♕xg7 26 ♖g1
♕b2 27 ♗b4 f6 28 ♖e1 0-0-0 29
♖xe6 ♔b8 30 ♕xf6 ♕a2 31 ♕d4
♖c8 32 ♗d2 ♔a8 33 ♗e3 ♖xc2+
34 ♗xc2 ♕xc2+ 35 ♔e1 ♕b1+ 36
♔d2 ♕a2+ 37 ♔d1 ♕b1+ 38 ♔e2
♕c2+ 39 ♗d2 ♖f8 40 ♕xd5 **Black
resigned.**

The second GM-norm

It took some time before Judit gained
more experience facing real strong
grandmasters. After her first GM-norm
in Amsterdam in July 1989, it took her
until October 1991 to be ready to make
the second norm.

A year after her first magnificent result in Amsterdam, she repeated it by
sharing first place with GM Tukmakov
in a very strong field. Unfortunately, she
was short the GM-norm by half a point.

In this tournament Judit played the
following game:

☐ **Judit Polgar**
■ **Wolfgang Uhlmann**
Amsterdam 1990
French Defense

1 e4 e6 2 d4 d5 3 ♘c3 ♗b4 4 e5
♘e7 5 a3 ♗xc3+ 6 bxc3 c5 7 ♕g4
0-0 8 ♗d3 f5 9 exf6 ♖xf6 10 ♗g5
♖f7 11 ♕h5 h6 12 ♗g6 ♖f8 13 ♘f3
♘bc6 14 0-0 ♕c7 15 ♗xe7 ♕xe7 16
♖ae1 ♕f6 17 ♘e5 cxd4 18 f4! dxc3

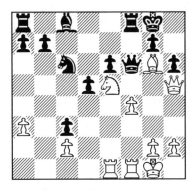

19 g4! (another of her famous g2-
g4 moves!) **19...♕e7 20 ♗d3 ♕e8 21
♘g6 ♗d7 22 g5 ♖f7 23 gxh6 gxh6
24 ♔h1 ♘e7 25 ♖g1** and Judit won in
53 moves, despite missing a way of finishing the game more quickly.

In 1991, we both played a strong GM
tournament in Munich, and had many
interesting games. Here is Judit's victory
against the Indian genius, Anand:

☐ **Judit Polgar**
■ **Viswanathan Anand**
Munich 1991
Ruy Lopez

1 e4 e5 2 ♘f3 ♘c6 3 ♗b5 a6 4

♗a4 ♘f6 5 0-0 ♘xe4 6 d4 b5 7
♗b3 d5 8 dxe5 ♗e6 9 c3 ♗e7 10
♘bd2 ♕d7 11 ♗c2 ♘xd2 12 ♕xd2
♗g4 13 ♕f4 ♗xf3 14 ♗f5 ♕d8 15
♕xf3 ♘xe5 16 ♕e2 ♕d6 17 ♖e1
♘c6 18 ♗g5 ♔f8 19 ♗e3 g6 20
♗h6+ ♔g8 21 ♕g4 ♕f6 22 ♗c2
♗f8 23 ♗g5 ♕d6 24 ♗f4 ♕d8 25
♖ad1 ♘a5 26 h4 c6 27 h5 ♘c4 28
hxg6 hxg6 29 b3 ♘d6

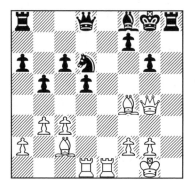

30 ♗xg6! fxg6 31 ♖e6 ♖h7 32
♗xd6 ♗g7 33 ♖de1 ♖h6 34 g3 ♕d7
35 ♗f4 g5 36 ♗xg5 ♖g6 37 ♕f5
♖xe6 38 ♕xe6+ ♕xe6 39 ♖xe6 ♖c8
40 ♗d2 ♔f7 41 ♖e1 c5 42 ♔f1 c4
43 bxc4 ♖xc4 44 ♖c1 ♔e6 45 ♔e2
d4 46 cxd4 ♗xd4 47 ♗e3 ♗b2 48
♖xc4 bxc4 49 ♔d2 ♗g7 50 ♔c2
♔d5 51 f3 ♗f6 52 ♗h6 ♗e5 53 g4
♗d4 54 ♗d2 ♗b6 55 ♗c1 ♗a5 56
a4 ♔e5 57 ♗g5 ♔d5 58 ♗d2 ♗c7
59 ♗c3 ♗f4 60 ♗f6 ♗g3 61 g5
♗h4 62 ♗d8 ♗f2 63 g6 ♗d4 64
♗a5 ♔e6 65 ♗c3 Black resigned.

Judit finally made her second GM-norm
in Vienna, Austria. It was quite a strong
invitational (category XII) with the ten
participants including six grandmasters.
The tournament was held in an amazing

setting in the City Hall.

At first, I was just going to drive Judit, Sofia (who played in the open section) and my mother to Vienna, but after we arrived I decided to stay and help my sisters with the preparation for their games.

After making 4/7 in the previous rounds, Judit needed 1½ points from her last two games. Here is the game from the penultimate round that was crucial in the fight for the GM norm:

□ **Vladimir Epishin**
■ **Judit Polgar**
Vienna 1991
King's Indian Defense

1 d4 ♘f6 2 c4 g6 3 ♘c3 ♗g7 4 e4
d6 5 ♘f3 0-0 6 ♗e2 e5 7 0-0 ♘c6
8 d5 ♘e7 9 ♘d2 a5 10 ♖b1 ♘d7 11
a3 f5 12 b4 ♔h8 13 f3 axb4 14
axb4 ♘g8 15 ♕c2 ♘gf6 16 ♘b5
♘h5 17 g3 ♘df6 18 c5 ♗d7 19
♖b3 ♗h6 20 ♖c3 fxe4 21 fxe4 ♗h3
22 ♖e1 ♕d7 23 ♘f3 ♗xc1 24 ♖xc1
♘f4 25 ♘g5 ♘xe2+ 26 ♕xe2 ♗g4
27 ♕c4 ♘e8 28 ♖f1 ♖xf1+ 29
♕xf1 ♔g8 30 h3 h6 31 c6 bxc6 32
dxc6 ♕e7 33 hxg4 hxg5 34 ♖f3

34...d5 35 exd5 ♕xb4 36 d6 ♘xd6 37 ♘xd6 cxd6 38 ♖f6 ♕b3 39 ♔h2 ♔g7 40 ♖xd6 ♖h8+ White resigned.

The Hungarian Championship 1991 – beating Bobby Fischer's record

The 1991 Championship was held in the center of Budapest at the Beke-Radisson Hotel, a place where numerous chess events have been hosted over the years. After Judit won her final game, versus GM Tibor Tolnai, I felt that this was our biggest success and happiest moment. I remember the atmosphere was totally euphoric. We were hugging each other and everybody was congratulating Judit and our family.

From the time when nobody believed that women could compete with men, many doubting that we were for real, this really felt like the best answer. It was unprecedented for any woman to win a national championship, especially in one of the strongest chess countries in the world.

And yet another Guinness record for Judit: at the age 15 years, 4 months and 28 days, she made her third required GM norm, beating Bobby Fischer's 33-year record as the youngest Grandmaster in the world.

Stagnation – 'almost' at the top

As the new overall Hungarian Champion, the highest rated woman player in the world, and the youngest grandmaster of all time, in 1992 (and in 1993) Judit was invited to many strong tournaments, but not yet to the absolute elite events in the in the world. She had steadily good results, though not as outstanding as in 1988 or in 1991. Finally, in July 1993, the breakthrough came when Judit passed the magic 2600 rating mark.

Defeating the World Champions

Besides playing World Champions in various tournaments, Judit also had two exhibition matches against two former World Champions.

Firstly, in 1993, Judit played a serious (classical time limit) ten game match against Boris Spassky in Budapest. It was hosted by the Hotel Intercontinental and sponsored by the same Jugoskandic Bank as the second Fischer-Spassky match in Yugoslavia.

It was a fantastic event with a crowd of about a thousand spectators daily. At critical moments in the games, one could feel the tension, people holding their breath, and you could almost cut the air. There was also a nightly 20-minute report on the games on Hungarian national television.

GM Lev Psakhis helped Judit in the preparation for the match, as well as during the match itself. Judit reached the necessary 5½ points for victory after the ninth game. Even though the match had a winner already, they played out the tenth game anyway to please the spectators. Spassky played well, sacrificed a knight for just two pawns and better mobility of his pieces, and won in 74 moves. Here is Judit's best game from that match (game 2):

| □ **Judit Polgar** |
| ■ **Boris Spassky** |
| Budapest 1993 |
| *Ruy Lopez* |

1 e4 e5 2 ♘f3 ♘c6 3 ♗b5 a6 4

♗a4 ♘f6 5 0-0 ♗e7 6 ♖e1 b5 7
♗b3 0-0 8 c3 d6 9 h3 ♘b8 10 d4
♘bd7 11 ♘bd2 ♗b7 12 ♗c2 ♖e8
13 ♘f1 ♗f8 14 ♘g3 g6 15 b3 ♗g7
16 d5 ♗f8 17 ♗g5 h6 18 ♗e3 c6
19 c4 a5 20 ♕d2 ♔h7 21 ♘h2 b4
22 ♘g4 ♘xg4 23 hxg4 ♕h4

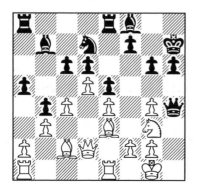

24 g5 c5 25 ♘f1 f6 26 g3 ♕h3 27
f3 fxg5 28 ♖e2 ♘f6 29 g4 ♕xf3 30
♘h2 ♕h3 31 ♖f1 ♘xg4 32 ♖f7+
♗g7 33 ♘xg4 ♕xg4+ 34 ♖g2 ♕h3
35 ♖xb7 ♖f8 36 ♗xg5 hxg5 37
♕xg5 ♕h6 38 ♕xh6+ ♔xh6 39
♖h2+ ♔g5 40 ♖xg7 ♖f3 **Black resigned.**

The other match Judit played was
against Anatoly Karpov in 1998, also in
Budapest. This was played at a rapid
time limit (30 minutes per player for the
entire game) and was a best of eight
challenge.

As one could imagine in this match,
the time factor had a significant importance. Judit probably had better time
management and succeeded in defeating
the former world champion 5-3, winning
games 2 and 3 and drawing the rest.

Over the years Judit has defeated the
following world champions, in individ-
ual games at various tournaments:
Vassily Smyslov, Boris Spassky, Anatoly
Karpov, Garry Kasparov, Viswanathan
Anand, Alexander Khalifman, and
Ruslan Ponomariov.

On the Super Circuit
In 1994, Judit was invited for the first
time to *the* Linares tournament, where
she had that infamous incident I described earlier. It was a very long and
tough tournament with no easy opponents. Judit started with a respectable 2
out of 4, and then the incident occurred
with Kasparov. She never really recovered from it psychologically during the
entire tournament. In the end she
scored only 4/13. It was a tough and
painful lesson, but perhaps a necessary
experience to get to the next step.

Just two months later in Madrid, Judit had her first victory in a super tournament. She finished 1½ points ahead of
a category 15 field, which included
grandmasters Shirov, Kamsky, Ivan
Sokolov, Tiviakov, Salov and Bareev.

Here is a fine performance by Judit
from that event:

> ☐ **Judit Polgar**
> ■ **Sergei Tiviakov**
> Madrid 1994
> *Sicilian Defense*

1 e4 c5 2 c3 d5 3 exd5 ♕xd5 4 d4
♘f6 5 ♘f3 ♘c6 6 ♗e2 cxd4 7 cxd4
e6 8 0-0 ♗e7 9 ♘c3 ♕d6 10 ♘b5
♕d8 11 ♗f4 ♘d5 12 ♗g3 a6 13
♘c3 0-0 14 ♖c1 ♘f6 15 h3 b6 16
a3 ♗b7 17 ♗d3 ♖c8 18 ♗b1 b5 19
♕d3 ♘a5 20 ♘e5 ♘c4 21 ♖c2 ♘d6
22 f3 g6 23 ♗f2 ♖e8 24 ♗a2 ♗f8

25 ♖e2 ♗g7 26 ♖fe1 ♘d5 27 ♘xd5 exd5 28 ♕d1 a5 29 h4 ♕c7 30 h5 ♘c4

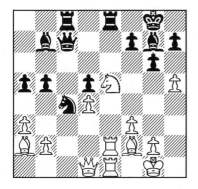

31 h6! ♗xh6 32 ♘g4 ♖xe2 33 ♘xh6+ ♔g7 34 ♖xe2 ♔xh6 35 ♕e1 ♔g7 36 ♖e7 ♕b6 37 ♗xc4 bxc4 38 ♕e5+ ♔g8 39 ♗e3 f6 40 ♕f4 ♔f8 41 ♖xh7 ♔e8 42 ♕h6 Black resigned.

In the mid nineties Judit played a lot of tournaments in Spain, some on a yearly basis, such as in Dos Hermanas and Madrid. At one point, Spain organized most of the strongest events in the world. Besides the big Linares super-tournaments, many of the formerly 'just strong' tournaments also became top level events.

In 1995, in the Kazakh capital, Alma Ata, they held the first (and so far only) lightning World Championship in two minute chess. Judit tied for first with Anatoly Karpov and they were announced co-winners, although Judit won the play-off games.

The same year she won a small 4-player double round tournament in Stornoway, on the Scottish island of Lewis, ahead the then British No.1, Nigel Short.

In 1996, Judit played a match against the Brazilian No.1, Gilberto Milos, which she won 2½-1½. Here is the following decisive fourth game:

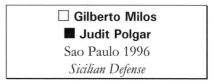

□ **Gilberto Milos**
■ **Judit Polgar**
Sao Paulo 1996
Sicilian Defense

1 e4 c5 2 ♘f3 d6 3 d4 cxd4 4 ♘xd4 ♘f6 5 ♘c3 a6 6 ♗e3 e6 7 f4 b5 8 ♕f3 ♗b7 9 ♗d3 ♘bd7 10 g4 h6 11 a3 ♖c8 12 0-0 ♗e7 13 ♖ae1

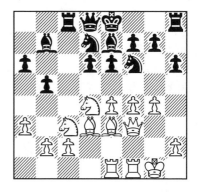

13...g5! 14 f5 ♘e5 15 ♕h3 ♔d7 16 ♗e2 h5 17 fxe6+ fxe6 18 gxh5 g4 19 ♕g2 ♖xc3 20 bxc3 ♗xe4 21 ♕f2 ♘xh5 22 ♗f4 g3 23 hxg3 ♘xf4 24 ♕xf4 ♖h1+ 25 ♔f2 ♖h2+ 26 ♔e3 ♗g5 27 ♔xe4 ♗xf4 28 gxf4 ♖h3 29 ♘xe6 ♔xe6 White resigned.

In 1998, Judit took a temporary break from the super circuit and played in the US Open in Hawaii. She was in the lead throughout the event, but the title still depended on her last round game against GM Joel Benjamin. Joel played the Berlin Defense, heading for the endgame right from the opening, and trying to minimize Judit's strength by avoiding middlegame complications. But Judit proved that she can play a 'squeeze' type of game when she has to, winning the game, and sharing first place with GM Boris Gulko.

Judit absolutely loved the trip to Hawaii and the kiss she got from a dolphin... Of all her travels around the world, Hawaii is one of the very top ones on her list.

Every year since 1997, there has been a special tournament in Holland, in which the players play with glass chess pieces. The tradition has been to invite the highest-ranked woman player, the World Junior Champion, a Dutch grandmaster, and a former World Champion (or challenger); the four play each other twice, six games altogether. Since its inaugural edition, Judit has taken part in all of them, except in 2004 when she was absent because of her newborn baby. She tied for first in 2001, and won clear first in both 1998 and 2003.

Here is a nice game from the 1998 edition:

□ **Tal Shaked**
■ **Judit Polgar**
Hoogeveen 1998
English Opening

---

1 c4 ♘f6 2 ♘c3 c5 3 g3 ♘c6 4 ♗g2 b6 5 e4 ♖b8 6 ♘ge2 d6 7 0-0 e5 8 d3 ♗e7 9 h3 a6 10 a4 0-0 11 f4 ♘d4 12 g4 ♗b7 13 ♘xd4 cxd4 14 ♘e2 ♘d7 15 b4 a5 16 b5 ♘c5 17 ♔h1 ♘e6 18 f5 ♘c5 19 ♘g1 ♗g5 20 ♖a3 f6 21 ♘f3 ♗xc1 22 ♕xc1 ♕e7 23 ♖g1 ♖bc8 24 ♘d2 g6

25 ♗f3 ♔h8 26 ♘f1 gxf5 27 gxf5

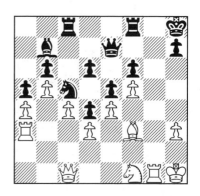

27...d5! 28 exd5 e4 29 dxe4 ♘xe4 30 ♕h6 ♘g5 31 ♖xg5 fxg5 32 d6 ♕e2 33 ♗xb7 ♕xf1+ 34 ♔h2 ♖xf5 White resigned.

In 1999, Judit participated in the FIDE knockout World Championship in Las Vegas. She got all the way to the quarter-finals, beating GMs Nielsen, Magem Badals and Zvjaginsev, and losing only to the future winner, GM Alexander Khalifman.

Here is one of her victories from that event:

□ **Judit Polgar**
■ **Peter Heine Nielsen**
Las Vegas 1999
Petroff Defense

---

1 e4 e5 2 ♘f3 ♘f6 3 ♘xe5 d6 4 ♘f3 ♘xe4 5 d4 d5 6 ♗d3 ♘c6 7 0-0 ♗e7 8 c4 ♘b4 9 ♗e2 0-0 10 ♘c3 ♗f5 11 a3 ♘xc3 12 bxc3 ♘c6 13 ♖e1 ♗f6 14 ♗f4 ♘a5 15 cxd5 ♕xd5 16 ♘d2 ♕d7 17 ♗f3 ♖fe8 18 ♘e4 ♗e7 19 ♘g3 ♗g6 20 ♗g4 ♕c6 21 ♗f3 ♕d7 22 ♖a2 ♗f8 23 ♖ae2 ♖xe2 24 ♕xe2 c6

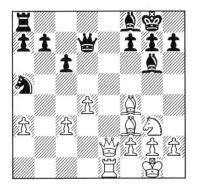

25 h4! h6 26 h5 ♗h7 27 a4 ♖d8 28 ♗g4 f5 29 ♗h3 ♕f7 30 ♕d3 ♘c4 31 ♗xf5 ♗xf5 32 ♘xf5 ♘b2 33 ♕h3 ♘xa4 34 ♖e3 ♘b6 35 ♖g3 ♔h7 36 ♗e5 ♖d5 37 ♕g4 ♘d7 38 ♕e4 Black resigned.

At the European Championship in Batumi, Judit represented Hungary on board two. She scored 6½/9 and won the gold medal for the best performance on her board, helping Hungary take the silver medals. Here is a cute queen trap:

□ **Judit Polgar**
■ **Sergey Volkov**
Batumi 1999

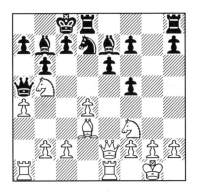

14 ♘b5! ♖hg8 15 c3 c5 16 g3 a6 17 ♘d2 axb5 18 axb5

and White soon won.

At the 2000 Chess Olympiad in Istanbul, Judit scored 10/13, the second highest points total in the entire Olympiad, with a rating performance of 2772. In the games and combinations section you can find two of Judit's masterpieces. Here is another cute short game which she won:

□ **Zbynek Hracek**
■ **Judit Polgar**
Istanbul Olympiad 2000
Sicilian Defense

1 e4 c5 2 ♘f3 e6 3 d4 cxd4 4 ♘xd4 ♘c6 5 ♘c3 ♕c7 6 ♗e3 a6 7 ♗d3 b5 8 ♘xc6 ♕xc6 9 0-0 ♗b7 10 a3 ♘f6 11 ♕e2 h5 12 f4 ♘g4 13 ♗d2 ♗c5+ 14 ♔h1 ♗d4 15 ♖ae1 0-0-0 16 ♘d1 f5 17 ♗a5 ♖df8 18 c3 ♗a7 19 e5 g5 20 c4 bxc4 21 ♗xc4 gxf4 22 ♖f3 ♖hg8 23 b4 ♘xe5 24 ♕xe5 ♕xc4 25 ♘b2

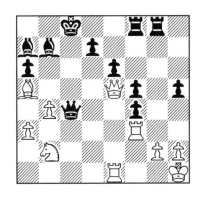

25...♗xf3! 26 gxf3 ♕c2 White resigned.

Judit also did well at the 2001 European Championship, in arguably the strongest open tournament ever held. She finishing on 9/13, tying third with Azmaiparashvili, just half a point behind the two winners, Sutovsky and Ponomariov.

Here is her game from round 11:

□ **Judit Polgar**
■ **Sergei Tiviakov**
Ohrid 2001
Sicilian Defense

1 e4 c5 2 ♘f3 ♘c6 3 ♗b5 d6 4 c3 ♘f6 5 ♕e2 ♗d7 6 d4 cxd4 7 cxd4 a6 8 ♗xc6 ♗xc6 9 d5 ♗d7 10 ♘c3 g6 11 0-0 ♗g7 12 ♗e3 0-0 13 ♗d4 ♗g4 14 h3 ♗xf3 15 ♕xf3 ♖c8 16 ♖ac1 b5 17 ♕e3 ♕d7 18 ♘e2 e6

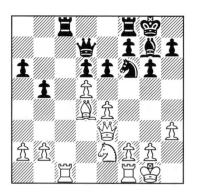

19 dxe6 ♕xe6 20 f3 ♖xc1 21 ♖xc1 ♕xa2 22 ♖c6 ♖d8 23 ♕c3 ♘e8 24 ♗xg7 ♘xg7 25 ♘f4 ♘e6 26 ♕f6 ♖e8 27 ♘d5 a5 28 ♖xd6 ♕c4 29 ♖d7 ♕c5+ 30 ♔h2 Black resigned.

In 2002, Judit was invited to represent the world in the Russia vs. Rest of the World rapid match in Moscow. Although she did not do particularly well

in this event, she did defeat Garry Kasparov for the first time. (See the supplementary games section.)

At the end of the year at the Olympiad in Bled, Slovenia, Judit won a silver medal with the Hungarian team. She also won an individual Bronze for her performance on board two.

Here is a nice miniature from that Olympiad:

□ **Judit Polgar**
■ **Shakhriyah Mamedyarov**
Bled Olympiad 2002
Ruy Lopez

1 e4 e5 2 ♘f3 ♘c6 3 ♗b5 a6 4 ♗a4 ♘f6 5 0-0 ♘xe4 6 d4 b5 7 ♗b3 d5 8 dxe5 ♗e6 9 ♘bd2 ♘c5 10 c3 d4 11 ♘g5 ♗d5

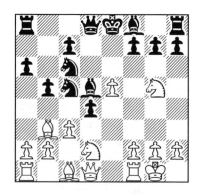

12 ♘xf7! ♔xf7 13 ♕f3+ ♔e6 14 ♕g4+ ♔f7 15 ♕f5+ ♔e7 16 e6 ♗xe6 17 ♖e1 ♕d6 18 ♗xe6 ♘xe6 19 ♘e4 ♕e5 20 ♗g5+ ♔d7 21 ♘c5+ ♗xc5 22 ♕f7+ ♔d6 23 ♗e7+ ♔d5
Black resigned

It is mate after 24 ♕f3+ ♔c4 25 b3.

Finally breaking 2700!

In 2003, Judit cleared another hurdle.

After being in the top twenty in the world for about a decade, Judit finally entered the top ten and crossed the magic 2700 barrier. She had a great tournament in Wijk aan Zee finishing second only to Anand. See her victory against Anatoly Karpov in the games section.

She had another good tournament in our home-town of Budapest. Judit and Nigel Short were in the chase for first place until the last round, but unfortunately she lost their individual game at the end. Nevertheless, she finished second, ahead of Peter Leko, Boris Gelfand and others.

In August of that year, the Chess Classic in Mainz, Germany, held a special rapid match between Vishy Anand and Judit. As chessbase.com commented about Judit: 'She is greatly feared by her colleagues as a dangerous attacking player who tends to go for mate right out of the opening.'

The spectators who want to see 'blood' could not be disappointed, as all eight games had decisive results. Judit took the lead in the first game after a win with the white pieces in a Sicilian Najdorf, but Anand bounced back in the next game on the white side of a Petroff. Judit won game 3, this time as

Black, choosing the Najdorf variation herself. In game 4, Vishy equalized by also winning with Black, in a queen, rook and opposite-colored bishop endgame. Judit took the lead once more by winning the fifth game quickly in another Najdorf. In the sixth game Judit was on the black side of the same opening and again White won and the score was tied.

Unfortunately, on the last day Anand won both games. Judit had a good position in game 7 almost until the very end, but then she made some inaccuracies in the endgame that cost her a full point. In the last game, Anand understandably switched from the sharp Sicilian to the calmer Ruy Lopez. Judit tried hard to win but over-pressed, and finally lost the match 3-5.

After such a wonderful year, Judit and her husband Gusztav decided to start a family, and Judit took time off from serious competition during her pregnancy. She gave birth on August 10th, 2004, to a healthy and cute baby boy called Oliver. As I write these lines, she is back competing with the world's best players in Wijk aan Zee. In her first game, she defeated a fellow 2700+ player, GM Peter Svidler!

Games and Combinations

Games

Game 1
□ **Judit Polgar**
■ **Krunoslav Hulak**
Amsterdam 1989
Sicilian Defense

---

1 e4

This was a very special event for Judit, in one of our favorite countries, the Netherlands. Judit was just turning 13 and performed sensationally well in the tournament. The press was writing things like 'Polgarmania Conquers Holland' and other similar headlines. This was one of her six victories there.

1...c5

Judit's opponent is a well-known Croatian Grandmaster.

2 ♘f3

A lot of British players like 2 f4, the so-called Grand-Prix Attack.

2...e6

2...d6 and 2...♘c6 are other moves.

3 d4

Judit is always ready for a challenging Sicilian battle.

3...cxd4

This is the normal and natural response, and usually people play it without much hesitation. One of the main ideas in the Sicilian is for Black to trade the c-pawn for White's central d-pawn.

4 ♘xd4

In the Sicilian the game is unbalanced very early on. White often gets a target in the d6 pawn and/or a kingside attack against the enemy king, while Black tries to obtain counterplay on the queenside. The king's pawn openings (1 e4 e5) are a lot more solid for Black.

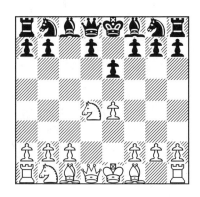

4...♘c6

4...♘f6 and 4...a6 are also playable.

5 ♘c3

The other main move is 5 ♘b5, leading to a positional struggle. It's no surprise that Judit preferred the more aggressive choice.

5...♕c7

Taking control of the h2-b8 diagonal. In some variations, Black can even follow it up with ...♗d6 gaining even more power over the dark squares along that diagonal.

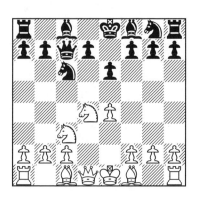

6 ♗e2

In those years, this was Judit's favorite set-up as Black. So here she had to play against her own opening.

6...a6

This is a very typical move in the Sicilian, preparing ...b7-b5.

7 0-0

A natural follow-up to White's previous move.

7...♘f6

Finally Black develops on the kingside too.

8 ♗e3

Judit has played a number of games, both as White and as Black, with 8 ♔h1 when play usually continues 8...♘xd4 9 ♕xd4 ♗c5.

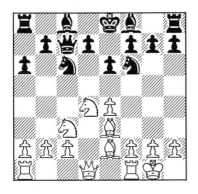

8...♗e7

This move switches back to the Scheveningen variation. To stay within the Paulsen variation, Black would continue 8...♗b4. A much later game of Judit's against the long time Dutch No.1, GM Jan Timman, at Wijk aan Zee 2003, continued 9 ♘a4 ♗e7 10 ♘xc6 bxc6 11 ♘b6 ♖b8 12 ♘xc8 ♕xc8 13 ♗d4 d5 14 exd5 cxd5 15 c4 0-0 16 ♖c1 dxc4 17 ♖xc4 ♕b7 18 ♕c2 ♘d5 19 b3 ♖fd8 20 ♕b2 ♘b6 21 ♖c2 ♘a4 22 ♕a1 ♕e4 23 ♖d2 ♗c5 24 ♗xc5 ♘xc5 25

♕c3 ♖xd2 26 ♕xd2 g6 27 ♖c1 ♕e5 28 f4 ♕f5 29 ♕d6 ♖c8 30 b4 ♕e4 31 ♕d2 and Black resigned.

9 f4

Now White is threatening to gain more space with e4-e5.

9...d6

Black prevents the pawn push and clears the path for the bishop on c8.

10 ♕e1

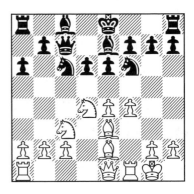

In this variation, White has to make a decision at some point whether to play a2-a4 or not. In most of her games, Judit preferred the direct attack which allows ...b7-b5. Another typical prophylactic move is ♔g1-h1 either here or in the next few moves.

10...♗d7

Developing the bishop. 10...b5 would open the long diagonal at the wrong time. White is better after 11 ♘xc6 ♕xc6 12 e5 followed by ♗e2-f3.

11 ♕g3

That is where the queen was heading!

11...0-0

Black had to protect the g7-pawn. 11...g6 would weaken the dark squares, while 11...♖g8 would strip Black of the right to castle on the kingside.

12 ♖ae1

Bringing the last undeveloped piece to the kingside. Its main purpose is to support the future e4-e5 advance.

12...b5

This is Black's primary counterplay, threatening to chase the white knight from c3 with ...b5-b4.

13 a3

Now the knight on c3 is safe for a while.

13...♘xd4

Black makes this trade to release the c6 square for the bishop.

14 ♗xd4

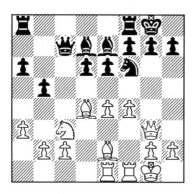

Now the white bishop on d4 is quite powerful. It is sort of pinning the knight on f6, since if the knight moves towards the center, the a1-h8 diagonal is opened up and White checkmates with ♕xg7.

14...♗c6

Black moves the bishop to a more active position and puts pressure on the e4 pawn. Although this pawn is not really under attack because of the pin on the f6 knight against the g7 square.

15 ♗d3

Even though White did not have to protect the pawn, she wanted the bishop pointing towards the black king.

15...♖ab8

The idea is to further support the b5 pawn with the plan of ...a6-a5 followed by ...b5-b4.

This position was also reached in a later game between Judit and the Hungarian chess legend, GM Lajos Portisch, in Monaco 1994. He continued more accurately with 15...♖ae8 16 ♕h3 e5 17 ♗e3 ♕d7 and drew the game.

16 e5

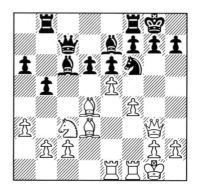

After all her preparation White is ready to open the position and start the real attack.

16...♘e8

White is better after 16...dxe5 17 ♗xe5 ♕b6+ 18 ♔h1 ♖bd8 19 f5.

17 f5!

Opening more files for the white rooks. One of White's threats is 18 fxe6 fxe6 19 ♕h3 with a dual attack on the e6 and h7 pawns.

17...exf5

Black had no choice since f5-f6 was also a scary threat.

18 ♖xf5

Bringing the rook closer to the black king. In many variations, the rook can go to g5 or h5.

18...dxe5

Black is trying to simplify the position with some exchanges.

19 ♕h3

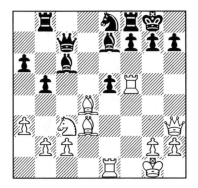

This was Judit's key idea! After 19 ♖exe5 Black can defend with 19...♗f6!. On the other hand, White perhaps has an even bigger advantage after 19 ♗xe5 ♗d6 20 ♗xd6 ♘xd6 21 ♖c5, and not 20...♕xd6? because White has a cute combination to win a piece with 21 ♖xe8! ♕xg3 22 ♖xf8+ ♔xf8 23 hxg3.

19...h6

There are some beautiful combinations after other responses. For example:

a) 19...g6 20 ♗xe5 ♕b6+ 21 ♔h1 threatening 22 ♕xh7+! ♔xh7 23 ♖h5+ ♔g8 24 ♖h8 mate.

b) If Black pins with 19...♗d7, White concludes the attack with 20 ♘d5 ♕d8 21 ♘xe7+ ♕xe7 22 ♕xh7+! ♔xh7 23 ♖fxe5+.

c) If Black accepts the sacrifice with 19...exd4, another pretty move follows: 20 ♖xf7!, and if Black accepts the gift, the game ends with a very quick checkmate, either by 20...♔xf7 21 ♕e6 mate or 20...♖xf7 21 ♕xh7+ ♔f8 22 ♕h8 mate, although Black can improve and

hang on with 20...♘f6.

20 ♗xe5

White has regained the pawn back and things look pretty bad for Black. White's pieces are well co-ordinated and the bishop pair are pointing right at the black king. But as Garry Kasparov said: 'You have to make several mistakes in chess to lose'.

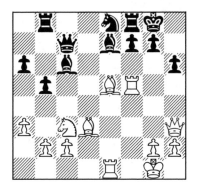

20...♕a7+?

If 20...♕b6+ 21 ♔h1 ♗d6 22 ♖g5, the difference on the game is that Black can take with 22...♗xe5, since 23 ♕xh6? loses to the discovery 23...♗xg2+!. However, White can improve with 22 ♗xg7! ♘xg7 23 ♕xh6 and a strong attack. So Black's best chance would have been to play 20...♗d6, and if 21 ♕g3 ♖d8.

21 ♔h1

Suddenly the rook on b8 is under attack.

21...♗d6

Knowing what happened in the game, 21...♖d8 would have been a better try.

22 ♖g5!!

This is an impressive move. The direct threat is ♕xh6, thanks to the just created pin.

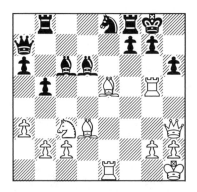

22...♛f2

Attacking the rook on e1. White has a crushing attack after 22...♝xe5 23 ♛xh6 g6 24 ♜exe5.

23 ♜f1

Moving the rook away from the queen's attack, and now the rook is attacking the queen. It would have been a blunder to do the same from the other side, i.e. 23 ♜e2? ♛f1 mate.

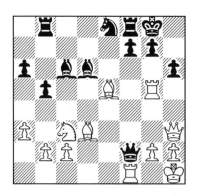

23...♛xf1+

Black could not save the queen, since if 23...♛d2 24 ♛f5 g6 25 ♜xg6+ fxg6 26 ♛xg6+ mate.

24 ♝xf1

Black gets two rooks for the queen, but White's attack is not over.

24...hxg5

Materially speaking, Black is OK, but his king is still in trouble.

25 ♝d3!

Threatening mate in one.

25...f5

25...g6 is not possible because of 26 ♛h8 mate, while if 25...f6 26 ♝g6 and the king cannot escape.

26 ♝xf5

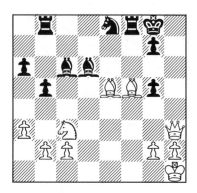

Another small combination, sacrificing the bishop on e5.

26...♝xe5

Black has just won a piece, but he cannot celebrate for long.

27 ♛h7+

This continuation is a lot better than 27 ♝e6+ ♜f7 or 27 ♝h7+ ♚f7 28 ♛f5+ ♝f6.

27...♚f7

Now the king is chased out of safety.

28 ♛g6+

With this check White wins the bishop back.

28...♚e7

If 28...♚g8 29 ♝e6+ and the game is over quickly, e.g. 29...♚h8 30 ♛h5 mate, or 29...♜f7 30 ♛xf7+ ♚h8 31 ♛h5 mate.

29 ♛e6+

29 ♕xc6 would be a mistake because Black can also capture with 29...♖xf5.

29...♔d8

And now White regains the piece.

30 ♕xe5

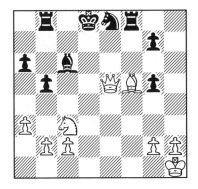

White has evened up the materials and the black king is still in a very vulnerable position.

30...♖b7

Trying to defend along the second rank.

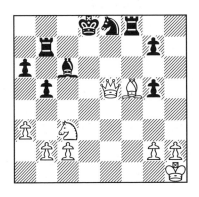

31 ♔g1!

31 ♘d5 was also good, but ♔g1 is a smart move from a practical point of view. It frees up the bishop on f5, since White no longer has to worry about a back rank mate with ...♖f1; for example,

31 ♕d4+ could have been answered with 31...♖d7.

31...♖bf7

With little time left on the clock Black tries to create some counterplay.

32 g4

The immediate 32 ♕b8+ was perhaps even more precise.

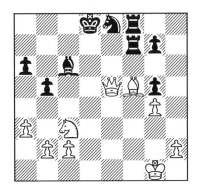

32...g6

Black is hoping for 33 ♗xg6 ♖f1 mate.

33 ♕b8+

Of course capturing the g6 pawn would have been suicidal.

33...♔e7

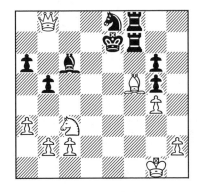

Black is suffering because his king can find no safety in the middle of the board. Now comes a final combination:

34 ♘d5+!

A pretty move! White involves her last inactive piece.

34...♗xd5

Black has no choice but to capture.

35 ♕e5+

This fork wins the bishop and more.

35...♔d8

The king has no other place to go.

36 ♕xd5+

The co-operation between the queen and bishop is very effective.

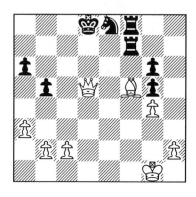

36...♔c7

Running to the other side is no better: 36...♔e7 37 ♕d7+ ♔f6 38 ♕e6+ ♔g7 39 ♕xg6+ ♔h8 40 ♕h6+ ♔g8 and 41 ♗e6 pins the rook on f7.

37 ♕c5+

Continuing the chase.

37...♔b8

If 37...♔d8 38 ♕d6+ wins, while after 37...♔b7 the white bishop gets to participate with a check by 38 ♗e4+.

38 ♕b6+

Now Black is forced to block the check.

38...♖b7

If 38...♔a8 39 ♗e4+ mates.

39 ♕d8+

An important intermediate check,

saving both the queen and the bishop.

39...♔a7

As the two black rooks are no longer doubled on the f-file, White can safely capture the pawn.

40 ♗xg6 Black resigned

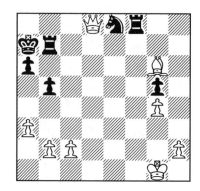

Black could have played on, but the result would be the same. White has too many pawns.

Game 2
□ **Alexander Chernin**
■ **Judit Polgar**
New Delhi 1990
King's Indian Defense

This game is from a major tournament in India. During our visit, we had the honor to meet the then prime minister, Rajiv Gandhi, who was present at a special banquet dinner held for the participants of the tournament. (Sadly, he was assassinated shortly afterwards).

1 c4

Grandmaster Alexander Chernin's favorite opening move.

1...g6

In those days Judit played the King's Indian almost exclusively. Therefore, she steered the game in that direction.

2 d4

White could also hold back d2-d4 and play the English Opening.

2...♘f6

Now we are back to a standard KID.

3 ♘c3

White develops the knight and prepares e2-e4.

3...♗g7

Another alternative is 3...d5, reaching a Grünfeld Defense.

4 e4

White has a perfect presence in the center. Black's plan is to provoke White to over-extend and then launch a counter-attack.

4...d6

Preventing e4-e5 and opening the diagonal for the bishop on c8.

5 h3

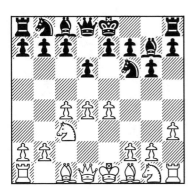

A modern approach. Until not long ago White mostly chose between 5 ♘f3, 5 ♗e2, 5 f3 and 5 f4. The idea of h2-h3 is to control the g4 square, both to prevent the black bishop or knight coming there, and even at times to play g2-g4. (See my game versus Hulsey for this variation.)

5...0-0

Safety first! A simple but important rule.

6 ♘f3

Continuing with normal development.

6...e5

The most typical theme for seeking counterplay in the King's Indian. The other approach is the Benoni style ...c7-c5.

7 d5

White locks up the center. After 7 dxe5 dxe5 8 ♕xd8 ♖xd8 9 ♘xe5 White could not keep the extra pawn for long: 9...♘xe4 10 ♘xe4 ♗xe5 wins it back with a favorable position for Black.

7...♘a6

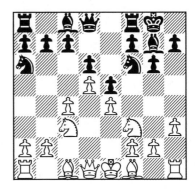

This is one of those exceptions when it is OK to develop the knight to the side of the board, as it is on its way to c5. There are two key advantages in using the route via a6 rather than d7: on a6 does not block the diagonal of the bishop on c8, and it also prevents b2-b4.

Black must make sure, however, that the knight will actually get to c5, and will not be stuck on a6 as a spectator after a possible a2-a3 and b2-b4.

8 ♗e3

Another option is 8 ♗d3 and after 8...♘c5 9 ♗c2.

8...♘h5

Black has to look for ways to get some activity. This move prepares ...f7-f5 and also eyes the f4 square.

9 ♘h2

An awkward-looking move. However, after the natural 9 ♗e2, Black achieves a good position with 9...♘f4. The game move prepares against both black ideas.

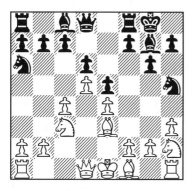

9...♛e8

Now if 9...♘f4 White can kick the knight straight back with 10 g3, as 10...♘xh3 11 ♘f3 would land the black knight in trouble. 9...f5 is also flawed since White can respond with 10 exf5 and Black cannot recapture, because 10...gxf5 leaves the knight on h5 hanging, while after 10...♗xf5 or 10...♖xf5 White forks with g2-g4.

10 ♗e2

Finally White develops the light-squared bishop.

10...f5

An open invitation for White to capture on h5. The alternative 10...♘f4 followed by ...f7-f5 also gives Black good chances.

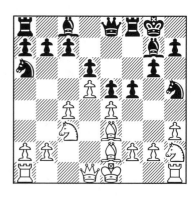

11 exf5

In games where White played 11 ♗xh5, Black got a very strong attack along the open g- and f-files, giving more than enough compensation for the weakness of the doubled pawns.

11...♘f4

Judit gladly sacrifices a pawn for the initiative, opening more files and diagonals.

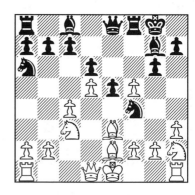

12 ♗xf4

If White wants to win a pawn, he has to trade the bishop first because the pawn on g2 was under attack. After 12 0-0 ♗xf5 Black has a very nice active position.

12...exf4

The bishop that was locked in behind the e5 pawn becomes alive and powerful.

13 fxg6

White is up a pawn, but for a price: Black has a pair of bishops and can create a strong attack against the white king.

13...♕xg6

Attacking the pawn on g2. White cannot play 14 0-0 because of 14...♗xh3 using the pin.

14 ♔f1

After this White has a chronic problem with his king's safety; But if 14 ♘g4 Black responds with 14...h5, while 14 ♗g4 ♗xg4 followed by ♖ae8+ would force the king to move anyway.

14...♘c5

It is time to bring the knight closer to the action in the center and on the kingside.

15 ♖c1?!

Judit did not think that it was important to defend against ...♗xc3. Better was 15 ♘f3 right away, when she planned to continue simply with 15...♗d7.

15...♗f5

The bishop is a lot more active here than on d7, controlling the important

b1-h7 diagonal. It also clears the eighth rank for the rook on a8 to get into the game.

16 ♘f3

A good and logical move, bringing the knight back closer to the center. The threat is also to play ♘f3-h4 and exchange one of Black's bishops.

16...♗f6!

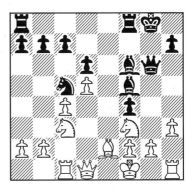

Preventing ♘f3-h4 and also clearing the g-file. Black does not want to allow the trade of one of her bishops.

17 ♔g1?!

A logical idea, trying to castle artificially by playing ♔g1-h2 and then getting to rook out from h1, but it seems very slow. 17 ♘d4!? would have been a better defense, when Judit planned 17...♗xd4 18 ♕xd4 and now sacrificing a second pawn with 18...f3! 19 ♗xf3 ♖ae8 20 ♔g1 ♘d3, or if 19 gxf3 ♖f7 preparing ...♖g7.

17...♔h8!

Clearing the g8 square for the rook. 17...♖ae8 also looked tempting.

18 ♔h2

The white king arrives at its natural destination, but this does not solve all the problems.

18...♖g8

Threatening an immediate mate.

19 ♖g1

After 19 ♗f1 Black can continue the attack with 19...♘d3, while 19 ♕g1? is a cute self-mate in two: 19...♕g3+ 20 fxg3 fxg3 mate!

19...♕h6!

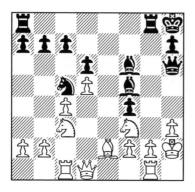

Another great attacking move, creating a direct threat!

20 ♗f1

If White plays a careless, such as 20 b4, Black strikes straight away with 20...♖xg2+! 21 ♖xg2 ♗xh3 and if 22 ♖g1? ♗f1+ and mate on the following move. Of course White can defend better with 22 ♘e1, but Black has a winning advantage anyway after 22...♗xg2+ 23 ♔xg2 ♖g8+ 24 ♗g4 ♕h4.

After the solid, but embarrassing-looking 20 ♕f1, Judit planned to play 20...a5 to solidify the knight's position on c5.

20...♖g7

Judit does not waste time getting ready to double the rooks. This is the critical moment of the game. After the next two active moves, White is lost.

21 b4

This move chases the knight back but creates additional weakness on the queenside. Instead, the centralizing 21 ♘d4 would fail to 21...♗xh3! 22 gxh3 ♖xg1 23 ♔xg1 ♕g7+ 24 ♔h2 ♗xd4, winning the pawn back while maintaining the attack. After the passive 21 ♕d2, Black can continue with 21...♖ag8 22 ♖d1 ♗g4 23 ♗e2 and now a quiet, but powerful move 23...♖g6!, threatening 24...♗xh3! 25 gxh3 ♕xh3+!! 26 ♔xh3 ♖h6+ and mate on the next move.

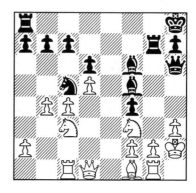

21...♘d7

A temporary retreat. The knight will soon reappear on another active post at e5.

22 ♗d3

This is certainly a mistake, as it allows the following combination. There are many more fascinating lines here. It is worth spending some time to figure out the exact variations. Of course computer software is a good aid here!

Just to give an example: On 22 ♘d4, Black's best answer is 22...♗xd4 23 ♕xd4 ♘e5, threatening 24...♗xh3! 24 ♔h1 f3! with an unexpected discovered attack on the rook on c1. It also destroys the wall of defense of the white pawns. After 25 ♕e3 ♕xe3 26 fxe3 and now the cute 26...f2 traps the rooks.

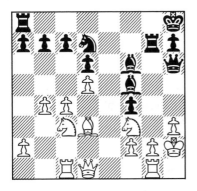

22...♖xg2+!!

The start of a beautiful combination which decides the game.

23 ♖xg2

If the king takes, Black mates in one with ...♕xh3.

23...♗xh3

Now after 23...♕xh3+ 24 ♔g1 and White would be safe.

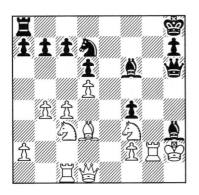

24 ♘e4

Again the rook cannot be saved with 24 ♖g1 because of 24...♗f1+, while after 24 ♔g1 Black wins all the sacrificed material back and more with 24...♗xg2 25 ♔xg2 ♗xc3, as the bishop cannot be taken because of the fork with 26...♕g7+.

24...♘e5!

This is a very important move, bringing new forces to the attack. The direct 24...♗xg2+ 25 ♔xg2 ♖g8+ 26 ♔f1 ♕h1+ is not good enough, as White escapes with 27 ♔e2.

25 ♘xe5

If 25 ♘xf6 either 25...♗g4+ or 25...♘xf3+ 26 ♕xf3 ♗g4+ wins.

25...♗xe5

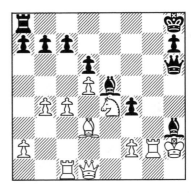

Threatening another discovered check with 26...f3+.

26 ♘g5

If White stops the ...f4-f3+ threat with 26 f3, Black can force mate with 26...♗xg2+ 27 ♔xg2 ♖g8+ 28 ♔f1 ♕h1+ 29 ♔e2 ♖g2+ 30 ♘f2 ♖xf2+! 31 ♔xf2 ♗d4+ 32 ♔e2 ♕g2+ 33 ♔e1 ♕f2. Instead, all of a sudden White threatens checkmate himself with 27 ♘f7!.

26...♗xg2+

It was a mistake to continue with 26...f3+ anyway, because after 27 ♔g1 ♗xg2 White forks with 28 ♘f7+.

27 ♔xg2

White was in a check so there was really no choice.

27...♕xg5+

All the clouds have cleared. Black won everything back and has an extra pawn, while White's key problem is still the lack of cover for the king.

28 ♔f3

If 28 ♔f1 f3! is winning. The white queen cannot take on f3 as the rook on c1 needs protection.

28...♖g8

Finally the queenside rook can also participate in the attack.

29 ♔e2

After 29 ♔e4 Black mates in two with 29...♕g2+ 30 ♔f5 ♕g6.

29...f3+! White resigned

After 30 ♔e1 ♗f4 or 30 ♔xf3 ♕g4+ 31 ♔e3 ♗f4+ White's position is hopeless.

A truly remarkable game! GM Chernin is one of the most solid players in the world and is rarely outplayed in such fashion.

> *Game 3*
> □ **Judit Polgar**
> ■ **Jordi Magem Badals**
> Madrid 1992
> *Caro-Kann Defense*

1 e4

This game is from one of the many big tournaments that Judit played in Spain.

1...c6

This is the Caro-Kann Defense.

2 d4

Just as against the French or the Pirc, this is the best response.

2...d5

Black must fight for the center.

3 exd5

3 ♘c3 or 3 e5 are the other common choices.

3...cxd5

Recapturing with the queen is out of the question, as White would gain time developing by attacking the queen with ♘c3.

4 c4

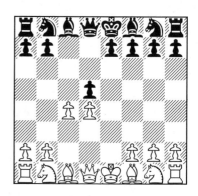

This is the Panov variation. White willingly goes for a middlegame with an isolated pawn, hoping for a strong initiative.

4...♘f6

Black develops the knight supporting the center.

5 ♘c3

White does the same.

5...e6

Opening the diagonal for the bishop on f8. 5...g6 is another, less popular way.

6 ♘f3

After 6 c5, Black puts the king in safety and then breaks with ...b7-b6, e.g. 6...♗e7 7 ♘f3 0-0 8 ♗d3 b6.

6...♗b4

Pinning the knight. Black is waiting for White to develop the king's bishop before capturing on c4. 6...♗e7 is a more popular move.

7 cxd5

White did not want to move the bishop on f1 and then have to waste another to recapture after ...d5xc4.

7...♘xd5

7...exd5 also seems playable, and after 8 ♕a4+ ♘c6.

8 ♕b3

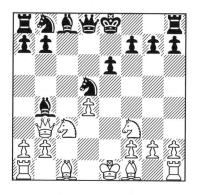

Protecting the knight on c3. In most games, White has preferred the more solid 8 ♗d2.

8...♘c6

Black continues developing and putting pressure on the d4 pawn.

9 ♗d3

Getting ready to castle.

9...♗e7

A few months later in Aruba, the former World Champion Vassily Smyslov made a significant improvement over Black's last move in 9...♕b6, followed by 10 ♗d2 ♗a5 with equality.

10 0-0

The white king is now in safety, while Black is invited to win a pawn.

10...♘db4?!

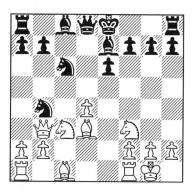

The beginning of an incorrect plan. We shall soon see why it is wrong.

11 ♗e4

In this case it is more important to keep the bishop than the d4 pawn.

11...♘xd4

Black is greedy; it is far too risky to accept this sacrifice, as the king will now be stuck in the center.

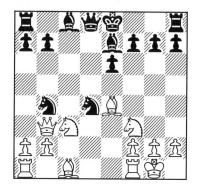

12 ♘xd4

With this trade White gains time to put the rook on the open file with tempo.

12...♕xd4

If Black had just one more move and could castle, everything would be fine. But it is White's turn.

13 ♖d1

A very important move. The immediate 13 ♕a4 does not achieve the goal, as Black could block with 13...♗d7.

13...♕e5

White's answer would be the same against other queen moves.

14 ♕a4+

Forcing the black king to move.

14...♔f8

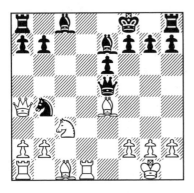

White has tremendous compensation for the sacrificed pawn. Besides the black king being stuck in the middle, Black also has trouble developing both rooks and the light-squared bishop.

15 ♗e3

Mobilizing the last undeveloped piece.

15...f5

Black clears some space for the king to move up and let the rook on h8 out.

16 ♗f3

Black has a hard time finding a decent plan, whereas White will improve her position little by little. The next piece that needs to be improved is the rook on a1.

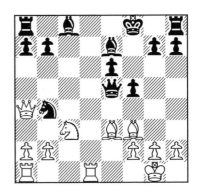

16...♖g8

Getting the rook off the a1-h8 diagonal. The following variation explains why: if 16...♔f7? right away, White has 17 ♗h5+ g6 (or 17...♔g8 18 ♕e8+ ♗f8 19 ♗f7 mate) 18 ♗d4 with a winning skewer.

17 a3

Kicking the black knight back.

17...♘a6

On 17...♘c6 White could just capture with 18 ♗xc6, but 18 ♗f4 ♕c5 19 ♘b5 is even better.

18 ♖ac1

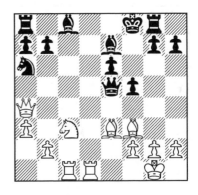

Now the white pieces totally dominate the board. Black has a problem with the bishop on c8 and his king is in a very awkward position.

18...&f7

Trying to let rook out.

19 &b5

Taking even more squares away from Black. The knight also attacks the pawn on a7.

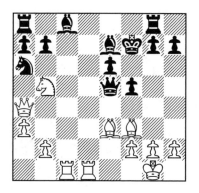

19...&f8

Black wants to artificially castle with ...&g8.

20 &d4

Chasing the queen away from its central location.

20...&f4

Staying away from b8 for now.

21 &b3

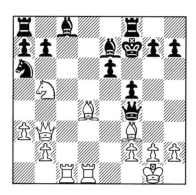

Keeping an eye on the e6 pawn.

21...&d8

If Black tries to hide the king with

21...&g8, White has a winning combination: 22 &xc8! &fxc8 23 &xe6+ &f8 24 &xg7+ &xg7 25 &xe7+

22 g3

22 &e3 is also good.

22...&b8

This move is equivalent to resigning; although after the more stubborn 22...&g5 23 &e3 Black's position is hopeless too.

23 &e3

Threatening 24 &e5 trapping the queen.

23...&f6

Stopping the threat, but this move has other flaws.

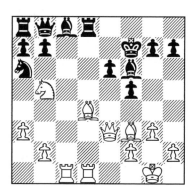

24 &xf6

It is 'cash in' time.

24...&xd1+

A necessary intermediate move as the rook is under attack.

25 &xd1

Now the rook takes control of the open d-file.

25...&xf6

Black is still a pawn ahead but suffers a miserable queenside.

26 &d8 Black resigned

If 26...&e5 27 &f8+ or 26...&e7 27 &g5+ wins.

> *Game 4*
> □ **Alexei Shirov**
> ■ **Judit Polgar**
> Buenos Aires 1994
> *Sicilian Defense*

1 e4

When I asked Judit which is her all time favorite game, she said it is hard to choose. However, this game is certainly one of the very first on her list.

1...c5

Shirov is one of the sharpest and most imaginative world-class players in chess history. It is a real challenge facing him in the sharpest opening.

2 ♘f3

Shirov always responds with this move against the Sicilian. In fact, the only game I found in my database where he played differently (with 2 c3) was against Judit in 1997.

2...e6

This game was played as part of a very special tournament, which was held on the honor of the late Lev Polugaevsky's 60th birthday. He was a great grandmaster and in love with the Sicilian Defense; a variation has even been named after him. In this unique tournament all the games had to start as a Sicilian Defense. Tournaments with opening restrictions used to be popular about a century ago, but went out of fashion long ago.

3 d4

This move was still part of the 'tournament rules'.

3...cxd4

The best response.

4 ♘xd4

This is the beginning of the Open Sicilian. From here on, the players were free to play any move they wanted.

4...♘c6

Starting out as the Taimanov variation.

5 ♘c3

5 ♘b5 is another good continuation.

5...d6

This is a rare move in this specific position. 5...♕c7 or 5...♘f6 are more common.

6 g4

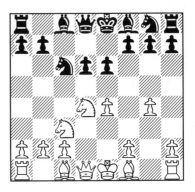

This looks a little strange to me. In the Keres Attack, everything is the same, except that instead of the knight from b8 being on c6, the other knight from g8 is on f6. In that case the 6 g4 move is a lot more logical, intending the chase away the knight with g4-g5.

6...a6

In some other games Judit started with 6...♘ge7 and played 7...a6 next, resulting in pretty much the same position.

7 ♗e3

White continues with development.

7...♘ge7

A smart choice, considering that White has already showed his cards by

---

playing g2-g4, 7...♘f6 would certainly justify White's plan. After the game move, on the other hand, it is not so clear what was the purpose of the early advance of the g-pawn.

With her last move Black also connected the two knights and therefore ...b7-b5 will be possible next.

8 ♘b3

In several later games (including against Judit), Shirov instead played 8 f4 as an improvement.

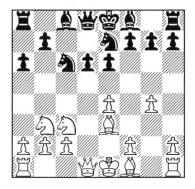

8...b5

8...♘g6 reaches a position between these same opponents at the 1996 Yerevan Olympiad. That wild game ended in a draw after the following moves: 9 ♕d2 b5 10 0-0-0 ♘ge5 11 g5 ♘a5 12 f4 ♘ec4 13 ♕f2 ♖b8 14 f5 ♘xe3 15 ♕xe3 ♕b6 16 ♕g3 ♗e7 17 ♘xa5 ♕xa5 18 e5 d5 19 f6 ♗b4 20 ♘xd5 exd5 21 e6 ♖b7 22 exf7+ ♔xf7 23 fxg7 ♖e8 24 g6+ ♔xg7 25 gxh7+ ♔h8 26 ♖g1 ♖xh7 27 ♕g6 ♕d8 28 ♗d3 ♕e7 29 ♕xh7+ ♕xh7 30 ♗xh7 ♔xh7 31 ♖xd5 ♗f8 32 ♖dd1 ♖e2 33 ♖de1 ♖xh2 34 ♖h1 ♖xh1 35 ♖xh1+ ♔g6 36 ♖h8 ♔g7 37 ♖h1 ♔f7 38 ♔d2 ♔e7 39 ♖h7+ ♔e6 40 ♖c7 ♗d7 and a draw was agreed.

9 f4

A year earlier, Shirov played 9 ♕e2 against Salov.

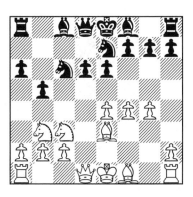

9...♗b7

A lovely place for the bishop.

10 ♕f3

So far Shirov has followed his game vs. Kasparov from a few months before.

10...g5!

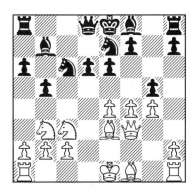

This novelty won a lot of awards. It is a beautiful, long-term pawn sacrifice with the idea of gaining control of the crucial central e5 square. Garry played 10...♘a5 in the above-mentioned game.

11 fxg5

After 11 0-0-0 Judit planned 11...gxf4 12 ♗xf4 ♘g6.

11...♘e5

Centralizing the knight and attacking the queen at the same time.

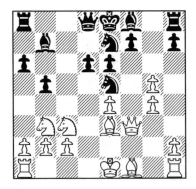

12 ♕g2

Holding on to both the e4 and g4 pawns. If 12 ♕e2, Black would chase the knight on c3 by 12...b4, and then capture the e4 pawn, e.g. after 13 ♘a4 ♗c6 14 ♘b6 ♗xe4.

12...b4

Forcing the knight to move to a less active square.

13 ♘e2

If 13 ♘a4, Judit planned the fancy 13...♘d5!.

13...h5!!

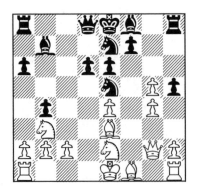

A very impressive sequence: 10...g5! and 13...h5!!. This move aims to clear the f5 square for the other knight. In-

stead, after 13...♘c4 14 ♗d4 e5, White has 15 ♘g3!.

14 gxh5?!

A mistake! After the game Shirov suggested giving the pawn back with 14 0-0-0 as an improvement. If 14 gxh6 Black can choose between 14...♗xh6 15 ♗xh6 ♖xh6 with compensation or the even wilder 14...f5!? with immense complications.

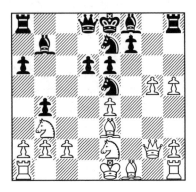

14...♘f5!

This move is possible because the pawn on e4 is pinned.

15 ♗f2

Keeping control of the h4 square. After 15 ♗f4 ♘h4 would follow.

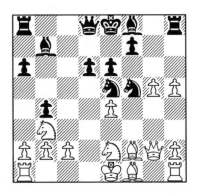

15...♕xg5!

A cute little combination. If White

captures with 16 ♕xg5 ♘f3+ forks and wins the queen back with a superior position after 17 ♔d1 ♘xg5.

16 ♘a5?

Shirov overlooked Judit's next move. White's position was bad no matter what, but this move makes Black's task easier.

16...♘e3!!

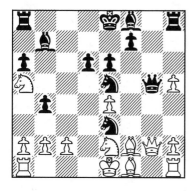

The prettiest move of the game!

17 ♕g3

If 17 ♕xg5 ♘f3 mates, while after 17 ♗xe3 ♕xe3, White does not have time to capture the bishop with 18 ♘xb7 because of 18...♘f3+ and White has to give the queen up, otherwise 19 ♔d1 ♕d2 mate ends the game.

17...♕xg3

Now Black simply gathers up the fruits of the attack.

18 ♘xg3

Protecting the e4 and h5 pawns.

18...♘xc2+

Forking the king and the rook on a1.

19 ♔d1

19 ♔d2 would allow Black a potential ...♗h6+.

19...♘xa1

Now the only thing Black has to be careful about is to rescue the knight from a1.

20 ♘xb7

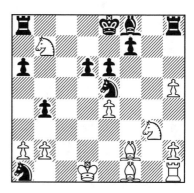

After all the clouds have cleared, White is down an exchange.

20...b3

Black immediately gets the knight out of the corner.

21 axb3

Otherwise the knight could escape via c2.

21...♘xb3

The rest is easy. Now White has to hurry up and rescue the knight on b7.

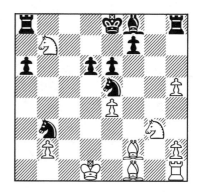

22 ♔c2

The game is hopeless at this point.

22...♘c5

Black is happy to trade pieces because she has a material advantage.

23 ♘xc5

A tiny success for White, forcing Black's d-pawn to the c-file.

23...dxc5

Now the c-pawn is isolated.

24 ♗e1

Trying to relocate the bishop to c3.

24...♘f3

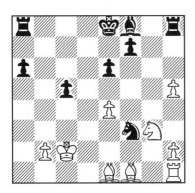

Switching to another center square, d4.

25 ♗c3

Moving away from the knight's attack while aiming at Black's rook.

25...♘d4+

There is no need to move the rook away.

26 ♔d3

26 ♗xd4 cxd4 was no better.

26...♗d6

One of many good choices.

27 ♗g2

On 27 b4, Judit planned 27...♔e7 28 bxc5 ♗xc5 29 ♗xd4 ♖hd8 30 ♘e2 e5 winning the bishop.

27...♗e5

Black is slowly improving the position of her pieces.

28 ♔c4

Attacking the c5 pawn.

28...♔e7

Black connects the rooks and sacrifices the pawn.

29 ♖a1

Capturing the pawn with 29 ♔xc5 would be walking the king into a mating net: 29...♖hc8+ 30 ♔b6 ♖ab8+ 31 ♔a5 ♖c4.

29...♘c6 White resigned

Shirov was tired of defending this lost position. Maybe some players would still continue on a little, but against somebody of Judit's caliber, the result would not change.

Game 5
□ **Judit Polgar**
■ **Michael Adams**
Dortmund 1996
Ruy Lopez

---

1 e4

In this game, Judit's opponent is the British super-grandmaster 'Mickey' Adams. I first met and played him at the World Junior Championship in Australia, when he was only 15 and already very talented. Now for many years he has belonged to the world's elite.

1...e5

Steering towards a more peaceful

game, which is no surprise against Judit.

2 ♘f3

Until her early teenage years Judit mostly played the romantic King's Gambit, 2 f4. Then with her coach at the time, IM Laszlo Hazai, she started to study the more conservative Ruy Lopez. Analyzing the more positional middlegames greatly helped her overall understanding of the game, which is necessary to get to the top.

2...♘c6

The Petroff (2...♘f6) is another very popular opening.

3 ♗b5

This is the Ruy Lopez. In my World Championship match against Xie Jun, I played the Scotch with 3 d4.

3...a6

The main line. 3...♘f6 straight away is also possible, leading to a different type of game. (See Judit's victory over Kasparov in the supplementary games section.)

4 ♗a4

Bobby Fischer's favorite used to be the Exchange variation with 4 ♗xc6 dxc6 5 0-0. After 5 ♘xe5 Black would win the pawn back immediately with 5...♕d4.

4...♘f6

A standard developing move which also attacks the e4 pawn.

5 0-0

White does not need to worry right now about protecting the e4 pawn and can proceed to put the king in safety.

5...♗e7

Black can capture the pawn on e4, which is the Open variation of the Ruy Lopez, but would not be able to keep the extra pawn for long. After 5...♘xe4

White could win the pawn back with 6 ♖e1, although White usually continues with 6 d4.

At the Bled Olympiad in 2002, Judit won a very nice game against Mamedyarov after 5...♘xe4 6 d4 b5 7 ♗b3 d5 8 dxe5 ♗e6 9 ♘bd2 ♘c5 10 c3 d4 11 ♘g5 ♗d5? 12 ♘xf7! ♔xf7 13 ♕f3+ ♔e6 14 ♕g4+ ♔f7 15 ♕f5+ ♔e7 16 e6! (see page 210).

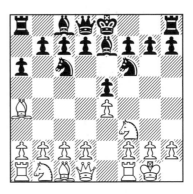

6 ♖e1

With this move White protects the e4 pawn, and now threatens to win a pawn with 7 ♗xc6 and 8 ♘xe5.

6...b5

Preventing the above threat and clearing space for the bishop on b7.

7 ♗b3

The white bishop had to retreat, but to a good place.

7...0-0

Keeping the option open of playing the Marshall Attack with 8 c3 d5. The main alternative is 7...d6.

8 h3

If Black plays 8...d5 now, the difference is that White has not weakened the d3 square with c2-c3, but has a more important pawn move in h2-h3 instead. Nevertheless, 8...d5 is still playable.

8...♗b7

Adams did not want to sacrifice the pawn here, but preferred a more conservative approach.

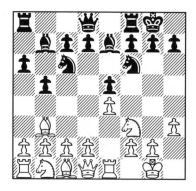

9 d3

Opening up the c1-h6 diagonal for the bishop on c1.

9...h6

An inaccuracy. It was more important to play 9...d6, protecting the e5 pawn, and then follow with ...♘a5 and ...c7-c5.

10 ♘c3

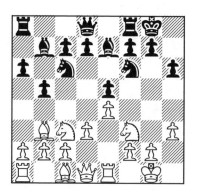

White focuses on the central d5 square. In an earlier game in 1993 Adams reached an OK position after 10 ♘bd2 ♖e8 11 c3 ♗f8 12 a4 ♘a5 13 ♗a2 c5. However, in 1999 Topalov improved on this for White (also against Adams) and got an advantage after 12 a3 d6 13 ♗a2 ♘b8 14 ♘h4 d5 15 ♕f3.

With the game continuation the white knight can also later arrive on f5, albeit via a different route: c3-e2-g3.

10...♖e8

After 10...d6 White would continue 11 a4 ♘a5 12 ♗a2 b4 13 ♘e2 c5 14 c3 bxc3 15 bxc3 c4 16 ♘g3 cxd3 17 ♕xd3 ♗c8 18 ♘h4 with a clear advantage.

11 a3

Opening an escape square for the bishop on a2, in anticipation of ...♘a5.

11...♗f8

A typical move in this opening, to defend the kingside and clear the e-file for the rook. Black often tries to relocate the bishop on g7 after ...g7-g6. 11...♗c5 was interesting too.

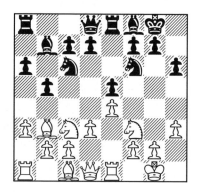

12 ♘d5

White offers a trade to improve her position.

12...♘a5

Chasing the bishop away. After the exchange on d5, White recaptures with the pawn and would have a better position since the black pawns are weaker than White's.

13 ♗a2

Naturally White does not allow the trade with ...♘xb3.

13...♗xd5?

This was a major strategical error; Black will miss the pair of bishops. 13...c5 was better.

14 exd5

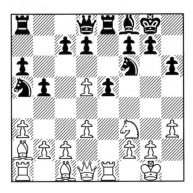

As useless as White's bishop on a2 seems, it is still a better piece than Black's knight on a5.

14...d6?!

Black was already in a difficult situation and this move makes things worse, further weakening the light squares on the queenside. Maybe 14...♗d6 would be the lesser evil.

15 b4

Chasing the knight to its worse place on the board.

15...♘b7

Here the knight is really limited in potential, going eventually to d8, and then where next?

16 c4

Now it is time to open the position. The target is the c-file.

16...♕d7

Black connects the rooks. White would welcome the trade on c4, straightening out her pawn formation

after 16...bxc4 17 dxc4.

17 ♗e3

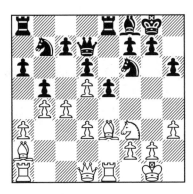

At last developing the bishop, clearing space for the rook, and also assisting to prepare the c4-c5 advance.

17...♘d8

Black dreams of one day bringing the knight to f7. If he tries to get activity with 17...c5, then the white bishop on a2 is revived after 18 dxc6 ♕xc6 19 ♖c1 with White's advantage.

18 ♖c1

Judit follows the plan of opening the c-file.

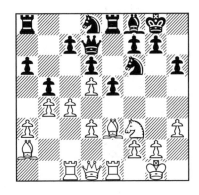

18...c6

Not waiting until White breaks with c4-c5.

19 ♘d2!

Preventing any potential counterplay with ...e5-e4, and also thinking about relocating the knight to a5 via b3. After 19 dxc6 Black would get some air, although White is still better.

19...cxd5?!

A number of analysts have criticized this move, as it plays along with White's plan. However, it is hard to suggest a real improvement. For example, after 19...♘h7 20 dxc6 ♘xc6 21 ♕f3 White is clearly better because of the weakness of the light squares in Black's camp; while if 19...g6? White wins material after 20 ♕f3 ♘h7 21 dxc6 ♘xc6 22 cxb5.

20 cxd5

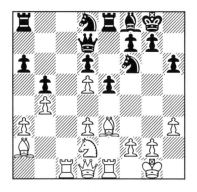

Now that the c-file has opened, White's goal is to enter with a rook via c6 or c7 to attack Black's weaknesses.

20...♘h7

20...a5 would get rid of Black's weakness on a6 but create another one on b5. White would answer by putting the bishop on a safe square on b3.

21 ♗b6

Now White threatens ♖c7.

21...♖c8

21...♕b7 would not change things much after 22 ♗a5.

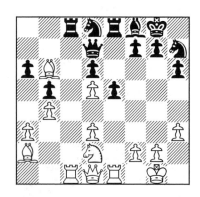

22 ♖xc8

White does not lose focus on the target: control of the c-file.

22...♕xc8

It seems that Black has taken over the c-file. But not for long!

23 ♕c1

White offers a trade of queens to regain control of the open file.

23...♕b7

If 23...♘b7, the plan is 24 ♕c6.

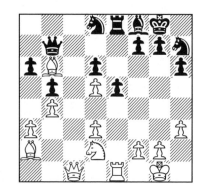

24 ♕c7

White has to play energetically, otherwise Black may regroup with ...f7-f5, ...♘f7 and ...♖c8.

24...♕xc7

On 24...f5 White has a cute move, 25 ♕c6!, based on the discovered check after 25...♘xc6 26 dxc6+.

25 ♗xc7

White's plan remains the same: ♖c1 and get to the weak pawns via the c6 square.

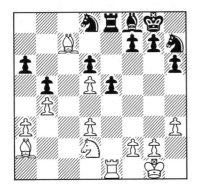

25...♘b7

After 25...f5 26 ♖c1 ♘f6 27 ♗b6, for example, the rook will be ready to enter on c8, c7 or c6 depending on response.

26 ♖c1

Mission accomplished!

26...♖c8

Pinning the bishop.

27 ♖c6

Putting the rook on a protected square.

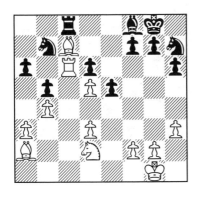

27...♘d8

Adams gets tired of defending and gives the pawn up.

After 27...f5? White has a nice combination in 28 ♗xd6!! ♘xd6 29 ♖xc8 ♘xc8 30 d6+ (discovered check) 30...♔h8 31 d7 and the pawn is unstoppable.

If Black tries to hold on to the pawn with 27...♘f6, White will slowly squeeze by 28 ♗b6 ♖a8 29 ♖c7 ♘d8 30 ♘e4 ♘xe4 (if 30...♘e8 31 ♖d7 traps the knight) 31 dxe4 ♖b8 32 ♗e3 ♖a8 33 ♖a7 ♖xa7 34 ♗xa7 and Black is helpless in this endgame because, after a3-a4 and the trade of the a-pawns, Black will not be able to save the pawn whether it is on a6 or b5.

28 ♗xd8

White could not capture the pawn on a6 immediately as she would lose the bishop on c7.

28...♖xd8

The only move.

29 ♖xa6

Now it is safe to capture the pawn. The next target will be the pawn on b5.

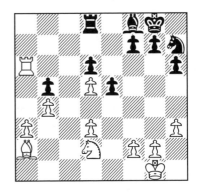

29...♖c8

The first active move in a long time! Black threatens 30...♖c2, but it does not help. Black's position is very bad.

30 ♖c6

Preventing the threat and again taking control of the c-file.

30...♖a8

Black could not trade rooks because the resulting passed pawn could not be stopped from promoting.

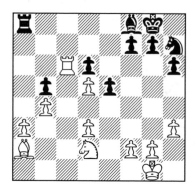

31 ♘b1

Protecting the pawn on a3 and also eyeing the c3 square, from where the knight can eventually attack the b5 pawn.

31...♘f6

Getting the knight back to the center.

32 ♔f1

In the endgame the king should be an active participant in the battle. After 32 ♖b6, Black again plays 32...♖c8.

32...♗e7

A waiting move to see how White improves her position. It also clears the way for the black king to move towards the center.

33 ♔e2

Now White is already threatening to go after the b5 pawn with 34 ♖b6, because after 34...♖c8, the white king is close enough to stop the black rook coming in with 35 ♔d1.

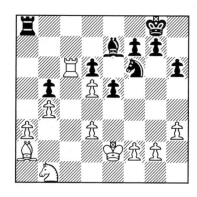

33...e4

Black still has a glimmer of hope, because there are opposite-colored bishops on the board, which often give the defending side chances to save the game, even two or sometimes three pawns down.

34 ♗b3

Securing the c2 square.

34...exd3+

The first and only check Black gives in the game! But it has no importance.

35 ♔xd3

The white king gets closer to the battleground.

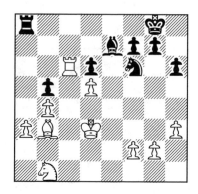

35...♘d7

Threatening to fork with ...♘e5+. 35...♖b8 would keep the b5 pawn, but

not for long. After 36 ♘c3 g6 37 ♖a6
♘e8 38 ♘xb5! ♖xb5 39 ♖a8 ♔f8 40
♔c4 ♖b7 41 ♗a4 wins the knight back
and the game

36 f4

Another preventive move. After 36
♖c7 Black escapes the skewer with
36...♘e5+.

36...g5

A last trick! If 37 fxg5 then
37...♘e5+.

37 ♖c7

The attacked knight cannot move
because then the bishop falls.

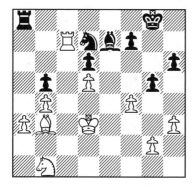

37...♖d8

The only move to avoid losing a
piece.

38 ♘c3

And now the b5 pawn cannot be
protected.

38...gxf4

Black gets a pawn temporarily.

39 ♘xb5

The connected a- and b-pawns have
no resistance in their path.

39...♘e5+

Otherwise the black rook is tied
down guarding the knight.

40 ♔e4

Going after the f4 pawn.

40...♖e8

If 40...♗g5 41 ♘xd6 wins another
pawn.

41 ♗a4 Black resigned

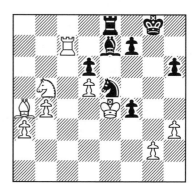

After 41...♗d8 42 ♘xd6 White has
too many passed pawns.

What a great positional masterpiece
by Judit!

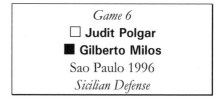

Game 6
□ **Judit Polgar**
■ **Gilberto Milos**
Sao Paulo 1996
Sicilian Defense

1 e4

This game was the first of a four-
game match against the top Brazilian
grandmaster.

1...c5

The Sicilian is certainly an invitation
to an interesting battle. In another game
between the same opponents during the
same trip, GM Milos surprised Judit
with the Alekhine Defense (1...♘f6).

2 ♘f3

Judit plays this move in most of her
games. In a few games, as a surprise,
she also played 2 c3.

2...e6

Judit played 2...d6 as Black in both games of the match.

3 d4

3 d3, followed by g2-g3, would transpose to a King's Indian Attack.

3...cxd4

An almost automatic response.

4 ♘xd4

The normal move is to recapture the pawn. Another rare choice is to play a gambit variation with 4 c3.

4...♘c6

Judit also likes to play this as Black.

5 ♘c3

White could get a Maróczy Bind type of position with 5 ♘b5 d6 6 c4.

5...♕c7

The Paulsen variation is an old favorite of all three Polgar sisters. In this game, Judit has to play against it.

6 g3

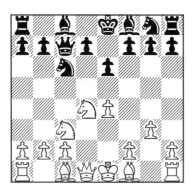

In most openings the g3 system is considered more positional and less ambitious. However, should Black make even a small mistake, White often gets a long-term steady advantage.

6...a6

This prevents any future ideas of ♘b5 and also prepares the ...b7-b5 advance.

7 ♗g2

This is a good place for the bishop, as long as there is potential to advance the e4 pawn.

7...♘f6

The best post for the knight.

8 0-0

Now that the king is in safety, the next mission is to increase the power of the light-squared bishop by preparing e4-e5.

8...d6

The standard theoretical move, although 8...♗c5 is interesting too.

9 ♖e1

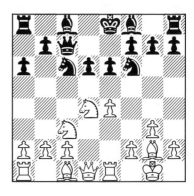

Preparing a cute tactic. If 9...♗e7 10 ♘xc6 bxc6 then 11 e5 dxe5 12 ♖xe5! is possible, because after 12...♕xe5? 13 ♗xc6+ White wins a pawn.

9...♗d7

Preventing the above idea, but perhaps 9...♖b8 is a better way to accomplish it.

10 ♘xc6

With this seemingly harmless trade, Judit has set a trap.

10...bxc6

If 10...♗xc6 then 11 ♘d5! improves White's position, since after 11...exd5 12 exd5+ regains the piece with advantage.

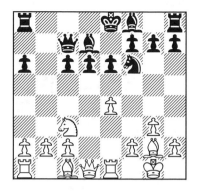

11 ♘a4

At first it looks strange to put the knight on the side of the board, but White is preparing to gain space by playing c2-c4; after that the knight can return to c3.

11...♖d8

Moving the rook off the long diagonal. On the immediate 11...c5, White would have the discovery 12 e5.

12 c4

This restricts Black's activity.

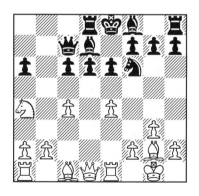

12...c5

With the idea of activating the bishop on c6, and also dreaming about getting the knight to d4.

13 ♗f4

If White plays too slowly, for exam-

ple with 13 ♘c3 ♗e7 14 ♗f4 ♗c6 15 ♕e2 0-0 16 ♖ad1 ♘d7, then Black would be OK.

13...♗e7

The natural 13...♗c6 would be dubious, because White gets a strong attack after 14 ♘xc5! e5 15 ♘xa6 ♕b6 16 b4.

14 e5

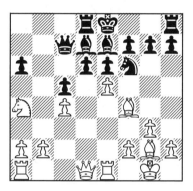

Finally it is breakthrough time!

14...dxe5

Black has no choice but to ruin his pawn structure.

15 ♗xe5

Now White is strategically better. She has two chains of healthy pawns, whereas Black has pawns in three islands and two of them are isolated.

15...♕a5

The queen would get trapped after 15...♕c8 16 ♘b6.

16 ♘c3

The knight has accomplished its goal and now goes back to c3.

16...0-0

Black has finally managed to castle too. White has a small, but steady advantage, because of her superior pawn structure and the difference in activity between the white and black bishops.

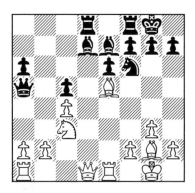

17 ♕f3

The queen had to get out of any potential discovered attack by the bishop on d7. It also clears the d1 square for the rook.

17...♗c8

Opening the d-file for the rook.

18 ♖ad1

Usually, when the opponent has control of an open file, it is best to try to fight for it by offering a trade.

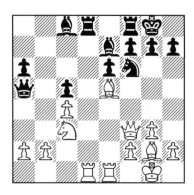

18...♖xd1

Black wants to exchange all four rooks.

19 ♖xd1

Naturally recapturing with the rook, because that is the piece which belongs on the open file.

19...♖d8

Continuing the fight for the d-file.

20 h3

A precautionary move. After the trade of rooks, there will be none left to cover the first rank, leaving the worry of a potential back rank check. 20 h3 move opens a 'luft' for the king to escape.

20...♖xd1+

Sooner or later, the exchange of the rooks along the d-file was inevitable.

21 ♕xd1

When there are no rooks on the board, the queen takes over the role of controlling the open file.

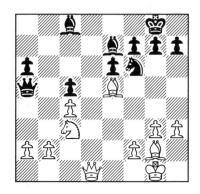

21...♘d7

After 21...♕d8, offering to swap queens as well, 22 ♕xd8+ ♗xd8 would result a difficult endgame for Black, because of the two weak and isolated pawns on the queenside.

22 ♗f4

As the white bishop is more active than its counterpart, it makes sense not to exchange it with 22 ♗d6.

22...♛b4?!

Attacking the white pawns on b2 and c4. If instead 22...♗f6, the d6 square becomes available for the white queen to enter.

23 ♛e2

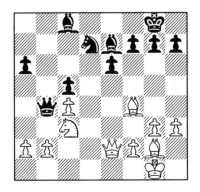

A very good move which protects both pawns. But it is not a purely defensive move. It also creates a pin enabling the threat of ♘c3-d5.

23...♗f8

The bishop moves to a protected square and therefore avoids ♘d5. If Black protects the bishop with 23...♚f8 then 24 ♛e4 ♛xb2 25 ♛c6 and the bishop on c8 is trapped, since if 25...♘b6 26 ♘a4!.

However, 23...♘b6 was a better defense. After 24 ♗c7 Black has to be careful to avoid 24...♘xc4? 25 ♘d5! exd5 26 ♛xe7, and because of the weakness of the back rank, Black has no time to save his bishop. Instead Black

should play 24...♗f6 25 ♘e4 ♛xc4 26 ♛xc4 ♘xc4 27 b3 with only a small advantage for White.

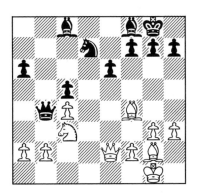

24 ♘e4

Now the positional threat is ♘d6, trading the knight for one of the bishops.

24...♛b6

Protecting the d6 square. 24...e5 solves the problem of the hole on d6, but creates another on d5. After 25 ♗c1, White's knight comes to d5 via c3.

25 ♛d2

Not giving up the fight over the d6 square.

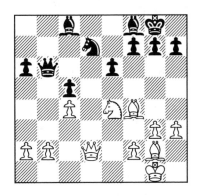

25...♘f6?!

Black was already in a tough situation. He could only decide between several unpleasant choices:

(i) allowing ♘d6;

(ii) playing 25...e5, weakening the d5 square; or

(iii), the game continuation, which weakens the kingside pawn structure and the black king's position.

Perhaps the second option was the least damaging choice.

26 ♘xf6+

This forces Black to double his pawns on the f-file.

26...gxf6

White is clearly better on all fronts. All of White's pieces are better placed than Black's; the black king is in danger; and Black's pawn structure is horrible.

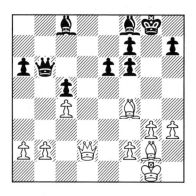

27 b3

A harmless-looking, but important move, which frees up the queen from protecting the b2 pawn and also secures the pawn on c4.

27...♗e7?!

This is not the right square for the bishop. Black would have been better off putting it on g7.

There is a nice line after 27...♗b7 28 ♗xb7 ♕xb7 29 ♕d8 (threatening 30 ♗h6) 29...♔g7? 30 ♗h6+! ♔xh6 31 ♕xf6+ ♔h5 32 g4 mate.

28 ♕d1!

Relocating the queen to g4.

28...f5

The threat of ♕g4+ followed by ♗h6 was serious, so Black had to prevent it. Possibly 28...e5 was a better choice.

29 g4!

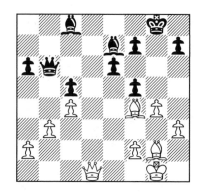

A very good move! It is true that it gets rid of Black's doubled f-pawns, but here Judit is going for the king, so it is a priority to get the queen closer.

29...e5

Opening his third rank, trying to get the queen to the kingside. After 29...fxg4 30 ♕xg4+ ♔h8 31 ♕h5 ♔g8 32 ♗e4 White's attack prevails.

30 ♕e2

30 ♗xe5 was perhaps simpler.

30...f6

Protecting the e5 pawn. After 30...exf4 31 ♕xe7 Black's position is hopeless.

31 ♗d5+

A very unpleasant check, especially in time pressure.

31...♔h8

This move makes White's job a little easier. If 31...♗e6 White wins a pawn with 32 gxf5. The most stubborn defense would have been 31...♔g7, when White could continue similarly to the game with 32 g5! (but not 32 gxf5 ♗xf5 33 ♕h5 ♗g6 34 ♕h6+ ♔h8 and Black is holding on) 32...♕d6 33 ♕h5 fxg5 (if 33...exf4?? 34 ♕f7+ ♔h8 35 ♕g8 mate) 34 ♕f7+ ♔h6, and now the peaceful 35 ♗e3. Here, Black's best defense is to trade queens with 35...♕f6 36 ♕xf6+ ♗xf6, but then White takes the pawn on c5 and reaches a won endgame because her pawns will much faster.

32 g5!!

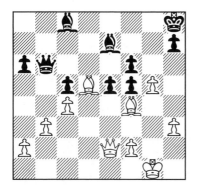

A very nice move, serving two purposes at once. It weakens the e5 pawn and opens the diagonal for the white queen to h5.

32...♕c7

This only defends against one of the two threats. 32...♕d6 doesn't help either, because of 33 ♕h5! fxg5 34 ♕f7 and mate in a few moves is inevitable.

33 ♕h5!

Now there are again two threats: 34 ♕e8+ ♔g7 and 35 ♕g8 mate, as well as 34 g6 with the idea of 35 ♕xh7 mate.

33...♗f8

If 33...fxg5 34 ♕f7 (threatening mate on g8) 34...♕d8 35 ♗xe5+ wins.

34 gxf6! Black resigned

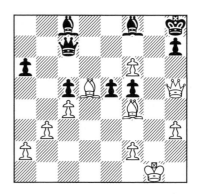

After 34...gxf4 35 ♕e8! ♕d6 36 ♕f7 followed by 37 ♕g8 mate is killing.

A wonderful performance by Judit!

Game 7
□ **Judit Polgar**
■ **Viswanathan Anand**
Dos Hermanas 1999
Sicilian Defense

---

1 e4

We first met Viswanathan Anand in Holland in 1990 and quickly became friends. After the tournament, he came to visit us in Budapest and stayed for about a week. We played a lot of chess and had a fun time. Some years later, 'Vishy' became the sixteenth World Champion. He has revolutionized chess in his homeland of India. All these years we have known him, our personal friendship has never affected any of our games, which were always full of fighting spirit and very interesting.

1...c5

Besides the Sicilian, Anand often employs 1...c6 (the Caro-Kann) and 1...e5 as well.

2 ♘f3

Judit plays the most popular choice.

2...d6

In about a dozen games between these opponents, when playing the Sicilian as Black, Anand always answered this way.

3 d4

3 ♗b5+ is another opening choice for White.

3...cxd4

As expected.

4 ♘xd4

Only in one of their encounters has Judit played differently with the alternative capture 4 ♕xd4.

4...♘f6

Developing and attacking the e4 pawn.

5 ♘c3

Protecting the pawn.

5...a6

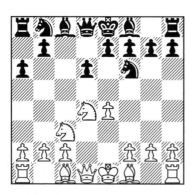

This is the Najdorf variation, named after the legendary Polish born, Argentine Grandmaster, 'Don Miguel' Najdorf. Anand has also experimented with the Dragon (5...g6) and the Rauzer variation (5...♘c6) against Judit.

6 ♗e3

In 1991, Judit played 6 ♗c4 against Vishy and won. Then in 1994, she played 6 f4 and lost.

6...e6

The year before at Wijk aan Zee, Judit won a nice game after Vishy played 6...e5.

7 g4

I remember this variation of the Najdorf being fashionable back in the early 1980s. It was invented by a small group of local Hungarian players (IMs Perenyi and Szalanczy), and is a gambit variation involving a piece sacrifice.

7...e5

This is a double attack. Besides hitting the knight on d4, the pawn on g4 is also hanging.

8 ♘f5

This move protects both.

8...g6

Chasing the knight away, but if the knight moves, White loses the g4 pawn.

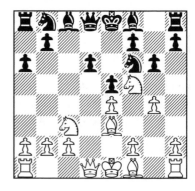

9 g5

White counter-attacks!

9...gxf5

Black has to accept the challenge. Other alternatives only give Black a bad game.

10 exf5

This is the whole point! White does not take the knight but makes a long-term sacrifice. After 10 gxf6 f4 Black is better, because the f6 pawn will not stay alive for long.

10...d5

The best reply, threatening to fork with ...d5-d4. In the early games when Black moved the knight, White did very well.

11 ♕f3

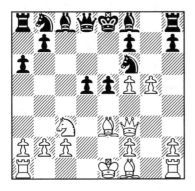

This was Perenyi's original idea. White protects the pawn on f5 and clears the road for queenside castling. Nowadays 11 gxf6 d4 12 ♗c4 is more popular.

11...d4

Here is the game, Perenyi-Schneider, in which this variation first started, back in 1978: 11...♘e4 12 ♘xe4 dxe4 13 ♕xe4 ♘c6 14 ♗c4 ♗d7 15 0-0-0 ♕c7 16 ♖he1 f6 17 ♖xd7 ♕xd7 18 gxf6 ♗d6 19 ♗e6 ♕c7 20 f7+ ♔d8 21 ♖d1 ♖c8 22 ♕xe5 and Black resigned, because after 22...♘xe5 23 ♗g5+ ♕e7 24 ♖xd6+ White has a winning advantage.

12 0-0-0

This creates a pin on the d-file, so Black cannot capture either piece.

12...♘bd7

Black is significantly behind in development, so there is no time to move the other knight.

13 ♗d2

13 gxf6!? dxc3 14 ♗c4 ♕xf6 15 ♖hg1 with compensation is the other interesting option.

13...dxc3

The most natural answer; 13...♕c7 is the main alternative.

14 ♗xc3

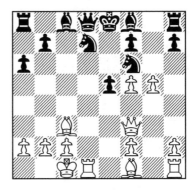

White has sacrificed two knights, but Black's king is stuck in the middle of the board and most of his pieces are undeveloped, whereas White has a very active position with all the pieces ready to attack.

14...♗g7

Black is trying to get ready to castle on the kingside.

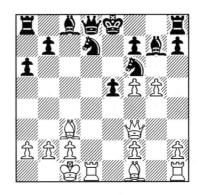

15 ♖g1

Better than the immediate 15 gxf6 ♕xf6.

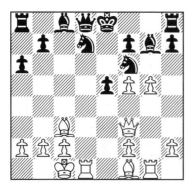

15...0-0?

A mistake! It is too dangerous to put the king on the g-file that is about to open. Judit suggested 15...♕c7 as an improvement, when she planned 16 gxf6 ♗xf6 17 ♖g4 with a strong attack.

16 gxf6

Finally getting a knight back.

16...♕xf6

As both the knight and bishop were pinned, this was the only possible recapture.

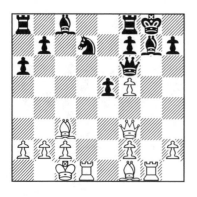

17 ♕e3

A strong move, clearing the path for the f2 pawn to advance.

17...♔h8

A logical move, getting out of the pin while liberating the dark-squared bishop. If 17...♕xf5? 18 ♗h3 and White wins the second piece back as well.

18 f4

Trying to eliminate the e5 pawn.

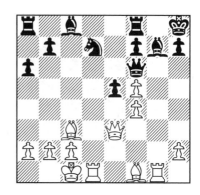

18...♕b6?!

A wrong decision. Black is trying to trade queens, which would be great, but of course White does not have to go along that plan. In fact, the white queen is sent where it wanted to go anyway.

This is a complicated position with a lot of interesting variations. Here are some of them:

a) 18...♕e7? 19 ♖xg7 ♔xg7 20 fxe5, ♔h8 21 ♕h6 f6 22 ♖xd7! ♗xd7 23 exf6 ♕f7 24 ♗c4! wins.

b) 18...♕h6 19 ♗c4 f6 20 ♗b4 ♖d8 (if 20...exf4 21 ♕e7) 21 ♕b6! ♕xf4+ 22 ♔b1 ♖e8 23 ♕c7 and now if 23...♕xf5 24 ♗f7 or 23...b5 24 ♗f7 ♕xb4 25 ♗xe8 ♕c5 26 ♕xc5 ♘xc5 27 ♗c6 wins.

c) 18...♖g8 19 ♖xg7! ♕xg7 (if 19...♖xg7 20 fxe5 ♕xf5 21 ♗c4! ♕g6 22 e6 fxe6 23 ♖g1 ♕xg1+ 24 ♕xg1 e5 25 ♕f2 or 22...f6 23 ♖f1!) 20 fxe5 ♖e8 21 e6 f6 (if 21...♘f6 22 exf7) 22 ♖d2 ♕e7 23 ♖g2 with a winning attack.

d) 18...♖e8 19 ♖xg7! ♕xg7 20 fxe5 ♘xe5 21 f6 ♕g6 was the best defense.

19 ♕g3

Now Black must defend against the immediate checkmate. Black would be fine after 19 ♕xb6 ♘xb6 20 f6 ♗h6 21 ♗xe5 ♗f5.

19...♕h6

Another move that makes things worse. 19...♖g8 was better, when Judit would respond with 20 ♗c4! ♕f6 21 fxe5 ♗h6+ 22 ♔b1 ♖xg3 23 exf6 ♖xg1 24 ♖xg1 ♘c5 25 ♗xf7 ♗xf5 26 ♗e8! ♖xe8 27 f7+ and mate on the next move.

20 ♖d6!

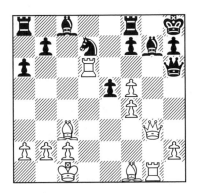

A beautiful deflection move!

20...f6

Of course the rook was indirectly protected (20...♕xd6 21 ♕xg7 mate). After 20...♗f6 21 ♔b1 e4 22 ♖xf6 ♘xf6 23 ♕h3 wins, while if 20...♘f6 21 ♗xe5 ♗xf5 22 ♕xg7+ ♕xg7 23 ♗xf6 ♕xf6 24 ♖xf6 and White is pawn up.

21 ♗d2

Protecting the f4 pawn and threatening the discovery f4xe5.

21...e4

Trying to close the position. If 21...♘c5 22 fxe5 ♘e4 23 exf6!! ♘xg3

(or 23...♖xf6 24 ♖d8+ ♖f8 25 ♖xf8+ ♗xf8 26 ♕g8 mate) 24 fxg7+ ♕xg7 25 ♖xg3, Black is forced to return the queen (otherwise 26 ♗c3 comes), and after 25...♕xg3 26 hxg3 ♗xf5 27 ♗c3+ ♔g8 28 ♗c4+ is winning for White.

22 ♗c4

Finally the last force enters the attack.

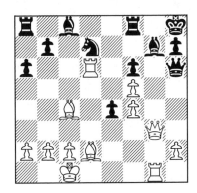

22...b5

There are some nice attacking lines after 22...♘b8 23 ♗c3 ♗xf5 (or 23...♘c6 24 ♖xf6 ♖xf6 25 ♕xg7+ ♕xg7 26 ♗xf6 ♕xf6 27 ♖g8 mate) 24 ♗xf6 ♗g6 (if 24...♗xf6 25 ♕g8+ ♖xg8 26 ♖xg8 mate) 25 ♗xg7+ ♕xg7 26 ♕h4 and ♖xg6 cannot be prevented.

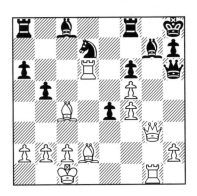

23 ♗e6

Attacking the knight.

23...♖a7

Protecting the knight. After 23...♘c5 24 ♗e3 ♘xe6 25 fxe6 Black is in bad shape.

24 ♖c6!

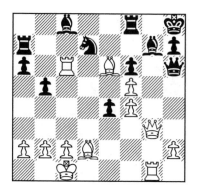

A strong move further paralyzing Black's position!

24...a5

After 24...♖b7, White would slowly improve with 25 ♗e3 and ♖d1.

25 ♗e3

Clearing the d-file.

25...♖b7

If 25...♖a8 then 26 ♖d1.

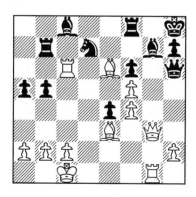

26 ♗d5

Creating a discovery threat with the rook.

26...♖b8

Moving away from the threat. If 26...b4? 27 ♖xc8 ♖xc8 28 ♗xb7 wins a piece.

27 ♖c7

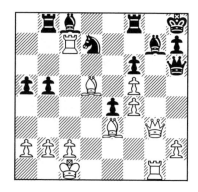

Even though Black still has a material advantage, White is able slowly to prepare the final blow.

27...b4

White threatened ♗e3-a7 trapping the rook, so Black makes space for it on b5.

28 b3

It is remarkable that White has time for everything. This was probably not the only way to win, it certainly is demoralizing for Black who, amazingly, is almost in Zugzwang!

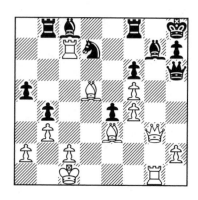

28...♖b5

Finally, an active move!

29 ♗c6

Forking the rook and the knight.

29...♖xf5

Black wins a pawn but loses a knight.

30 ♖xc8

The simple 30 ♗xd7 ♗xd7 31 ♖xd7 was good too.

30...♖xc8

Black has only a very temporary material advantage.

31 ♗xd7

Forking both rooks.

31...♖cc5

After 31...♖fc5 32 ♗xc8 ♖xc8 33 f5! wins.

32 ♗xf5

Better than capturing the other rook.

32...♖xf5

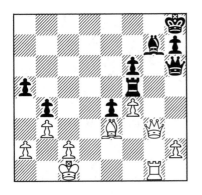

Finally, for the first time since very early in the opening, there is material equality. But Black is lost because his king's defenders are completely misplaced.

33 ♖d1

Now the rook comes in on the d-file.

33...♔g8

If 33...♗f8 34 ♖d8.

34 ♕g2 Black resigned

The e4 pawn is lost. Then the co-operation between the white queen and rook will be deadly.

> *Game 8*
> ☐ **Judit Polgar**
> ■ **Ilia Smirin**
> Istanbul Olympiad 2000
> *Pirc Defense*

This game is from the Istanbul Olympiad, where Judit played on board three for the Hungarian (men's) team, below GMs Peter Leko and Zoltan Almasi. In this match she was on board two.

1 e4

As usual, Judit starts with the king's pawn.

1...g6

This is the Modern Defense. Most of the time, it transposes to the Pirc Defense after Black plays ...d6 and ...♘f6, but it can have had an independent life if Black delays the development of the knight on g8 or plays ...d7-d5 instead of ...d7-d6.

2 d4

It is a good idea in the opening to occupy the center with both e- and d-pawns when allowed.

2...♗g7

The dark-squared bishop is a key piece in this opening. If Black manages to activate it properly, it can become extremely dangerous along the a1-h8 diagonal.

3 ♘c3

The most natural developing move.

3...d6

Black is happy to transpose back to the Pirc Defense. 3...c6, planning ...d7-d5, is an alternative, as Shirov played against Judit in 1995 (see Combination 16 for the end of that game).

4 f4

This has been my sisters' favorite line since childhood. You can find two of Sofia's games in her section with the same opening moves.

4...♘f6

Preparing to castle.

5 ♘f3

Now the two knights combine to control all the center squares!

5...0-0

The king has reached safety. Black has the exact same set-up as in the King's Indian Defense against 1 d4. Van Wely played 5...c5 against Sofia (see her Game 3).

6 ♗e3

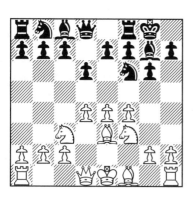

A rare move. The idea is to prepare queenside castling right away. Sofia played the more common 6 ♗d3 against Safranska (see her Game 8).

6...b6

Black is preparing the double fianchetto with ...♗b7.

7 ♕d2

Clearing the way for the king.

7...c5

The correct approach: counter-attacking in the center.

8 0-0-0

Judit went all out in this game, as she used to do in her teenage years. Castling on opposite sides usually involves taking a lot of risk. Instead, 8 d5 is also interesting.

8...cxd4

Opening the c-file.

9 ♗xd4

A somewhat unusual recapture. It is more customary in similar positions to have a knight on d4. But Judit has something special in mind. And here 9 ♘xd4 ♗b7 10 ♗d3 (or 10 e5 dxe5 11 fxe5 ♘g4) 10...♘bd7 looks fine for Black.

9...♘c6

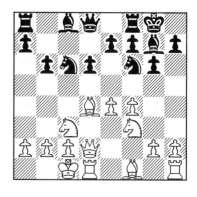

Now the position resembles more a Sicilian Dragon than the Pirc. With his last move Black plans the trade a knight for White's bishop.

10 ♗xf6

It is quite impressive how dangerous White's attack becomes in a couple of moves.

10...♗xf6

Black has gained the advantage of the bishop pair, but here that is not so important. The key question will be whether the black king can survive the attack or not.

11 h4!

This is what Judit had in mind when she started her plan several moves ago. She was focusing on opening the h-file at all cost. This is where her home preparation stopped. The rest is all over-the-board brilliancy.

White gets nothing with 11 e5 dxe5 12 ♕xd8 ♖xd8 13 ♖xd8+ ♘xd8 14 fxe5 ♗g7 15 ♘d5, because after 15...♗b7, White cannot capture with 16 ♘xe7+ as the knight has no way to escape after 16...♔f8.

11...♗g4

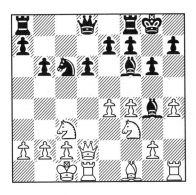

This is always a dilemma for Black in such situations: whether to allow h4-h5 or to prevent it by playing ...h7-h5. Here, after 11...h5!? I like 12 f5 with good attacking prospects for White.

But hasn't Black's last move also stopped the pawn advance?

12 h5!

It seemed so, but not really! White is willing to sacrifice the h-pawn and more.

12...♗xh5

After 12...gxh5 Judit planned 13 ♘d5 ♗g7 14 ♗b5.

13 ♖xh5!

This long-term exchange sacrifice is a shocker!

13...gxh5

Black gained material, but had to damage the shield in front of his king.

14 ♕d5

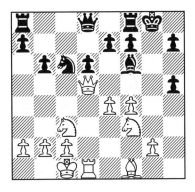

An energetic move which wins a pawn back and, even more importantly, swings the queen over close to the enemy king.

14...♖c8

According to Judit, this was the first mistake in Black's defense. She suggested

14...♗xc3!? as an improvement. I can understand that, psychologically, it had to be very difficult for the Soviet/Israeli GM to give up the only piece guarding the king. In that case, Judit's plan was 15 bxc3 ♕c8 16 ♕xh5 ♕e6 17 ♗b5 ♘a5 18 ♖h1 ♕g6 19 ♕h4, or 15...♘a5 16 ♕xh5 f6 17 e5 ♕e8 18 ♕h4. In both variations, Black is a clear exchange up, but White maintains a strong attack on the kingside. Objectively speaking, Black probably can hold but, with limited time on the clock, it would be unpleasant to defend.

15 ♕xh5

Now 15...♗xc3? is too late because 16 ♘g5! decides immediately.

15...♗g7

White's attack prevails after 15...♘b4 16 e5 ♗g7 17 a3 ♘c6 18 ♗d3 h6 19 ♕f5 ♖e8 20 e6 fxe6 21 ♕xe6+ ♔f8 22 ♗h7 or 21...♔h8 22 ♖h1.

16 e5!

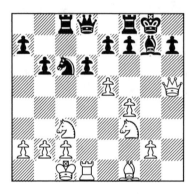

The right move order. White wants to storm the h7 pawn by playing ♗d3, e4-e5 and ♖h1. The direct 16 ♗d3 would not be so good because of 16...♘b4.

16...♕e8

A tricky move. The idea is to be able to play ...f7-f5 while avoiding the possibility of an en passant reply. Nevertheless, 16...h6!? was a somewhat better defense, when Judit had in mind 17 ♘h4 e6 18 ♖xd6 ♕e7 19 ♘d5 exd5 20 ♘f5 ♕c7 21 ♘xh6+ or 18...♕e8 19 ♗b5. Also good was 17 ♗d3 ♘b4 18 ♗e4 with the idea of ♕f5.

17 ♕h3!

A fine move, making sure the queens will not be exchanged after a future ...f7-f5. When you are on the at-

tack, usually the most important piece is the queen! Instead 17 ♗d3 f5 was Black's hope.

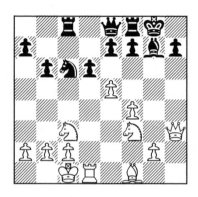

17...h6

Now if 17...f5 18 ♗c4+ ♔h8 19 ♗e6 would be the answer, while after 17...dxe5 there is a pretty way to win: 18 ♘g5! h6 19 ♕f5! hxg5 20 ♗d3 f6 21 ♕h7+ ♔f7 22 ♗g6+ ♔e6 23 f5 mate.

18 ♗d3

Threatening 19 ♕f5.

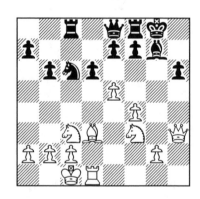

18...♘b4

If Black prevents ♕f5 with 18...e6, White would have continued 19 ♘e4 ♘b4 (or 19...dxe5 20 ♘f6+! ♗xf6 21 ♕xh6) 20 ♘f6+ ♗xf6 21 exf6 ♘xd3+ 22 ♖xd3 ♔h7 23 ♘g5+ ♔g6 24 ♘e4 with an overwhelming attack.

19 ♗e4

It is crucial to keep this bishop on the board. White maintains the same threat of ♕f5.

19...e6

Stopping the threat ♕h3-f5. If 19...d5 20 ♘xd5 ♘xd5 White does not waste time capturing the knight, but wins as planned with 21 ♕f5.

20 f5!

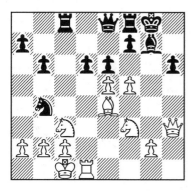

Just when it seems that Black is holding, Judit brings more forces into the attack. The new threat is 21 f6!.

20...♖xc3

An attempt at counterplay. Here is what would happen on some other responses:

a) 20...dxe5 21 f6! ♗xf6 22 ♕xh6 followed by 23 ♕h7 mate.

b) 20...f6 21 exd6 threatening 22 d7 and 22 fxe6.

c) 20...♘xa2+ 21 ♘xa2 ♕a4 22 ♖d4 ♕xa2 23 f6 ♕a1+ 24 ♔d2 followed by 25 ♕g4.

21 f6!

The most straightforward way to continue the attack. White is also better after 21 bxc3 ♘xa2+ 22 ♔b2, but not 22 ♔d2? dxe5 23 f6 which would allow 23...♕d8+!.

21...♕b5

Black is whole rook ahead, but still cannot save the game. If 21...♕a4 22 bxc3 ♘xa2+ 23 ♔b2 ♘xc3, White wins with 24 ♖d4.

22 ♕g3! Black resigned

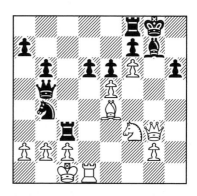

After 22...♖xc2+ 23 ♗xc2 ♘xa2+ 24 ♔d2 ♕b4+ 25 ♔e2 the white king is able to escape the checks.

A really impressive, pure attacking game!

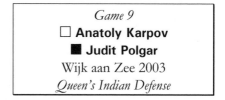

Game 9
□ **Anatoly Karpov**
■ **Judit Polgar**
Wijk aan Zee 2003
Queen's Indian Defense

1 d4

Most grandmasters usually stick either to 1 e4 or 1 d4. Only the greatest are able to play both successfully. Karpov is one of those players.

1...♘f6

Judit has played many games against the great World Champion, Anatoly Karpov, during her career. Although she beat him in their 1998 rapid match, this was the first time she won at the classical time control.

2 ♘f3

This move order rules out the Nimzo-Indian Defense after 2 c4 e6 3 ♘c3 ♗b4.

2...e6

For many years, Judit was famous for her results in the King's Indian Defense with 2...g6. Only in recent years has she switched to the more conservative 2...e6.

3 c4

White fights for the central d5 square.

3...b6

This is Queen's Indian Defense.

4 a3

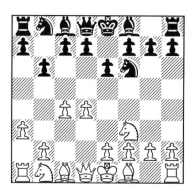

And this is the Petrosian variation, named after the late Armenian World Champion. The basic idea is to prevent ...♗b4.

4...♗b7

An ideal place for the bishop, controlling the d5 and e4 center squares on the long diagonal.

5 ♘c3

Now that the ...♗b4 pin is no longer possible, White can conveniently develop the knight.

5...d5

If Black does not play this move,

then White would most probably play d4-d5 herself.

6 cxd5

Against Judit in Linares two years earlier, Anatoly had played 6 ♗g5, which led to a very complicated game.

6...♘xd5

This leaves the diagonal open for the bishop on b7. The other main line is the pawn recapture, 6...exd5, the advantage of which is that Black has better control of the center than after the game move.

7 ♕c2

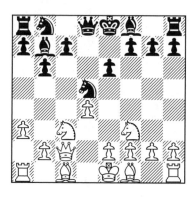

For many years until the early 1980s, White used to play the more natural-looking 7 e3 here. By that time theory had found ways for Black to equalize in those variations, so Garry Kasparov then came up with the move 7 ♕c2, which he has popularized.

The immediate 7 e4 would be a mistake, because Black wins a pawn after 7...♘xc3 8 bxc3 ♗xe4.

7...♘xc3

7...c5 or 7...♗e7 are also playable.

8 ♕xc3

In the same tournament GM Krasenkow played the more popular 8 bxc3 against Judit; the game was drawn in 24 moves.

The first meeting with Bobby in 1993 in Kanizsa in his Hotel room.

Playing some friendly blitz with Garry June 2003

Susan as a guest commentator on ESPN2 during the Kasparov-Deep Junior match with Jeremy Schapp, GM Seirawan and GM Ashley January 2003

Susan with Paul Truong and Judit, New York July 15, 2001

GMs Lev Alburt, Susan, USCF Executive director Frank Niro, Judit, Michael
Khodarkhovsky, Yona Kosashvili, Boris Gulko after dinner New York 2003

GMs Palatnik, Alburt, Al Lawrence, Boris Spassky and Susan at the Chess
Hall of Fame Florida March 2003.

Outdoors, after a hard day of training with Garry June 2003

Susan and NY Governor Pataki (Sep 2004)

Susan with Members of Hawaii State House Members, Honolulu 2004

The three sisters in 'casual mode' in Budapest November 2004

Susan giving a 41 board simul at the All-Girls National
Championship Chicago May 2004

Susan vs. Karpov (1st ever Clash of the Titans - Battle of the
Gender match), Lindsborg, Kansas - Sept 2004

Jana Robbins, producer of the Broadway hit Little Women, Multi-Platinum Recording
Superstar Josh Groban, Tony-Award Winner Sutton Foster and Susan, April 2005

8...h6

Preventing ♗c1-g5. In an earlier game as Black, Karpov played 8...♘d7, allowing 9 ♗g5 ♗e7 10 ♗xe7 ♚xe7. As ugly as it looks with the black king stuck in the middle, White is not able to take advantage.

9 e3

The main line here is 9 ♗f4. In this game, White decides to develop the bishop on the a1-h8 long diagonal instead.

9...♘d7

A rarely-played move. It is more common to develop the bishop on f8 first.

10 b4

10 ♗b5 would be logical, trying to exploit the weakness of the c6 square, but Black equalizes after 10...♗d6 11 ♗c6 ♗xc6 12 ♕xc6 0-0 13 b4 e5 14 ♗b2 ♕e7.

10...♗e7

Time to prepare to castle.

11 ♗b2

Play for the discovery against the g7 pawn by 11 d5 is suicidal, because of the skewer with 11...♗f6.

11...0-0

Now we can understand why Judit

developed the bishop to e7 and not to the more active d6 square. If White threatens to checkmate with 12 d5, it is important to have ...♗f6 as a response.

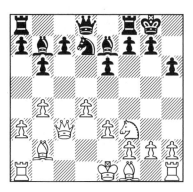

12 ♖d1

This aims to prevent Black's main counterplay with ...c7-c5. But it has a drawback too: The rook moves away from the a-file.

12...a5

During her pre-game preparation, Judit planned to play 12...♖c8 here. But she changed her mind at the board as she really liked the game move.

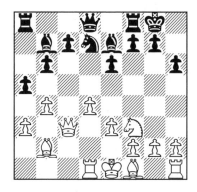

13 b5

White must keep the a-file closed. Otherwise Black would trade with ...a5xb4 and benefit from having the rook on a8 already, without wasting time to get to the open file.

13...罝c8

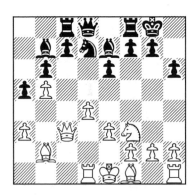

At this point, Judit already felt very good about Black's position, because she had a big lead in development.

14 豐b3

The start of an incorrect plan. Better was 14 豐d2, and after 14...c6 15 bxc6 奧xc6, then 16 奧a6 followed by castling with a close to equal position, although Judit even then slightly prefers Black.

14...c6

Now Black already has a small advantage.

15 bxc6

On 15 奧e2 Black would continue with 15...cxb5, and if 16 奧xb5 奧e4 or 16 豐xb5 奧c6 followed by 17...b5.

15...奧xc6

The correct recapture. It is vital to have the b5 square under control.

16 奧b5?

This is a serious mistake. 16 奧a6 罝c7 17 0-0 was clearly better. However, Black would have a small advantage anyway after 17...b5 18 奧xb5 and 18...罝b7 19 a4 豐b8 20 奧c3 奧xb5 21 axb5 罝xb5 22 豐a4 奧b4. Alternatively, 17...a4 looks promising too, and if 18

豐d3 豐a8 19 豐e2 罝b8 (with the idea of ...b5 to trap the bishop on a6) 20 奧b5 奧xb5 21 豐xb5 豐a5.

16...奧b4+!

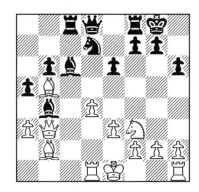

Karpov probably missed this move. Seemingly, all it does is trade a pair of bishops. But the point is that it also will stop White from castling.

17 axb4

The check has cut off the white queen from protecting the bishop on b5.

17...奧xb5

White is in serious trouble with his king stuck in the middle of the board.

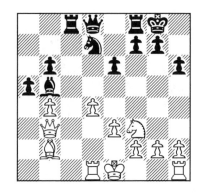

18 bxa5

The most natural move. If White plays 18 d5, Judit would have responded 18...a4 19 ♕a3 and now 19...e5! with a clear advantage for Black.

18...♗c4

Black could not recapture on a5 without this intermediate move, because the bishop on b5 was unprotected.

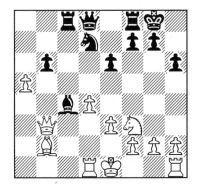

19 ♕a3

Judit was expecting 19 ♕a4 and after 19...bxa5 20 ♗c3. The following variations (from Judit) demonstrate the difficulties White has to face: 20...♕f6! (20...♗e2 is insufficient for an advantage after 21 ♔xe2 ♖xc3 22 ♖c1 and White is not in danger anymore) 21 ♕xd7 (if 21 ♗xa5 ♕f5!) 21...♕g6 22 d5 (if 22 ♖g1 ♕c2) 22...♕c2 23 ♗d2 ♖fd8 24 ♕e7 ♖xd5 25 ♕b7 (if 25 ♕a3 ♗a6 26 e4 ♖dc5 27 ♕e3 ♖c3 28 ♕f4 ♖b3 29 ♘d4 ♕c4 or 26 ♘d4 ♕g6 27 ♖g1 e5 28 ♘e2 ♖c2 with a huge advantage for Black) 25...♕d3 26 ♕xc8+ ♔h7 27 ♕xc ♕xc4 and Black is better, because it is very difficult to stop the a-pawn.

19...bxa5

Regaining the material. The next plan is to mobilize all the black pieces on the queenside, while making sure the white king does not reach safety.

20 ♕d6

According to Judit, this is another mistake. White should have tried to consolidate his position. I believe 20 ♗c3 would have been the best try, although 20...♕f6 prepares to attack on the light squares after ...♕g6. Even if White can save the game, it is awfully difficult to find the only moves at the board with limited time.

Instead, after 20 ♘d2, Black wins in a pretty way by 20...♕g5 21 g3 ♗a6 22 ♕a4 ♕g4 23 f3 ♘e5!! 24 fxg4 ♘d3+ 25 ♔e2 ♘xb2+.

20...♗b5!

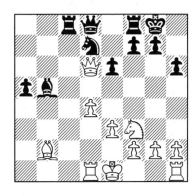

A very fine move! In Judit's opinion, White is lost at this point because there are too many threats to face. White is losing the game on the light squares, and also because of his bad king.

21 d5

If White tries to stop ...♖c2 with 21 ♖d2, Black continues again with the ...♕f6-g6 plan.

21...♖c2

Judit was so happy with her position after 21...♖c2, she did not calculate carefully enough the other (superior) choice 21...♘c5, when White could not prevent the very unpleasant ...♘d3+.

22 ♖d2

This is the only move. After 22 ♘d4

Black transposes to a winning rook endgame with 22...♖xb2 23 ♘xb5 ♖xb5 24 dxe6 fxe6 25 ♕xd7 ♕xd7 26 ♖xd7, and now wins a pawn with 26...♖b1+ 27 ♖d1 ♖xd1+ 28 ♔xd1 ♖xf2.

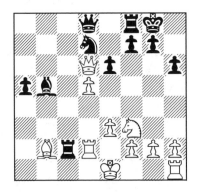

22...♕c8

22...♖xd2 first was also good. The game move threatens 23...♖xb2 24 ♖xb2 ♕c1 mate.

23 ♕a3

On 23 dxe6 Judit's plan was 23...♖xb2 24 ♖xb2 ♕c1+ 25 ♕d1 ♕xb2 26 exd7 ♖d8. Judit said she was pretty sure that this position should be winning for Black, because all her pieces are better than White's and she even has a passed a-pawn.

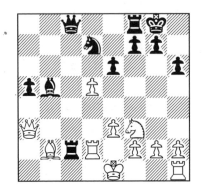

23...♖xd2

Judit said: 'At this point, my problem was that I had too many promising options.' She spent some time calculating 23...♕c4!, the most natural move. After 24 ♘d4 (or 24 ♖xc2 ♕xc2 25 ♘d4 ♕b1+ 26 ♗c1 ♖c8 27 ♘c6 ♘e5 wins) 24...♖xd2 25 ♔xd2 ♕xd5 26 ♕xa5 ♖b8 White is also hopeless.

24 ♔xd2

If 24 ♘xd2 ♘c5 would win easily.

24...♘b6

The most precise move. 24...♕c4 would give White some hopes of survival after 25 ♕c3.

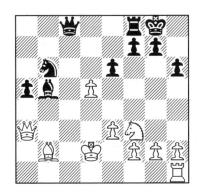

25 ♕c3

25 ♕b3 was no better, as 25...♘c4+ 26 ♔e1 and then simply 26...♘xb2 27 ♕xb2 exd5 gives Black a huge advantage.

25...♘c4+

Considering the white king's position, it is in Black's best interest to avoid the exchange of queens.

26 ♔c2

Trying to let the rook on h1 out.

26...e5

Black had to defend against the mate on g7.

27 ♔b1

It seems there is no safe place for

the white king in this game.

27...♕g4

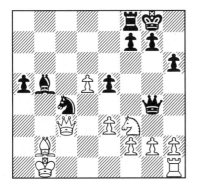

Attacking the pawn on g2 and, even more importantly, clearing the rook's way to b8.

28 ♖c1

White loses after 28 ♘xe5 ♘xe5 29 ♕xe5 ♗d3+ 30 ♔c1 ♖c8+ 31 ♗c3 f6.

28...♖b8

The best move to get the rook in action. 28...♕xg2 is OK too.

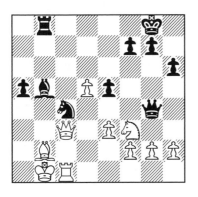

29 ♖c2

If 29 ♔a1 then 29...♗a6 was Judit's intention.

29...f6

To avoid any counter-chances.

30 d6

A last trick.

30...♕xg2

30...♘xd6 would be a mistake because of 31 ♕c7.

31 ♘d2

The knight was under attack.

31...♕h1+

Not the only way, but the best way.

32 ♔a2

After 32 ♖c1 Black would continue with 32...♘xd2+ 33 ♕xd2 ♕e4+ and after 34 ♔a1 ♕a4+ 35 ♔b1 ♗c6 wins. There is also a cute alternative given by Judit: 35...e4 36 ♖c3 ♗d3+ 37 ♔c1 ♕a1+! 38 ♗xa1 ♖b1 mate.

32...♘xd6

Black is two pawns ahead.

33 ♕c5

If 33 f3, ...♗e8 and ...♗f7+ is strong.

33...♖c8 White resigned

If 34 ♕xd6 then 34...♖xc2 35 ♕b8+ ♔h7 36 ♕xb5 ♖xd2 wins.

Game 10
□ **Judit Polgar**
■ **Ferenc Berkes**
Budapest 2003
French Defense

---

1 e4

This game was played at probably

the strongest tournament ever held in our home-town of Budapest.

1...e6

Judit's opponent was the young and upcoming star, who won the 2002 World Under-18 Championship. In this game he chose the French Defense.

2 d4

Just as in the Pirc Defense, here too it is best to occupy the center with both pawns.

2...d5

Black must also have a presence in the center to avoid problems.

3 ♘c3

Protecting the pawn on e4. Other common ways to solve that problem are 3 ♘d2, 3 e5 or 3 exd5.

3...♘f6

Putting more pressure on the e4 pawn. Pinning with 3...♗b4 would also serve the same purpose.

4 ♗g5

Indirectly protecting the pawn by pinning the knight on f6. 4 e5 is another popular choice.

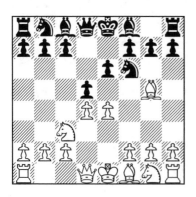

4...dxe4

The other two theoretical moves are 4...♗e7 and the less favored 4...♗b4.

5 ♘xe4

This move is possible because if the black knight captures on e4, the black queen will fall.

5...♗e7

Unpinning the knight. Now Black threatens to capture the knight on e4.

6 ♗xf6

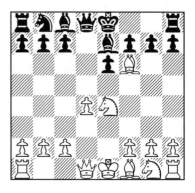

This is another case where it is favorable to trade a bishop for a knight. The white knight on e4 is nicely centralized and will also have the option to trade for Black's dark-squared bishop in the future.

6...♗xf6

A couple of decades ago recapturing with 6...gxf6 used to be quite popular (a little surprisingly to me). In that case, Black voluntarily doubles the f-pawns, while the king can no longer find safety on the kingside. However, the compensation will be potential counterplay along the open g-file.

7 ♘f3

Developing and protecting the pawn on d4.

7...0-0

Black is fully developed on the kingside. The pieces on the queenside should follow next.

8 ♕d2

Preparing to castle to the queenside and start a kingside attack.

8...♞d7

White also gets a dangerous attack after 8...b6 9 ♞xf6+ ♛xf6 10 ♗d3 ♗b7 11 ♞g5 g6 (or 11...h6 12 ♞h7) 12 0-0-0 ♖d8 13 h4 ♖xd4 14 h5.

9 0-0-0

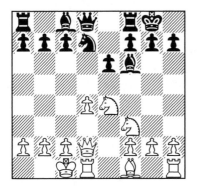

The most ambitious continuation, which also prepares the d4-d5 push.

9...♗e7

Black wants to keep his pair of bishops.

10 ♗d3

A good and very natural developing move. Bobby Fischer instead played 10 ♛f4 against Pal Benko at the Curacao Candidates tournament in 1962. 10 ♗c4 is also interesting, with the idea of 11 d5.

10...b6

In this opening one of the biggest problems for Black is developing the light-squared bishop to an active post.

11 ♞eg5

An aggressive attacking move. It is not bad, though it had actually more psychological effect than real strength. 11 h4 or 11 ♛f4 are also logical moves.

11...h6

11...♞f6 would be less weakening.

12 ♗h7+!

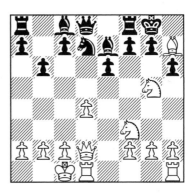

Very interesting! White deliberately loses a tempo to force the black king to the h-file and away from the f7 pawn.

12...♔h8

There was no other choice.

13 ♗e4

Attacking the rook on a8, but it is not that simple.

13...hxg5?

This move cost Black the game. After 13...♖b8 Judit planned to continue 14 h4. The correct move was 13...♗xg5! 14 ♞xg5 and now 14...♖b8 when White's attack is stuck, and after 15 ♞f3 ♞f6 16 ♗d3 ♗b7 Black has equalized.

14 g4!!

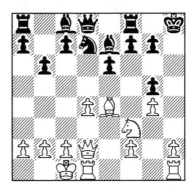

A brilliant idea! It reminds me of Judit's teenage years when g2-g4! was her trademark in almost every opening! The main purpose of the move here is to prevent what would happen after 14 ♗xa8?, that is 14...g4 and if the knight moves away then 15...♗g5 pins the white queen.

Instead, Judit wants to open the h-file and checkmate! She was even willing to spend a precious tempo to accomplish that task.

14...♖b8

Judit had the following ideas after other moves:

a) 14...♗a6 15 h4 gxh4 16 g5 ♔g8 17 ♕f4 f5 18 ♕xh4 fxe4 19 ♕h7+ ♔f7 20 ♕h5+ g6 21 ♕h7+ ♔e8 22 ♕xg6+ ♖f7 23 ♖h7.

b) 14...c6 15 h4 gxh4 16 g5 f6 17 ♘xh4 ♔g8 18 ♘g6.

In both variations, White prefers to keep the bishop on the b1-h7 diagonal to assist the attack, rather than win material.

15 h4

Black is up an entire bishop, but his king is in serious jeopardy. Now Black cannot avoid the opening of the h-file.

15...g6

After 15...gxh4, White would con-

tinue as before with 16 g5 followed by ♕f4.

If instead 15...♗b7 16 hxg5+ ♔g8 17 ♗xb7 ♖xb7 18 ♕f4 (threatening 19 ♕e4 attacking the rook and mate on h7) 18...♖b8 19 ♔b1! (getting out of any checks on the c1-h6 diagonal; the immediate 19 ♕h2 would give Black some hope after 19...♗xg5+ 20 ♔b1 f6) 19...♗d6 20 ♘e5 ♗xe5 21 dxe5 ♖e8 22 ♖d3 and the other white rook will appear on h3 with decisive effect.

16 hxg5+

This discovered check opens the h-file.

16...♔g7

16...♔g8 would be even worse, because the black rook on f8 would not have access to the h-file.

17 ♕f4

This move is planning a beautiful rook sacrifice!

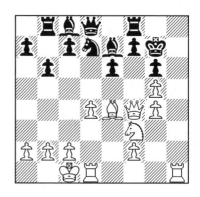

17...♗b7

If Black plays the natural 17...♖h8 (17...♖g8 loses straight away to 18 ♖h7+ ♔xh7 19 ♕xf7+), the attack would continue with 18 ♖xh8 ♕xh8 19 ♘e5 (attacking the f7 pawn, and preparing ♖h1) 19...♕g8 (or 19...♘xe5 20 ♕xe5+ ♔g8 21 ♕xc7 trapping the rook on b8)

20 ♖h1 ♗d6 and now 21 ♖h7+!! ♕xh7
(or 21...♔xh7 22 ♕h2+ ♔g7 23 ♕h6
mate) 22 ♕xf7+ ♔h8 23 ♘xg6+ and
White is winning.

Also, after 17...♗d6, White answers
18 ♘e5 ♗xe5 19 dxe5 ♖h8 20 ♖xh8
♕xh8 21 ♗c6 ♕d8, and now the calm
22 ♔b1! puts Black almost in zugzwang;
e.g. 22...a5 23 a4 ♔f8 24 ♖h1.

18 ♖h7+!!

Judit sacrifices a whole rook to gain
one tempo!

18...♔xh7

If Black does not accept the gift, the
game ends quickly after the variation
18...♔g8 19 ♖dh1 f5 20 gxf6 ♗xf6 21
♖h8+ ♗xh8 22 ♖xh8+ ♔xh8 23 ♕h6+
♔g8 24 ♕xg6+ ♔h8 and now 25 ♕h7
is mate.

19 ♕h2+

The queen comes to the h-file with
check.

19...♔g8

After 19...♔g7 White wins with 20
♕h6+ ♔g8 21 ♗xg6! (21 ♖h1? is not so
good, because of 21...♗xg5+! 22 ♘xg5
♕xg5+ 23 ♕xg5 ♗xe4) 21...♗xg5+ 22
♘xg5 ♕xg5+ 23 ♕xg5 fxg6 24 ♕xg6+
♔h8 25 d5! ♗xd5 26 f3! ♗xf3 27 ♖xd7
and mate is unavoidable.

20 ♖h1

Threatening to mate on h7 or h8.

20...♗xg5+

Black captures the pawn with check,
but it does not help.

21 ♘xg5

Otherwise the black king would get
a chance to escape with ...♔g7.

21...♕xg5+

There was a pretty checkmate after
21...♔g7 22 ♘xe6+! fxe6 23 ♕h7+ ♔f6
24 g5+! ♔xg5 25 ♕h4.

22 f4

A very important move that Judit
had to foresee, at least prior to sacrificing her rook. Now Black has to give up
the queen or else get mated.

22...♕xf4+

White's attack also prevails after 22...♕h5 23 gxh5 ♗xe4 24 hxg6 ♔g7 25 ♕h6+ ♔f6 26 ♕g5+ ♔g7 27 ♖h7+ ♔g8 28 ♕h6.

23 ♕xf4

Threatening 24 ♕h6.

23...♗xe4

Now White cannot play 24 ♕h6 because the rook on h1 will be captured.

24 ♕xe4 Black resigned

White has a queen against rook, knight and pawn, which purely by numbers is an equal material distribution. However, White has an overwhelming advantage here, because the attack on the h-file still exists, as well as other threats such as ♕c6.

Combinations

> *Combination 1*
> □ **Jonathan Tisdall**
> ■ **Judit Polgar**
> Reykjavik 1988

At the time of this game Judit was just 11 years old. Her opponent is a well-known Norwegian International Master (now a grandmaster). This was our (the whole family's) first visit to

Iceland. It is amazing how that small nation has loved and supported chess ever since the famous Fischer-Spassky match, which was held in 1972 in Reykjavik. Iceland has the highest number of chess grandmasters per capita in the world!

The position seems about even. However, Judit found a tricky way to take advantage of the lack of defense near the white king.

32...♖1h3!

Attacking the queen.

33 ♕e2

The only place where the queen protects the rook. After 33 ♖g3, Black trades on g3 and then picks up the other rook for free.

33...♕a4+!! White resigned

After 34 ♖xa4 ♖xa4+ 35 ♔b1 ♖h1+ the mate in two is unavoidable. A beautiful combination to end the game!

> *Combination 2*
> □ **Judit Polgar**
> ■ **Pavlina Chilingirova**
> Thessaloniki 1988

This game won the brilliancy prize at the 1988 Chess Olympiad, where Judit scored an incredible 12½ out of 13 and became an instant world sensation. This game is from the Hungary-Bulgaria match.

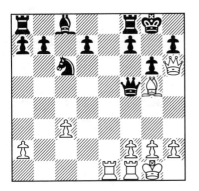

Judit reached this position after just 16 moves. White to move and mate in three!

17 ♕xf8+! Black resigned

If 17...♔xf8 18 ♗h6+ ♔g8 19 ♖e8 mate.

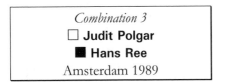

Combination 3
□ **Judit Polgar**
■ **Hans Ree**
Amsterdam 1989

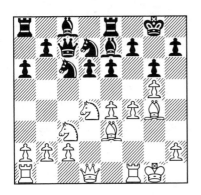

This game is from the same tournament as Judit's wonderful victory against GM Hulak (see Game 1 above). She was around 13 years old at the time.

Here Judit implemented a nice version of a typical Sicilian sacrifice against the famous Dutch grandmaster.

14 ♘xe6!

A sacrifice to destroy Black's pawn defense near his king and open some diagonals.

14...fxe6

If Black does not capture, White just has succeeded in winning an important pawn, while maintaining the attack.

15 ♗xe6+ ♔h8

If 15...♔f8 16 f5 opens the f-file for the rook.

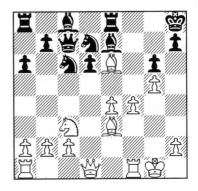

16 ♘d5

An obvious move to improve the position of the knight with tempo.

16...♕b8

After 16...♕d8 17 ♗d4+ ♘de5 the queen gets trapped by 18 ♗b6.

17 ♗f7!

17 ♗d4+ was also good enough, but this is even more accurate.

17...♖f8 18 ♗d4+ ♘de5 19 ♘xe7!
♘xe7 20 fxe5 dxe5 21 ♗c5 ♔g7

If 21...♕c7 22 ♗d6 ♕b6+ 23 ♔h1 and Black is in trouble.

22 ♗xe7 ♕a7+

Or 22...♖xf7 23 ♗f6+ ♔g8 24 ♕d8+ ♖f8 25 ♕d5+ ♖f7 26 ♗xe5 ♕a7+ 27 ♗d4 and Black is lost.

23 ♔h1 ♗h3

If 23...♖xf7 24 ♕d8 followed by ♗f6+ wins.

24 ♕f3 Black resigned

Combination 4
□ **Judit Polgar**
■ **Lars Bo Hansen**
Vejstrup 1989

Another pearl from Judit's jewel box. This game is from an international tournament in Denmark.

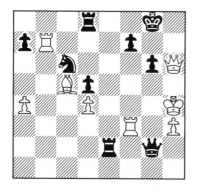

33 ♕g7+!! and **Black resigned**, because the end is inevitable after 33...♔xg7 34 ♖fxf7+ ♔h8 35 ♖h7+ ♔g8 36 ♖bg7 mate.

Combination 5
□ **Alon Greenfeld**
■ **Judit Polgar**
Haifa 1989

The 1989 European Championship was the first in which both Judit and I represented our native Hungary in the overall competition. Judit's opponent is an Israeli Grandmaster.

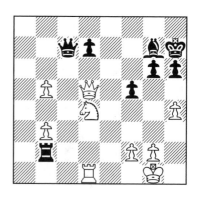

29...♖d2! 30 ♖e1

After 30 ♖xd2, Black forks with 30...♕c1+ 31 ♔h2 ♕xd2 and the knight cannot escape because of the pin.

30...♖xd4 and **White resigned** ten moves later.

Combination 6
□ **Judit Polgar**
■ **Peter Sinkovics**
Hungary 1990

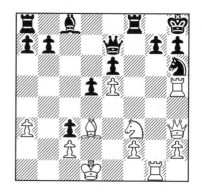

This game is from the Hungarian Team Championship. Leagues are common in many European countries. We played for many years in those friendly, but competitive team events. It was an important part of our chess experience.

As we can see Judit has gone all out, burning all the bridges behind her. The white king is stuck in the middle and Black is also ahead two pawns. She placed everything on the attack against the king.

20 ♖xg7!!

This sacrifice opens up the files against the black king. Black suffers because the bishop on c8 and the rook on a8 never developed and therefore cannot participate in the defense.

20...♔xg7

After 20...♕xg7 21 ♖xh6 ♖f7 22 ♘g5! ♕xg5 23 ♖xh7+ ♔g8 24 ♖h8+ and mate on the following move, or 21...♖f5 22 ♗xf5 exf5 then again the same idea: 23 ♘g5! ♕xg5 24 ♖xh7+ ♔g8 25 ♖h8+ ♔f7 26 ♕h7+ ♕g7 27 ♕h5+ ♔e6 28 ♕e8+ ♕e7 29 ♖h6+ and White is winning.

21 ♖xh6 ♖h8 22 ♖f6

This rook maneuver is not the only way to win, but it is certainly cute.

22...♔g8 23 ♖f4!

Threatening 24 ♕g3+ ♕g7 25 ♖g4 to pin and win the queen.

23...h5 24 ♖f6! Black resigned

He is helpless against the threat of 25 ♕g2+ ♕g7 26 ♖g6.

Combination 7
□ **Judit Polgar**
■ **Aurelien Mathe**
Fon du Lac 1990

This is a nice finish from the World Under-14 (Boys) Championship. It was the second World Youth Championship Judit won, after previously winning the World Under-12 in 1988. Judit's opponent is the French representative.

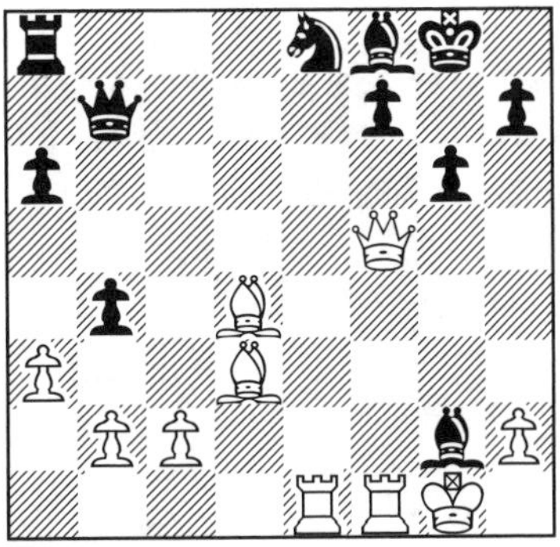

Black is attacking the white queen and rook. But White comes first.

27 ♕xf7+! Black resigned

After 27...♕xf7 28 ♖xf7 Black cannot capture the rook with 28...♔xf7, due to 29 ♗c4+ ♗d5 30 ♗xd5 mate.

Combination 8
□ **Rob Bertholee**
■ **Judit Polgar**
Amsterdam 1990

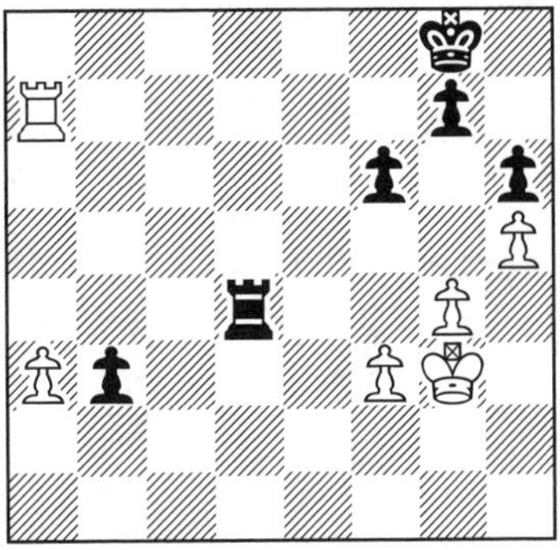

It seems that White can save the game, since if 35...b2, the white rook gets behind the pawn with 36 ♖b7. However...

35...♖b4!

...changes everything!

36 axb4 b2

The pawn is unstoppable.

37 ♖a5 b1♕ 38 ♖f5 ♕xb4 39 ♔g2 ♔f7 40 ♔f2 ♔e6 41 ♔g2 ♕b2+ 42 ♔g3 ♕b1 43 ♖f4 ♕b8 White resigned

He is losing the rook.

Combination 9
□ **Judit Polgar**
■ **Lev Polugaevsky**
Aruba 1991

This is the first game of a best of eight match between these two players. It was sponsored by one of the nicest people in the world, the great chess enthusiast, Mr. Joop van Oosterom. At the time, he was residing in the beautiful Caribbean island of Aruba. That was the reason for this great venue.

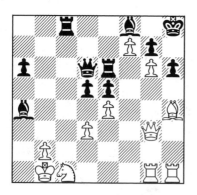

34 ♗f6!

A very impressive move, although the nice-looking 34 ♗e7! worked too; for example 34...♖xc1+ 35 ♖xc1 ♕xe7 36 ♖c8.

34...♖xc1+

Trying to deflect the rook from g1.

After 34...♖xf6 White sacrifices another rook and mates with 35 ♖xh6+! gxh6 36 g7+ ♗xg7 37 ♕xg7.

35 ♖xc1!

35 ♔xc1? would spoil it all, as after 35...♕c7+ 36 ♔d2 ♕c2+ 37 ♔e3 d4+ 38 ♔f3 ♖xf6+ then Black wins!

35...♖xf6

35...gxf6 36 g7+ ♗xg7 37 ♖xh6+! ♗xh6 38 ♕g8 mate is another pretty variation.

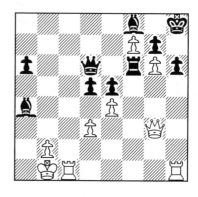

36 ♖cg1!

A quiet, but deadly move! White renews the threat of ♖xh6+. Instead, Black would escape after 36 ♖c8 ♖xg6 37 ♖xf8+ ♔h7.

36...♖f1+

The only move to delay the end.

37 ♖xf1 dxe4 38 ♖fg1

Back again to the same threat, for the third time!

38...♕xd3+ 39 ♕xd3 exd3 40 ♖e1 ♗c2+ 41 ♔c1 Black resigned

Combination 10
□ **Judit Polgar**
■ **Evgeny Bareev**
Hastings 1992/93

This game was played in the English

seaside town of Hastings, where they have an old (since 1895!) chess tradition of elite tournaments. The event always starts around Christmas time and ends in the first days of the New Year.

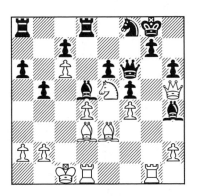

25 ♖xg7+!

Another nice combination with similarities to the one against Sinkovics (see Combination 6).

25...♔xg7

After 25...♕xg7 26 ♕xh4 Black has no good defense against 27 ♖g1.

26 ♖g1+ ♔h8

If 26...♔h7 27 ♘g4! ♕g7 (or 27...♕g6 28 ♕xh4) 28 ♘xh6! ♕xh6 29 ♕f7+ ♔h8 30 ♕g8 mate.

27 ♘f7+ ♔h7 28 ♘xh6! Black resigned

After 28...♕xh6 29 ♕f7+ ♔h8 30 ♕g8 mates as in the previous variation.

> *Combination 11*
> □ **Judit Polgar**
> ■ **Leon Pliester**
> Aruba 1992

This was our second trip to the beautiful island of Aruba. It was a special practice tournament with good prizes and great conditions, sponsored by Mr. Van Oosterom and organized by me. Judit's opponent is a Dutch International Master.

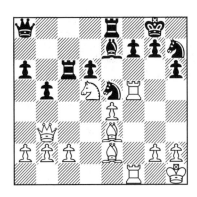

20 ♖xf7!!

The first of two sacrifices on the same square, based on a following discovered check.

20...♘xf7 21 ♖xf7! ♔xf7

Declining the sacrifice does not help. For example:

a) 21...♗f8 22 ♖a7! ♕d8 23 ♘f6+ ♔h8 24 ♕g8 mate.

b) 21...♗g5 22 ♖a7 ♕xa7 23 ♘e7+ ♔f8 24 ♘g6 mate.

c) 21...♕d8 22 ♘xe7+ ♖xe7 23 ♖xe7+ and White is winning.

22 ♘b6+

Unfortunately for Black, there is more trouble coming than "just" losing the queen.

22...♔g6

If 22...♔f8 23 ♘d7 mate, or 22...♔f6 23 ♘d7+ ♔g6 24 ♗h5+ ♔xh5 25 ♕f7+ g6 26 ♕f3+ ♔h4 27 ♕h3 mate.

23 ♗h5+!

Another sacrifice to force checkmate.

23...♔xh5 24 ♕f7+ Black resigned

In view of 24...♔h4 25 ♗f2+ ♔g5 26 ♕f5 mate.

Combination 12
□ **Jonathan Mestel**
■ **Judit Polgar**
Oviedo 1993

This position was from a rapid game, with both sides having very little time.

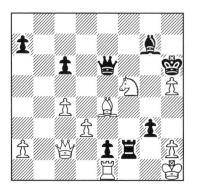

Judit found a cute finish in seconds.
35...♕xf5! 36 ♗xf5 ♖xh2+ White resigned

Mate follows after 37 ♔g1 ♗d4.

Combination 13
□ **Judit Polgar**
■ **Jose Fernandez Garcia**
Dos Hermanas 1993

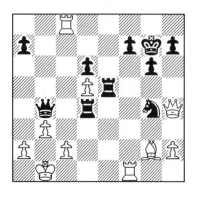

This combination reminds me of Combinations 1 and 4. In both of those examples, as in this one, Judit nicely coordinated the attack with two rooks on the king by means of a queen sacrifice.
35 ♕xh7+!!

There was a second solution to the puzzle: 35 ♖xf7+! ♔xf7 36 ♕xh7+ ♔f6 37 ♖f8+ ♔g5 38 h4 mate. But Judit choose the prettier way!
35...♔xh7 36 ♖xf7+ ♔h6 37 ♖h8+ Black resigned

37...♔g5 38 h4 mate would end the game.

Combination 14
□ **Vadim Ruban**
■ **Judit Polgar**
Groningen 1993

This game was played at the PCA World Championship Qualifying Tournament

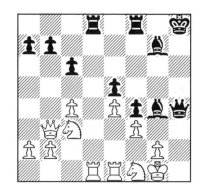

Judit has played her favorite King's Indian. It seems that White is OK, but Judit proved otherwise.
24...♗xf3!

A sacrifice to open the g-file.
25 gxf3 ♖g8 26 ♘h2

To make a hiding place on h1 for

the king. On 26 ♖xd8 the discovered check with 26...♗f8+ decides.

26...♗f8+

A discovered check to get the rook involved in the attack, and to swing the bishop over to more important diagonal.

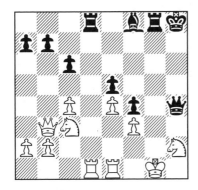

27 ♔h1 ♗c5!

To bring additional control over the g1 square.

28 ♖e2

After 28 ♕c2 Black has a nice win by doubling the rooks on the g-file: 28...♖d7! 29 ♖f1 (29 ♖xd7 leaves the rook on e1 unprotected, allowing 29...♕xe1+) 29...♖dg7 30 ♘a4 ♕h3 31 ♘xc5 ♖g2 winning.

28...♖d7! 29 ♘a4

If 29 ♖f1 ♕g3 forces mate..

29...♗f2! White resigned

If 30 ♕c2 ♕xh2+! 31 ♔xh2 ♖h7 or 31 ♖xd7 ♖g1 mates.

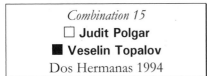
> *Combination 15*
> □ **Judit Polgar**
> ■ **Veselin Topalov**
> Dos Hermanas 1994

Here Judit's opponent is the Bulgarian super-grandmaster.

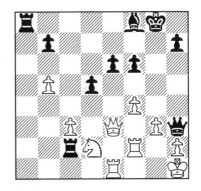

33 ♘e4! ♖aa2

If 33...♖xf2 34 ♘xf2 and White wins the pawn on e6.

34 ♘xf6+ ♔h8?

But if 34...♔f7 White proceeds with 35 f5!, cutting the black queen off the e6 square, and then 35...♖xf2 36 ♕xe6+ ♔g7 37 ♕g8+ ♔xf6 38 ♕xf8+ ♔g5 39 ♕g7+ ♔h5 40 ♕xh7+ ♔g4 41 ♕g8+ ♔xf5 42 ♕e6+ wins.

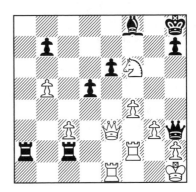

35 ♕e5!

A quiet move, creating a threat of discovered check.

35...♖xf2

If 35...♗g7 36 ♕b8+ exploits Black's back rank problem.

36 ♘g4+ ♔g8 37 ♕xe6+ Black resigned

The end would come after 37...♔h8 38 ♕e5+ ♔g8 39 ♕xd5+ ♔h8 40 ♘xf2 ♖xf2 41 ♕d4+ and wins the rook.

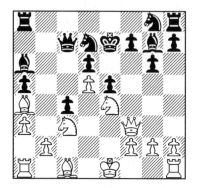

Combination 16

□ **Judit Polgar**

■ **Alexei Shirov**

Amsterdam 1995

Here Black is in trouble because the king failed to castle. Judit nicely exploited this problem.

15 ♘xd6! ♕xd6

If 15...♔xd6? 16 ♘e4+ ♔xd5 (or 16...♔e7 17 d6+) 17 ♕xf7+ ♔xe4 18 ♗c2+ ♔d4 19 ♗e3 mate.

16 ♘e4 ♕xd5

Others are no better, e.g. 16...♕b6 17 d6+ ♔f8 18 ♘g5 or 16...♕b8 17 d6+ ♔e8 18 ♗xd7+ ♔xd7 19 ♕xf7+.

17 ♗g5+

All the white pieces get to participate in the attack.

17...♘df6 18 ♖d1 ♕b7

If 18...♕e6 then 19 ♖d7+ ♔f8 20 ♘xf6 and the rook on a8 is hanging.

19 ♖d7+ ♕xd7 20 ♗xd7 h6?

After the more stubborn 20...♗b7, Judit had a nice hidden move planned: 21 a4! making space for the queen to appear on a3; e.g. 21...h6 22 ♗b5! hxg5 23 ♕a3+ ♔d8 24 ♕d6+ ♔c8 25 ♘c5 and White has a winning attack anyway.

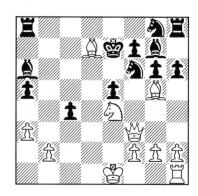

21 ♕d1! Black resigned

The following variations explain why Shirov resigned: 21...hxg5 22 ♕d6+ ♔d8 23 ♗b5+ ♔c8 24 ♕c6+ ♔b8 (or 24...♔d8 25 ♕b6+ ♔c8 26 ♘d6 mate) 25 ♕b6+ ♗b7 26 ♘d6 ♖a7 27 ♕d8+ ♗c8 28 ♕xc8 mate. It is a rare occurrence for somebody of Shirov's caliber to lose in only 21 moves.

Combination 17

□ **Judit Polgar**

■ **Vladimir Epishin**

Geneva 1996

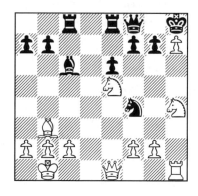

Again has Judit castled on the opposite side to her opponent. Here she found an impressive move to finish the game quickly.

28 ♕b4!

I have to add, though, that the less fancy 28 ♕e3 did the job too.

28...g5

If Black captures 28...♕xb4, White plays 29 ♘hg6+! followed by 30 ♘f7 mate.

29 ♕d4

Threatening mate in one.

29...♔g7

After 29...♕g7 White mates in two by 30 ♘hg6+ fxg6 31 ♘f7.

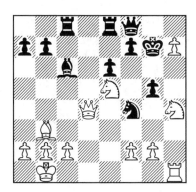

30 ♘f5+! exf5 31 h8♕+

Here 31 ♘d7+ or 31 ♘g4+ leads to an even swifter end.

31...♕xh8 32 ♘xf7+ Black resigned

Combination 18
□ **Valery Salov**
■ **Judit Polgar**
Madrid 1997

It seems that White is in good shape, having a bishop and two pawns for the rook. But Judit created a miracle out of nothing in this boring-looking endgame.

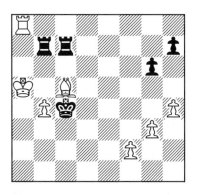

51...♖c6!

Cutting the king off from the sixth rank. All of a sudden White is lost.

52 ♗f8

Others do not help:

a) 52 ♖a6 ♖b5+ 53 ♔a4 ♖xa6 mate.

b) 52 ♖a7 ♖xc5+ 53 bxc5 ♖xa7+.

c) 52 ♗e3 ♖xb4.

d) 52 g4 ♖b5+ 53 ♔a4 ♖cxc5! 54 bxc5 ♖b1 55 ♔a5 ♖a1+ 56 ♔b6 ♖xa8 and even though White manages to promote the c-pawn, the arising pawn endgame is lost: 57 c6 ♔d5 58 c7 ♔e4 59 ♔b7 ♖f8 60 c8♕ ♖xc8 61 ♔xc8 ♔f3 62 g5 ♔xf2 63 ♔d7 ♔g3 etc.

52...♖b5+ 53 ♔a4

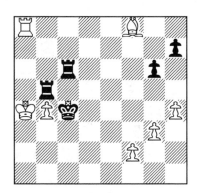

53...♖b8!! White resigned

If 54 ♖xb8 ♖a6 mate.

In this game Judit was representing Hungary's national team against France.

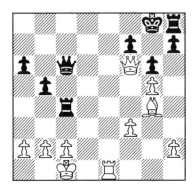

29 ♗e6!

Black is ahead in material, but the rook on h8 does not have full value in its current position.

29...fxe6

29...♖xc2+ 30 ♔b1 ♖c1+ 31 ♖xc1 ♕xe6 leads to a winning pawn endgame for White after 32 ♕xe6 fxe6 33 ♖c8+ ♔g7 34 ♖xh8 ♔xh8 35 ♔c2.

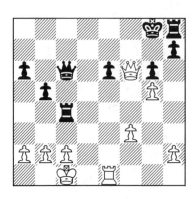

30 ♖d1 Black resigned

After 30...♕e8 31 ♖d8 ♕xd8 32 ♕xd8+ ♔g7 33 ♕f6+ ♔g8 34 f4, the black rook on c4 will soon have to go to an unprotected square, where it will be forked after a few checks. If 30...♖xc2+ 31 ♔b1 ♖c1+ 32 ♖xc1 ♕d7 33 ♖e1 and Black will lose the e6 pawn and the game.

This game is from the European Championship.

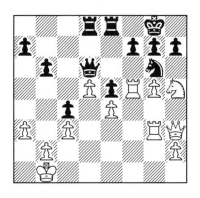

33 ♘xg7!

Another sacrifice on g7, this time with the knight!

33...♘f4

If Black accepts the piece with 33...♔xg7, the attack continues 34 ♕h6+ ♔g8 35 ♖h3! ♘f8 (if 35...♖e7 36 ♖f6 ♕c7 37 ♕xh7+ ♔f8 38 ♕xg6), and now the main point of the whole combination: 36 g6! fxg6 37 ♖xf8+! ♕xf8 38 ♕xh7 mate or 36...♕xg6 37 ♖g3 wins.

34 ♘xe8 ♖xe8

Black survived the immediate checkmate, but only at the costly price of of losing the exchange and a pawn.

35 ♕h6 ♕d7 36 ♖g1 ♘xd5 37 g6! ♘xc3+

If 37...fxg6 38 ♖xg6+! hxg6 39 ♕xg6+ leads to mate.

38 bxc3 ♕d3+ 39 ♔b2 Black resigned

Combination 21
□ **Judit Polgar**
■ **Felix Izeta Txabarri**
Santurtzi 2003

This finish comes from a special Blindfold exhibition match, between the top players from the Basque country and a selection representing the rest of the World.

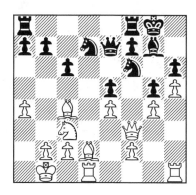

15 ♗xg5!

Destroying Black's defense in front of the king.

15...hxg5 16 h6 ♘b6

If the bishop retreats with 16...♗h8, White wins by 17 h7+ ♘xh7 (or 17...♔g7 18 ♕h3) 18 ♖xd7! ♕xd7 19 ♕h3.

17 ♗b3 ♖fd8 18.hxg7 ♖xd1+ 19 ♘xd1 Black resigned

After 19...♔xg7 20 ♘e3 White's attack is too powerful.

Combination 22
□ **Judit Polgar**
■ **Anatoly Karpov**
Hoogeveen 2003

This was played in the "glass tournament", where games were conducted on a wooden board with glass pieces.

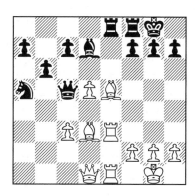

25 ♗xh7+!

A version of the famous double bishop sacrifice invented by Emanuel Lasker.

25...♔xh7 26 ♕h5+ Black resigned

26...♔g8 27 ♗xg7! leads to mate after 27...♔xg7 28 ♖g3+ ♔f6 29 ♕g5 mate, or 27...f6 28 ♗xf6 ♖xf6 29 ♖g3+ ♔f8 30 ♕h8+ ♔f7 31 ♕g7 mate.

Supplementary Games

Game 11
□ **Tibor Tolnai**
■ **Judit Polgar**
Budapest 1991
Sicilian Defense

This was the final round of the Hungarian Championship which Judit won, and thereby also became the youngest Grandmaster in the world, beating

Bobby Fischer's long-standing record.

1 e4 c5 2 ♘f3 e6 3 d4 cxd4 4 ♘xd4 a6 5 ♘c3 ♕c7 6 f4 b5 7 ♗d3 ♗b7 8 ♕f3 ♘f6 9 ♗e3 ♘c6 10 0-0-0 b4 11 ♘ce2 ♘a5 12 g4 d5 13 e5 ♘d7 14 ♔b1 ♘c4 15 ♗c1 0-0-0 16 h4 ♘c5 17 b3 ♘a3+ 18 ♔a1 f6 19 c3 fxe5 20 fxe5 ♘c4 21 ♘xe6 ♘xe5 22 ♕g3 ♘xe6 23 ♗f5 ♕b8 24 ♗xe6 bxc3 25 ♘xc3 d4 26 ♖hf1 ♗b4 27 ♘a4 ♖he8 28 ♗f5 ♗c6 29 ♗b2 g6 30 ♗b1 ♗xa4 31 bxa4 ♗c3 32 ♗xc3 ♕xc3+ 33 ♕xc3 dxc3 34 ♖c1 ♖c8 35 ♖f4 ♖c5 36 ♖b4+ ♔a7 37 ♖b3 ♖ec8 38 ♗e4 ♖8c7 39 ♖cb1 ♘c6 40 ♗xc6 ♖5xc6 41 ♖b4 ♖c4 42 a3 ♖xb4 43 axb4 ♖c4 44 h5

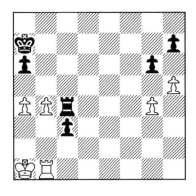

44...a5!

A nice move based on the idea that if 45 bxa5, then 45...♖a4 is mate.

45 hxg6 hxg6 46 ♔a2 ♖xb4 47 ♖g1 c2 48 g5 ♔b7 White resigned

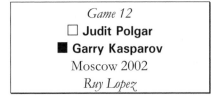
This game was part of the World vs. Russia rapid match. It was the first time that Judit managed to defeat one of the greatest ever players, Garry Kasparov.

1 e4 e5 2 ♘f3 ♘c6 3 ♗b5 ♘f6 4 0-0 ♘xe4 5 d4 ♘d6 6 ♗xc6 dxc6 7 dxe5 ♘f5 8 ♕xd8+ ♔xd8 9 ♘c3 h6 10 ♖d1+ ♔e8 11 h3 ♗e7 12 ♘e2 ♘h4 13 ♘xh4 ♗xh4 14 ♗e3 ♗f5 15 ♘d4 ♗h7 16 g4 ♗e7 17 ♔g2 h5 18 ♘f5 ♗f8 19 ♔f3 ♗g6 20 ♖d2 hxg4+ 21 hxg4 ♖h3+ 22 ♔g2 ♖h7 23 ♔g3 f6 24 ♗f4 ♗xf5 25 gxf5 fxe5

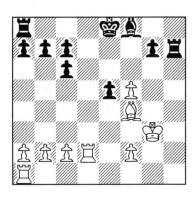

26 ♖e1!

This fine move makes the difference. Even though there are not many pieces left on the board, the black king is in serious trouble.

26...♗d6 27 ♗xe5 ♔d7 28 c4 c5 29 ♗xd6 cxd6 30 ♖e6 ♖ah8 31 ♖dxd6+ ♔c8 32 ♖d5 ♖h3+ 33 ♔g2 ♖h2+ 34 ♔f3 ♖2h3+ 35 ♔e4 b6 36 ♖c6+ ♔b8 37 ♖d7 ♖h2 38 ♔e3 ♖f8 39 ♖cc7 ♖xf5 40 ♖b7+ ♔c8 41 ♖dc7+ ♔d8 42 ♖xg7 ♔c8 Black resigned

CHAPTER FOUR

As a Family

Parental support and sacrifices

Needless to say, without the support, encouragement, sacrifices and discipline from our parents, none of this fairytale story would have happened.

In the 1970s, we were a typical Hungarian family, with a total income of around $200-$300 a month. I remember that, when I was a child, my father worked very hard at some point, even three jobs at once, practically day and night. Both my parents worked as teachers. For many years, my father would rather take the night shift, so that he could play with me or teach me chess during the daytime.

Unlike many families, my parents gave up on a lot of things to support our chess careers. For example, until the last decade or so, they never bought a car, or a week-end house; they rarely went out to a restaurant or the movies or to the theater. They also preferred to spend time with us rather than with their friends. I only understood to appreciate their sacrifices much later when I became a mother myself.

Polgaria – travels around the world

We used to travel together as a family a lot to different parts of the world to compete in chess tournaments. There was one very special type of event we always used to feel great about. That was when my sisters and I played as a team, and challenged other teams. These matches used the so-called Scheveningen system, where each sister would play each member of the opposing team, but not against each other.

In 1989-91, we played a number of 'Sister challenges':

Young England versus Young Hungary, 1989

This rapidplay match took place in November 1989, at the Barbican Centre in London, as part of the 'Britain Salutes Hungary' Festival. Our opponents were three very strong players: Michael Adams, David Norwood and Stuart Conquest. We had a slow start and trailed after two days, but fought back on the last day and tied the match 9-9.

Greece vs. Polgar sisters, 1990

In the summer of 1990, we received an invitation to play the Greek national team, as part of the preparation for the upcoming Olympiad in Novi Sad. The venue was the beautiful island of Corfu. After our great memories from the 1988 Olympiad in Thessaloniki, it was our absolute pleasure to return to the land of Gods and Goddesses.

The mountainous island at the entrance of the Adriatic Sea is very beautiful. Our hosts made sure we will remember Corfu forever, with its beaches and clear blue water, delicious food and, most of all, the Greek hospitality. We almost felt 'ashamed' not to be such good guests on the chess boards, because we won the match 11½-6½.

Vojvodina vs. Polgar sisters, 1990

In the autumn, not too long before the start of the Novi Sad Olympiad, the local organizers set up another Scheveningen-style match. Vojvodina is a province of Yugoslavia and has a large Hungarian speaking population. Our opponents were the best local players and included GM Petar Popovic. The score was 10-8 in our favor.

Slovenia vs. Polgar sisters, 1991

Something unthinkable happened at the beginning of the nineties. Hungary's southern neighbor, Yugoslavia, went through a civil war and the country was falling to pieces. It was quite shocking to us, as we knew a lot of people and we had a lot of friends in Yugoslavia. We could never have imagined that things could escalate to such horrible and bloody fights.

The organizer of the match was Boris Kutin (currently president of the European Chess Union), who drove us from Budapest through Croatia to Slovenia. The war was still going on and we were a little worried about getting there safely. However, once we arrived in Slovenia everything was peaceful.

The match was divided between two cities: the famous harbor resort of Portoroz on the Adriatic Sea, and Nova Gorica on the Italian border between the Alps and the sea. The Slovenians invited the Italian IM Ennio Arlandi and Russian future World Champion Alexander Khalifman as guest players to strengthen their team. All three sisters drew 1-1 with GM Khalifman; Judit and I each won one game, while Sofia made two draws. We all did quite well overall and the final score was 12-6 in our favor.

USA vs. Polgar sisters blitz match

The match was hosted in Boston, as part of the Harvard Cup event organized by Danny Edelman and Chris Chabris. In this blitz exhibition, our opponents were two former US Champions, GMs Boris Gulko and Patrick Wolff, and a young master Jorge Zamora. The event drew a large crowd and was also taped by ESPN. We won all three matches.

Other Sports

When I was growing up, my parents did not put too much emphasis on physical exercise. However, some time around 1987, we started to play table tennis in a club. All three of us took lessons for a while and practiced on an almost daily basis. We all had our 'shining days' at ping-pong. My greatest accomplishment was at the 1993 Maccabi Games, where my partner and I reached the quarter-finals of the mixed doubles; Judit was once in the top 32 in Hungary for her age group; and Sofia won the silver medal in Brazil... Of course we never took table tennis half as seriously as chess.

In the early 90s, we started to play tennis for fun. Nowadays, in the winter time, Judit is a keen skier; and a few years ago she used to compete at shooting too.

After I moved to New York, I joined my (ex) husband in working out in the gym regularly. I also started running several times a week.

Hobbies

All three of us enjoy going to the movies and the theater; we love listening to music, dancing, sightseeing, doing sports, going to the beach, hosting parties, shopping, and of course have fun with our kids. At one point Judit was very interested in photography. Sofia enjoys arts, especially painting. While both my sisters are good cooks, I love to cook and bake the most.

Three sisters on three continents

The three sisters were extremely close growing up, even more so than a 'normal' family where siblings are very close to each other. There are several reasons for this. First of all, the fact that we all three were home-schooled, logistically resulted in us being together practically 24 hours a day for many years. Then later, as we all started to play chess around the world, we collected countless (mostly good) memories together. Also we played as a team many times, including representing our motherland.

It is rather ironic and unfortunate that, as of right now, we live in three different parts of the world. Judit is in Budapest with her husband and newborn son, close to our parents. Sofia got married to an Israeli and lives in Rishon Le Zion, raising her two boys (currently 4 and 1½). I moved to US around ten years ago when I got married. In the meantime, I have been separated from my husband for the last three years (we are in the process of a divorce) and I am raising my two sons in New York.

Our parents still live in Budapest. Usually they spend at least a few months in Israel, too, especially in the wintertime. My children and I miss them the most, as we see them least.

Future plans

The most important thing for me in the foreseeable future is definitely to make sure my boys, Tommy and Leeam, grow up healthy, happy and well educated.

My future plans in chess focus mostly on promoting the game for children, and especially girls, on behalf of the Susan Polgar Foundation. I have big dreams, such as introducing chess in all schools in the United States, to help all children learn valuable life skills through chess, such as logical thinking, concentration, discipline, planning, being responsible for your actions, and many more. This will be part of the 'Excel Through Chess' program that I have just started. I also hope to raise respect and recognition for chess as a sport, and for professional chess players. After breaking through so many barriers so far in my life, I hope I'll be successful again in my new mission!

CHAPTER FIVE

The Ultimate Breakthrough

The Ultimate Breakthrough from another person's view by Paul Truong

Ever since Susan was four years old, she has played chess and loved the game with a passion. And over the next few decades, she dedicated her life to achieving excellence in the royal game in spite of many roadblocks. No matter what obstacles were placed in her way, she was able to knock them all down, breaking through countless age, gender, religious and social barriers in chess.

After winning her fourth World Championship in 1996, to become the first and only woman or man to win the triple-crown in chess (world blitz, rapid and classical championships), Susan slowly expanded her goals. In 1997, she decided to fulfill her childhood dream of owning and running her own chess club. Shortly afterwards, the Polgar Chess Center in Queens, New York, was opened to give something back to the community. Since then, she has worked with countless young players of all ages at her chess center.

In the next several years, her efforts were split between preparing for a title defense (supposed to be in early 1998) that never took place, fighting FIDE in court, and having a family of her own. After the birth of her second son at the end of 2000, some thought was given towards accomplishing more chess goals. That was the beginning of many new changes in her life. One of the stories in 2001 was the success of the prestigious New York City Mayor's Cup international tournament, which Susan organized with the support of the office of the Mayor and the Sports Commissioner of New York. Both Mayor Giuliani and Commissioner Podziba were on hand for the opening ceremony.

Susan and I have known each other for more than 15 years, but we had never worked on any chess project together. In fact, we tried hard not even to discuss the topic of chess, since I had completely left the game more than a decade ago. She was always busy with her chess playing career, while I was running my own companies. But during the Mayor's Cup, we had a chance to sit down and talk about the world of chess and we both expressed our desires of making the game better.

One of the first projects we collaborated on was writing the *Teach Yourself Chess in 24 Hours* book, which was published by MacMillan in March 2002. A few months later, things started to change drastically. One day in the summer, Susan received a phone call from WIM Beatriz Marinello (who she has known for a while), telling her that the Executive Director of the United States Chess Federation, Mr. Frank Niro, wanted to schedule a meeting at the Polgar Chess Center. She said "of course, no problem." They made an appointment for an afternoon in the following week.

This meeting was the beginning of the ultimate breakthrough that may impact on chess in America for decades to come. Mr. Niro is a great chess fan and his love for the game is endless. He also had a similar vision of helping to develop chess in the United States. During the meeting, he and Ms. Marinello addressed to us their concerns about chess in America. It seems that there were almost as many girls as boys playing chess at a young age, but for some reason at around the 3rd or 4th grade (age 9-10), the number of girls playing chess dropped dramatically. The Federation did not have an answer to this problem. So Susan was asked to do some research and help find a solution.

In addition, she was asked by Mr. Niro to help raise the visibility of US chess. There was no bigger name in chess in the United States, and Susan is the only World Champion living there. He stressed that US chess was in a very special time and the USCF needed to do something to take advantage of the chess boom. Since both of these projects were also of great interest to Susan, her answer was yes.

In the coming months, Susan made numerous appearances on behalf of the USCF to promote chess. During these trips, both she and I discovered something we were never aware of before. Since Susan was a young girl, she was trained to compete to be the best. Her focus was always on winning and being No.1. She also believed that there was no obstacle great enough to stop a woman from competing equally against men. (She was, of course, the first woman who succeeded in breaking through many barriers.) But what we discovered was that there are countless girls out there who do not think or look at chess the way Susan does.

To figure out why so many girls quit chess it is necessary to understand why they started playing in the first place. For many of them it is because they regard chess as a game. Chess is fun and gives them opportunities to travel, learn new cultures, make lasting friendships, etc. But as they grew older, they started to face the typical social stigma that girls are not supposed to play chess. You cannot be beautiful and smart at the same time. And rather than waste energy fighting the system, they just walked away.

One beautiful, energetic, cheerful teenager from Utah, named Stephanie, gave a chilling and truthful answer. On being asked why, when she was in the 9th and 10th grade (age 15-16), she refused to have her name published in the school yearbook for being a good chess player, she said that she did not want anyone to know she plays chess. She did not want to show the kids in her school that she is smart and that she can beat them. She said that boys do not like smart girls because they are intimidated by them. She wanted to protect her social standing in school.

When Stephanie reached the 11th grade (age 17), she began to gain the self-confidence needed to be herself. Otherwise she would have been just another girl in the statistics who quit chess. She credited chess for helping build her self-esteem and confidence. She is now in her first year of college and still plays chess, and is also teaching chess on a part-time basis to younger children in a nearby school. Because she decided to stay in chess, she is making a tremendous impact future generations of kids in her area.

Another young woman from California recounted a similar story. Elisha said: "When I first started playing chess, I was afraid, with so many boys..." She continued: "Preconceptions of playing ability inundated the tournament halls: 'No woman has ever beaten a healthy man.' I started believing that I lacked the endurance and the intelligence fundamental to the game simply because I was born XX instead of XY." Elisha also added: "I was weak; I abhorred the things people would say, and I almost stopped playing. Only the few games I did win kept me in the competition. The thrill of checkmate rushed through my fingers and *that* was indispensable. I had to stay."

In January 2002, Elisha won the high school girls' championship, but it wasn't considered a great accomplishment because "girls can't play as well as boys", so it was not a big deal. That May, she competed in the annual Memorial Day tournament in San Francisco. She won her first three games and felt somewhat nervous before the fourth round.

Elisha sat down and saw that her opponent had already come to the board. His notation sheet was set beside the board and his black leather jacket hung on the chair. A few minutes later, he returned carrying a cup of water. A faint smile emerged when he saw Elisha. "I immediately knew what he was thinking: *this is going to be an easy game*. I had seen the hidden half-smile enough times to decipher it. After lost games, it reappeared mockingly: *not many girls can play chess*." How badly she wanted to beat him and how badly she wanted to prove that her last three wins weren't just good luck. She did it! She won! Her queen and rook worked in unison to crush his king. As her opponent resigned, he said to Elisha, "I have never lost to a girl before."

There were countless stories like these. Many young girls cannot withstand the social prejudice against girls playing chess. They were scared to admit that they love the game. Many of these girls were teased by their classmates, teased by other chess players, ridiculed by society. Many of them felt uncomfortable being one of only a few girls in a predominantly male environment. And the worst part is that many of them quit because they could not handle the severe pressure. Many of them thought they were abnormal because they play and love the royal game.

Susan faced many similar problems when she was younger; she admits that it was very tough for her; she was alone so often in many of these fights. But her difficulties also helped motivate her; they made her a stronger person. But she was also lucky enough to be raised in a family with two very supportive parents, in a country where chess is a lot more popular than it is in the United States.

That is why Susan felt strongly that these girls needed a voice. She did not want them to face the same things she had. She felt that they needed a hero, a role model; someone who could understand their dilemma and make them feel that they were not alone. Therefore, she committed herself to making a difference.

With the full support of Frank Niro and the Executive Board of the USCF, the plan was off to a good start. But to revolutionize the game, to motivate the countless girls who play to stay in chess, and do something that has never been done before, would require a lot of work. It was impossible for Susan, with two young sons at home, to accomplish this task without a full-time co-ordinator, and so she asked if I would be interested in helping her. After many successful years in business, marketing and promotion, I felt that I could assist Susan in her mission and that it was a worthwhile vision.

The next step was to set up a non-profit organization to raise funding – which was when the Susan Polgar Foundation was born. The aim of the foundation is to promote chess throughout the United States, with all its social, educational and competitive benefits for young people of all ages, especially girls.

Three of the main goals of the foundation are as follows:

- Introduce chess to as many youngsters as possible, with special emphasis on young girls.
- Find ways to excite and motivate these youngsters (especially girls) to stay in the game, even just as a hobby.
- Create a program to assist those who have the talent and desire to excel and be the best with special emphasis on women's chess.

To accomplish these goals, several serious and critical chess projects had to be created. The first on the list was an all-girls national event. There was not a single national event for girls existing in the United States. How could we expect to motivate and excite the young America women to stay in chess if we had no tournament available for them?

During a National Scholastic Event in Nashville, Tennessee, in early 2003, Mr. Dewain Barber (a major scholastic chess supporter), Frank Niro, Susan and I had a breakfast meeting. During this get together, the inspiration of the Denker Tournament of High School Champions gave Susan the idea of doing something similar for the girls. The plan was immediately well received by everyone at the table and the Susan Polgar National Invitational for Girls was born.

However, some modifications had to be made. The Denker Tournament is only open to high school students. The problem with the girls is that most of them quit around the 3rd or 4th grades. If we wanted to reverse this trend, we must inspire and motivate the girls at a much younger age. That is why Susan decided to have the tournament for all girls under 19 and not restrict it to only High School students.

The winner of the Denker event receives a $40,000 scholarship to the University of Texas in Dallas (UTD). We wanted to offer the same for the girls. Therefore, Susan and Dewain contacted Dr. Tim Redman, a professor and head of the chess program at UTD. After consulting the appropriate parties, UTD graciously agreed to support the Susan Polgar National Invitational for Girls and offer the same scholarship as for the Denker event.

The next step was to present this idea officially at the 2003 USCF scholastic meeting, as well as the delegates meeting in Los Angeles during the 2003 US Open. At the scholastic meeting, the idea of the girls' national invitational was hotly contested by a few prominent US chess personalities. For whatever reasons, they did not want to see this tournament get off the ground. This was not the first time some people objected about activities and events for girls. They don't like changes, especially when the changes are not their own ideas. But Susan never gave up a fight in her life and she was not about to give up now. She kept on battling for the girls and eventually a majority of people supported the idea and this major project passed the first hurdle.

Since the Susan Polgar Foundation was brand new, Susan had not had time to do proper fund-raising. Therefore, she personally guaranteed the players' stipends and additional scholarship totaling over $6,500 annually. Mr. Dewain Barber and his company agreed to sponsor the cost of the tournament medallions and the opening ceremony. Frank Niro and I volunteered to take care of all promotional and organizational aspects of the event. We were happy and honored to support Susan's mission to change the game for the better.

Even though we faced many serious obstacles, in August 2004 the first annual Susan Polgar National Invitational for Girls took place as planned in Fort Lauderdale, Florida. We had incredible support from parents, coaches and young female players all over the country, and an outstanding 34 players from all over the United States took place in this historic event. Most people were betting on there being around 20 players in the first year. This was a tremendous breakthrough for young female players across America.

But just how do the girls get a spot in this prestigious event? Each year, each state is entitled to nominate one player to participate. Although states are encouraged to run a girls' qualifying event to bring more girls into chess, each state can decide instead to nominate the highest-rated girl that meets the age criteria, based on what their budgets allow. The main idea is for us is to reach out to young female players in all 50 states.

After the success of the 2004 inaugural event, Susan never stopped wanting to make things better. She hoped to create more excitement and motivate even more girls to play chess than ever before. Therefore, she decided to create some additional events to spice things up. The three new additions were:

- Susan Polgar National Invitational Blitz Championship for Girls
- Susan Polgar National Invitational Puzzle Solving Contest for Girls
- Susan Polgar National Invitational Chess Training Program for Girls (to help girls improve their chess and life skills)

Because of Susan's vision, we expect nearly 3000 young women to compete in regional qualifying events for a chance to represent their states in the Championship. Furthermore, additional scholarships and prizes will be awarded to countless young female players across the US. For the first time in the history of women's chess in America, there is a sense of optimism. The girls finally feel that they have a voice in the game. Susan received a lot of support and praise from parents and coaches and the young girls themselves.

The third item on Susan's list was to create a program to assist those with the talent and desire to excel and be the best, again with special emphasis on women's chess. That was the beginning of the US Women's Olympiad Program – another part of the original discussion between Frank Niro, Susan, Beatriz and me.

We had a good nucleus of young, talented, top-level female players in the United States, such as Irina Krush and Jennifer Shahade. But in order for the team to be a serious contender at the Olympiad, we needed veteran leadership. That was one of the reasons why Mr. Niro and the Executive Board fully supported the idea of Susan switching federations to help the United States, her new permanent home.

However, this was an agonizing decision for Susan. Very few players of her strength actually change federations; in addition, Susan is a national hero in her native Hungary. She broke through many gender barriers and brought pride to her country. By changing federations, Susan understood that she might face some harsh criticism from the Hungarian nationalists. But the challenge of transforming women's chess in an entire country, the USA, and making positive impacts for decades to come, was hard for her to turn down.

The next step was to assemble other players for the Women's Olympiad Program. Invitations were emailed to the top six women by rating. Four accepted, and the first-ever training squad was formed. These were IM Irina Krush (US Women's Champion), WGM Anna Zatonskih (two-time Ukrainian Women's Champion), WIM Jennifer Shahade (US Women's Champion), and WGM Rusa Goletiani (three-time World Junior Champion and European Junior Champion), three of whom also had Olympiad experience.

The idea was great as far as it went, but we needed a lot of support. Susan, who agreed to represent the US team in the 2004 Olympiad, and I presented the idea of the team and the program to the USCF Executive Board in March 2003. The board unanimously endorsed the idea and warmly greeted the entire group. It was a great experience, but we still needed additional financial backing. At that point, besides the USCF and the US Chess Trust, we had sponsorships and assistance from IBM, the

World Chess Network, *ChessBase*, the Susan Polgar Foundation, and International Chess Marketing. But this was not enough. We still needed more.

During the Kasparov-*Deep Junior* Match in January 2003, and the US Amateur Team East in February, we had several meetings and discussions about sponsorship with Michael Khodarkovsky, a friend and confidant of Garry Kasparov. Michael is also a famous coach with extensive top-level experience. After consulting with Garry and the Kasparov Chess Foundation, the answer was more than we could have hoped for. Not only did the Foundation agree to assist our program financially, Michael also offered his wisdom and experience as the team training consultant. To top things off, Garry Kasparov, one of the strongest World Champions ever, also agreed to offer his incredible chess knowledge to our women players. We finally were on our way!

The US Women's Olympiad Training Program, led by Michael (our head coach) and Susan, conducted six sessions over eighteen months, the first from March 17th-20th 2003, the sixth and last on September 1st-3rd 2004, just before the Olympiad. In each session we were greatly helped by strong guest grandmasters: Boris Gulko (sessions 1&2), Gennadi Zaichik (session 2), Garry Kasparov (sessions 3&5), Alexander Chernin (session 4), Sam Palatnik (session 6). Each trainer was wonderful in their own special way. The general idea was to enhance each player's strength and improve each player's weaknesses.

Garry Kasparov also offered specific suggestions for the team about what to work on and how to improve. At the end of session 3, he went over his overall impression with Michael and me and suggested a specific course of action to get the team ready for the Olympiad. The one point that Garry made over and over was the word "team". He was very impressed with the unity of our team and how well everyone respected and got along with each other. This is one of the key ingredients for success.

These were Susan's perceptions and thoughts about the 2004 US Women's Olympiad Training Program: "I have spent my entire life trying to make a difference in chess. In my native Hungary, the Polgar sisters inspired a whole new generation of wonderful chess players. As for women's chess, I am very proud to have made a big impact in changing how women are perceived as chess players.

"Now my goal is to bring a new attitude to women's chess and chess in general in America. The best way to lead is by example. That is why I have agreed to play for the US in the next Olympiad. I want to inspire the next group of young players to follow their dreams. I want them to understand the message that anything can be accomplished if you want it badly enough and if you are willing to work hard for it.

"I am very proud of this group of young players (Irina, Anna, Jennifer and Rusa) who fully committed themselves for two years for a chance at the gold medal in 2004. They are giving their all to be role models for the next generation.

"I am also very thankful for the incredible support from Michael (Khodarkovsky), Garry (Kasparov), who is not only a great player but great coach and person, the

USCF, you (Paul Truong), Frank (Niro) and many others. This is what chess needs. We need people working together if we want to make a difference. The politics, pettiness, and selfishness should be replaced by team work, hard work, and professionalism. We want to bring the 'Three Es' to American chess: Energy, Excitement and Enthusiasm! Our goal is nothing short of the gold medal in 2004 and we are can do it!'"

The 2004 Women's Olympiad

At the USCF Executive Board meeting on March 16th, 2003, four-time Women's World Champion and three-time Olympic Champion, GM Susan Polgar, made it official that she would indeed lead the US Women's Olympiad Team to go for the gold medal in the 2004 Chess Olympiad in Spain.

The rest of the squad consisted of the stars of women's chess in America: US Women's Champions, IM Irina Krush and WIM Jennifer Shahade; two-time Ukrainian Women's Champion, WGM Anna Zatonskih, and three-time World Junior Champion WGM Rusudan "Rusa" Goletiani.

The US Women's Team has never won a medal at the Chess Olympiad in the past. However, this team would be considered as one of the top three favorites to win the gold medal in 2004.

The 36th World Chess Olympiad officially began on October 15th, 2004, in the beautiful island of Mallorca. There were 128 men's and 87 women's national teams taking part in the most prestigious team chess event in the world. Everyone arrived in Spain with the same dream and goal in mind: to capture the gold medal.

The women's section was especially strong, because just about all of the top women players in the world were competing. China came in as the favorites and were clearly a notch above all of the other teams. They included a superstar in GM Xie Jun, who is the greatest woman player in the history of China, and who basically revolutionized chess in her country. On board 2 was the dynamic WGM Xu Yuhua, followed by the very talented World Junior Champion WGM Zhao Xue on board 3.

The second-ranked women's team was the 2002 silver medalists, Russia, with IM Alexandra Kosteniuk, the reigning European Women's Champion on board 1, the young Russian Women's Champion WGM Tatiana Kosintseva on board 2, and Women's World Championship finalist, WGM Ekaterina Kovalevskaya on board 3. Russia's reserve was another powerful young player, WGM Nadezhda Kosintseva, the older sister of Tatiana.

The United States team was seeded number three, which was the highest pre-tournament ranking for any US women's team. Our board 1 was GM Susan Polgar; on board 2, IM Irina Krush, the youngest US Women's Champion ever at the age of 14; with WGM and IM-elect, Anna Zatonskih, on the third board. Two-time US Women's Champion, WIM Jennifer Shahade, was the reserve.

Other notable top women's players at the Olympiad were: former World Champion GM Maia Chiburdanidze, reigning Women's World Champion GM Antoaneta Stefanova, former European Women's Champion GM Pia Cramling, and the French superstar IM Almira Skripchenko.

Round 1 – October 15, 2004

In the first round, the US women's team was paired against Venezuela. Because Irina Krush had only arrived the day before, having important classes at the university that she could not skip, she was given a day off to get over the jetlag. Anna Zatonskih was moved up to board 2 and Jennifer Shahade played board 3. Even though the Venezuelan team was out-rated by a good margin, they put up a very tough fight. But in the end the US won as expected. Susan and Anna both won their games and Jennifer drew, thus giving the US women's team a respectable start with the score of 2½/3.

Round 2 – October 16, 2004

Both the US men's and women's team were paired against Lithuania. Our women's line-up was back to the normal rotation: GM Polgar, IM Krush and WGM Zatonskih. This time Irina and Anna both won, while Susan was held to a draw by IM Viktorija Cmilyte in an opposite-colored bishop endgame. So again the final score was 2½-½ and we were in a good position. Incidentally, the men's team scored four draws against the Lithuanians.

Round 3 – October 17, 2004

On the third day, the tournament got tougher as strong teams were paired against each other for the first time. The match up of the day was India vs. Bulgaria, featuring the World Junior Champion, GM Humpy Koneru, against the reigning Women's World Champion, GM Antoaneta Stefanova.

The US faced a young and confident Slovenian team with the sensational WGM, Anna Muzychuk, on the top board. This was the team that had just demolished France, one of the tournament favorites, by the score of 2½-½. Our line-up remained the same.

Our entire team arrived a little late for the round because no team bus was available and there was no taxi in sight. The walking distance between our hotel and the tournament hall was about an hour. I had to arrive at the playing hall 30 minutes earlier than the rest of the team each day, because I needed to bring all their purses and pocketbooks through the metal detector and security checkpoint. The line was long and the security was very tight; no one gets in and out anywhere without their Olympiad ID badge. As you can imagine, I was pacing like an expectant father when I did not see our team at the start of the round. Thankfully, everyone was able to get to their boards only 2-3 minutes late.

All the games were fairly calm until the second hour. Susan Polgar slightly misplayed the position and her talented young opponent took advantage of it immediately. Anna Zatonskih was a pawn up in a fairly easy rook endgame, while Irina Krush was slightly better and focused on one of her opponent's isolated pawns. As the third hour approached, Susan managed to get out of trouble and reach another opposite-colored bishop draw. Irina finally won the isolated weak pawn, and Anna converted her rook endgame into a win, giving the US team a third consecutive 2½-½. victory.

In the meantime, the Chinese team continued rolled on with a perfect 3-0 score over Latvia, and the German team continued their Cinderella ride by beating Kazakhstan 2½-½. So after three rounds, China and Germany were both on 8½/9. The US team was in a third-place tie on 7½ with Russia and Hungary. Incidentally, the game between GMs Koneru and Stefanova ended in a draw.

Round 4 – October 18, 2004

In the fourth round, the US women's team (seeded three) were paired against the second seeds and 2002 silver medalists, Russia, who had an average rating of 2491. The board match-ups were: Kosteniuk vs. Polgar; Krush vs. Kosintseva, and Kovalevskaya vs. Zatonskih. This was the premier match of the tournament so far. Once again, difficulties over transportation led to our team arriving at the tournament hall with only seconds to spare. This was a serious problem, especially in view of the fast 90/30 time control where every second counts.

All three games were intense from the first moment, right until to last minute. After the first hour, our three boards were all in good shape, complicated but looking promising. As the second hour approached, Irina was heading towards a favorable double rook endgame; on board 3, Anna's position looked solid, while Susan was battling in a complicated endgame resulting from the Berlin.

But despite Susan's efforts, the game fizzled out to a draw as IM Kosteniuk managed to keep checking her king. In the meantime, Irina, trying hard to win the double rook endgame, unfortunately blundered under the fast time control and lost. After seeing her team-mate's defeat, Anna gave her all to level the match, but the opposite-colored bishops ultimately ensured the draw.

So, what had started out as promising positions on all three boards, netted us only one point and we fell out of the medal placement. We had a lot of work to do to get back into the medal hunt.

Round 5 – October 19, 2004

After our unfortunate loss to Russia, the US women's team was paired against Sweden, led by the former European Women's Champion, GM Pia Cramling. IM Krush requested a day off to recuperate from her painful defeat. So our line-up was Polgar, Zatonskih and Shahade, vs. Cramling, WIM Agrest and WIM Johansson.

With the black pieces against a friend she had known for more than 20 years, Susan decided to play a very sharp line of the Queen's Gambit Accepted. For the first time in her career, Anna played 1 d4! which really shocked her opponent. Jennifer engaged in the black side of the Nimzo-Indian. Sharp positions arose right out of the opening, with both Polgar and Zatonskih sacrificing a pawn for the initiative.

After the first hour, Jennifer spent 35 minutes on one key move, contemplating a possible sacrifice to create an attack; but it was not a sound plan and her opponent developed a kingside attack herself which ultimately won the game. As we approached the second hour, Anna Zatonskih won a piece, after which it was just a matter of being careful in order to net the full point. Meanwhile Susan had sacrificed a second pawn to take her opponent's queen out of play. At the turn of the third hour, it was still stuck in the heart of the black queenside, but the white queen could not be trapped and the players eventually repeated moves for a draw. Therefore, we ended up tying with Sweden 1½-1½.

In the meantime, China steam-rollered England 3-0, showing the difference between amateur and professional players. In China, chess is supported by the government, the way it used to be in the old Soviet Union. The success of Xie Jun and the Chinese Olympiad team has helped create interest for millions of new young players, especially girls, and China keeps on producing young talents year after year. The Chinese teams take the Olympiad very seriously; leading up to the tournament they spent a lot of time training chess daily; they worked hard to come to the Olympiad and win.

Unfortunately, we do not have this type of backing in America, so our national federation is unable to create such a professional program. Our limited training schedule was only supported by a few individuals, companies and organizations. Even with the involvement of Susan Polgar and Garry Kasparov, our team training program was faced with tremendous opposition from many people. What these opponents fail to understand is that the success of US players and teams translates into greater popularity for chess in America, and hence to greater membership. But until proper support is given, we can only fight teams like China, Russia, Ukraine, Georgia, etc. with sheer willpower and determination.

Round 6 – October 20, 2004

After two mediocre rounds, we needed to do well in Round 6 to get back on track. Nevertheless, instead of getting easier competition, we now had to face the fourth seeds, Georgia, headed by former Women's World Champion, GM Maia Chiburdanidze, and their young superstar WGM Nana Dzagnidze. The Georgian team was also considered one of the pre-tournament favorites for a medal. We returned to our main line-up of GM Polgar, IM Krush, and WGM Zatonskih facing WGM Lela Javakhishvili on board 3.

Our chief theoretician, GM Chernin, and head coach, IM Khodarkovsky, worked hard all night to come up with strong opening choices for our players to use against our powerful opponents, while I worked with GM Polgar to counter Maia Chiburdanidze. We scanned through all Maia's games from the past three years, and even some earlier ones. At around 12.40 pm, I suggested a novelty with g2-g4 against the Queen's Indian. I checked all of our databases and the move seemed new. Susan immediately liked it. First of all, it would give her a psychological edge, since it seemed certain to stun her opponent; secondly, with the crazy 90/30 time control, it might land her opponent in time trouble, having to find a solution against the dangerous attacking plan. Michael, our head coach, also liked the idea and the three of us continued to work, analyzing countless lines.

At 3.30 pm sharp, the round began. GM Chiburdanidze played exactly what we had anticipated and Susan uncorked the novelty on move 9. In the meantime, both Irina and Anna obtained reasonable positions against their opponents. Everything looked fine for the moment. As the first hour approached, GM Polgar sacrificed her knight to mount a fierce kingside attack, while IM Krush established a very good position with the black pieces; but here WGM Zatonskih fell way behind on time.

Right before the second hour, a nice combination left Susan the exchange and a pawn ahead and an easily won position. This was one of the most brilliant games of the Women's Olympiad and was published in countless newspapers, websites and magazines around the world. Irina was also a pawn up. However, Anna was now a pawn down and had only seconds left on her clock. She fought valiantly to try and save the game, but ultimately it could not be salvaged. At the turn of the third hour, Irina, still a pawn up, managed to trade off the rooks to reach a knight vs. bishop endgame. The win was by no means easy, but IM Krush displayed her magnificent endgame technique and there was soon no hope for her opponent, who eventually resigned.

With this 2-1 victory, we moved back into a tie for third place (with five other teams) on 12 points, behind China (16) and France (13). The next day was our only day off and then we would play India, headed by the young superstar GM Koneru. After only six rounds, we had already faced the No.2 seeds, Russia, and the No.4 seeds, Georgia, and would now play the No.6 seeds, India. But this is what the Olympiad is all about, facing the best of the best!

Round 7 – October 22, 2004

After a badly needed day off, we were back to work. Our opponents were an extremely tough India headed by GM Humpy Koneru. She was ranked among the top 5 in the world and was only the fifth woman player to earn the male GM title through normal over the board performance. The match-ups were: Polgar vs. Koneru, Krush vs. IM Vijayalakshmi, Zatonskih vs. WGM Harika.

We had a very unusual start to the round. After the first few moves, Harika, probably surprised by the opening and fearing some preparation, decided to repeat moves as White. Since Anna would have had the worse game had she played something different, she had no choice but to accept the draw by repetition.

On board 1, GM Koneru played very solidly and maintained a slight space advantage; while on board 2 Irina had a slightly better position in our one game with the white pieces. However, there was one crucial factor involved. The two Indian players had more than 90 minutes on their clocks, whereas Susan and Irina were already 30 minutes behind before the first hour approached as they both tried to find ways to play for the win.

As the second hour loomed, GM Koneru's position was still very solid and Susan could not get anything out of it. After Humpy forced the trade of queens, the two players agreed a draw. On board 2, Irina was still a little better, but she now had only 17 minutes left on her clock against more than an hour for her opponent. Rather than risk another blunder in time trouble, Irina offered a draw, giving the teams a 1½-1½ split.

Once again our team was facing serious problems with the time control. As I pleaded with the USCF Executive Board some months before, we should have held more 90/30 events, especially the 2004 US Women's Championship. There was no serious event in the US with this time control, and it does not matter how much you practice at home, it is never the same as when you face world-class competition. Unfortunately, the federation did not agree and the lack of practice meant that our players were constantly in time trouble, which was a big disadvantage for our team.

The news of the India-USA match was reported worldwide by the Indian media. They considered this a premier contest in the Women's Olympiad. After the game, Susan saw Anand while he was giving an interview to the media. They are old friends and Anand immediately asked Susan how she had done. She replied 'draw'. One of the media, surprised, asked Anand: "Do you know who she played?" Anand just looked at him with an expression of "How could anyone not know?" and then said Humpy of course! And of course Humpy is the best woman player that India has ever produced; she is on course to become a future world champion.

In the meantime, China once again trounced their latest victim, this time France, by the score of 2½-½. It seemed that no team was able to hold off China.

Round 8 – October 23, 2004

We were now in the second half of the 36th Olympiad and the entire playing hall was filled with tension as crunch time grew nearer. The US team faced Armenia, the reigning European Women's Team Champions. The day's match-ups were: Polgar vs. IM Danielian, Krush vs. IM Mkrtchian, Zatonskih vs. WGM Aginian.

After the first hour, there was very little movement on any of the boards. All three positions were still in the early stages. An hour later, they were still totally unclear. Susan was spending a lot of time trying to make something happen; Irina was also trying to create some kind of an advantage from the black side; Anna's position was extremely difficult.

As we approached the second hour, the tension mounted even higher. Not a single game on the top nine boards had finished. Everyone was still playing and fighting hard, knowing that every game and every match could play in big role in determining the medal winners. In the meantime, Susan sacrificed a pawn to create tactical opportunities; Irina had reached a rook and opposite-colored bishop endgame; Anna was finally up a pawn but had to carefully consolidate her position to avoid danger. Any wrong move could have lead to a disastrous result.

At the three and a half hour mark, the Georgian team finally won their match to produce the first result on the top boards. At this point, IM Danielian seemed to have consolidated her extra pawn, but missed a trick allowing Susan to force a draw by repetition. Anna beautifully simplified her position and achieved connected passed pawns on the queenside; her opponent resigned shortly after that. Irina traded rooks to reach opposite-colored bishop endgame a pawn, but her opponent was able to sacrifice her bishop to reach a standard rook's pawn and wrong-colored bishop draw. A 2-1 win was not what we had hoped for but it was a solid result to keep us in contention for a medal.

A minor incident took place today: both world champions Anand and Polgar were asked to leave the tournament hall by the arbiters. They had finished their games and wanted to spend a few minutes to look at their team-mates' games. Unfortunately, the organizer had the silly rule that the moment a player finishes their game, they must leave the playing area *immediately*. Meanwhile, non-playing VIPs were free to roam around anywhere they wished. Many players complained about this rule, but to no avail.

Round 9 – October 24, 2004

Round 9 was the most exciting one so far for both US teams. The men's team faced Spain 'A' led by super-GM Shirov. The women faced the 2002 bronze medalists, Poland. Our line-up was: Polgar vs. WGM Radziewicz, Krush vs. WGM Socko, Zatonskih vs. WGM Zielinska. We had high hopes in this round to move ahead of the pack.

Susan obtained a slight advantage out of the opening, which she slowly increased. Monika Socko played a speculative gambit in the Sicilian, sacrificing two pawns for a dangerous initiative. By the second hour Irina's king was shuffling between f6 and g6 in the line of heavy attack. Meanwhile, Anna's position was in a deadlock, and her opponent was very good at playing this type of closed game.

As the third hour approached, GM Polgar was two pawns up in a bishop vs. knight endgame; her opponent soon resigned giving us a 1-0 lead. This was the beginning of an incredible second half of the Olympiad for Susan. Meanwhile Irina had managed to shuffle her king across from g6 to b8 and relative safety, However, she now had about one minute left on her clock. Anna was now a pawn up, but her clock was down to just a few minutes as well. It looked like we could win 3-0 or lose 1-2.

When Irina only had about 30 seconds on her clock, her opponent offered a draw. Objectively Irina's position was much better, but with so little time anything can happen, and she made the right decision by accepting the draw. In a team competition, the rule of thumb is to avoid losing at all costs.

At the same time, Anna, with only seconds left on her clock, blundered the pawn back and now faced a much worse position. Around the four hour mark, she was down three pawns, but there were still a lot of complicated tactics and her opponent was now also having to play at a blitz tempo. The battle went up and down like mountains and valleys. With the 30-second increments, there was not much time to think about great moves while also having to write them down. (It is not like in the

USCF rule where the players can stop notating when they have less than 5 minutes.) The players just tried not to blunder and hang pieces. Anna managed to win back a couple of pawns and then simplified the position to just rook and pawn vs. rook and two. It was quite simple to draw, but of course her opponent had to try and win to even the match score. By now, even the cleaning ladies were standing in the back room waiting to clean up the room and prepare for the next round.

Eventually, Anna won another pawn and we were down to rook and one pawn each, but there was still no draw offer. The four arbiters looked helplessly at me, wanting to say can we just end this game, we all want to go home. A short time later, Anna sacrificed her last pawn to reach a dead drawn endgame. But her opponent did not give up trying. We were at about move 100 when Zielinska finally offered a draw. It was immediately accepted giving us a 2-1 win and a tie for second place on 17½ with Russia, India and Hungary.

The contest was not getting easier. The next day we would face China, the No.1 seeds and the runaway leaders of the tournament. China had a perfect 9-0 match score and were way in front on 23½. They had just beaten Lithuania 3-0, winning the board in only 15 moves, and that despite having rested Xie Jun for this match. So far, no team had managed to stop them.

Round 10 – October 25, 2004

I said that Round 9 was our most exciting so far. I take that back. Round 10 was our most incredible round. Up until then, the professional Chinese team had knocked over every opponent put in front of them, including Russia and France. Their match score was an amazing 9-0 and they were leading the tournament by 6 points. We now had to face this seemingly invincible team.

To make matters worse, we had Black on boards 1 and 3. The line-up was as follows: GM Xie Jun vs. Polgar, Krush vs. WGM Xu Yuhua, WGM Zhao Xue vs. Zatonskih. Both Michael Khodarkovsky and Alexander Chernin worked hard all night long and until 30 minutes before the round to prepare our players. Meanwhile, I had to double-check every line that Susan might encounter against her old adversary, GM Xie Jun. We analyzed some of the variations 30-35 moves deep. This was a big match and nothing could be left to chance.

When Xie Jun and Susan sat down at their board, the media surrounded them, taking pictures. The last time these two great players met was in their historic 1996 World Championship match, which also happened to be in Spain. Eight years later, these two World Champions were now ambassadors for their sport. Xie Jun had revolutionized chess in China, while Susan has been doing the same in America. They are now both mothers, too, so they had plenty to share before the round started. It was wonderful to see the warm respect and admiration they have for each other.

My strategy for this match was very simple. Since we had Black in two games, I wanted to equalize the color odds immediately and put pressure on the Chinese team. Therefore, after about ten minutes, I instructed our board 1 to offer a draw. After she had consulted the Chinese captain, GM Xie Jun accepted. Five minutes later, I instructed our board 3 to offer a draw as well. While I had some expectations that their board 1 might accept, I was absolutely sure that their board 3 would not, since she was in contention to win an individual gold medal (as she had done in 2002).

So why did I make this decision? The idea was to throw our opponents off their rhythm and to confuse them. After long consideration, their board 3, as expected, turned down the draw. But Anna was now up more than 30 minutes on the clock. In the meantime, Irina had maintained a slight space advantage as White. As the second hour approached, I was quite confident about both boards; we were also ahead on time, which was a key factor. Anna managed to lock up the position, while Irina continued to have a good game.

As the third hour came, Anna's opponent, Zhao Xue, was just shuffling the pieces around, unable to break through. Irina was now much better: she had the bishop pair, while her opponent had a very weak pawn structure. Irina soon forced a queen trade and reached a completely winning endgame, giving us a lead of 1½-½. The last task in hand was to hold the position on board 3. After 88 moves, 66 of them without a single pawn move, Anna offered a draw and her opponent accepted.

So China were finally halted as we became the first team in this Olympiad to score a match point against them. All of us went out to a local Chinese restaurant to celebrate, but as soon as we came back to the hotel, it was business as usual. Preparation started immediately. We could not afford to take any team for granted just because we had beaten China.

The scores were now China 24½, Hungary 20, Georgia, India, USA 19½. Georgia had recovered from their loss to us in Round 6 and moved back into contention with a 3-0 win over Sweden. Meanwhile, the Hungarian team, led by IM Ildiko Madl, had actually gone ahead with a 2½-½ win over Latvia.

Round 11 – October 26, 2004

After a big victory against China, we tried to avoid a let down against a good Slovakian team. Once again we used the same line-up. The match-ups for the day were: WGM Repkova vs. Polgar, Krush vs. WGM Pokorna, IM Hagarova vs. Zatonskih.

After the first hour, all three boards were even. Susan's opponent played a very unusual opening with b2-b3 against the Sicilian – a system she had been using successfully for three years. Because of this, Susan had to be very cautious not to fall into any home-cooked variations. In the meantime, Irina had a slight space advantage in her game, while Anna had a solid position.

As the second hour approached, the evaluations were much the same. GM Polgar was now cautiously defending against a vicious kingside attack. IM Krush continued to improve on her advantage and launched a standard minority attack on the queenside. WGM Zatonskih was still level and was working at creating some weaknesses in her opponent's position.

By the time we approached the third hour, many things had changed. Irina's minority attack had netted a pawn. Her opponent then hung a knight in time pressure and immediately resigned. Susan was now up on material, having completely refuted her opponent's piece sacrifice. Repkova's position soon collapsed, giving us the second full point of the day. Meanwhile, Anna continued to push for a win, while her opponent tried to force a repetition. Both players were in time pressure. Unfortunately, having playing almost 190 moves in the past two days, Anna was tired and made an incorrect exchange sacrifice. She was soon down even more material and inevitably lost. The final score was USA 2 Slovakia 1.

After being stunned by us, China played very cautiously to maintain their overall lead. They ended up drawing all three games against Hungary. You can say that China were taking it easy towards the finish line. It is like being up 5-6 runs in a baseball game, and you trade a run for an out in the 8th or 9th inning.

India, who had not lost a match in this Olympiad so far, now had a disastrous day. With her team trailing ½-1½ to Georgia, GM Koneru tried very hard to win a superior endgame against GM Chiburdanidze. All of sudden, Koneru dropped a bishop and lost the game. With this shocking 2½-½ match win, Georgia moved into second place on 22 points, behind China on 26. We were in a tie for third place on 21½ points with Hungary, whom we would play next.

This pairing gave us a big dilemma. Prior to going to the Olympiad, Susan had told me that she would not play against Hungary. Her family still lives there and she was afraid for their safety if she played against her own native country. In fact, during the first day of the Olympiad, she had received death threats from fans about playing against Hungary. Furthermore, Susan risked losing hundreds of thousands of dollars in endorsement and other revenue sources in Hungary, if she played against them.

The problem was that, without Susan, our medal hopes would immediately evaporate. This US Dream Team and the US Women's Olympiad program was her brainchild. She had brought in Garry Kasparov, Michael Khodarkovsky, the Kasparov Chess Foundation and me to help with this project. She had agreed to switch federations from Hungary to the United States to help chess in this country. So what to do? To play or not to play against Hungary? She called her family to ask their opinions and it was a right down the line split. The situation was a nightmare.

Susan made up her mind. She would play against Hungary. She would give her all to help US chess. This was a very painful but courageous decision from a great World Champion. On behalf of all chess fans in the United States and around the world, I would like to thank Susan for this monumental decision. To be honest, I do not know what I would do in the same situation.

Round 12 – October 27, 2004

Hungary were very motivated for this match. Since Round 7 they had been ahead or else tied with us on points. In the previous round they had held the powerful Chinese team to three draws. Their top board, IM Ildiko Madl, was a two-time Olympic gold medalist and a team-mate of the Polgar sisters at the 1988, 1990 and 1994 Olympiads.

All the Hungarian women had a lot of experience in Olympiad competition. They also had something to prove against their famous compatriot on the US top board.

The line-ups for the round were: Polgar vs. IM Madl, WGM Anita Gara vs. Krush, Zatonskih vs. WGM Nikoletta Lakos.

After the first hour of play, all three boards had complicated positions. Susan started an attack with g2-g4-g5, h2-h4, etc. Irina's position was slightly cramped, while Anna had a comfortable game. As the second hour approached, Susan continued to forge ahead on the kingside. At this point Irina was in trouble; her pieces had very little space to maneuver. Anna had a very nice set-up but her opponent's position was also very solid. The question was how could she break through? One wrong step and the scale could tip against her.

As we reached the third hour, Susan had finally opened up the kingside and was simultaneously making play on the queenside. Her opponent was in big trouble as she could not defend both sides and soon resigned, giving the US a 1-0 lead. In the meantime, Irina had managed to defend her position, though it was still full of danger. On board 3, Anna was strategically shifting pieces to ideal squares as she awaited developments.

At the three and a half hour mark, WGM Lakos, now under severe time pressure, lost patience and decided to break open the position. Anna immediately took advantage and scored a full point giving us a 2-0 lead. While this was taking place, in a time scramble on the other board, Irina's opponent made an unsound sacrifice for an attack. Unfortunately, with only seconds left, Irina was unable to find the refutation; instead she returned the material, and the players soon agreed a draw, making the final score 2½-½ to us.

Meanwhile, China had lost again, this time 2-1 to Georgia. Russia and France had moved back into contention beating Slovenia 3-0 and England 2-1 respectively. So after 12 rounds the scores were China 27, Georgia, USA 24, Russia 23½, France 23. From being 6 points down to China with four rounds to go, we were now only 3 points behind with two rounds to go. But we had to win big in the last two rounds to have a chance at the overall gold medal.

Round 13 – October 28, 2004

In the crucial penultimate round, everyone could sense the tension in the tournament hall. There were now even more media than before and everyone was paying very close attention to the US women's team. Many people mumbled the phrase "Dream Team" when they talked about us. I guess we had proven that marketing does work for chess.

There were some very important match-ups in this round. China took on the No.6 seeds India, with Xie Jun facing the young GM Humpy Koneru. No.4 Georgia played the No.2 Russia, with GM Maia Chiburdanidze squaring off against the young IM Alexandra Kosteniuk. We had to face the No.8 seeds, France. Our pairings were: IM Skripchenko vs. Polgar, Krush vs. IM Sebag, WGM Collas vs. Zatonskih.

After the first hour, we had difficult positions on all three boards. Susan had to be very careful dealing with a kingside attack from IM Skripchenko. Irina and Anna were also caught in very sharp openings. Then the French board 3 suddenly offered a draw. Anna asked me if she should accept. In Olympiad competition the players are allowed to ask the advice of their team captain on whether to accept or reject draw offers. I instructed Anna to play on but feel free to offer a draw if she became uncomfortable with her position.

As we approached the second hour, things got even more difficult. Anna was now really low on time, so she offered a draw, to which her opponent immediately agreed. Irina continued to have problems, while Susan, after very careful calculation, accepted a pawn sacrifice from her opponent. At the third hour mark, the tide turned in this game. IM Skripchenko failed to break through on the kingside, and now Susan created a very strong counter-attack, eventually winning a bishop and chasing the white king to g3. In a completely hopeless position, her opponent resigned to give us a 1½-½ lead. Unfortunately, Irina was unable to save her position and the match ended in a tie. This was a bad result for us because it cost us any breathing room.

In the other top games, GMs Xie Jun and Koneru agreed a quick draw as China won 2-1 against India. GM Chiburdanidze also drew against IM Kosteniuk in the Georgia-Russia match. Unfortunately, in a dynamic game on board 3, the Georgian WGM Javakhishvili blundered a rook in time trouble and lost, giving Russia the match 2-1 and allowing them to catch us on points. Hungary bounced back from their defeat in the previous round to beat England 2-1.

So the placings with one round to go were China 29, Russia, USA 25½, Georgia 25, France 24½, Hungary, Slovakia 24, India 23½. China could no longer be caught. But there were still the silver and bronze medals to play for.

The question was, who would be our final opponents? Our tough draw in the Olympiad so far meant we had already played all our nearest rivals, from India upwards. Now we could only be drawn against one of the teams behind on 23 points: Ukraine, England or Vietnam.

Ukraine were the No.5 seeds with a 2454 average rating, but had underperformed at the Olympiad. In joint second place after Round 5, they then lost 2-1 to France. With another loss in Round 9, this time to India, and four draws against lower-ranked teams, they had never figured in the medal hunt again. After a 3-0 drubbing by China in Round 5, England (average rating 2308) were never really in contention either; although IM Hunt had a fine tournament on the top board. Vietnam (average rating 2293) were the real surprise. They had come up out of nowhere with four successive big wins (3-0, 2½-½, 2½-½, 3-0 against Bolivia, Venezuela, Kazakhstan and Latvia) and were now riding high on confidence. Vietnam were to be our final opponents. China would play Slovakia, while Russia and Georgia faced France and the Ukraine.

Round 14 – October 29, 2004
Before the round started, I congratulated GM Xie Jun of China for leading her coun-

try to another Olympiad victory. Then it was the last minute pep-talk to our players. We were dead even with Russia and only half a point ahead of Georgia and there were still too many teams right behind us. Our match-ups were: Polgar vs. WIM Nguyen, Krush vs. WIM Le, Zatonskih vs. Hoang.

At 3:30 pm sharp, the chief arbiter announced the start of play. The drama had begun.

Right around the first hour mark, the Vietnamese board 1 offered a draw in an even but dangerous position. GM Polgar felt she was worse. She turned to me and asked if she should accept the draw. This was the normal protocol at the Olympiad.

In front of the players, my answer was an immediate, loud and firm: "Absolutely not!!!! Play on!" I did this on purpose for psychological reasons: to show confidence in our players, to give them a mental and psychological boost, and to create self-doubt in their opponents' minds. Being from South Vietnam originally, I understood how opponents like China or Vietnam think. They are very tough mentally and I had to help our players break through this. But it was not without risks, and could backfire big time if our players became over-confident.

As the second hour approached, we had nothing on any of the three boards. In the meantime, Russia had already scored 2-0 against France on boards 2 and 3. Our players did not realize this and I didn't tell them. I did not want to give them more pressure than they already had.

At the third hour mark, Georgia were up 1½-½, while China had already won 2-1. For us, GM Polgar was a pawn up in a rook and opposite-colored bishop endgame. IM Krush's position was very tight, and WGM Zatonskih had a slight space advantage. Soon after this, Susan demonstrated fine endgame technique and won her game, giving us a crucial 1-0 lead. Irina could not do much in her position and it ended in perpetual check. The score was now 1½-½ in our favor.

But at the same time, tragedy happened for us. IM Lahno of the Ukraine, two pawns up in a completely winning rook and bishop endgame, hung her rook and immediately resigned. This gave Georgia a match score of 2½-½ and they were suddenly back in the hunt for Silver and Bronze. They had moved passed us and tied with Russia in the standings. But we still had one game in hand. So did Russia.

At the last, WGM Zatonskih, in severe time pressure with only seconds left on the clock, defeated her opponent. Our match score was now 2½-½ as well, and we had once again moved past the Georgians. This guaranteed us a medal, though we still had no idea what color it would be.

It all came down to the last game between France and Russia: IM Almira Skripchenko vs. WGM Tatiana Kosintseva. In a queen and rook endgame with equal material both players were trying to win. Victory for Russia would mean Bronze for us. A draw or win for France would mean Silver. Finally, on move 77, with only seconds remaining, IM Skripchenko won the game for France. And so the final placings in the 2004 Women's Olympiad were: 1st China (31 points), 2nd USA (28 points), 3rd (on tie-break) Russia (27½ points), followed by Georgia 27½, France 25½, Hungary, Slovakia, and England 25.

History had been made! We had won the Silver medal! The 2004 US Women's Olympiad Team had captured the first ever medal for the United States!

This medal came from incredible team work. When GM Polgar was having a difficult time with the time control, IM Krush and WGM Zatonskih carried her. Then Susan carried the team towards the finish line as any great champion would do. It was like Michael Jordan taking the last jump shot in the final seconds to give his team victory. Every team member contributed to this achievement. Michael and Alex also worked very hard.

The performance of Susan Polgar was the talk of the Women's Olympiad. After disappearing from the world stage for 8½ years, she came back to score the overall best performance (2622) of the Women's Olympiad, ahead of World Champions Xie Jun, Maia Chiburdanidze, Antoaneta Stefanova, GMs Humpy Koneru, Pia Cramling and many other top players. She also finished No.1 on points scored with 10½ and second in percentage on board 1 with 75%. That left people scratching their heads wondering how she had done it.

A few more facts that people may not have known:

1. GM Susan Polgar played all 14 games on board 1 without a break in the four Olympiads in which she participated (1988, 1990, 1994 and 2004).

2. In each of these four Olympiads, she captured both team and individual board medals.

3. She has played 56 consecutive games in the Olympiads without a single loss. (This is comparable to Joe DiMaggio's incredible hitting streak in baseball.) In fact, Susan has never lost a game at the Olympiads.

These are amazing statistics that very few players in the world can match.

GM Polgar had shown America what a serious Olympiad training program with proper management and no politics can do for women's chess in America. We had succeeded despite opposition from countless US chess politicians. The real question was: Would the USCF continue to support a US Women's Olympiad program that could forever change US Chess for the better? Or would they go back to politics as usual?

We went out to celebrate in a local restaurant. There we met the Icelandic team. During our dinner, a waiter came by with two bottles of champagne and chilled glasses, and handed Susan a note from the Icelanders congratulating us! It was an incredible gesture from them. I asked the waiter to bring more glasses for them and let us all have a toast together.

After dinner, Irina, Jennifer and Anna went dancing. Michael, Alex, Susan and I went back to the hotel to answer all the email from fans. We were also congratulated by the USCF President Beatriz Marinello, Don Schultz, Steve Doyle, Bill Kelleher and his wife, many members of the US men's team and their captain Boris.

Before ending this segment I would like to thank: our head coach, IM Michael

Khodarkovsky; our very special chief theoretician, GM Alex Chernin; Garry Kasparov and the Kasparov Chess Foundation; GMs Boris Gulko, Gennadi Zaichik and Semon Palatnik; our many other sponsors, Frank Niro, John McCrary (and his board for supporting this program), Harold Dondis, Frank Berry and Ken Gordon; our team, Susan, Irina, Anna and Jennifer; our biggest fans at the USCF Headquarters in New Windsor; and all of the fans in the US and around the world who supported us and sent us encouraging emails throughout the two weeks. We would not have made it without all your wonderful support and encouragements. History had been made!

Politics as usual

As I mentioned earlier, winning the team Silver, one individual Silver, two individual Golds, and making history at the Olympiad proved that, if chess is run the right way without politics, great success can follow for the United States.

However, as we all suspected and feared, politics usually takes center stage in American chess. The Chinese Women's Team were warmly greeted at the airport by the president of their federation and countless media sources. They were presented with a big bonus check. They came home as heroes. The bronze medalist team, Russia, were invited to Moscow for a big celebration with high level politicians and treated like stars. For the US Women's Olympiad Team, it was politics as usual. After 18 months of sweat and tears, we had made history, but the reception we received was chilling. There was no official letter from our federation to congratulate us. What we got was a registered letter notifying us that the US Women's Olympiad Program had been officially canceled!! Yes, let me repeat! You did not read this wrong. Our reward for making history was to have the Olympiad Program officially canceled!!!

In addition, more than six months had passed and our players were yet to receive their bonuses from the federation. And one wonders why no other US women's team ever won a single Olympiad medal. This is now another obstacle that has to be broken through for the benefit and growth of chess in America. I am confident it will give Susan more motivation than ever to change things for the better. After all, she has never given up a fight, no matter how many hurdles were put in front of her.

We did have a wonderful team celebration with Garry Kasparov and the board members of the Kasparov Chess Foundation. And prior to that, the team was invited to New York Governor Pataki's office in Manhattan. Governor Pataki is of Hungarian descent and has been fully supportive of Susan and her initiatives. Thank you Garry for your tremendous support! Thank you Governor Pataki for supporting chess and Susan's vision!

CHAPTER SIX

Women's Chess:
Questions, Comments and Answers

Over the past few years, Susan has given many lectures, conducted many Question and Answer sessions, and written many articles in various chess publications and on websites. Below are some of the questions related to women's chess that were asked at various events, as well as on her Chess Café column.

Kevin C. asked: "Where are the women and girl coaches? While young girls in particular frequently derive benefit from education or training in temporary isolation from boys, a key element to the boosting of self confidence Susan mentions often consists of a teacher who is a woman, or a mentor who is an older girl, particularly in the US where female primary school teachers still outnumber males by six-to-one or more."

Susan: Excellent point Kevin! There are not enough women coaches out there. Why?

Let's ask the same question about hockey? Do you see many minority coaches in professional hockey? No. If you have very few players in the game who are part of the minority group, it hard to find future coaches from this small pool of talent. This is the same problem in chess. If there are fewer women playing chess at a higher level now, there will be fewer women who will be coaches in the future. The current problem we have now is a direct result of the past.

Why are women coaches important? There are a number of reasons. In some cases, women coaches can relate, understand and motivate young girls better. Many male coaches do a great job too. Another reason is many parents are not comfortable leaving their young teenage daughters alone with male coaches. I can tell you from my own experience growing up, my parents would be sitting right in the next room for as many hours as my sisters and I were training with male coaches. That was a time-consuming process and not all parents have the time to do that. Is that necessary for every case out there? No. But that is how things work. We cannot change everything at once.

Let me add that I began training one young girl at age 6 when she had no idea of the difference between a knight and a bishop. She was my first ever student when I opened my chess center in Rego Park, New York. Now she is 13 and is helping me with coaching duties at my club. She is also rated on USCF best women players list. My Olympiad team-mates IM Irina Krush, WGM Anna Zatonskih, WGM Rusa Goletiani and WIM Jennifer Shahade are all working as chess trainers, while training hard to win the gold at the 2004 Olympiad. There are many women players who are fine coaches. Their number is still very small. But I am working hard to change that.

John S. wrote: "When it comes to chess, there is not enough difference between the sexes to justify any special outlook for women – not in training, nor in tournaments. The women's world heavyweight boxing champion will never beat the men's heavyweight champion; but the best woman player in the world could and did beat the best male player (and Judit Polgar may beat Garry Kasparov again). Special titles such as WGM, etc., are ridiculous. The best tournaments are open to the best players, and this includes women. If women want to do better against the men, they are simply going to have to sacrifice even more, like the men do. I seriously doubt whether men are the best chess players because of any special or superior attributes stemming from their gender; they are better because they are more obsessive..."

Susan: You are right John. Many men are more obsessive than women in chess. And yes, Judit did beat Garry once out of more than a dozen times. But let me add a few points to your arguments. You are looking at chess today in the USA.

In some countries, women were not allowed or were not encouraged to play chess. I can tell you from my own experience growing up. I was not allowed to do many things in chess because I was a girl. I was not allowed even to travel to the West to compete, even though I was already a superstar in my own country. If you have a chance to check out the recent article by Frederic Friedel of *ChessBase*, he wrote that he was the person who had to go to Budapest to negotiate with the officials and make a lot of noise to get my own federation to allow me to play chess in the West. Without him and a few other friends and supporters, maybe my sisters and I would still be unknown to you and the rest of the world.

Yes, I made a lot of sacrifices from the age of 4. While other girls played in the yard, I studied chess. I was determined to be the overall world champion. But how would you feel if you did all that and were then told that you would not be allowed to enter the big dance? Let me point out the fact: I was the first woman ever to qualify for the Men's World Championship Zonal Tournament. The key word is "men's". No one would ever have thought a woman could qualify until I did. And after I qualified, the answer was basically "Sorry, you are a woman. You cannot play in the men's world championship cycle."

Well, I was denied the opportunity to compete, but eventually FIDE changed the rule to allow women to compete, and now it is called the World Chess Championship and not the Men's World Chess Championship. By the way, not all the best tournaments are open to all women players. Aside from Judit and me, when I was competing actively, how many other women were invited to super tournaments? Recently, GM Sergey Karjakin (age 13) was invited to play in super tournaments when his rating was in the low to mid-2500 Elo range. No woman has been invited, not even GM Antoaneta Stefanova who was rated higher at 2560. Thank you for your input John.

Tony H. wrote: "Susan argues that society (social and peer pressure) and boys create unbearable pressure on girls who play chess, which results in a decrease in the number of girls that want to play chess after grade 4. I seriously question this as a cause for the lack of women in chess. Boys are not at fault for girls leaving chess. There are a variety of reasons, but to put it on men or boys is misleading and not going to solve the problem. Unless there are some recent studies I am unaware of, there is no reason that girls cannot compete equally with boys. If this is the case, why separate boys and girls at all? Separating "girl" chess from "boy" chess only seems to reaffirm a subconscious belief that girls can't compete with boys. I fail to see how avoiding playing a particular group can increase a person's confidence. Would not playing and defeating boys after attending the same training increase a girls confidence even more? Saying that girls need special training or special anything just adds to the current batch of misconceptions."

Susan: Excellent point, Tony, and thank you for your input! There is no need for separate training for all girls, just some girls. Different people handle things differently. My point is not a scientific argument. There is no single reason for girls dropping off after grade 4. There are many reasons for that. But rather than trying to be a politician and promising to fix everything at once, I would just offer an initial choice for parents and young girls to attend some separate training. Even if this would help increase girls retention in chess by 20-30% or more, it is worth it. Confidence is contagious for everyone, especially for a young player. This program may help some young girls to have a good start.

By the way, Tony, I was one of the first women to compete against all men and I was severely criticized and attacked by other players, organizers and even some people in my own federation at that time. How times have changed! My sisters and I handled it fine. But not all girls are this way, especially those who do not have the luxury of having parents fully supporting them emotionally and psychologically. If some young girls feel that they can handle the pressure and want to learn and compete against boys only, thumbs up to them and they will have my full support. I just don't want to leave any girl in the middle of the road. I am not fighting the issues for me but for the next generation.

Tom F. wrote: "I do not, however, think that it follows that pressure "caused by society and other boys" is the reason girls lose interest in chess. At least in my little neck of the woods here in the mid-western USA, I believe it is more complicated than that. In 2001 in one of my classes, 3 of the top 4 players were 10-year-old girls; in 2002, upon advancing to the middle school, none of them continued to play chess. This despite the fact that at the end of the 2001 school year all three said they planned to continue. And I know for sure that none of them lacked chess confidence, at least relative to others their own age. I also question the notion that the girls need "an option and opportunity to improve their chess in a more friendly and normal environment." I don't notice unfriendliness generally in my classes or at tournaments, and I specifically don't notice unfriendliness by boys directed at girls. And I have been looking for it. I have, however, noticed the following which I find interesting. At ages of approximately 4-6 girls seem not to care whether they play recreational chess with a boy or girl opponent. Beginning at about age 6 or 7, many girls seem to prefer playing other girls."

Susan: As I mentioned above, each girl handles things differently. One example from one of the questions above: "Boys are more obsessive." That is correct. Many boys play chess to win, to conquer, to dominate. I love chess for a different reason. I love the beauty of the game. I love the grace and creativity in chess. My sister Judit on the other hand is different. She is much more into winning. Even as sisters, and I was her first coach, she took a different direction. So my point is why not have both? Let the young people decide for themselves.

As coaches or parents, I urge everyone to allow the youngster to make her own choices, to study and compete with the boys, or start off with the girls and merge with the boys later. It is always helpful to have an option and that is all I am suggesting. Even Garry Kasparov and his Chess Foundation are supporting the idea of having a branch of their training program dedicated to girls only.

Now, I would like to update you with some progress in women's chess. The US Women's Olympiad Program took a turn for the better. Through the co-operation between team training consultant, Michael Khodarkovsky, and the team captain and business manager, Paul Truong, our team members were very happy and honored to spend 3-4 days recently training with Garry Kasparov.

Everyone agrees that it was a most incredible experience to see how Garry trains and analyzes. It helped all the team members to better understand how to study and improve their chess. The team also worked with GMs Boris Gulko and Gennadi Zaichik. I also worked with the team members. Each of us helped the players in a different area.

Jennifer J. asked: I have heard many people say that you were the first woman to earn the men's grandmaster title. Is that true?

Susan: Yes, I was the first woman who broke the gender barrier to earn the grandmaster title. What that means is that I earned my three grandmaster norms in tournament play like other male players. Approximately one year after I earned the title in 1991, my sister Judit earned her grandmaster title, and after Judit my good friend Pia Cramling from Sweden earned it. Judit was also the youngest grandmaster at that time, breaking Bobby Fischer's long-time record.

Recently, two new women have earned the grandmaster title. They are Antoaneta Stefanova of Bulgaria and Humpy Koneru of India.

There are also other women who received the grandmaster title for winning the Women's World Championship, such as Nona Gaprindashvili, Maia Chiburdanidze, Xie Jun and Zhu Chen. They are all good champions. I hope many more women can earn this prestigious title in the near future.

Mary D. asked: Many people have said that chess helps children. Can you explain how can chess do that

Susan: Over the past few decades, numerous scientific studies have clearly shown that chess helps children in many ways. Chess can help a child develop logical thinking, decision making, reasoning, and pattern recognition skills, which in turn can help math and verbal skills.

In addition, chess also teaches the important values of hard work, concentration, focus, objectivity, commitment, and patience. Chess has been used to enhance self-confidence and self-worth in children, especially in young girls. These are just some of the qualities that, in most cases, have not been reached by traditional educational methods and means. Among the educational benefits are improved mental discipline and better planning skills. Chess educators have argued that chess is beneficial, not just for the intellectually gifted, but also for the learning disabled and hyperactive children.

Jennifer C. asked: My two daughters really love chess. However, because of the ratio of boys versus girls playing chess (about 10 to 1 in their school) they got frustrated and no longer want to play outside of our home. What do I do?

Susan: Unfortunately, there is no magic wand that can change this instantly. I am trying to correct this problem by creating programs and tournaments specifically for girls. I will post as much information as possible on the websites: www.SusanPolgar.com, www.SusanPolgarFoundation.org and www.USScholastic-Chess.org.

Girls and boys approach the game very differently. Many boys see chess as a form of competition and brute force. They want to win at all cost! Many girls view chess as an art form. They are less worried about the results and more concerned with the beauty of the game.

I was the same way; I did not perceive chess as an egotistical competition as many of my male counterparts did. I wanted to win just like anyone else, but that was not my top priority. I am happiest when I produce a beautiful, artistic chess game.

Many girls also like to attend different tournaments to meet and make new friends. By understanding that girls have different priorities and interests; it may make it easier for parents to motivate their daughters. I have seen many parents who are too preoccupied with the win-loss records for their daughters, and that may not be the way to maintain their interest in the game.

This is also one of the reasons why I like separate classes for some, but not all, girls. It helps them build camaraderie, friendship, self-confidence, and self esteem before competing against the boys. It also improves the chances of girls preserving an interest in chess.

Anita M. asked: What is the Susan Polgar Foundation?

Susan: The Susan Polgar Foundation is a non-profit organization. Its mission is to promote chess, with all its social, educational and competitive benefits, throughout the United States, for young people of all ages, especially girls.

- Chess develops decision making, critical thinking, logical thinking, evaluating, planning, problem solving, and perseverance skills.
- Chess improves concentration, memory and self-control.
- Chess promotes independence, imagination and creativity.
- Chess inspires self-motivation, self-esteem and self-confidence.

That is why we should do much more to introduce chess to children. There are three major areas we need to concentrate on:

- Getting more young players involved in chess.
- Motivating more young players to stay in chess, even if only for personal enjoyment.
- Help the most talented and most motivated young players to reach the top level.

The foundation has created the Women's Olympiad Program, sponsored the Annual Susan Polgar National Invitational for Girls, started regional training programs for gifted young players and will eventually expand this training program nationwide. I hope that we will be able to do a lot more for US chess in the coming years and beyond.

We heard that you originally decided not to play against Hungary in the Olympiad. What made you change your mind?

Susan: I have to say that this was one of the most difficult decisions of my life. I said to the team captain before going to Mallorca that I would *not* play against Hungary. That was my condition. No matter that I have lived in the United States for around ten years and am now a US citizen, I will always be a Hungarian. I am proud of my country and am proud of what my sisters and I have done for Hungarian chess. Nothing can ever change that.

Unfortunately, there is something much bigger that I must deal with. My sole purpose of coming back to chess is to help US chess and then chess worldwide. If the US team can bring home the first ever medal, it will give a big boost to chess in this country. It can help bring in a lot of sponsorships for chess and chess players. This will benefit my colleagues.

If we had faced Hungary in the early rounds, I would definitely sit out. But when we face each other in round 12, what can I do? I cannot allow my personal feelings to stand in the way of the welfare of countless chess players out there. I see so many chess players struggle to make a living in the game. I must do everything I can to change that. I must do everything I can to help them.

I cried all night. It was a very painful decision for me. But just as I had to face my sisters in the 1992 World Rapid and World Blitz World Championships, we had no choice. We had to play. I hope that everyone can understand my decision. This is for the best interest of chess. As an ambassador for chess, I have to do what is best for the game.

Question: "Can women play chess as well as men?"

Susan: The answer is yes and no. If we talk about pure abilities and skills, I believe there should be no reason why women cannot play as well as men. Then why aren't there as many top-level women players as there are men? I would like to offer my personal point of view, especially as it may apply to women's chess in America:

1. Cultural and Social Acceptance

Whether we like it or not, or whether it is politically correct or not, cultural and gender bias exist in our society every day. All you have to do is look at the world of sports and you will see what I am describing. How often do you see minorities in professional tennis, golf or hockey, etc.? Not often – there are only a handful. On the other hand, what about in professional basketball, football, or baseball? These sports are dominated by minorities. Is this just a coincidence? I don't think so.

What would parents think if boys were interested in playing with Barbie dolls, and girls were interested in playing with cars, trucks or collect Pokemon cards? This is cultural and gender bias at its best. As a result, it is a problem for girls who may be interested in chess at an early age. It is generally not accepted or at least not endorsed by our society. I remember the same problem in my own experience growing up as a young female chess star. I was not well received. Many people thought it was absurd for a little girl like me to play chess.

As I improved and showed promise in chess as a young girl, some even went as far as to imply that I may have been forced to play chess or that it was a form of child abuse. But luckily for me, I had supportive and loving parents who helped me battle many of these serious obstacles. I believe it is a lot more acceptable now for young girls to play chess. In the schools that I teach, there are quite a number of young girls wanting to learn to play chess. This is a good trend. Unfortunately, boys still outnumber girls by a large margin.

2. Biological clock

Women athletes, regardless of the sport, face the same dilemma. Their bodies are created differently than men. When a woman reaches the age between 20 something to 30 something, she must ask a simple question: Which is more important? To have a family or to have a long (chess) career?

So far, the choice for many top women players, including myself, has been to have a family. Unless science can discover a way for women to have healthy children any time they wish, a woman athlete must choose one or the other. This in itself limits the longevity of any player. Therefore, it is rare to see women with as long a career as, for example, Smyslov, Korchnoi, Portisch, etc.

This is not an excuse. This is a pure fact. After bringing a child into the world, being a full-time mom is quite a job itself. It is hard enough to be a top woman player, competing against other male professionals. It is even harder when you have to nurture your children 24 hours a day. Imagine sitting across the board from Kasparov or Karpov playing a game, while thinking if your child needs a diaper change or if he/she is hungry. In addition, women have to face a "monthly problem". For some women, it is devastating and it can affect them very negatively. For others, it is just unpleasant.

3. Setting standards

For years, women have set much lower standards than men. I remember a time when no women player was above 2400. When you set low goals and expectations, chances are the results you achieve will be very low. The problem is that many women do not look at chess as a full-time profession. Many do not regard at it as seriously as male players do. Therefore, the results are obvious. If you do not put in the same work, you can't compete at the same level. It is as simple as that!

4. Opportunities

In chess, if you want to improve, one of the many things you have to do to improve is gain experience by competing at a higher level of competition. Many girls do not have this opportunity. This adds to the dilemma. When I was growing up, my father only wanted me to compete against men. I think this is the right approach.

However, to receive an invitation to an all male tournament was not an easy feat. If you look at the top women players in the world today, they all have experience playing in men's tournaments. But for the next generation, without the opportunity to compete on the same level, women simply cannot catch up to men.

5. A numbers game

When the number of boys who play chess at the early age is far more than girls, then purely statistically there will be more top male players than women players. If you have a hundred boys playing chess for every ten girls, what will the future bring? When the amount of young girls playing basketball and soccer increased substantially, new opportunities opened up. So the WNBA (Women's National Basketball Association) and the WUSA (Women's United Soccer Association) were born. Unless there are initiatives to change the image of chess for young girls in America and throughout the world, I don't expect to see many changes.

6. Confidence

When you add all of the above factors, the pressure for a young girl to succeed in this men's dominated game is incredible. When you are one of the few to reach the higher level in chess, the eyes of the world are on you. If a male player does badly in a tournament, people will say that player just had a bad tourney. But if a woman is competing in a men's tournament and does badly, people will have much more criticism. Some people just can't wait for a woman player to do badly to say she is not good or she is totally outclassed. So the pressure to succeed in the men's game is even greater.

Chess has a lot to do with psychology, and the fear of being singled out does not help one's confidence.

So what is my conclusion? Well, I think women can compete as well as men in chess. However, if a woman wants to succeed, she must put in the same amount of work and make the same amount of sacrifices. There is no other way around it. There are no excuses and there should not be.

Rachel Kramer Bussel asked: As one of the most prominent women in the world of chess, have you experienced sexism, and if so, how have you combated it?

Susan: Yes, and I am not the only one. When a man wins, people say: "Do you see how great he played? That was a great game!" When a woman wins, many times people would say: "Wow, doesn't she look hot!" and they go on with more sexist remarks or comments. Many men still do not take women playing chess seriously. I just ignore it and prove myself on the board. I don't think sexism will ever change. Therefore, I decided that the best thing to do is show that one can be beautiful, graceful and smart as well.

Rachel Kramer Bussel asked: You, along with your sisters Judit and Sofia, are credited with breaking many of the gender barriers in chess, but there is still a large disparity between the top female and top male players in chess. What do you think can be done to ameliorate this situation? Are there inherent differences in chess-playing skill by gender, or is it simply that fewer females enter and stay in the game competitively?

Susan: There is no reason why women cannot compete against men on an equal footing in a given game. However, a woman's career is generally a lot shorter due to the fact that they may decide to have a family. There are also some other issues that can affect a woman during a two-week long tournament. Many things have to change in order for this to happen. The first thing would be to change to social acceptance. Many girls are still very intimidated playing chess against boys. Their approach to the game is different. Most girls like to play for to have fun while boys are a lot more competitive.

From 1st-3rd grade, the numbers of boys and girls playing chess are similar. However, at around 4th grade and up, the number of girls starts to drop off. That is why I want to change that through the work of my foundation.

CHAPTER SEVEN

Special Women's World Champions

Vera Menchik, Nona Gaprindashvili, Maia Chiburdanidze, and Xie Jun! What do these have in common? They are the names of four Women's World Champions that have made a special impact on chess and for their countries, each in their own special way. These are the women who made tremendous breakthroughs in the world of chess.

Vera Menchik

Vera Menchik, born in Moscow and later residing in England, became the first official Women's World Champion in 1927. Even though she never reached the same level as other top male players, she was the first modern woman to regularly defeat male grandmasters, in an era when chess was not so popular among women. Some of her wins included victories over world champion Max Euwe, Samuel Reshevsky, Mir Sultan Khan, etc. She was tragically killed in an air raid on London in 1944.

Nona Gaprindashvili

Nona Gaprindashvili, from Georgia (part of the former Soviet Union), was the first woman player to achieve good results competing against male grandmasters. She marks the beginning of the Georgian dominance of the women's chess scene in 1962, when she became the Women's World Champion by defeating Elisaveta Bykova. Some of her best results were: equal first at Lone Pine in 1977 (with GMs Panno, Balashov, and Sahovic), and at Wijk aan Zee in 1987 (with GMs Farago and Winants).

Maia Chiburdanidze

Maia Chiburdanidze, also from Georgia, continued the long tradition of Georgian (and old Soviet) dominance in women's chess by becoming the Women's World Champion by defeating Gaprindashvili in 1978; she held the title until 1991 when she lost to Xie Jun. Maia had some excellent results during her career, and also met and defeated many male grandmasters. Some of her best results included finishing first at New Delhi in 1984 and Banja Luka in 1985.

Xie Jun

Xie Jun became the first Chinese to become a World Chess Champion, when she defeated Maia Chiburdanidze in 1991, ending decades of Georgian and Soviet dominance. Asia, and China in particular, is known more for Xiangqi (Chinese Chess), not for Western chess.

What she has done for chess in China and Asia overall is remarkable. With a formidable career as a Xiangqi champion, Jun made a smooth transition to Western chess and put China in the map as one of the chess powerhouses. Her celebrity in China is often compared to that of Michael Jordan in the US

She has often competed against male grandmasters with good results. Her crucial win against one of the top American GMs, Alexander Shabalov, in fact gave China a 1-point victory over the United States in the recent China-US Summit match.

Jun is known for her positive, cheerful outlook on life. With her accomplishments in chess, she has cleared a path for a whole new generation of young Chinese girls. And with the support from the Chinese government, I fully expect China to be a dominant force in women chess for years to come.

FIDE Women's World Champions

1927 - 1944:	Vera Menchik	USSR/Czechoslovakia/UK
1950 - 1953:	Liudmila Rudenko	USSR
1953 - 1956:	Elisaveta Bykova	USSR
1956 - 1958:	Olga Rubtsova	USSR
1958 - 1962:	Elisaveta Bykova	USSR
1962 - 1978:	Nona Gaprindashvili	USSR
1978 - 1991:	Maia Chiburdanidze	USSR/Georgia
1991 - 1996:	Xie Jun	China
1996 - 1999:	Zsuzsa "Susan" Polgar	Hungary
1999 - 2001:	Xie Jun	China
2001 - 2004:	Zhu Chen	China
2004 -	Antoaneta Stefanova	Bulgaria

INDEX OF OPPONENTS

Numbers refer to pages. Bold type indicates that the Polgars had the black pieces.

INDEX OF OPENINGS

Numbers refer to pages. Bold type indicates that the Polgars had the black pieces.

Descriptive Openings

ECO index